Elizabeth Sprague Coolidge

CYRILLA BARR

Elizabeth Sprague Coolidge

AMERICAN PATRON OF MUSIC

FOREWORD BY GUNTHER SCHULLER

Published in Cooperation with the Music Division of the Library of Congress

SCHIRMER BOOKS
An Imprint of Simon & Schuster Macmillan
NEW YORK
Prentice Hall International
LONDON • MEXICO CITY • NEW DEHLI • SINGAPORE • SYDNEY • TORONTO

Schirmer Books
An Imprint of Simon & Schuster Macmillan
1633 Broadway
New York, New York 10019

Library of Congress Catalog Number: 97-31635
Printed in the United States of America
Printing number
1 2 3 4 5 6 7 8 9 10

Library of Congress Cataloging-in-Publication Data
Barr, Cyrilla.
Elizabeth Sprague Coolidge : American patron of music / Cyrilla Barr.
p. cm.
Includes bibliographical references and index.
ISBN 0-02-864888-9
1. Coolidge, Elizabeth Sprague, 1864-1953.
2. Music patrons—United States—Biography. I. Title.
ML429.C64B37 1998
780'.92—dc21 [B] 97-31635
CIP
MN

This paper meets the requirements of ANSI/NISO Z39.48-1992 (Permanence of Paper).

FRONTISPIECE
Elizabeth Sprague Coolidge, circa 1896. Courtesy of Elizabeth Coolidge Winship Private Collection, Library of Congress.

To the Coolidge family,
keepers of the legacy,
and
to the loyal friends whose
support and encouragement have
helped to bring this work
to fulfillment

Contents

Foreword

THE WHOLE HISTORY of Western music has been profoundly affected and nurtured by patronage, whether it was the patronage of the church early in this millennium, or later royal patronage, or in our time the support of private patrons. It is an uncommon vocation, not given to many people to practice, but one that is as necessary to the creation of new art as the artists themselves. Therefore, whoever cares about the future of music as well as music's early-twentieth-century history should know about Elizabeth Sprague Coolidge, one of the greatest music patrons of all time. The hundreds of masterpieces that she commissioned over a period of many decades are to a remarkable extent the basic staples of our twentieth-century repertory, particularly in chamber music. They are also de facto the foundation on which the future of music will be built. Her vision as patron is in its spirit as universal as the music of those many unique talents which she supported.

The work of the arts patron, the music patron, is often not sufficiently recognized, let alone celebrated. It is work that is done mostly behind the scene, so to speak. If the work is a success, it is the composer who receives all the accolades. Rarely is sufficient recognition given to the person or commissioning body that initially generated the work. And so, Coolidge's work was for many years either scantily recognized, particularly in the public arena, or appreciated only by a small inner circle of composers and contemporary music professionals.

And yet the musical masterpieces which she helped bring into the world are by now legendary. My generation certainly grew up on them, learned from them, built further upon them, was inspired by them. My awareness of Coolidge began when as a teenager I began to study the works of Bartók, Milhaud, Honegger, Schoenberg, Stravinsky, Webern, Copland and so many others, when I saw in the front pages of the scores the name Elizabeth Sprague Coolidge. She remained a mystery to most of us, her work being performed quietly and unostentatiously in the background. Who was she, we sometimes thought, but not too long. We were more interested in devouring the scores themselves than wondering who this wonderful mystery lady was.

The great musical treasures we held in our hands were the gifts of genius. And they were the great art created during the period between the two world wars, in retrospect seemingly miraculously brought into the world in spite of a prevailing general indifference, perhaps even hostility, to such things. We vaguely knew that these works had probably been paid for, but in our minds such pragmatic considerations cast Coolidge in that dubious half light to which all young, aspiring, and usually poor artists tend to see persons of wealth and power. And our only vague memories were of far-off legendary patrons such as Mozart's Archbishop of Salzburg or Wagner's Mad Ludwig of Bavaria.

Of course, a few of us knew better, but it was not in those days usually the business of composers to probe the motives of donors. In response to one disparaging remark about Coolidge, Stravinsky replied, "But she pays." Besides the platitudes that politeness requires, that is for the most part the only honest tribute a patron receives.

Cyrilla Barr has brought her subject out of that half-light, and has enabled us to see several related and important human qualities in that proud and at times imposing woman. For one thing, we learn that Coolidge was one of the most qualified patrons of music, for she was not only an accomplished pianist, but a composer, as well. When, in her old age, she had a recording made of her own string quartet, she played it for Harold Spivacke, then chief of the Music Division in the Library of Congress, through which institution her most enduring work was accomplished. They both knew that at the conclusion he would have to tell her what he thought.Well, he is reported to have said, you have commissioned worse.

It was a judgment with which she was fully satisfied. Her musical ability in no way led her to assume superiority or to impose her own tastes on those she commissioned, nor did it lead her to assume powers of judgment that, in her wisdom, she knew she lacked. Her understanding of music did not help her to appreciate the music of Ives, from whom, on advice she obtained from an esteemed composer, she did *not* commission a piece; and she was disappointed in the String Quartet, op. 28, of Webern, which she *did* commission, because of its brevity. Her close friendships with Bridge and Malipiero, together with her own music, reflect a generally conservative outlook. Yet her commission of Schoenberg's Fourth String Quartet was certainly not predicated on any misgivings she might have had about its predecessor, the Third, which she also commissioned. Year after year she thought and planned so that possibilities might, through her financial assistance, become realities. Furthermore, and as important, her labors were concerned not only as we learn from this biography strictly in the sphere of creating works, but also played a critically important role in enabling refugee composers and musicians to find sanctuary in America.

It was, no doubt, only in part because of her musical training, and the enjoyment as well as the intellectual perspective it gave her, that Coolidge was sufficiently secure not to be daunted either by her own fallibility or those uncertainties over which she had no control. Beyond the inherited wealth and talent with which she was born, there was the stamp of strong character that enabled her to grow where such unearned gifts might have diminished another. The first half of her life, which saw, besides the birth of her first and only child, the building in the Berkshires of a magnificent home designed for extensive musical entertainment, was also marked by the protracted illness and decline of her beloved husband. An orthopedic surgeon who had knowingly performed an operation on a patient suffering from the unmentionable syphilis, he cut himself accidentally during the procedure, and became infected. From that day until his death, the Coolidges experienced, with only occasional periods of hope, the gradual and necessarily secret realization of their deepest apprehensions. It was a tragedy whose outcome might have reduced a less resilient spirit than Coolidge's to seek thereafter a sheltered and unenterprising retirement. Instead of ashes, however, she found fertile ground and roots for her famous philanthropic ventures, and so the first half of her life became the preparation for the second.

This biography will help to dispell some stereotypes of the patron. Coolidge was a product of her age, but also a shaper of that age. She stands, in our own time of ambivalent support for the arts, as a model of informed benevolence. She and we, who have enjoyed directly and indirectly the heritage of her patronage, deserve this telling of her story.

– GUNTHER SCHULLER

Preface

GRAM WAS A SURVIVOR!" These were the first words that Dr. John C. Coolidge spoke to me as I walked into the dining room of the ancestral home in Cambridge in December of 1988. The table was piled high with photograph albums, scrapbooks, cartons of letters, and other memorabilia—a veritable private archive of material documenting the life of the very complex lady who was his grandmother.

Somehow, after having already spent several years researching the activities of this rather formidable woman whom I had gotten to know largely through documents that are public record, hearing her referred to so familiarly as "Gram" seemed almost irreverent. Yet I knew she truly was a survivor—in a literal sense—for it required only a simple calculation to discover that she had indeed survived eighteen presidents, from Lincoln to Eisenhower, and had lived through wars from the Civil to the Korean. She was born when Victoria was Queen and lived to see Elizabeth II ascend the throne of the country from which her forebears had come. She died in her ninetieth year, her life encompassing incredible advances in science and technology that far outpaced any previous period of nine decades.

Besides the many scientific advances that occurred in her time, her life spanned a vast diversity of styles and "isms" in the arts as well. She was brought up in the heyday of romanticism, lived on to hear experiments with aleatory and electronic music and, in fact, commissioned some of the most avant-garde works of the early twentieth century. Her circle of friends included practically every major composer and performer from the first half of this century, and her munificence brought beauty into the lives of literally millions of unnamed music lovers who heard the broadcasts and attended the free concerts that she sponsored.

To many she appeared to be a woman of contradictions, a woman who could happily give away hundreds of thousands of dollars and yet castigate a piano tuner who overcharged her one dollar; one who unabashedly demanded a rebate from her corset maker when she lost weight and could no longer wear the garments, yet never failed to bestow generous perquisites on those who offered her the simplest courtesy. She could turn a phrase like an Oxford don when protocol required it, and in the next breath sally forth with great relish into a verbal sparring contest that betrayed not only a marvelous sense of humor, but a lexicon that, though never offensive, was often spiced with the most apt and colorful of descriptive adjectives. She was the imperious dowager who could speak in the majestic plural when occasion required, but was also capable of the greatest tenderness, allowing only a chosen few to glimpse her surprising vulnerability—the soft underside of a complex personality full of surprises. In the words of Anna Malipiero, a member of that privileged inner circle, "One had to *learn* to know her. . . . There were so many sides to her character. Her quick brain was allied to an equally quick sense of dry humor. And even her wrath had the nature of Greek tragedy."[1] The humor and the wrath! These may explain the contrasting attitudes of those who still remember her.

These seeming incongruities in her behavior only superficially mask the resoluteness of purpose that characterized her ironclad and unchanging dedication to her art. She chose to call it "fidelity to standards," a phrase that runs throughout her correspondence like a battle cry and is lived out in action through her work. She once remarked to Roy Harris, "The love and fidelity that I feel toward Art are high priestesses in the service of the only religion which I know."[2] And indeed throughout her correspondence, "Art," "Truth," and "Beauty" are consistently capitalized as is proper for references to the Deity.

Elizabeth Sprague Coolidge was born more than a century and a quarter ago, and over forty years have passed since her death. Her major philanthropic works are common knowledge among musicians, but what has been known of Coolidge's life up to now does little to enlighten our understanding of the person behind the public image, for she jealously guarded her privacy. And even in her career as a patron there are innumerable silent benefactions, both large and small.

The surviving photographs of Coolidge that grace the trade journals of the music profession document only her later years and perpetuate the image of a frumpy, amazonian old lady in orthopedic shoes, swathed in layers of shawls and sweaters, with her hearing aid as prominently displayed on her imposing bosom as were the ubiquitous pearls. Her firmly set jaw and penetrating eyes only serve to underscore her reputation as one who did not suffer fools gladly.

Who then was this woman whose struggle for self-identity came fully to fruition only in mid-life? Coolidge was reared within the strictures of the Victorian ethic that frowned upon public careers for young ladies of her social standing, and although she became an accomplished pianist, there could be no thought of her pursuing a life on the stage. The fact that such well-known female concert artists as Fanny Bloomfield-Zeisler and Teresa Carreño were both close family friends of the Spragues only added to the tensions that plagued Elizabeth's early adulthood and dictated that her aspirations must be channeled into the only respectable realms available to her class and gender—the women's clubs. With her marriage to Frederic Shurtleff Coolidge she once and for all relinquished any serious thought of a career and devoted herself to becoming the proper wife and mother—and ultimately her husband's long-suffering companion throughout his tragic illness. Coolidge's early years were as different from her well-known public life as the late photos are from those of the young Elizabeth Sprague, the tall, blond, willowy beauty who so utterly captivated the heart of young Fred Coolidge in his last year of medical studies at Harvard. Fred Coolidge belonged to what Oliver Wendell Holmes, Sr., characterized as America's "untitled aristocracy," the caste of Boston Brahmins.

Had life progressed as Elizabeth undoubtedly expected it would at the time of her marriage in 1891, the course of American music might well have been quite different. Between January of 1915 and March of 1916 Elizabeth lost her father, husband, and mother and suddenly found herself not only alone and emotionally bereft, but the sole heiress of the Sprague fortune, with no experience in the world of finance. The strength of will that had characterized her even as a stubborn child, and the single-minded dedication to music that had seen her through so many difficult times, now became her refuge and her defense. With a brittle sort of courage she began her first philanthropic work in support of the art that had sustained her and that she so passionately loved.

Inspired by the example of her father, Albert Arnold Sprague, whose hard work and industry had built an empire out of the wholesale grocery business in Chicago, she set about to create her own trajectory to success. As the Sprague business prospered the family acquired both considerable wealth and prestige in the commercial and artistic life of Chicago. By 1884 the Spragues had built a fine home on fashionable Prairie Avenue, in the heart of what was then Chicago's "Gold Coast," where neighbors included Marshall Field, Pullman, Armour, McCormack, Potter Palmer, the Glessners, and Kimball (of the Kimball piano company). While the Sprague home was the center of much social, intellectual, and musical activity, through it all Elizabeth's parents retained their deeply ingrained Puritan values and work ethic that dictated concern for the less endowed. It was an example that she emulated as even in her most affluent years she was known to stretch a dollar.

Sprung suddenly as she was into the world of finance, Elizabeth was something of a parvenu, a vibrant original who created an idiosyncratic style of giving that in many respects allowed her to live vicariously the career she would love to have had. Having suddenly acquired wealth and a certain attendant power, she quickly went about establishing her own style of giving. As a female and a maverick in her new-found role she ignored some time-honored traditions and created a career that was unique in many ways—not the least of which was her determination to involve the government in the support of the arts.

Donald Leavitt accurately observed that it was "a combination of keen intellect, solid musical background, an irrevocable commitment to music, and an indomitable will—all of these, far more than money—that made her a person to whom few could say 'no.'"[3]

Coolidge's story as told here attempts not only to explore the legacy of her patronage, but also to reveal the person of the patron. The richest source of information on her early life is the diary kept by her mother, Nancy Ann Atwood Sprague, from 1854 to her death in 1916 (now in the Schlesinger Library, Radcliffe College). In it she faithfully recorded daily entries from that period and preserved hundreds of letters, programs, menus, and other memorabilia. Elizabeth herself never kept a journal other than the early travel diaries of 1882–83 and 1888, but she was a prodigious correspondent, and the present work draws heavily upon her letters. Indeed some of the most enlightening of them have nothing to do with music but reveal a good deal about her thorny character.

The biography is divided into two parts. The first traces her private life in simple chronological fashion, but the nature and diversity of her professional activities dictate different organization and procedure for the second part of the book, which necessarily combines a chronological, geographical, and topical arrangement.

In the context of feminist studies in the 1990s the question inevitably arises, "Was Elizabeth Sprague Coolidge an early feminist?" I would simply observe that she was acutely conscious of her singular position as a woman entrepreneur in a traditionally male-dominated arena and enjoyed the uniqueness of it. It is a stance that Oscar Sonneck observed very early on in his association with her. When it became apparent that she was warming to the idea of an alliance with the Library of Congress, he wrote to Carl Engel, his successor as chief of the Music Division there, "Do not *cherchez la femme.* Mrs. Coolidge will not object, I presume, to a man, but she would object to another woman. Who then, among us men, are the available candidates?"[4]

Convinced of the value and importance of her work, Coolidge seemed to give little consideration to the question of gender, as far as it affected her own professional activities. She dealt largely with men, and counted among her friends men of all ages. It is well known that bestowal of a nickname by Coolidge meant benediction and initiation into her most intimate circle. Although she had some close women friends, she appears—consciously or otherwise—to have maintained these relationships quite separate from her professional life. Perhaps most significant of all is the obvious absence of women from the list of composers that she supported: Rebecca Clarke was the only woman that Coolidge ever commissioned, and no woman ever received the ultimate accolade—the Coolidge Medal.

If there is a sense in which Coolidge may be said to have influenced the feminists of our time, it is in the courage that she manifested in taking charge of her life, creating it anew after the tragedies visited upon her. What Carolyn Heilbrun has said of Dorothy L. Sayers might well be applied to Coolidge's example: "[H]er life . . . teaches us about the possible hidden lives of accomplished women who were educated enough to have had a choice and brave enough to have made one."[5] History can only be grateful that Coolidge made that choice.

Acknowledgments

MANY DEBTS ACRUE in the course of writing a life. Of these without a doubt the greatest is to the Coolidge family. The relatives of the subject of a biography can be the greatest obstacle or the greatest gift to a biographer. In the Coolidge family I have been singularly blessed, for over the years that I have worked on this book I have been made to feel like one of the family. I am especially indebted to Dr. John C. Coolidge and his wife, Melba, for granting me unrestricted access to his grandmother's personal papers, and for sharing their wonderfully vivid recollections and countless anecdotes that have enlivened my perception of Elizabeth Sprague Coolidge. To their son Jeffrey Coolidge I am indebted for the numerous photographs that he has supplied for this work, and for facilitating the deposit of the private family archive at the Library of Congress. I am likewise indebted to Elizabeth Coolidge Winship for graciously allowing the photo album created for her by her grandmother and namesake to be reproduced at the Library of Congress for inclusion in this book. Without the cooperation of the family this work would be limited to a study of Elizabeth Sprague Coolidge's public life as a patron and would necessarily provide only a limited understanding of this truly remarkable woman.

During the course of my research the Library of Congress has become a kind of second home. Dr. James Pruett, during whose tenure as chief of the Music Division this work was begun, and Mr. Jon Newsom, the current chief, have not only been unfailingly supportive by their interest, encouragement, and friendship, but have offered invaluable suggestions and practical help as well. To them and to the staff of the Music Division I owe an enormous debt of gratitude. I wish to acknowledge in a special way Kevin LaVine, Kate Rivers, and Ray White for their good-natured and patient guidance through the vast dusty labyrinth of Coolidge memorabilia, still unsorted and uncataloged at the outset of this research.

My sincerest thanks go also to the following librarians and archivists without whose help this biography would be incomplete. In Aldeburgh, England, The Britten-Pears Library, Dr. Donald Mitchell, Rosamund Strode, and Paul S. Wilson; in Boston, Kathleen Green Meyer of Shepley Bulfinch Richardson and Abbot architectural firm; in Cambridge, Sarah A. Polirer and Michael Raines, Harvard University Archives, Pusey Library; Richard J. Wolfe, Curator of Rare Books and Manuscripts, Countway Medical Library, Harvard; Jane Knowles, Archivist, and Elizabeth Shenton, Assistant Director, The Schlesinger Library, Radcliffe College; in Chicago, John Smith, Archivist of the Art Institute of Chicago; Eileen Flanagan and Archie Motley of the Chicago Historical Society; Cynthia H. Peters of the Newberry Library; the late William Kona, Rush-Presbyterian-St. Luke's Medical Center Archives; Evelyn Meine, the Chicago Symphony Special Services Manager; in Florence, Laura Dallapiccola for access to her husband's papers at the Archivio Contemporaneo Bonsanti, and Fiamma Nicolodi for access to the private archive of her grandfather, Alfredo Casella; in Hartford, to Beverly Zell of the Mark Twain Memorial; in London to Tim Day of the Recorded Sound Division of the British Library, to John Bishop of the Frank Bridge Trust, and to Christopher Bonnet of the Royal College of Music; in Los Angeles, to Marsha Berman, Ann Caeger, and Carole Prietto of UCLA, to Virginia Steele of the University of Southern California, and to Rusty Balah and Mel Rosenberg of the Los Angeles Public Library; in Montpelier, to Barney Bloom of the Vermont Historical Society; in New York City to Jim Qian of the New York Historical Society; in Pittsfield to Jean Bousquet, Ruth Degenhandt, Emilie Piper and Kathleen Reilly of the Berkshire Athenaeum; to Christopher Husted of the University of California, Santa Barbara; to Gladys Hansen of the San Francisco Public Library; in Venice to Dottoressa Maria Teresa Muraro of Fondazione Giorgio Cini; to Bernard Schermetzler, Archivist of the University of Wisconsin, Madison; and to Judith Schiff and Nancy A. Young of the Sterling Memorial Library Archives, Yale University.

In countless other ways various individuals have contributed to this research. While working on this book I had the good fortune to discover that Ralph Locke of the Eastman School of Music was doing similar research on a woman patron of music, Isabella Stewart Gardner. Our shared frustration over the lack of scholarly attention to women's support of art music ultimately led to our cooperation in editing a book on the subject. I have profited greatly by that shared experience and am grateful for Professor Locke's support, good counsel, and friendship.

Others who offered enthusiastic encouragement in the early stages of this work include Gillian Anderson, Adrienne Fried Block, Dena Epstein, Judith McCulloh, and Wayne Shirley. For their guidance in directing me to the many Sprague connections in Chicago I am deeply indebted to Mary Alice Molloy and to Joan Campbell. Similarly by providing me with introductions to the families of Alfano, Casella, Malipiero, Dallapiccola, Respighi, and Pizzetti, Professor John C. G. Waterhouse, University of Birmingham, England, has rendered invaluable assistance. To Martha Blum and the late Gunnar Johansen I am indebted for information on Coolidge's connection with the Pro Arte Quartet; to Dorothy Indenbaum for material related to Mary Howe, and to Margery Lowens on MacDowell. Others who have generously shared information are Elise Kirk on Lou Henry Hoover, Liane Curtis on Rebecca Clarke, Louise Spizizen on Roy Harris, and Philip Tacka on Copland and *Appalachian Spring.* I am likewise indebted to Jeanice Brooks for calling my attention to materials in the Recorded Sound Archive of the British Library, London, and to Mary Di Quinzio for obtaining materials in the Biblioteca Nazionale, Florence.

I owe a special debt to my capable graduate student assistants—David Hildebrand, who for two years spent every Friday at my side as we made our way through sixteen linear meters of Coolidge correspondence at the Library of Congress; Gail Miller, who applied her considerable detective skills to the difficult assignment of constructing the list of Coolidge commissions and prize-winning compositions; and Anthony DelDonna for assistance in obtaining permissions to quote.

Others who have contributed their personal reflections include Laura Dallapiccola, Giuliette Malipiero, Fiamma Nicolodi, Luther Noss, and Carleton Sprague Smith. Invaluable criticism and suggestions have been provided by various colleagues and friends who have read the manuscript at different stages. They include Gillian Anderson, Barbara Henry, Kelly McGillis, and James Pruett. I am especially indebted to

John Collins Harvey, M.D., Ph.D., for his critique of those portions of the manuscript that deal with medical problems.

For their advice, encouragement, and good counsel, special thanks are due to the editorial staff of Schirmer Books, especially Andrew Libby, Dan Mausner, and Richard Carlin.

Some of the information contained in chapters 11 and 12 has appeared in substantially altered form as articles in the *Journal of Musicology* and *American Music*, as a chapter in *Cultivating Music in America; Women Patrons and Activists since 1860* (University of California Press, 1997), and as a monograph entitled *The Coolidge Legacy* (Library of Congress, 1997).

Research in various libraries and archives in this country and in Europe was made possible through grants from the American Council of Learned Societies and the National Endowment for the Humanities, as well as sabbatical leaves and Faculty Research Grants from the Catholic University of America.

On a more personal level it is a pleasure to express my sincere thanks to the friends who by their hospitality have seen to my physical needs during my research expeditions: Ann Sears, Bill Macartor, and James David Christie for hospitality and good times during my forays into Cambridge, Boston, and Montpelier; Douglas and Rosemary Moore at Williamstown and Pittsfield; the late Lorraine Casella, in New York; the Larsons—Willard, Joyce, and Mary—during my expeditions in Wisconsin; Rosamunde Strode, Aldeburgh, England; and Virginia Browne-Wilkinson, whose lovely flat in Florence's Oltrarno has always been my home away from home during my many research trips to Italy.

Lastly, to my colleagues and students too numerous to mention, my thanks for their support and encouragement during the course of this work.

Abbreviations

SOURCES

ACBF	Archivio Contemporaneo Bonsanti, Florence, Italy
AS Col.	Alexander Schneider Collection, Library of Congress
BL	British Library, London
BPLA	Britten-Pears Library, Aldeburgh, England
CHS	Chicago Historical Society
C. Col.	Coolidge Collection, Library of Congress
EPSD	Elizabeth Penn Sprague Diary of Grand Tour
FCV	Fondazione Giorgio Cini, Venice, Italy
GJ	Glessner Journals, Chicago Historical Society
HHPL	Herbert Hoover Presidential Library, West Branch, Iowa
HJ	Hindemith Journal, Paul Hindemith Collection, Yale University
LC	Library of Congress
MDCP	MacDowell Colony Papers, Library of Congress, Manuscript Division
NASD	Nancy Atwood Sprague Diaries, Schlesinger Library, Radcliffe College
NL	Newberry Library, Chicago
NYCHS	New York City Historical Society
PM	Nancy Atwood Sprague, *Pleasant Memories*
SMLA	Sterling Memorial Library Archives, Yale University
TL	Lucy Sprague Mitchell, *Two Lives*
YUA	Yale University Archives

NAMES

AAS	Albert Arnold Sprague
ASC	Albert Sprague Coolidge (Sprague)
CE	Carl Engel
EPS	Elizabeth Penn Sprague (references written before her marriage are cited by the initials of her maiden name)
ESC	Elizabeth Sprague Coolidge (for references after her marriage)
FG	Frances Glessner
FSC	Frederic Shurtleff Coolidge
HP	Herbert Putnam
NAS	Nancy Atwood Sprague
OS	Oscar Sonneck

Editorial Procedures

LETTERS

Many letters are undated. In those cases for which the envelope survives and the postmark is legible that date is used. In some cases only a portion of the date is provided—for example, Sunday, 19 May. In other cases, when the letter is undated and no postmark survives, but the date can be determined from the context of the letter, the date is given in brackets thus: [1898]. If a portion of the date is provided and the remainder can only be ascertained from the content of the letter, it is indicated thus: 19 May [1898]. If a reasonable assertion is possible but not certain from the context, the date will be indicated along with a question mark enclosed within brackets thus: [1898?]

LACUNAE

Since much of the research was done from handwritten letters and diaries some portions are occasionally illegible. Such lacunae are indicated in the text by empty brackets thus: [ ]. Comments inserted by the author are indicated in parentheses thus: ( ).

CLIPPINGS

Many of the clippings from newspapers and periodicals among Coolidge's memorabilia are undated, and many fail to identify the source. In some instances it has been possible to determine the publication, but the majority of these are simply identified here according to the collection in which they are contained.

PART ONE

No one should live as you and I do without devoting a part of our opportunities to the world.

– ELIZABETH SPRAGUE COOLIDGE TO HER SON, ALBERT SPRAGUE COOLIDGE, 20 FEBRUARY 1924

CHAPTER ONE

Prelude: The Atwoods and the Spragues

I recall that beautiful October day when
your voice first chimed with the Sabbath church bells.
– A.A. SPRAGUE TO ELIZABETH, 28 OCTOBER 1904

THE PROFOUND SILENCE of the crowd that lined the streets that May morning in 1865 was broken only by the measured steps of the soldiers and the ceaseless tolling of the bell from the courthouse tower. It had rained steadily for days, and although the sun broke through at dawn, the streets and sidewalks were still thick with mud. Major General Joseph Hooker, his head bared in a gesture of respect, rode before an honor guard of young women dressed in white, followed by endless ranks of soldiers, religious leaders, civic groups, and hundreds of schoolchildren. They had walked all the way from the train station at Park Row, and although they moved steadily and without pause—nowhere fewer than four abreast—it required four hours for the procession to pass the point where a slight young woman stood holding her infant daughter. Unlike the many women who had fainted away and had to be carried from the scene senseless,[1] Nancy Ann Atwood Sprague endured the long wait and that night inscribed in her diary: "When the vast procession marched through the streets I stood on the sidewalk with my baby who weighed a ton, it seemed."[2]

It was fitting that the young mother should bring her baby to this historic event, for the child's forebears had been much a part of the fabric of colonial history: They had served their country in the War of

Independence, the War of 1812, and the conflict that still raged when Elizabeth Penn Sprague was born on 30 October 1864 in a fashionable section of Chicago. It was a critical moment in history to which the child, though still but an insentient bystander, was a witness, for the "vast procession" that her mother described in her diary was Lincoln's funeral cortege as it passed through the streets of Chicago before the slain president was laid to rest in Springfield.

You might say she was born making music, as her first robust cries formed a curious counterpoint with the pealing bells of the neighborhood church. Hindsight might declare it a portent of things to come.

She came from a long line of survivors, for the Atwoods and the Spragues were a hardy lot, sprung from Puritan stock and formed by the beliefs and traditions of ancestors who had faced the uncertainties of the New World and had not only survived, but flourished. Both parents came from respected old families with lineage dating from colonial times. Her mother, Nancy Ann Atwood (1837–1916), descended from the Atwoods near Bristol in Gloucestershire, England, where the family name appears in public records as early as the fourteenth century.[3] And stately grandmother Atwood delighted in recounting how in the thirteenth century an Atwood held a high and important position in the royal household.[4] The patriarch of the family in the New World was John Atwood (1614–76), who came to Massachusetts around 1635 or 1636 and quickly assumed a place in the government of the Plymouth Colony, becoming governor assistant in 1638 and treasurer from 1641 until 1644.[5] Seven generations of Atwoods, all of whom produced large families, figure prominently in the history of New England both as active civic leaders and as enterprising farmers who acquired a sizable homestead. John's son, Nathaniel (1651–1724), was a deacon and farmer in what is now Carver, and his son, "Lieutenant" Nathaniel (1693–1767), lived on the homestead that was held in a direct line of descent for five generations until "Captain" Ebenezer (1773–1841) moved the family to

Barnard, Vermont.[6] Here Elizabeth's grandfather, also named Ebenezer (1802–69), was born. Like his ancestors he became a prominent public official, serving as a delegate to the General Assembly from 1837 to 1838 and as a member of the state militia.[7] In 1824 he married Elvira Tucker of Barnard, who bore him thirteen children, the eighth of whom was Nancy Ann (Nan), Elizabeth's mother.

Elizabeth's paternal side can be traced to Edward Sprague (ca. 1576–1614), a fuller from Upway, a small village in County Dorset, England. Edward's three sons, Ralph, Richard, and William arrived in the New World in 1628 and immediately settled on the north side of the Charles River on land granted to them by Governor Endicott.[8] The location of their new settlement, which they called Charlestown, now lies within the city limits of Boston. It was there, in the Great House they helped to build, that the first Thanksgiving was celebrated.[9]

By 1631 Ralph (ca. 1603–50), from whom Elizabeth's line descends, was a freeman of the colony and member of the militia, rising rapidly through the ranks to become its captain, and by 1634 he was first selectman of Charlestown. The seven generations of Spragues following Ralph produced a succession of freemen, representatives to the General Court, officeholders in colonial government, and commanders of the militia. But the Spragues were equally well known for their piety, and when Edward (1663–1715, third generation) moved to Malden, he became tithingman and was responsible for watching over "moral welfare," preserving order in the meeting house, and enforcing general observation of the Lord's day.

It was Jonathan (1739–1822, fifth generation), a noted carpenter and joiner, who in 1792 moved the family from Massachusetts to Vermont after spending a short time in Hanover, New Hampshire, where he distinguished himself by laying out and building one of the Dartmouth College buildings solely by square rule.[10] His son Edward (1779–1858) settled on a farm east of Randolph and before the advent of the railroads began freighting country produce to Boston in exchange for merchandise to bring back to Vermont. As a deacon of the Free Will Baptist Church, Edward became widely known for the efficacy of his prayers—it was reported that when he prayed, "the blessings fell right down."[11]

Edward's oldest surviving son, Ziba (1806–67), was a prosperous farmer who, like his father, became deacon of the Free Will Baptist

Church and later representative from Randolph to the General Assembly.[12] The three children born of his union with Caroline Arnold would all figure importantly in the lives of the Atwoods in nearby Royalton. Of these, Albert Arnold (1835–1915), the oldest, was Elizabeth's father.

Both families originated in the southwestern part of England, but their histories did not intersect until their respective wanderings brought them to within fifteen miles of one another near the White River in central Vermont. While their lives are parallel in time and more or less contiguous in space, much more is known about the family life of the Atwoods. This is largely because of Nancy's memoirs, written in the last year of her life and published by Elizabeth after her mother's death under the title *Pleasant Memories of My Life.*

Although she claimed to be shy, Nan developed into a feisty, proprietary, and practical young woman whose personality seems to have been very much influenced by her position in the large family. While her older sister, Elizabeth, was away at school and before the last child, Lucia, was born in 1849, Nan was the solitary girl amid ten brothers and a doting father for whom she admits she was something of a pet and plaything.[13] She proved to be very capable of holding her own with her brothers and became an efficient helper to her busy mother too, learning to cook and sew and tending the babies who arrived at respectable two-year intervals.

The children were all educated at the local country school in Barnard, but when George, Thomas, and Lizzie had mastered all that the common school could offer, Ebenezer sent them to nearby Royalton Academy, where they boarded during the week with the local deacon for the handsome sum of $6 for the three. However, when this proved to be too serious a drain on the modest family income, the enterprising Ebenezer moved his entire family to Royalton to a farm within walking distance of the two poles that were ever to be the axis of the Atwood's existence—church and school.[14]

Study was not relegated solely to the schoolhouse, however, for Elvira Tucker played an important part in her children's education at home. She was an avid reader, "by nature scholarly and studious . . . with an intelligence which in spite of the duties and cares of a large family, never grew dull." Whenever she could steal a few precious moments she delighted in gathering her children around her, drilling them in spelling, and parsing *Paradise Lost* or *The Lady of the Lake.*[15] Above all, she was well informed in matters of politics and enjoyed spirited debate on the subject, though it was necessarily restricted to short intervals between baking bread and rocking the cradle.

The Atwood home may have been lacking in material comforts, yet it provided a yeasty intellectual environment for the brood growing up there. Work was hard, time for study was scarce, and discipline was strict, but the home was a warm and hospitable place, always filled with music and open to friends and neighbors. Praying and singing together were daily occurrences, and Nan, who could sing before she could read, recollected that "We learned music as we learned to walk, in fact, we did not have to learn it, we got it, just as we got teeth when 'twas time."[16]

All of the children sang, and most played instruments as well. At the end of the day Ebenezer would gather the children, give the pitches with his tuning fork, and lead the singing from one of the much-used hymnals that lay on an old-fashioned table in the parlor. New anthems and glees were anxiously sought after, and on one occasion, when an especially coveted collection became available but proved beyond the Atwood budget, Ebenezer traded a cord of wood for the book.[17] In time father Atwood also formed a family choir that became quite famous in the area and much in demand for special occasions, from Fourth-of-July celebrations to weddings and funerals. And it was not surprising that Royalton's Congregational Church boasted the best music in town, for Ebenezer Atwood was director of its choir and most of his children were members.

Of all the children, the most musically gifted appear to have been Thomas, Lizzie, and Lucia. Perhaps because as a child he was lame and could not participate in the rowdy play of his brothers, Thomas spent much time whittling little fiddles. When Ebenezer finally managed to provide a real violin for Thomas he applied himself so diligently that he not only taught himself to read music, but also became quite skilled as a performer. He was eventually sent off to a singing school where he became proficient enough that in time he opened his own singing school to which "scores of men and women all through the towns of New England owed their knowledge."[18] Thomas's most memorable achievement occurred in 1869, when his choir—including several of his siblings—was invited to participate in the much-publicized and gargantuan Peace Jubilee organized in celebration of the end of the Civil War.[19]

Lizzie, the eldest girl, was the only one of the Atwoods given the opportunity for a higher education. She attended Mt. Holyoke Female Seminary, where she came under the influence of Mary Lyon, the school's founder and a pioneer for the cause of women's education. Following Lyon's example Lizzie taught until she married at the age of thirty: A year later she died in childbirth. One other girl would be born to the Atwood family, the last of the thirteen children: Lucia Elvira, born in May of 1849. Nancy at once claimed the baby as her own, assumed the care of the infant, slept in her room, and even made her clothes. It was a special bond that would grow ever closer over the succeeding years.

The simple life of the Atwood family was inexorably changed when on 12 April 1861 Confederate troops fired on Fort Sumpter in Charleston Harbor, plunging the nation into the Civil War. Three days later President Lincoln announced blockades of all southern ports and called for a force of 75,000 volunteers to help to restore federal authority in the South. Three of Nancy's brothers responded to the call and joined the Union Army; only one would return. The early 1860s found the family circle diminished by five—the three boys had gone to war, Lizzie had died, and now, in 1862, Nancy was about to leave the nest. It is not known exactly how or when Nancy actually met Albert Arnold Sprague. Neither her memoirs nor her diary shed any light on the question. It seems likely that Albert knew Nan's brothers, for she speaks of Albert's brother Otho Sprague as an old friend of her brother Thomas.

Albert, the eldest son of Ziba and Caroline Sprague, was born on the family homestead in Randolph, Vermont, on 19 May 1835, and after studying in the common school there went on to Kimball Union Academy in Meridan, New Hampshire, in 1850.[20] He entered Yale College at age nineteen and graduated with honors, earning his A.B. degree in the classical curriculum in 1859. Although little is known of his years at Yale, it is clear from his later life that many treasured friendships were forged there. John Haskell Hewitt, a classmate and friend, who years later delivered an address on the occasion of the dedication of Sprague

Nancy Ann Atwood Sprague, Elizabeth's mother

Jeffrey Coolidge Photography, Boston

Albert Arnold Sprague, Elizabeth's father

Jeffrey Coolidge Photography, Boston

Hall at Yale, described Albert as a handsome, blue-eyed blond with a gentle and lovable disposition that attracted many friends.[21]

Without a doubt the closest and most enduring of these friendships was with classmate Joseph H. Twichell, who went on to Yale Divinity School and was ordained to the Congregational ministry in 1863.[22] During his pastorate in Hartford, Twichell became an intimate friend of Mark Twain, with whom he often traveled. The Spragues frequently socialized with the Twichells and two of their European tours were made together. Albert's regard for his old friend is perhaps most patently demonstrated by his will, which provided $50,000 in trust to Twichell and his family.[23]

After Yale Albert contemplated a career in law, but a brush with tuberculosis led doctors to prescribe a more physically active life for him. He returned briefly to Randolph—long enough to regain his strength and make the acquaintance of Nancy Ann Atwood. While there he worked on his father's farm and thought about establishing a wholesale grocery business. Just at this time there was agitation in the country for a transcontinental railroad, and during the 1850s topographical engineers from the army had explored possible routes. The Civil War had demonstrated the need for more effective communication, especially to open the vast territory of the West to settlement and commerce. Accordingly, Congress passed and President Lincoln signed a bill in 1862 authorizing the construction of a railroad between the Missouri River and California.

Albert must have been aware of the ferment over the possibility of linking America's two coasts by a railway system. Although he was not trained for a commercial career, he demonstrated his keen intuition by choosing Chicago, the major rail junction of the country, as a place to make his fortune. In 1861 he borrowed $2,300 from his father and left to explore the city. Nan notes in her diary, "About the 9th (December) Albert, my fiancé, took dinner and spent evening to midnight, then said good-bye and left for Chicago to make his fortune and a home for us. 'Twas a sad parting and many bitter tears were shed. Chicago is a long way off."[24]

In his first letter back to Nan, Albert assured her, "The city has struck me very favorably indeed, and I am sure if I get into a good business I shall like it. It is a much clearer . . . healthier looking city than I supposed."[25] Albert settled quickly in Chicago and in less than one year returned to Vermont to claim his bride. On 29 September 1862 Nancy and Albert drove their own buggy to the meeting house, which was packed with family and friends, and were married in a short and simple service. The account is best told in Nancy's own words: "Albert and I walked up the aisle, unattended, and in a few words were married. Quietly, without flourish, we walked to the door, out to the road, and over to the station where we were to take the train for the wedding journey. . . . We were married at ten, and the train which we were to take arrived at eleven. So, right there on the platform we held our reception, and soon we had said good-bye and were off."[26]

It was a long journey, but Albert had thoughtfully planned to break it at several points, stopping at his alma mater to introduce his bride to old college friends and arranging surprise visits to two of Nan's brothers along the way. It was mid-October by the time they reached their new hometown; surprisingly Nan does not record her first impressions of Chicago in the diary that she so faithfully kept from 1854 until her death in 1916.

Their first home was a humble boarding house on West Adams Street. There, Elizabeth would be born and live until the age of two, when the family moved to a rented dwelling at 310 West Washington Street. With Albert's rapidly expanding business they soon were able to purchase their own home on the same street at number 464, which was closer to Union Park, the *Bois de Boulogne* of the west side. Here they would remain until they built their house on Prairie Avenue in 1884.

With his brother-in-law, Zerah Stetson (the widower of Nan's sister, Elizabeth) Albert had purchased a modest $200 stock of goods and opened his first grocery store with "bare board counters . . . and a dubious future."[27] Within a year Stetson sold his interest in the enterprise, and Albert was then joined by Ezra J. Warner, an old Vermont friend who, like himself, had been schooled at Kimball Academy. Meanwhile, Otho had been released from the 8th Vermont Volunteer Regiment on medical discharge and at Albert's invitation, and with an investment of $500, joined the firm now established at 14 State Street under the name Sprague Warner and Company.[28]

These three men, so unlike each other in temperament and talents, complemented one another ideally and brought to the business just the right combination of abilities to ensure the success of the venture. Otho, always the more adventurous and progressive of the two brothers, envisioned extending credit to retailers of small towns in the West and began exploring even those areas of the country not yet accessible by rail, thus expanding the business greatly.[29] Warner, with the instincts of an investment broker, managed the financial interests of the company very capably. Albert, the senior member of the firm, always remained the most conservative of the triumvirate and was noted for his even disposition, his ability to negotiate peaceably, and his having the sensibilities needed to run a well-oiled operation on the home front. With sound yet progressive merchandising methods reflected in the company's motto, "good measure, good quality, fair price,"[30] the enterprise flourished and distinguished itself by its efficient service and a consistently high quality of merchandise that included not only the staples of life, but such luxuries as exotic spices, truffles, fine imported olive oils, and a surprising variety of tobacco, coffee, and tea. The company published regular catalogs and by 1885 advertised that it sold no product that contained chemical preservatives.[31]

While important changes were taking place in the larger outside world of Chicago's commerce and society, the Sprague household underwent some changes on the domestic level with the arrival of baby Elizabeth Penn, named for Nan's late older sister. For the time being, and until she went east to study, she was called Lizzie.

Two years later Lizzie was joined by a baby sister, Carrie, and by another, Suzie, in 1869. Lucia had come to help Nan with the children during the winter months, and Otho, who had previously known Lucia only as Thomas Atwood's scrawny little sister, could not escape noticing that she had grown into a lovely, vivacious young woman. She was just seventeen, and Otho, ten years her senior, was smitten. As the youngest of the family, Lucia would remain with her aging parents as long as they lived. But with their deaths in 1869 and 1871 she was free and the following July she and Otho were married. Just as she had done so often when

Lucia was a little girl, Nan took charge of affairs; she arranged the wedding reception, prepared her sister's trousseau, selected all the hats and dresses, and had them made in Chicago at Otho's expense.[32] Nan always spent more liberally than her sister, whose pocketbook was cautiously eyed by Otho.

The establishment of Otho and Lucia next door on West Washington Street was the greatest joy to Nancy and Albert, for the two brothers had always been very close and the Atwood girls were bound by an unusually deep attachment. There was also a third alliance of sorts between the two families with the rather one-sided romance of Thomas Atwood and Caroline Amelia Sprague. Nan declared that "Thomas loved Amelia with a real and mighty love,"[33] but she, impressed with the success of her two brothers, was not willing to commit herself until Thomas established himself as a rich man. He had worked hard and saved enough money to attend college, but just at that time Ebenezer was in danger of losing his land. Only years later did Nan discover that Thomas had sacrificed his savings to salvage the farm and gave up college in order to stay at home to help his father.

Amelia selfishly prolonged the engagement for twelve years until Thomas had at last gone west and established himself in a business that met her expectations. But it was too late. Just as she finally consented to marriage Thomas was suddenly taken ill and died of meningitis. Amelia never married and continued to live in the household, spending six months of the year with Nan and Albert and the remainder with Lucia and Otho, stoically bearing the stigma of the spinster without a home of her own. The brothers provided her with a generous allowance and she in turn helped, especially with Lucia's children, whose pranks she tolerated and even loved. But she was a constant irritant to Nan, who confessed in her diary, "I can never forgive her."[34]

Just months after Lucia and Otho's wedding the two Sprague families were witness to one of Chicago's great calamities. At 2:00 on Sunday morning, 8 October 1871, neighbors awakened the Spragues to report that the city was ablaze. No rain had fallen for nearly three months and the combination of dry wells and near gale-force winds made it impossible to control the fire, which moved rapidly to the northeast until it reached the shores of Lake Michigan. Sprague Warner and most of the

Otho S. A. Sprague, Elizabeth's uncle, her father's partner in the firm of Sprague Warner and Company

Chicago Historical Society

Caroline Amelia Sprague (Aunt Amelia), Elizabeth's aunt who spent six months of the year living with Otho's family and six months with Albert's

Jeffrey Coolidge Photography, Boston

business district lay in the path of the conflagration. In an effort to salvage as much as possible, Albert and Otho immediately loaded a wagon with as much warehouse stock as they could and moved it to the lakeshore, only to have it consumed when the fire actually reached water's edge.[35]

Elizabeth, who was almost seven years old at the time, vividly recalled that every bed and lounge in the house was occupied by wounded and exhausted firefighters being ministered to by her mother and her aunt Lucia, while her father and uncle Otho kept a team of horses hitched and a wagon ready in the yard to evacuate the family in the event that the winds shifted.[36]

Despite massive destruction, Chicago's strategic position on the waterways and railway lines remained unchanged; and since the Sprague Warner business relied so heavily upon dependable means of transportation, rapid recovery was possible. Even as the fire still burned Albert located and rented new quarters and Otho had circulars printed announcing that the Sprague Warner Company was still in the business of food distribution.[37] Although the firm's stock had been wiped out, the Sprague brothers and their partner worked long hours to make a remarkable comeback and within a short time had moved back to Michigan Avenue.[38] Even as they struggled to save their own business, the brothers also worked vigorously with the Chicago Relief and Aid Society to help those left homeless by the fire.

Within a surprisingly short time Sprague Warner's volume of business expanded greatly as did its inventory of both domestic and imported goods. The many menus of teas, luncheons, and dinner parties described in both Nan's diary and the Glessner Journals of the same period are a vivid record of the luxury comestibles available to the wealthy: Exotic fruits are often found on mid-winter menus, and lobster, caviar, and other seafood not native to the Great Lakes were frequently served along with such delicacies as sweetbreads and fancy ices.

But the domestic life of the Spragues was not all parties and entertainment. In the period immediately after the fire both young families experienced their share of sorrows. As the arrival of each new baby increased the family circle, death visited Washington Street to claim another member. Within a year of the birth of Lucia's first child, Nan's youngest, Suzie, died of measles complicated by scarlet fever, and only a month after the birth of Lucia's second, Albert Arnold II, Nan lost her second child, Carrie, to tuberculosis of the brain.[39] By the age of eight, young Elizabeth had experienced firsthand the meaning of sickness and death. Her response was not recorded in the diary, but there is a good deal of evidence that Nan grieved excessively for her two little girls. Many years later Elizabeth recalled that her mother had repeatedly taken her by the hand to visit the family burial plot at Graceland Cemetery, where she wept over the small graves. Weary of these dismal pilgrimages, and perhaps feeling neglected, Elizabeth one day pointed to the space between the two headstones and said, "See, Mama, there's just room for me too."[40] Her none-too-subtle gesture was something of a rebuke to Nan but seems to have conveyed the message. Ever the good mother, Nan turned her grief into what became an almost equally intense outpouring of affection for her one remaining child, an attachment that would complicate the rocky relationship of mother and daughter for some years.

Soon after Carrie's death Elizabeth entered a world that would for the remainder of her long life be her joy, her refuge, and her unmistakable vocation: music. The occasion also marked the beginning of Elizabeth's association with the person who, next to her immediate family, would have the greatest influence on her—Regina Watson, née Cohn ("Ginka" to her friends), her teacher. Born in Breslau, Germany, in 1845, Regina came to the United States with her parents while still a child but returned to Germany as a young girl to study piano in Berlin with Carl Tausig, Liszt's favorite pupil. In Berlin she joined a circle of friends that included such notable figures of the musical world as Hans von Bülow, Anton Rubinstein, Eugen d'Albert, and Otto Lessmann. Others with whom she had at least an acquaintance were Clara Schumann and Joseph Joachim.[41]

Regina was "brilliant and scholarly," fluent in four languages, and showed great promise as a performer. But like so many women musicians of the nineteenth century, she gave up her ambitions for a concert career when she married and instead found her métier in teaching. (Teresa Carreño once described her as "the most prominent piano teacher in America."[42]) With her husband, Dr. Louis H. Watson, she settled

Elizabeth Penn Sprague, age ten, with her mother, Nancy Ann Atwood Sprague

Elizabeth Coolidge Winship Private Collection, Library of Congress

in Chicago around 1874 and almost immediately opened a studio on the south side of the city, calling it Mrs. Regina Watson's School for the Higher Art of Piano Playing.[43] At about the same time Amy Fay opened her studio on the north side of Chicago.[44]

It is a mark of Watson's character that, although her circle of intimates included many distinguished artists and musicians, she reached out to include the newest and the youngest of her pupils. Elizabeth was one of the first to enroll in Watson's program and was to be enormously influenced by her, for under her tutelage she not only developed into a very capable performer, but she found a warm-hearted and loving friend who would forever be a support and inspiration. Through her study with Watson Lizzie was, in a sense, joining a distinguished genealogy of pianists traceable to Tausig and ultimately to Franz Liszt.

It is easy to document her rapid progress from the programs of the "Class Reunion" recitals of Watson's studio. By the reunion of 1876 Elizabeth was already playing the simpler Mozart Sonatas and Bach English Suites,[45] and by the following year had progressed to more difficult works of Mendelssohn, Schubert, and Beethoven.[46] Nan's diary contains a particularly interesting entry from 1881, noting "the long talked of recital in which Elizabeth played a concerto (not identified). She gets many compliments and we are very proud and pleased. She commits everything to memory."[47] Pride in her daughter's accomplishments notwithstanding, there is evidence that Nan felt some resentment at Elizabeth's attachment to this new influence in her life. "Lizzie is daft over Mrs. Watson. Thinks and cares for her all the time—to my annoyance or anxiety."[48]

There was never any doubt about the deep love that Nancy and Albert Sprague had for their firstborn, and the pain they experienced over the loss of their other two little girls was only natural. That Elizabeth felt a need to remind them of the one treasure that they still possessed might have been merely the expression of natural sibling rivalry extended beyond the grave. At the same time it was a definite manifestation of her increasingly strong-willed nature. It was fortunate for all concerned that Elizabeth found a niche and a refuge in her musical achievements, for it was the beginning of a lifelong pattern of ever-reliable escape and sustenance in times of trouble.

While Nan learned to administer a smooth-running household and mastered the art of the gracious hostess, Albert was making a name for himself in the business world of Chicago. In 1877 he became a founding member of the Commercial Club of Chicago, which was distinguished by its conviction that men of means had a special obligation to contribute significantly to the city's development by using their combined power and wealth to address urgent social and fiscal needs. Albert was active in the club all his life and at various times served as president and as vice president.[49] At the same time he joined various fraternal organizations devoted to the cultivation and promotion of literature and the fine arts.[50]

While Albert had been privileged to receive a college education, Nan's formal schooling was minimal, but like her mother she was an inveterate reader. An inventory of the family library was made at the time of the dissolution of the household, which demonstrated an amazingly catholic range of interests.[51] Complete editions of classics such as Shakespeare and Molière, as well as such currently popular authors as Jane Austen, Emily Brontë, the Brownings, and George Eliot are found there along with musical scores, art books, political writings, and travelogues—everything from Dante to Disraeli and more.

Over the course of his life Albert Sprague would many times apply the entrepreneurial skills that he learned in the administration of his own business to the service of artistic endeavors in Chicago, particularly music, which he considered to be life's single most beautiful adornment. In 1882 he became a board member of the Chicago Musical Festival Association, a subscriber to the guarantee fund, and vice president of the business staff.[52] The first Chicago May Festival of that year was important to the Sprague family for personal reasons too, for it marked the beginning of their long and friendly association with Theodore Thomas, this country's first virtuoso conductor.

Whatever the artistic merits of the first Chicago May Festival, the balance sheet showed a financial loss of over $9,000; yet plans were soon underway to stage a second festival in 1884, and once again A. A. Sprague was a guarantor.[53] Advance publicity made much of the fact that three of Wagner's soloists from the second Bayreuth festival would be featured, as well as Christine Nilsson, the famous Swedish soprano who had sung

Marguerite in Gounod's *Faust* just the year before at the opening of the Metropolitan Opera in New York. Once again the festival expenditures exceeded receipts.

Undeterred by financial losses, the following year Chicago launched its first Opera Festival, with A. A. Sprague at the head of the board of directors. Its goal to produce fourteen operas between 13 April and 25 April would, even today, be an extremely ambitious undertaking. An impressive roster of great singers had been assembled, among them Adelina Patti, Sofia Scalchi, and Emma Nevada, for whom it was a Chicago debut. The festival was a stunning financial success, leaving a substantial balance in the treasury and making Chicago a contender for the musical leadership of the nation.

Although the boards of these organizations were made up exclusively of men, the women of Chicago society were making their mark as well, and a certain degree of emancipation is evident in the proliferation of different women's societies concerned with a variety of issues springing up at about the same time. The fact that these fledgling groups eschewed the title "club" suggests that this designation still carried with it a strong connotation of fraternal organization, bringing to mind an ambiance of great leather armchairs, cigars, and port.

The first notable organization established by and for women was the Fortnightly, founded in 1873 for the purpose of encouraging the social and intellectual development of its members. Membership was limited to 175, of which many were the wives of prominent businessmen, senators, physicians, and lawyers.[54] The Fortnightly, like the Amateur Musical Club that began informally around 1877, and the Friday Club, established in the following decade,[55] was to figure very importantly in the lives and activities of the Sprague women, particularly Elizabeth.

By the 1880s the Spragues found themselves in a world very different from their Vermont experience. How they adjusted says much about their character. Sprague Warner and Company had become a leader in the wholesale grocery business, not only in Chicago but in the nation.[56] The owners were recognized for their roles in civic affairs, and the spouses were taking their place in the social life of the city. To their credit the Spragues were not afflicted by the affectation and tasteless ostentation that often characterizes the nouveaux riches. The values and the work ethic inherited from their Puritan ancestors were so deeply instilled in them that the comforts and privileges that resulted from their new status only served to dictate a greater degree of responsibility, an awareness of morality in the stewardship of wealth. It was a lesson that Elizabeth was not too young to learn either—and one that neither Albert nor Nan would lose sight of even now, as they made plans for what was rapidly becoming the requisite of any family of means in that Gilded Age—the "grand tour."[57]

CHAPTER TWO

Coming of Age

Taking up Baedeker's Handbook of Northern Italy, she committed to memory the most important dates of Florentine history. For she was determined to enjoy herself on the morrow.

– E. M. FORSTER, *A ROOM WITH A VIEW*

THE SPRAGUE FAMILY library contained no fewer than thirty volumes of Baedeker's travel guides, and the detailed journals that both Nan and Lizzie kept during their tour of Europe suggest that they had assiduously done their homework in preparation for the trip. Lizzie's reaction to a morning gallery excursion in Vienna hints that she was fast becoming capable of making independent judgments. Noting that Baedeker gave several stars to the gallery, which she declared inferior to the Dresden collection, she mused that, "perhaps Mr. Baedeker had a hard bump once or twice, and put down stars in his guide book which he saw at the moment."[1]

At seventeen Elizabeth tottered between young womanhood and lingering adolescence, being both intellectually precocious and emotionally immature. Her chronicle of the journey betrays the contest within her as her ingenuous reactions to each new experience take wing in unbridled verbiage that quickly alternates with mature and realistic insights into the personalities of others—and above all an awareness of her own character flaws. She was, by her own admission, strong-willed, quick-tempered, and often unreasonable, while at the same time a perfectionist and her own severest critic. In matters less personal the journal reveals that her fine young mind was busy processing the staggering diversity of cultural experiences to which she was being exposed, and the critical sense that would characterize her judgments in later life was already emerging.

We know from the numerous pictures taken of her by Nan, who was an avid amateur photographer, that Lizzie was a pretty child. The photos often capture a petulant attitude but also document her development into a lovely young woman. Although the visa procured for her trip does not contain her picture, it does provide a valuable verbal description: "stature six feet and one half inch; forehead high; eyes blue; nose straight; mouth ordinary; chin pointed; hair light; complexion light; face oval."[2] She seems to have inherited the physical features of her tall, fair-haired father rather than her petite, dark-haired mother. It was often noted that she bore a striking resemblance to the famed opera singer Christine Nilsson.

Elizabeth's travel journal begins on 17 May 1882, the day of their departure on the Cunard liner HMS *Servie.* Despite a rough crossing the voyage was a glittering affair, with Elizabeth garnering a good deal of praise for her piano playing—especially at the party celebrating Queen Victoria's sixty-third birthday on 24 May. The following day they arrived in England, where they remained until mid-July, traversing the isle from Glasgow to the Channel and taking great satisfaction in locating the graves of ancestors and attending concerts, operas, and the theater.[3]

The next stop was Brussels, where "with Lizzie's French we manage[d]."[4] Her study of the language had been only a part of her grooming for the trip. Months before their departure she was being tutored in history by a Mr. Mathews who accompanied them on the trip and sometimes read poetry aloud, as on the day that he stood beneath a tree in the country churchyard at Stoke Poges and read Gray's elegy to his approving audience. Mathews was just one of ten in the traveling party, which included Albert's old friends the Twichells. Frequently it became difficult to procure rooms for so many in one place, and inevitable tensions arose. Nan found the months of togetherness trying and recorded her frustrations in her diary along with her accounts of their daily excursions to museums and art galleries. It was at this time that the Spragues began their collection of artworks, many of which would eventually be given to the Chicago Art Institute, of which Albert was a director.[5]

Lizzie also wrote at length of the art works that she saw, often adding her own critical comments to those of Baedeker. Not surprisingly,

Elizabeth Penn Sprague in 1882, at the time of her "grand tour"

Elizabeth Coolidge Winship Private Collection, Library of Congress

though, the lion's share of the chronicle, and certainly the most vivid portions, are her commentaries on the music that she heard in every place that they visited. Her developing good taste and critical faculties are revealed in her description of a performance conducted by Eduard Strauss, whose demeanor on the podium could at best be described as idiosyncratic. Lizzie found him "a rather peculiar, out of the way young man. He seems to be on the verge of dancing as he leads." And his habit of sometimes facing the audience as he conducted elicited her description of him as a "dandy" and a "smasher."[6] The accuracy of her perception is borne out by a no less well-informed and capable artist than the American violinist, Maud Powell, who declared him to be "simply ludicrous to look at, with a bow arm to make a violinist's eyes ache."[7]

Father, mother, and daughter were all devoted opera enthusiasts and attended performances wherever they went, often hearing the latest repertoire sung by the world's greatest artists and being escorted through the backstage areas of great opera houses. Two experiences in particular made a deep impression on Lizzie, and for very different reasons. The first was in Paris, where she was obviously more overwhelmed by the opulence of the Théâtre de l'Opéra than by the singing she heard. The performance by an unnamed soprano "with a pretty face but a thin voice" is breezily passed over in favor of a detailed description of the theater. The Opéra was still a very new building, for although it was begun in 1861, the Franco-Prussian War had delayed completion, and it was opened only in 1875. This time she agreed with Baedeker who declared it to be one of the finest in Europe. Lizzie's account gives the impression of one slightly overcome by the grandeur of it all. But with the second visit a week later, her journal suggests a frank, girlish delight not only in seeing the opera, but in watching the audience and being seen. "In the evening we attended the Grand Opéra House, hearing the opera of 'The Jewess' (Halévy's *La Juive*). . . . We had an opportunity to see the Grand Foyer, and Mama, Papa, and I remained out after the scene had begun again. . . . [B]ut before we had gotten upstairs, the bell rang for a signal, as it does before the music begins. . . . We did not go in even after that, but promenaded—the act was a long ways along."[8]

The only other musical experience to surpass the thrill of the Opéra was to come at Bayreuth, where they not only toured Wahnfried,

Wagner's villa, but attended a performance in the superb new Festspielhaus. This was indeed a very special occasion for it was the premiere of Wagner's last music drama, *Parsifal.* The Festspielhaus, so innovative in design, with its covered orchestra pit and superb acoustics, had been inaugurated in 1876 with the first complete performance of Wagner's Ring cycle. But the financial losses had been so great that the second Bayreuth festival had to be delayed until 1882, when the Spragues were there. The first performance of *Parsifal* had actually taken place on 26 July with the great Amalie Materna as Kundry, Hermann Winkelmann as Parsifal, and Theodore Reichmann as Amfortas. In the performance that Elizabeth and her parents saw on 14 August Marianne Brandt took Materna's place and Heinrich Gudehus sang the title role. Although it was not actually the first performance it was indeed the premiere production of the work.[9]

Elizabeth was primed for the occasion and noted in her journal on 14 August, "[We] start for Bayreuth this evening where we attend Wagner's opera house and hear his music performed by a band which he himself leads. Isn't it grand!"[10] She was, in fact, incorrect about Wagner conducting and noted her error at the bottom of the page. By this time the composer was quite ill and would die within six months. However, Lizzie cannot have been too disappointed, for Nan's diary entry confirms that Wagner was in the audience. "He was sitting in a box with his head bowed and was called out on stage. The event of a lifetime."[11] She had obviously prepared herself well for this experience, and understood that *Parsifal* "must not be called an opera; it is not like an ordinary opera; but is grand, oh magnificent, . . . a most sublime drama."[12]

Nan was very moved too but somewhat less effusive—perhaps influenced by the extreme length of the work, which she, with characteristic efficiency, had obviously timed. "Began at 4, Act 1, 2 hrs; interim ½ hour; Act 2, 1 and ½ hour, interim of 45 minutes; Act 3, 1 hour."[13] By her account the production would have been over at 9:45, a colossal five and three-quarter hours from start to finish.

In all, their tour lasted over eleven months and took them through nearly every country of Western Europe as well as parts of Africa. From Spain they crossed the Strait of Gibraltar to Tangier and eventually went on to Egypt, then retraced their steps northward to England. Both Nan's and Lizzie's accounts of the trip are filled with many anecdotes that, while trivial in themselves, reveal a good deal about the characters of the two. Nan's experience in Spain was colored by the fact that they were exposed to smallpox while there and had to buy sulfur to burn in braziers in their rooms. "I am sick of Spain," she wrote.[14] On occasion she became the jaded tourist too, affecting for example a blasé attitude to the Treasury of St. Stephen's Cathedral in Vienna. She commented, "The jewels are so numerous and big that they seem common."[15] Vienna redeemed itself, however, by providing another unforgettable musical experience, for it was here that they heard Brahms perform his own chamber music.

Not surprisingly, Nan was ever mindful of their wardrobes. By October when they again reached Paris she noted, "We are shabby and must buy some clothes. The first thing I do is go with Amelia and Lizzie to order corsets. . . . [We] buy hats, but shopping in Paris is no joke when you cannot speak French."[16] Lizzie recounted the same episode in her diary: "In the morning I take lesson in French by wrestling with a French corset maker; asking her to *parler plus lentement* and stumbling away myself to her."[17] Her progress is revealed in entries now generously and affectedly garnished with French phrases.

There is a certain girlish naiveté in some of Elizabeth's observations, such as her announcement that Marseilles reminded her of Chicago and one street in particular "looked quite a good deal like Wabash Avenue."[18] She loved Italy but when in Florence pronounced the unadorned façade of San Lorenzo to be "extremely uncouth." And her first experience of Catholic ritual in Rome is amusingly described in a letter to her cousin Lucy back in Chicago. "The ministers wear funny long dresses with very splendid embroidery over them. Sometimes they wear red gloves and large hats on their heads. When they read out of the bible they say their words in a sing-song . . . isn't that a funny way to have church?"[19]

On arriving in Zurich on 22 August Nan received a letter from Regina Watson urging her to take Lizzie to Berlin to study piano. She must have given the idea some serious consideration, for Elizabeth wrote home to her Aunt Em a short time later, "I think likely Mama and I shall be in Berlin this winter and I shall study with Reiff."[20] However,

Nan was growing weary and lonely for her friends at home and decided against the idea. She genuinely regretted the disappointment for her daughter, because she recognized that Elizabeth was "in just the right mood for it," but believed it best to return with Albert.

They booked passage home on 21 April and after nearly a year of travel returned to a multitude of receptions hosted by their many friends. The only blight on the whole event for Lizzie was the disappointment of being denied the opportunity to study in Berlin. The experience had been good for her, though: She had left Chicago a girl and returned a young lady with a patina of sophistication that the experience of the tour had added to her persona. It remained only to apply the last gloss of finishing school—in the East, of course.

It was with much trepidation that Nan took her daughter to New York, to Mrs. Sylvanus Reed's French and English Boarding and Day School, in the autumn of 1883. A number of Chicago girls were already enrolled there, but that was small consolation to her and to Lizzie, whom she describes as "tearful and homesick." It is quite clear that Albert Sprague recognized the need for some separation of mother and daughter as well as the value of this educational experience for Elizabeth. From Chicago he wrote urging Nan "to give Lizzie up to stay in New York and study."[21]

Mrs. Reed's School, founded in 1864, was located on East 53rd Street between Fifth and Madison Avenues. Although the school offered the usual training in the social graces of the "finishing school," these were only accessories to the basic curriculum in the humanities. Elizabeth was enrolled in the Collegiate Department, which offered a broad spectrum of courses in language and literature, philosophy, science, church history, and the arts.[22]

For a $900 tuition the school offered private accommodations for boarding students, common rooms with a pleasant ambiance, and a cuisine under the charge of a maître d'hôtel of reputation. Daily exercise and nature study were taken in Central Park, and the staff included a trained infirmarian. Above all Mrs. Reed kept a careful maternal eye on the girls at all times. Although she emphasized the importance of an intellectually challenging course of study for them—equal to that offered in the best colleges here and abroad—she also espoused the solidly Victorian attitude that "the aim of this higher education should not be to give to women the same training as to men, but to develop in them the highest type of womanhood. . . . It must not seek to make woman discontented with the position in the universe which nature has assigned to her, but to maintain the dignity and fulfill the responsibility of that position."[23]

Accordingly, the discipline was strict and students' lives were highly structured. Boarding students were never permitted to go into the streets of New York unattended by a governess or some responsible person, and girls could not receive visitors, "except those introduced by parents or guardians, and then only at the option of the Principal."[24] It is obvious that Nan worried over how her dutiful nineteen-year-old daughter, just returned from an extended European tour, would adapt to this strict new way of life. In her diary she wrote of Elizabeth's "morbidly conscientious nature. It is hard for my dear girl . . . to be like other girls . . . and I fear life will always be difficult for her."[25]

A part of the curriculum that undoubtedly was a factor in the choice of Mrs. Reed's School was the emphasis placed upon music. Courses in solfège were offered, and private instruction in singing and instrumental music were available as well. There were practice rooms with good pianos, and time for practice was carefully worked into the students' individual schedules. In addition they were taken to rehearsals and concerts of the New York Philharmonic Society and the Church Music Association.[26]

Elizabeth immediately settled into a highly structured routine: Whether it was self-imposed or dictated by her advisors is not clear. It may very well have been the only way that she could do justice to a demanding academic curriculum and still fit in her piano lessons and daily practice which, as it was, had to be broken into three periods. She was immediately enrolled in both French and German language courses, English literature, philosophy, psychology, elocution, and gymnastics. Her achievements are documented in her grade reports at the end of the year. "Logic excellent—of mind quite unusually acute. Ancient Art and Composition—excellent."[27]

As the title of Mrs. Reed's school suggests, the study of languages was stressed. The school employed five Parisian French teachers, and all of the American teachers were compelled to use French in conversation with their students so that "every pupil in the school was required to study and to speak French."[28] The satisfaction that Elizabeth had experienced in Europe of being able to communicate in another language, however imperfectly, apparently motivated her to immerse herself in French—which she did so enthusiastically that she was proclaimed the most serious student in the class. Later in life she would depend greatly upon her French to communicate with her many European friends. She seemed to take her German somewhat less seriously, yet by the second year she was reading works of E. T. A. Hoffmann in German.

Her frequent letters home recount experiences of a young lady who up to this time had neither cared for her own clothes nor done her own hair, but who now found herself responsible for such common domestic chores as darning stockings. There is an unmistakable sense of pride evident in the account of her bumbling and repeated efforts to mend her gloves and to manage her own finances. But as always, the place of primacy in her life was reserved for her music. And although she had already met her new piano teacher, Mr. Pinner, by the end of the first month, she was impatient at the slow start and disappointed with her own performance at the first lesson. "I did not do myself justice in all, but he will find out afterward what I can do. He thought I played too loudly, a fault for which Mrs. Watson has corrected me."[29]

Saturday afternoons were devoted to her piano lessons, which meant giving up opera matinees and concerts. So it was a rare treat when Mr. Hamburger, an old family friend, arrived in New York armed with a letter from Albert granting him permission to take her to the opera, where they sat in a box and heard Nilsson and Scalchi in *Faust.*[30] The Metropolitan Opera House had been inaugurated less than a month earlier with Gounod's *Faust* sung by the same cast. Surprisingly, Elizabeth does not offer her impressions of either the performance or of the spanking new theater with its profusion of crimson and gold leaf, as she had so ecstatically done the preceding year when she visited Paris's Opéra.

In fact her letters home begin to take on a less spontaneous character, as if she were writing an assigned essay. Whether this was the influence of her tutors or a self-imposed exercise in cultivating the deportment and style expected of a proper young lady of the Victorian era is not clear. At the same time her letters begin to reflect an increasing lack of self-confidence.[31] It may have been the natural consequence of having been tutored alone and now finding herself for the first time in competition with other bright students. Even more disturbing are the letters that indicate problems in relating with her peers. Growing up without siblings, Elizabeth had spent the greater part of her life with adults and now continued to do so by seeking the company of her teachers. At the same time her longing to be liked by her peers was impossibly constrained by her puritanical judgments of some of the other students' actions. In keeping with this serious tone, she expresses a growing attraction to the church.

Religious training was a very important part of the school's philosophy, and since Mrs. Reed's husband was an Episcopal priest, the resident students attended services in his church with Mrs. Reed and her family. For those girls who wished to worship elsewhere Reed provided a seat in the Presbyterian Church, Madison Square, where they went with a chaperone.[32] The Spragues were Presbyterians, and Elizabeth went to her own church, but she often attended Episcopal services as well because she found the music there to be much better.

That the adjustment had been difficult for Elizabeth is evident from the fact that by December she had lost even her zest for piano lessons. But with the beginning of the new year things seemed to improve. Critiques of musical performances again spice her letters, such as her estimation of a recital by a certain Madame Schiller. "I think very slightly of her playing. She pounded like a 40 horsepower triphammer," she wrote.[33]

Meanwhile back in Chicago Nan missed her daughter dreadfully, so it was determined at Christmas 1884 that Elizabeth would not go back to New York. "I keep her—I need her more than she needs more school. She does not come out this year, but will study at home."[34] The denial of a college education was something that Elizabeth would always regret deeply. Had she been born only a little later she might have had the same opportunities for a higher education as her cousin Lucy who attended Radcliffe College.

Undoubtedly one of the reasons that Nan wanted her daughter with her at this time was that the Spragues were building a new home. Prairie

Avenue on the South side was fast becoming Chicago's "Gold Coast." The industrialists Gustavus Swift, Philip Armour, and George Pullman all resided there now. Within an area of five blocks of Prairie Avenue, forty of the sixty members of the Commercial Club had their homes.[35] Albert began negotiating the purchase of land soon after returning from the European trip,[36] and in September of 1883 Nan inscribed in her diary the cost of the new house:

Lot	$16,000	Sold house on Washington St.	$16,000
House	46,000	Sold property on Ashland Ave.	11,000
Stable	6,137	TOTAL	27,000
TOTAL	$70,826	DIFFERENCE	$43,826

The designer of the house was Daniel Burnham, who over the years would distinguish himself as one of the finest architects of the era.[37] The Spragues moved into their new home just days before Christmas 1884, and the following December staged the elaborate coming out of their daughter. That it was a social event of some note is evident from the extensive coverage in the press, which dubbed it "a brilliant affair," with "all the elite of Chicago . . . represented."[38]

After the European trip and her studies in the East, Elizabeth resumed her lessons with Regina Watson and was soon performing in the Class Reunions again—programs that attest to progress made during the New York interim.[39] And now after her debut, her social life accelerated as well. Many a pleasant afternoon was taken up playing duets with Frances Glessner, the wife of industrialist John J. Glessner who made his fortune in the manufacture of farm implements. It was for Elizabeth a healthy association, for Fanny (as she was called by her friends) was a vigorous woman of many interests and an accomplished pianist. She was a self-styled critic of things cultural, with perceptions not unlike Elizabeth's—only honed to a more audacious candor by virtue of her added years, for she was fifteen years Elizabeth's senior. A noteworthy example of Mrs. Glessner's forthright—if opinionated—declarations was her reaction to the much-publicized visit of Oscar Wilde to Chicago in 1882. His lecture on "The Decorative Arts" evoked Fanny's opinion of him as "a great fool and humbug."[40]

Elizabeth's parental home at 2710 Prairie Avenue, Chicago, designed by Daniel Burnham. After her parents' deaths she gave the house to be used as a residence for nurses from Presbyterian Hospital

Jeffrey Coolidge Photography, Boston

John Glessner's wealth and position allowed Fanny the luxury to indulge her seemingly endless curiosity in an extravagant number of pursuits.[41] The journal that she kept from 1870 to 1921 provides a priceless look into the life of the wealthy in Chicago's Gilded Age and is rich in details related to the Spragues, especially during this critical period of Elizabeth's early adulthood. The Spragues begin to be mentioned around 1880, and it is clear that the two families socialized together often and even occupied adjacent boxes at the opera, where Fanny always sat hatless in defiance of both fashion and decorum.

During this period there were innumerable musicales, dinners, and all manner of theatrical and musical entertainment shared by the Glessners and the Spragues. The Chicago of that era offered an impressive array of great talent, and both Nan's diary and Fanny's journal read like a litany of great singers—among them Patti, Sembrich, Nordica, Calvé, Melba, Tetrazzini, Caruso, Materna, and the de Reszke brothers. They saw Sarah Bernhardt, Eleonora Duse, and Tommaso Salvini tread the boards speaking their parts in their native tongue in curious bilingual productions in which the rest of the cast spoke English. They were treated to orchestral performances conducted by Damrosch and Thomas, and heard such great pianists as Paderewski, Carreño, and Bloomfield-Zeisler—all of whom at times performed in the Glessners' home at private musicales attended by Elizabeth. Without a doubt Carreño and Bloomfield-Zeisler were inspirations to her and fueled her desire for a career—Carreño in particular, for she was an intimate friend of Regina Watson, to whom she gave much credit for her own career.[42]

The Glessners were friends with the Coolidge family of Boston. During their summer sojourns in the East, the Glessners regularly called on the Coolidges there, and the Coolidges spent time with the Glessners at their summer home, "The Rocks," at Littleton, New Hampshire. Elizabeth had met Isa Coolidge at The Rocks in 1883 and the two girls became friends.

In 1885 the Glessners engaged the renowned Boston architect Henry Hobson Richardson to design a home for them at 1800 Prairie Avenue. Richardson did not live to see the house completed; he died in 1886 shortly after finishing the final drawings. His successors in the firm, Shepley Rutan and Coolidge, brought the project to completion in accordance with Richardson's plans. Isa's brother Charles Allerton Coolidge was a junior member of the firm and made many trips to Chicago in connection with the project, furthering the association between the Glessners and the Coolidges.[43]

In the late summer of 1888 Elizabeth was again at The Rocks when the Coolidge family came, and the following summer, on her way to the Glessners, Elizabeth stopped to see Mrs. Stone at Beach Bluff, where the Coolidges were also visiting. Her animated letters home are the first evidence of her being paid attention to by young men. Clearly—at age 25—she was delighted and somewhat mystified by this newfound popularity with the opposite sex. "I have really been a howling belle. What has come over me is more than I can tell. . . . Among these men there is one with whom I have had quite an affair, and I think he is very seriously interested in me. . . . I cannot tell you all now but am dying to give you particulars in full when I reach home."[44]

The name of her mystery man is never revealed in writing, but soon enough the identity of this first love—the love of her life—would be quite clear.

C H A P T E R   T H R E E

Enter Frederic

The face of all the world is changed, I think since first I heard the footsteps of thy soul.

– ELIZABETH BARRETT BROWNING,
SONNETS FROM THE PORTUGUESE, VII

ELIZABETH AND ISA COOLIDGE had been friends for nearly six years by the time Elizabeth was wooed by the unnamed suitor in the summer of 1889. That winter Elizabeth visited Isa at the Coolidges' home at 114 Commonwealth Avenue in Boston's fashionable Back Bay. It was one of the worst winters in Boston history, and her stay was prolonged sufficiently for Frederic Coolidge, younger brother of Isa and Charles, to lose his heart completely. When the time for Elizabeth's departure came, Fred gallantly volunteered to see her to the train and attend to her baggage. He loitered as he settled her in the compartment, and when the train began to leave the station with Fred still on board Elizabeth realized that it was all a carefully laid plan. He rode with her as far as Pittsfield, the junction of the Boston-Albany Road and the New York Central's main line west to Chicago. There is no written account of what followed, but years later Elizabeth related to her grandson that in Pittsfield, Fred rented a sleigh, took her for a ride in the snowy woods, and proposed. With a twinkle in her eye she added, "You know, it was cozy under those buffalo robes!"[1]

Fred was the scion of a distinguished family, easily the equal of the Atwoods and the Spragues in lineage, claiming ancestors who had fought at Lexington and Bunker Hill. He belonged to the ninth generation of Coolidges, who traced their origin in the New World to John Coolidge (ca. 1603–91), who came to the Massachusetts Bay Colony from the village of Cottenham, Cambridgeshire, England, in 1630 on the *Arabella,* probably with Governor John Winthrop.[2] His son, Nathaniel (ca. 1634–1711), from whom Fred descended, was an enterprising man of considerable financial and political influence and was apparently the settlement's factotum. He was a tailor, farmer, miller, owner of a large fish weir in the Charles River, fence viewer, constable, keeper of the books, and even the town hangman. The Coolidges after him were mainly innkeepers, farmers, and officeholders in the colony.[3]

Fred's father, David Hill Coolidge (1833–1907), was a prominent attorney in Boston, trained at Boston Latin School and Harvard University. He became a member of the Boston Common Council and in 1865 was representative in the lower house of the Massachusetts legislature.[4] In 1858 he married Isabella Shurtleff, daughter of Dr. Samuel Atwood Shurtleff (1792–1873).[5]

Isabella could trace her ancestry from William Shurtleff, who came from Ecclesfield, near Sheffield in Yorkshire, England, when he was a child of ten, and was apprenticed to Thomas Clarke, a carpenter in the Plymouth Colony. By the time that the General Court of the Colony convened in Plymouth in June 1656, William was chosen one of the "Surveyors for the highwaies."[6] The succeeding generations of Shurtleffs were prominent civil servants and people of great piety.

Fred was the youngest child of Isabella Shurtleff and David Hill Coolidge and from his earliest years was characterized by all who knew him as "a boy of the sweetest possible disposition," affectionate yet manly, having "a great capacity for creating and freely giving friendship."[7] After attending Boston Latin he entered Harvard, where he took honors and for all four years was class president. Everything about him—his lineage, character, and reputation—was without blemish, yet his letters convey the distinct impression that he felt unworthy of Elizabeth, whose quick mind and musical talent he so admired. His feelings of inadequacy seem to stem from several sources, some real, others imagined, and they may have been unwittingly exacerbated by the prolonged engagement of two years.

Elizabeth carefully kept Fred's letters from the first to the very last. Fewer of hers to him have survived. Although he was a busy medical student, during the courtship years Fred wrote almost daily letters that

Isabella Coolidge Councilman (Isa), Fred's sister, through whom Elizabeth met Fred

Jeffrey Coolidge Photography, Boston

are filled with the outpouring of his love for Elizabeth and his highly idealistic aspirations. There is no question that the specter of Elizabeth's ubiquitous and possessive mother was a formidable obstacle for Frederic. His letters not only suggest that he felt guilty about writing daily to Elizabeth without Nan's permission, they also make it very clear that he kept their relationship secret from his own family as well. For Fred in his last year of medical studies at Harvard, it was difficult to carve out time to be alone with his reveries, which he soon learned to disguise as study time. "I have run away to . . . the hay loft of the barn with the wind whistling through the cracks, and my hands cold. . . . I read and reread your letters dear and have much to say in answer if I can find time. Confound it! Here come the boys and I must get out my study book and pretend to read it. . . . They think I am queer to stay here."[8]

One of the most endearing of Fred's qualities is the concern he felt for the integrity of the relationship between his sister and Elizabeth. Worried that he might fail in his "heart's desire" to marry Elizabeth, he could "pretend to be happy" more easily if none of the family knew, and there would be no danger of Isa blaming her.

Female bonding in the nineteenth century often found expression in unabashedly affectionate language, and Fred seemed to understand that the mutual affection of these two important women in his life was something sacred. His respect for their relationship says much for the quality of his own love for Elizabeth. Even in his daily contact with Isa at home he continued to maintain his silence with regard to Elizabeth and often reported to her his clumsy attempts at subterfuge. "Such a narrow escape, dearest . . . Isa just came upstairs and I had to toss your picture, which is always before me when I am writing, ignominiously into the table drawer, followed by your dear letter and this letter but by the time she got upstairs I was studying hard on a case of heart disease or something of the sort."[9]

By early spring of 1890 Fred was experiencing doubts concerning his lack of exposure to the kinds of cultural experiences that Elizabeth had had by this time while he had been immersed almost exclusively in his demanding medical studies. He admired her sophistication and above all her musical talents that he had observed from close range as he sat by her side at the piano for hours. During this self-conscious period he even resorted to collecting anecdotes and bits of news to enable him to make conversation more comfortably with her friends and family when he came to visit her in the summer. On a spiritual level they shared confidences in long letters that reveal similar high-minded aspirations and ideals for their future together. Fred acknowledged that "Meeting you, darling, my life has broadened and my aims must change, reaching higher and farther. What they are I know not yet in detail. . . . If you could trust your life to me, the working out of some more or less definite aims would be our holiest, happiest moments." At the same time he expresses a nagging awareness of the differences in their life experiences up to that time: "Now dear Elizabeth, you have to decide whether . . . coming down to plain earth again after all the excitement of society and the 'being as good as the next one' with their comfortable and self-satisfying needs, is not going to be the happier way of life."[10]

By early summer of 1890 Fred finally felt secure enough to suggest to his family that he might go to Chicago after medical school, and had even confided his intentions to Isa. While he was concluding his studies at Harvard and questioning his lack of time for cultural experiences, back home in Chicago Elizabeth was caught up in the stimulating round of social activities that revolved more and more around music. There were many musicales featuring Carreño, Bloomfield-Zeisler, and Julia Rivé-King. For Elizabeth the example of these women who were successful concert artists may have stimulated her own aspirations as a performer but at the same time created tensions within her as she contemplated marriage and considered her commitment to Fred's ideal of the "simple life" of service to others—not to mention the awareness of her social station as the daughter of a prominent and wealthy family in a period when careers for women in her class were frowned upon.

It was an exciting time in Chicago, with theaters and concert halls offering an abundance of great music and drama. D'Albert and Sarasate were performing there; Patti was appearing in *Il Barbiere di Siviglia,* and Francesco Tamagno could be seen as Otello, a role created by him under the direction of Verdi himself.[11] And when it was announced that Walter Damrosch would be conducting a performance of the entire Ring cycle of Wagner with the Metropolitan Opera Company, Messrs. Palmer, Glessner, McCormick, McVeagh, and Sprague petitioned him to lecture on the work in preparation—with Damrosch, of course, invited to dine with them afterward.[12]

Elizabeth was neither idle nor content to be merely a spectator. She played numerous musicales at the Glessners during this time and also performed at a charity concert sponsored by the Amateur Music Club. Meanwhile, Nan struggled with disparate emotions, on the one hand grateful at the prospect of seeing her daughter settled in a union with a fine young man who would cherish her and support her in a good life, but feeling at the same time a deep sense of deprivation at the thought of sharing Elizabeth's love. Her feelings all too often manifested themselves in downright selfish behavior—full of jealousy and hurt—always the occasion of headaches and hysteria. That she recognized the excessive degree of her attachment to her daughter is clear from her admission to Albert that "my relations with her are not common . . . you know how my love for E has grown to be a passion—a mania—and how when night comes I long for day, that I may be with her again. And when she goes from me I watch and wait till her return."[13] Aware too that she had often made a spectacle of herself with her uncontrolled emotional displays, she longed for understanding from those who had witnessed these outbreaks so that they might "not think I am all selfish and weak. I don't want to be but cannot think of my life separate from hers."[14]

It is not that Nan did not like Fred. She thought him "very sensible" and approved of his ambition to become a success in the medical profession. Behind the scenes Albert was the great peacemaker, a role he would so often be called upon to play. He assured Nan, "[Y]ou know I appreciate what it is to you to give up your idolized child. But I believe you agree with me that we are not giving her away, although another takes her."[15] Nonetheless, Albert was, in his own quiet way, taking measures to ensure Fred's worthiness and requested him to send a complete account of his grades and his extracurricular activities from Harvard. This scrutinizing could not have done much to bolster the young man's already fragile image of himself, but to his credit he complied in all docility and passed the test.[16] With the battle won, their engagement was formally announced in Chicago on 20 September 1890. Fred could not be there since he was now an intern on duty at Massachusetts General Hospital in Boston. But even from a distance he gradually managed to

Frederic Shurtleff Coolidge at the time of his marriage to Elizabeth, 1891

Jeffrey Coolidge Photography, Boston

Elizabeth Sprague Coolidge in her wedding gown, 1891

Jeffrey Coolidge Photography, Boston

win the love and confidence of the whole family, beginning with Nan, whom he obviously recognized as his foremost adversary. In time he had so softened her that she was able not only to acknowledge her bad behavior but actually came close to an apology. "If sometimes the selfish thought has come to me, that I can never let you take her from me, and that in return for my life's best devotion she and you must not leave me, it is not my heart's best and truest wish. . . . You have seen too many evidences (alas) from me to need to tell you how overflowingly full my fond heart is, but believe me, however selfish or weak I may appear, when the real test comes, I shall be ready to accept what is best."[17]

Meanwhile, Albert, realizing that it would not be a simple matter for a young and inexperienced physician to establish himself in a new city, took steps to create a niche for his future son-in-law. As members of the board of directors of Rush Medical College in Chicago, he and Otho used their influence to create a position there for Fred, who was specializing in orthopedic surgery, a relatively new field that seems to have appealed to the administration of the college.

Things just seemed to be approaching normal when Nan was called upon to assume another burden. She now became the caretaker of her sister's family, who by now lived directly next door on Prairie Avenue. Neither Lucia nor Otho was ever very robust, and several of their children were sickly. In 1889 Otho suffered a recurrence of tuberculosis, and doctors advised a complete rest in a mild climate, so he and Lucia left for nearly a year in the south of Europe while Nan cared for the children.[18] During their absence six-year-old Arnold died, and it became Nan's sad duty to inform the other children and to attempt to locate Otho and Lucia. To add to the stress, Lucia's second child and Nan's namesake, Nannie, had begun to exhibit serious signs of mental and emotional instability. Although her complete breakdown did not occur until several years later, Nan seems to have foreseen the seriousness of the situation and penned her own typically unvarnished prognosis: "Nannie gets worse and worse, and very irritable and strange, til it develops into insanity."[19]

Albert typically handled stressful situations with grace and equanimity, and Nan had come to rely on him as her acknowledged "rock," her "anchor." Though she describes herself throughout this period as "hysterical and lacking self-control to a frightful degree,"[20] with her husband's constant support and calming presence, she managed every detail of the wedding with meticulous care, for it was to be the social event of the season. Finally, in Chicago's Second Presbyterian Church on 12 November 1891, Albert's old classmate Rev. Joseph Twichell officiated as Elizabeth Penn Sprague and Frederic Shurtleff Coolidge pledged themselves to each other through sickness and in health until death should separate them.

CHAPTER FOUR

Marriage and Motherhood

As is the mother, so is her daughter.

– EZEKIEL, 16:44

IF NANCY SPRAGUE was anything she was honest; direct to a fault sometimes, but honest with herself as well. Her diary, which was undoubtedly never meant for the eyes of anyone else, was the one secret retreat where she could freely confess her failings and vent her often contradictory emotions. The confidences she recorded in it during the early 1890s offer valuable candid insights into her complicated relationship with her daughter and a discerning look at Elizabeth's unsettled emotional state in the early years of her marriage.

In one sense Nan was the victim of the sort of gender differentiation that more or less dictated the distinct spheres in which men and women could function acceptably in late-nineteenth-century society. Nan's life was typical in that she minded the domestic scene and cultivated a circle of close women friends while Albert went about becoming the successful business executive. But at home, where their two worlds met, she was atypical—Nan was the boss. Lucy Sprague, reflecting on the difference between the relationship of her own parents and that of Elizabeth's once commented that Nan "ruled Uncle Albert partly by her executive energy, which managed all things easily [and] partly by her uninhibited tongue." Despite her small stature she was a formidable presence, always sitting ramrod erect on a straight-backed chair. Once when she was feeling unwell Elizabeth had the temerity to suggest that she should lie down, to which she snapped back, "I don't feel equal to it."[1]

Hers was a kind of interior balancing act that sometimes found her deeply ingrained Puritan values and standard of conduct at odds with her new way of life. The Vermont farm girl who had sewn her own clothes by hand, made soap, dipped candles, and watched as a traveling cobbler came once a year to make shoes for the family from hides that they had tanned themselves, now had fashionable tailor-made clothes, servants, and leisure time.[2]

Traditional mother-daughter relationships of the period have been described as a kind of apprenticeship system in which mothers trained their daughters in the art of housewifery and motherhood.[3] But in the years since her return from Mrs. Reed's School Elizabeth had grown into an independent thinker. While she may have inherited her mild-mannered father's looks, in temperament she was her mother's child—nervous, strong-willed, short-tempered, and capable of harsh words at times. It was inevitable that there should be tensions between these two who were so much alike.

The wedding had been the supreme test of nerves for Nan as she struggled to accept the fact that her relationship with her daughter would never be quite the same again. Despite her best intentions she failed to allow the young couple much privacy even on their brief honeymoon.[4] They spent their wedding night at Hyde Park only to find Nan on the doorstep the next day. It was good that Fred's work required their departure from Chicago, and soon the young couple left for New York, where he worked as assistant surgeon at the New York City Orthopedic Hospital and Dispensary and Elizabeth began to study piano with Ferdinand Van Inten, who had high praise for her talent. He found her extremely well prepared, with "such reliable technique that there was no limit to what [she] could do."[5]

Since up to now there had not been time for a proper honeymoon, Albert booked passage for the newlyweds on the *Bismarck* on 2 June 1892, and when Fred finished his work in New York they left for Europe. But even now they were not alone, for Nan, Albert, Isa Coolidge, and Mary Sprague accompanied them, and the Twichells met them in London. Fortunately, Fred's work required him to remain in Vienna for four months: Here Elizabeth was able to indulge her musical interests while he visited hospitals. The others made their way through Europe and eventually to Egypt, where they all met to celebrate Christmas together. They returned home the following February and Nan at once took charge of finding a proper home for them, and selecting all the furnishings—all the while wondering why her daughter did not seem happy.[6] Elizabeth, meanwhile, found her escape in long hours at the piano.

It is true that in the early years of her marriage Elizabeth often succumbed to extreme moodiness and fits of crying. Whether this was brought on by her mother's interference in her life, a misunderstanding with Fred, or a combination of factors is not always clear. At any rate there is plenty of evidence of erratic emotional behavior, and it was Nan's perception that she was always considered to blame. "[E]verything at sixes and sevens with E and F. What the trouble is I cannot fathom. If I have done amiss I am in ignorance of what or how! *But they treat me as if I were a culprit.*"[7]

Perhaps it is unrealistic to expect Nan to have understood the conflict that churned within her daughter at this time. Nan had always found fulfillment in the acceptance of her proper womanly, wifely role. But for Elizabeth the tensions between ambition for a career, devotion to the husband she loved so deeply, and the weight of societal expectations seemed to decree an inevitable confinement. Elizabeth's already well-developed sense of responsibility to society and the idealistic goals of service that she and Fred had set for themselves were admirable objectives but difficult to attain within their sphere of life. The model of the upper-class Victorian wife was at odds with the ambitious spirit that dwelt within her. She had already savored the sweet success and adulation that her performance as a pianist had brought her—though admittedly within the limited circle of a partisan public. And now she was beginning to realize the unrealistic nature of her desire to emulate role models like Carreño and Bloomfield-Zeisler. The honeymoon was over, and it was time to step into that role for which mother and father had so carefully groomed her. There is no doubt that she enjoyed the comfort and privileges that her wealth and station brought her, but the longing for recognition and the creative outlet provided by her music would forever be circumscribed by the expectations of the society in which she was so comfortably installed. Moreover, she was about to become a mother.

It seems apparent that some of her moods were triggered by Fred's fishing and hunting excursions with a gang of old male friends. He was an expert marksman and while at Harvard had been an enthusiastic member of the Shooting Club. His favorite haunts were Talleston, in the intercoastal waterways of Georgia, and Pelee Island in Port Sheridan, Ontario, where members of the Chicago Commercial Club had built a lodge. He was often accompanied there by Uncle Otho, or his father, or brother David. Since Elizabeth's letters to him while he was away have not survived there is no way of knowing if she expressed to him her feelings about these trips. Fred, however, wrote long and affectionate letters to her almost daily during these times, assuring her that "anywhere without you dearest [I am] more or less ill at ease."[8]

The strained relations between mother and daughter were at least temporarily relaxed when in early May of 1893 Nan learned that she was to become a grandmother. She was immediately relieved to think that much of Elizabeth's moodiness was probably a result of distress in the early weeks of her pregnancy.

During this time Fred entered with great enthusiasm into his responsibilities at Rush Medical College and soon began to make a name for himself in his work. The forty-ninth *Annual Announcement* (1891–92) of Rush Medical College notes that "Dr. Frederick [*sic*] S. Coolidge, who has been carefully training himself by foreign study for his special work in Orthopedic Surgery, will begin his lectures after his return from Europe."[9] He was, in fact the first ever to lecture on orthopedics at Rush Medical College, and his growing involvement in his work there is testimony of his success.[10] Fred seemed supremely content with his work and was ecstatic at the prospect of becoming a father.

The summer of Elizabeth's pregnancy was marked by two events of special importance to the Spragues and Coolidges: the dedication of the new Art Institute and the opening of the World Columbian Exposition. President Cleveland came for the official opening of the fair and threw the golden switch that illuminated the "White City" on the beach, as guests—royal and otherwise—poured into the city. Daniel Burnham, the architect of the Sprague's house, had been appointed chief of construction and a committee of prominent artists and architects from all over the country worked on the project.

The fair was in many ways remarkable, but it was marred by its share of spats—the cause célèbre being the controversy over Paderewski's insistence upon using a Steinway piano for his appearance. The Steinway firm had refused to exhibit its instruments at the fair, and in response the commission placed a ban upon the use of any Steinway on the fair grounds. Because of his great friendship and admiration for Paderewski, Theodore Thomas defied the order and smuggled a forbidden instrument onto the premises during the night, which Paderewski then used in the concert. Thomas was accused of being an agent of Steinway and in consequence resigned as music director of the exposition.[11]

The Sprague families spent a good deal of time visiting the fair grounds in the course of the summer, but without a doubt for them the highlight of it all was Elizabeth's appearance in a special concert of "Illinois Amateurs" held in the Woman's Building on Saturday, 1 July 1893. The centerpiece and highlight of the program which began with several short works, was Elizabeth's performance of the Schumann Piano Concerto in A Minor. It was an unforgettable experience for her as she took her place at the piano—dressed in a fine new blue gown that Nan had insisted upon against Elizabeth's wishes—and launched into the opening chords accompanied by an orchestra led by Thomas himself. Here at last was a taste of the career that she had dreamt of.

Thomas had been lured away from New York in 1891 to establish a resident orchestra in Chicago that would rival those of Boston and New York. Charles Norman Fay, president of the Chicago Gas Trust Company, solicited fifty guarantors of $1,000 each for a period of three years to ensure an annual income for Thomas. A. A. Sprague was among them from the start, and just a month before Elizabeth and Fred's wedding the new Chicago Orchestra had made its debut in the huge auditorium designed by Adler and Sullivan.[12]

Thomas and his second wife, Rose (the sister of Norman and Amy Fay), soon became a part of the social life of the city and came to know some of the wealthy guarantors very well—especially the Glessners and the Spragues. Orchestra members were frequently called upon to provide elaborate entertainment in the homes of the well-to-do—for example, at Marshall Field's a dramatic reading of *Manfred* backed by some thirty musicians,[13] and at the Glessner home a reading of *Faust* for which Fanny had installed a Mason Hamlin Liszt organ and employed twenty-five orchestra members. On another occasion Thomas led the orchestra in Haydn's "Farewell Symphony" for a ball to which all came in eighteenth-century costume—powdered wigs and all.[14]

For the requisite post-concert receptions Rose Thomas had personally alerted Fanny to the fact that her husband seldom ate before conducting but after a concert had a robust appetite for good roast beef, ham, and brut champagne. He seems to have had an equal relish for good-natured horseplay too, his favorite party entertainment being a demonstration of how he could remove his vest without taking off his coat. Besides such diversions these occasions always provided an opportunity for delicious indulgence in gossip about the musical underworld. Guests were particularly keen to hear such tales as Paderewski's criticism of Walter Damrosch's conducting, for it pleased and entertained the proud partisans of the new Chicago Orchestra.

These same glittering years were eventful within the extended family of the Spragues and the Coolidges. Through his affiliation with H. H. Richardson and the completion of the Glessner house, Charlie Coolidge had become an important presence in the architectural scene of Chicago. There is good reason to believe that Albert Sprague was of some help to Charlie in obtaining the contract for the Chicago Public Library and also the Art Institute. Although the designs for the library were submitted as blind entries, it is clear from Nan's letter to Elizabeth that Albert knew which design was Charlie's; and as early as February of 1892 she mentions that Albert was "able to do a good turn now and then for Charlie—influencing men who have other buildings going up."[15]

In 1889 Charlie had wed Julia Shepley, the daughter of the senior member of the firm of Shepley Rutan and Coolidge, and now his success in Chicago brought him such steady work there that he made it his residence from 1892 to 1900. Fred had always been very close to his older brother, and now with Charlie present in the same city it was possible for the two young couples to be together much more. It was an attachment that Nan resented now and again but would come to appreciate only later. At the same time back in Boston Isa Coolidge was married to

Dr. William Councilman, a renowned physician in the city, who would also in time assume an important role in the lives of Fred and Elizabeth.[16]

On 4 January Elizabeth moved into her parents' home to await the arrival of her baby. It was a difficult birth, but finally on 23 January 1894, after long hours in labor, a healthy big boy was delivered. Christened Albert Sprague Coolidge after his grandfather, he would always be known simply as Sprague. The baby became the center around which the entire family life revolved, but at the same time his arrival provided grist for further disagreements between mother and daughter over matters of infant care. Elizabeth adopted a "go-it-alone" attitude, rejecting her mother's opinions and considerable experience, and attempted to train the baby to go to sleep alone. As she listened while the infant cried himself hoarse every night, Nan helplessly concluded that "the baby has his mother's persistence."[17]

Only a few days after the opening of the Columbian Exposition in 1893, the stock market had crashed and sent major cities, particularly in the East, into turmoil. Because of the added revenue brought into Chicago by the fair, the city was slower to feel the effects of the crash, but depression and unemployment were inevitable. The railroad industry was hit especially hard by the Depression and as a consequence canceled large parts of its orders from Pullman, who in turn decreased his employee's salaries by some twenty-six percent, yet made no reduction in the rentals and other fees charged to them in Pullman City, the self-contained industrial city he had built and owned. When workers attempted to discuss the matter with him, Pullman refused to meet with them. Instead, he summarily dismissed them all and threw them out of their homes the next day. Some 4,000 workers joined Eugene V. Debs's American Railway Union in the spring of 1894 and by May, 2,500 employees quit work. All attempts at arbitration failed.

The effects of the strike were soon felt nationwide so that by the end of June the entire country was involved. In Chicago the fear of violence by strikers was so intense that by 4 July President Cleveland intervened and ordered federal troops into the city. Anything involving rail transportation was, of course, of great consequence to the Sprague Warner business, and so it is not surprising that Nan's diary should reflect the concern. By her account, "everything was assuming a military air. . . . [T]he lake front was given over to troops and the strike is something terrible. Millions of properties are being destroyed—traffic is at a standstill—no communication with points west."[18] When Sprague Warner teamsters struck because they feared delivering goods to military quarters, Albert insisted, "they must deliver or consider themselves discharged."[19]

Jane Addams, the "civic savior of Chicago," came out on the side of the striking workers and in doing so alienated some of the wealthier citizens who had supported her work. She was the founder of the Hull House humanitarian settlement, where she carried out social work that reached beyond immediate ministrations to the bodily needs of the poor to include a campaign for social and labor reforms in the courts and legislatures. As a result Addams had established a reputation for radicalism: the Daughters of the American Revolution canceled her membership and the Fortnightly withdrew her invitation to speak.[20]

Both the Sprague brothers had supported Addams and the Hull House venture, and Otho had often encouraged Lucy to visit the settlement and hear Addams speak. Elizabeth, like her younger cousin, was experiencing a growing sensitivity to the gap between wealth and poverty, and a conscience that viewed the financial support of such men as their fathers as merely "efforts to uplift the lower classes."[21] However, when Addams openly supported the Pullman workers, the Sprague brothers and their daughters found themselves on opposite sides in the contest. Lucy, in particular, was profoundly shocked because her father had been an enthusiastic supporter of Hull House. His change of heart, in Lucy's opinion, had much to do with the fact that "she (Addams) was stepping out of her place. The fact that she was a woman only added to his indignation." The whole affair forever colored Lucy's relationship with her father.[22]

Elizabeth's immediate reaction has not been recorded, but from Lucy's writings as well as from what we know about Elizabeth's development, it is clear that on this one subject father and daughter did not see eye to eye. The strong social leanings that would characterize Elizabeth in her later life were already well implanted, and in the words of Lucy, they "were rather confusing to her conservative father, who greatly admired her, though a bit uncomprehendingly."[23] However disparate Elizabeth's and Albert's attitudes over this issue may have been, they did not allow it to strain their relationship in the way that it did that of Otho and Lucy.

In August Lucia and Otho's son, 11-year-old Otho Jr., died of typhoid. Lucia never quite recovered from this catastrophe—the loss of a second son within four years. The situation was further complicated when Nannie suffered a complete mental breakdown and had to be institutionalized. Lucia took to her bed and Otho sank into a deep depression, leaving Nan and Albert to become again caretakers of the extended family. Soon Otho suffered a serious hemorrhage that signaled a recurrence of his tuberculosis. Because of the illness, he decided to make California their permanent home. What must have seemed like the final dissolution of the family came shortly after Christmas, when Fred had to go to Harvard to fetch Lucia and Otho's only remaining son, Albert Arnold II. Although Nan does not actually describe this "new and terrible anxiety," indications are that the boy had developed a drinking problem.[24]

As if that were not enough, Amelia's condition was deteriorating and her presence in the household was becoming unbearable to Nan, who by 1897 would write: "No one begins to realize what a nerve-wracking thing it is to live with Amelia. . . . I can not bear it any longer."[25] Shortly thereafter she was taken to Geneseo, New York to live with a cousin, Alice Arnold.

Through it all there were two great joys that sustained Nan and Albert. The first was little Sprague, whose every move is chronicled with delight, and the other was the happiness that it gave them to provide a new home for their daughter. In April, Albert bought a lot at 2636 Prairie Avenue, where they would build a proper house for Fred and Elizabeth. The stretch of land between Elizabeth's parental home and her new house was close enough, Nan hoped, that they "can surely look after us as we grow old."[26] Charlie, of course, was called upon as the architect, and perhaps it is appropriate, given the circumstances, that the newspapers claimed the house looked "very much like Beacon St., Boston."[27]

In December 1895, with the house completed, Albert would formally convey the property to Elizabeth with this simple message: "We have had great pleasure in building a home for you and yours. In installing you as mistress, our happiness has been enhanced—our fond anticipation realized. Please accept, with best Christmas wishes, love and benediction, this deed conveying a good title to you, from Papa."[28]

CHAPTER FIVE

From the "Gold Coast" to the "Magic Mountain"

We are healed by suffering only by experiencing it to the full.

– MARCEL PROUST, *THE PAST RECAPTURED*

WHEN 1895 BEGAN, the year promised to be filled with blessings. Fred and Elizabeth's new home was rising steadily from the gaping hole in the empty plot at 2636 Prairie Avenue, Fred was earning recognition for his work at Rush Memorial Hospital, and Sprague's first birthday was suitably celebrated. Yet in only a matter of days after the festivities, that happiness was blighted by the onset of a strange and initially undiagnosed (or misdiagnosed) illness. Fred grew weak and ill in early February and by April he was very sick with an "infected arm." By Nan's account, he "was suffering a great deal" and "may have to have glands cut out."[1] After consultation the doctors advised surgery, which occurred on 19 April. Nan's successive diary entries throughout April and May record the progress of Fred's illness and testify that the operation was a serious one. Doctors declared Fred desperately ill, and not even Elizabeth was allowed to go to him. He was finally brought home from the hospital on 1 May, according to Nan, "a poor wilted, thin and pale chappie. . . . I believe we almost lost him."[2] Yet only a few days later he indulged in a game of tennis, a hazardous thing to do, and an action that would more or less be a pattern for the next fifteen years, as with each recovery he overtaxed himself—sometimes with work, sometimes play.

Doctors ordered a summer of rest, so by the end of May Elizabeth and Fred left for Marion, Massachusetts, a coastal resort on Buzzard's

Bay where Nan and Albert later also took a cottage.

Only the baby seemed predictably happy at this time. He was talking and showing a distinct response to music, singing and dancing excitedly much to the delight of all. It was at this time that he began to call his grandmother "Omama," a pet name by which he would refer to Nan for the rest of her life. He had learned it from Elizabeth's German maid, and with childlike invention extended it to include "Opapa" and even "Oparents."

The tender bond that developed between Sprague and his grandparents—especially Nan—unquestionably was enhanced by the nurturing role that Omama was called upon to assume during the long and trying years of Fred's illness, which demanded so much of Elizabeth's time, attention, and strength. Moreover, Elizabeth herself was frequently ill, and a progressive loss of hearing, which had already begun several years before, was by this time noticeably worse. At age thirty-one—at the onset of Fred's illness—Nan notes in her diary that "E's deafness has increased distinctly in this year."[3] There were periods when she went to New York for weeks at a time for treatment. Nan and Albert quietly stepped in for the ailing young couple as surrogate parents and at the same time lent moral support and love to the chronically ill Lucia and Otho and attended to the needs of their children. Although their caretaker responsibilities increased markedly over the years, their letters and Nan's diary reveal no hint whatsoever of resentment—only an occasional and understandable mention of fatigue.

On 11 September Elizabeth and Fred spent their first night in their new home. With Fred unable to work at this time Albert and Nan agreed to provide their children a quarterly allowance of $900. Elizabeth managed the household so well with this money that she earned Nan's praise for "the wonderful way she finds things at cheap prices, and shows a kind of ability we would have thought she didn't possess."[4] Now installed as the mistress of her own domain, Elizabeth went about the business of creating a real home, giving receptions and taking a more active part in the various women's organizations to which she belonged. Included were the Friday Club, the Amateur Music Club, and especially the prestigious Fortnightly, into which she was invited just at this time. The honor undoubtedly came as a result of the lecture that she delivered

Albert Sprague Coolidge (Sprague), age three

Jeffrey Coolidge Photography, Boston

Elizabeth Sprague Coolidge, circa 1896

Elizabeth Coolidge Winship Private Collection, Library of Congress

at a meeting of the Friday Club on 27 March 1896 entitled "The Evolution of the Dance"—a fifty page handwritten essay that survives in the Library of Congress collection. The thoroughness with which she launched into these undertakings is reflected in Nan's observation that Elizabeth "literally buried herself at the Newberry Library while researching the topic."[5]

By early January of 1897 Fred was again quite unwell. Although it was a great worry to all, to the casual observer it must have appeared that life in the Sprague and Coolidge households went on as usual. Actually, Elizabeth retreated into her studies, including a pursuit of genealogy that she had begun earlier.[6] At the same time she enrolled at the Art Institute, where she dedicated herself to lessons with such vehemence that Nan was moved to comment, "Queer how intense she is—I wish she could be more moderate."[7]

Meanwhile Nan and Albert remained the great nurturing support of the whole clan. In February they embarked upon what would become their annual pilgrimage to southern California for two months, visiting and helping Lucia and Otho and enjoying a round of socializing with other denizens of Chicago who sought the sun of southern California.

Throughout this period Elizabeth was frequently quite ill and finally on doctor's orders moved to Lakeside. There, on her wedding anniversary in November 1897, she delivered a stillborn baby girl.[8] Following close on the heels of this loss, Lucia arrived from California to dismantle the house that she and Otho had long ago built next door to Nan and Albert. This signified the end of proximity for the two sisters, who were bound by an unusually deep attachment. The only bright spot for Nan in this otherwise dismal period was the news that she had been elected to the Colonial Dames.

From this troubled period comes Elizabeth's first attempt at musical composition, a collection of twenty children's songs written specifically for Sprague and entitled *After Supper Songs.*[9] In a sense this collection represents the coming together of her various and considerable talents as musician, poet, and artist, for the texts are of her composition as is the music, and each song is preceded by an illustration of her making. In general, her poetic efforts might be characterized as "garden variety Victorian," but Elizabeth's many sketches and water colors that have survived indicate that she possessed considerable artistic talent. However, it was music above all that was Elizabeth's solace, her comfort in times of stress, sadness, and disappointment; and while the endless hours at the piano could not make the pain go away they did seem to blunt the rough edges and calm the disquietude.

The success of this first essay in composition, the joy of seeing the songs in print, and the enthusiasm they evoked from friends who heard them seem to have encouraged her to pursue the study of composition more seriously and to seek the advice of those more experienced in the craft. She turned—rather tentatively at first—to the most successful woman composer of the day, Amy Beach, and sent a copy of the *After Supper Songs* as a gift, perhaps hoping for her criticism. It is clear from Beach's note that the two women had already met; Amy Beach's husband was a physician who taught at Harvard and may even have been one of Fred's professors there. More importantly the Beaches, like the Coolidges, resided on Commonwealth Avenue in Boston's Back Bay, and it is likely that the families knew each other. Beach's response of 22 March 1902 was warm: "I can hardly tell you how much the whole idea of the volume appeals to me, remembering the talk I had with you about the little boy who inspired it. The verses are as charming as the music, and that is saying a great deal! . . . Let me congratulate you again upon the talent you have for characterization, which is indeed a rare one. Each little song here is as perfectly adapted to its subject as is possible, and suggests nothing else."[10]

The enthusiastic tone of the letter apparently gave Elizabeth the courage to submit to Beach a much more serious and complicated work that she had actually completed the previous year. To commemorate the tenth anniversary of her marriage to Fred she presented to him, on 12 November 1901, a cycle of ten songs on texts taken from Elizabeth Barrett Browning's *Sonnets from the Portuguese*—love poetry in the tradition of Dante, Sidney, and Spenser. It is evident from her handling of the poems that she was well acquainted with the texts—there were eighteen volumes of the Brownings' poetry in the Sprague library. Whatever her perception of the sonnets, the relationship of the fragile and constantly ailing Elizabeth Barrett and her attentive poet-husband resonated in Elizabeth's soul; she may have seen their roles reversed in Fred's and her marriage.[11] In fact, in a letter written near the end of her life Elizabeth makes it very clear that it was indeed her intention to be autobiographical in the cycle in an attempt "to apply the words to our own situation."[12]

The poems, as she set them to music, are necessarily truncated, and in some cases individual songs are set to texts that are actually cobbled together from several different sonnets. But whatever literary license she took with the poems, Elizabeth's rendering of them served her purpose well and in many instances effects an extraordinary concentration of emotion.[13]

Musically the cycle employs the harmonic palette of the late Romantics, characterized by the use of thick harmonies, widely spaced chords in the accompaniment, and abundant chromatic alterations. The compositional sketches of the work that have survived suggest that Elizabeth was influenced by Wagner, for there is a minutely worked out precompositional scheme of associative themes in the manner of the Wagnerian leitmotif, all identified in the sketches and developed in the songs. But a loose fragment found among her notes argues for a more contemporary and direct influence exerted by the French composer Gustave Charpentier, whose opera *Louise* employs the similar device of identifying melodic themes with characters and incidents in the drama. Elizabeth had carefully copied out and identified some ninety melodic fragments from Charpentier's opera, which she could have known only from study of the score for the work was premiered in Paris in 1900—at exactly the period when she was composing the cycle—and was not performed in the United States until Mary Garden created the role for New York in 1908.

The "Browning Cycle," as Nan always referred to it, was a much more ambitious undertaking than Elizabeth's previous little songs, and the repeated performances of it, which drew praise from her audiences in both Chicago and New York, are undoubtedly what gave her the courage to send them to Beach for criticism. Her evaluation not only speaks well for Elizabeth's talents, but reflects favorably her own ability as critic as well as her generous and open-hearted encouragement:

> *Many of the good qualities I admired in your "children's songs" are noticeable here, especially the faithfulness to the spirit of the words, and*

> *the generally admirable manner in which you have followed the accent of the text. . . . There is considerable ingenuity in the handling of your "leit-motifs." Many lovely bits of melody and harmony, many endings of phrases and songs that haunt by their weird beauty. That you have not yet acquired the skill to wield so great a mass of material into a perfectly homogeneous whole, is only to be expected from the comparatively short experience which you have had in composition.*[14]

It is apparent that Beach considered Elizabeth's talent worth cultivating, for she encouraged her to study composition seriously with a good teacher, saying "You will grow, I am sure, to be your own best critic, and in future years you will be able to rewrite these songs with full consciousness of what is strongest as well as weakest in their structure. Only, keep on. Hesitate at nothing."[15] The sequence of letters that passed between the two over the next few years reveals that Elizabeth continued to send work to her friend for critical comment. Beach's recommendations of a specific teacher, of instruction books that she valued, and her wish that she might have had the benefit of such a tutor, are revealing. "I cannot help wishing that you might take a course of study with just the right teacher, who would help you over the rough places of detail—teach you to have full command over your own ideas and power to express them to their best advantage—without destroying your individuality. Such teachers are rare, as you know!"[16] In Beach's opinion that rare tutor was the music pedagogue Percy Goetschius, whom she considered "a man of highest authority in Europe as well as America. . . . I know that he would be deeply interested in your work."[17] In the event that study with him personally was not possible, she recommended, "his books are the next best thing. I can only say I wish I might have had Goetschius' books when I was working out my own salvation so far as harmony and counterpoint are concerned."[18] To Elizabeth's thoughts of cutting certain parts of the work Beach responded: "I should cut nothing at present, nor would I attempt any revision or change until after study. You will be surprised to see how certain bits will clear themselves up in your mind after more growth and study."[19]

A letter nearly two years later indicates that Elizabeth had indeed continued to work on the cycle, for Beach comments: "It was deeply interesting to see how you had developed and crystallized your original ideas, and how closely you had followed the spirit of the words chosen. . . . Pray, keep on studying and making every effort to express what is in your heart and mind."[20] Elizabeth's plans to study with Goetschius did not materialize until much later, but in the meantime she found a tutor in Arthur Whiting, whose instructions are documented in his corrections and comments in one of her surviving exercise books. Elizabeth would eventually seek the tuition of other composers as well, but for the time being her life allowed no further excursions into that rarefied province.

The deterioration of Fred's health during the time that she was composing the Browning Cycle lends a special poignancy to the almost anguished expressions of love captured in her settings of the sonnets. As always it was Nan who faithfully recorded the family's ordeals—for that is mainly what they seemed to be throughout these difficult years. On 16 February 1899 Fred was once again operated on, but there is no indication of the nature of the surgery this time. By the following year his condition had deteriorated seriously, necessitating a series of three more operations in the space of one month.[21]

By April Fred's condition was grave and Elizabeth sought the counsel of Dr. Sanger Brown, who at once began the "heroic treatment"—massive doses of iodides. Fred's illness was syphilis, in fact, but it is not clear when this was recognized and to what extent the family shared in the knowledge or confronted the situation. Even in her diary Nan always referred to his sickness as "blood poisoning," perhaps euphemistically. There is evidence that Elizabeth faced the tragedy more squarely, but because mother and daughter were together throughout the early stages of the illness there are no letters, no written shared confidences on Elizabeth's part to clarify the issue—just Nan's circumspect and often cryptic allusions to the disease as entered in her diary.

The onset of the infection and the early surgery are clearly fixed as occurring in 1895, just one year after Sprague's birth. Fred' s still undiagnosed problem seems to have been arrested for the time being, for there are no references to it for a while in the diary, and in 1897 Elizabeth gave birth to a stillborn baby girl.

The repeated operations of 1900, however, did not prevent another relapse in April of the following year. Once again Sanger Brown prescribed the "heroic treatment." It seems clear from Elizabeth's subsequent pregnancy and from Fred's letter to Albert that he believed himself to be cured this time: "I never had the least doubt of my recovery."[22]

It is highly unlikely that Fred, a devoted husband who was acknowledged by his peers to be a brilliant physician, would knowingly expose his wife to the danger of contracting venereal disease if he knew the risk. The answer to the questions raised may lie partly in the circumstances of his contracting the illness, partly in the very nature of the behavior of the disease in its various stages, and partly in the state of late-nineteenth-century venereal therapeutics. These considerations, compounded by the almost inevitable moral judgments of society that caused Nan to treat the topic with such circumspection, make it difficult to arrive at the truth. But a careful chronology of the evidence casts some light on the subject.

Some time in 1895 Fred was called upon to perform surgery at St. Luke's Hospital upon a syphilitic patient. It is well known that the use of surgical gloves was not as yet a common practice, and it was not unusual for physicians to contract disease through accidents in surgery. In the course of the operation Fred had the misfortune to cut himself. Aware of his patient's chancres, and realizing the danger to himself, with the help of the assisting doctor he spent the night bathing the wound with mercury bichloride in an effort to stave off the infection, but apparently to no avail.[23]

It is the nature of primary syphilis that symptoms may appear as early as twenty-one days after the spirochete enters the bloodstream, but the range of incubation may vary from as little as ten days to as much as ten weeks, which would place the accident anywhere from the end of March 1895 to as early as January of that year.[24] Since the first manifestation of the primary chancre usually occurs near the site of entrance of the organism, the fact that Fred's arm was the first area infected, lends credence to the story of how the disease was contracted. Moreover, at this stage the neighboring lymph nodes often become enlarged and ulcerated. It is clear from Nan's diary as well as Fred's letter to Mrs. Glessner[25] that the initial operation on his arm which Nan refers to as "cutting out his glands" very likely indicates the removal of the lymph nodes. Moreover, it sometimes happens that the lesions caused by syphilis do not resemble typical chancres and the disease, especially at that stage, could easily have been misdiagnosed.

In secondary syphilis the signs and symptoms may be of wide variety, and commonly there is again a swelling of the lymph nodes. This may perhaps clarify the reference to the series of operations in 1900. Typically there is a latent period between secondary and the onset of tertiary syphilis that may extend over several years or even a lifetime, which period is characterized by the absence of any outward signs or symptoms of the illness. Serologic tests alone reveal the presence of the disease, but it was not until 1907 that the German bacteriologist, August von Wassermann, developed the first blood test for detecting the symptoms of syphilis. Also, during this latent period the disease loses some of its infectiousness and after the first few years is only rarely transmitted through sexual intercourse. The chronology of Elizabeth's two pregnancies in 1897 and 1901 would seem to suggest that they believed the disease to be cured.

After the operations of 1900 and until about 1905, Fred's syphilis seems to have been arrested, and he was able to carry on a limited medical practice. However, the sequence of events during that interval was anything but free from problems as one crisis after another presented itself.

The typically unvarnished reports and prognostications of Nan's diary read like a litany of disasters for this period. June brought a visit to Amelia in Geneseo which found her "a wretch . . . intelligence all gone."[26] And in September she pronounced her niece, Nannie, "a poor crazy girl."[27] The following February Elizabeth submitted to surgery of an undisclosed nature and recuperated in the East with the Glessners, and in early summer Nan nursed Albert through appendicitis.[28] By June 1901 Elizabeth had had her second miscarriage, and that autumn Nan's beloved sister Lucia arrived back in Chicago, where Nan nursed her in her last illness and was, for the most part, the only person Lucia wanted to see—including Otho.[29] Finally, on 25 September Lucia died. The sense of personal loss to Nan was intense, and coming at this particular time of crisis it must have been especially acute. Nan was now sixty-four years old and had in effect become the support of both her immediate and extended family with their numerous illnesses and psychological problems.

The crowning blow came in February of 1902, when Fred manifested worrisome symptoms of a nagging cough that refused to go away. On

26 May he had the first of a series of hemorrhages; doctors diagnosed him as having tuberculosis and recommended immediate departure for Saranac in New York's Adirondack Mountains, where Doctors Trudeau and Baldwin were having encouraging success in the treatment of tuberculosis. Fred and a nervous, worried Elizabeth arrived there on 10 June and were followed the next day by Albert, who went to find a home for them there.

In the last decade of the nineteenth century there were concerted efforts to control the spread of tuberculosis, and although the mortality rate in the United States had fallen by half—from 400 per 100,000 (in 1830) to 200 (in 1900)—the disease still remained the greatest killer of the human race at the time Fred was diagnosed. These otherwise faceless statistics were all too familiar to the Spragues and the Coolidges, for various members of both families had been victims of the disease. Now with tuberculosis coming so swiftly on the heels of Fred's syphilis, the future looked bleak indeed. Moreover, the prospect of treatment necessarily implied the wrenching of the little family from a comfortable life in a luxurious new home in exchange for a spartan existence in conditions that, by comparison, must have seemed primitive.

The village of Saranac Lake in the Adirondack Mountains, near the Saranac and St. Regis chains of lakes, was familiar territory to the Spragues, who often vacationed there. The area had become a popular summer resort and in winter attracted skiers in large numbers. In 1885 Dr. Edward Livingston Trudeau, himself a victim of tuberculosis, fortuitously discovered the restorative powers of outdoor life in the clean air of the mountains.[30] When his own case seemed hopeless he went to Saranac to await death in a congenial place where he had spent many happy vacations as a young man. Instead his condition steadily improved the longer he stayed. Encouraged by his own improvement and by the success of similar treatment attained by Brehmer in his sanitarium in Silesia in 1882, Trudeau was inspired to organize his own establishment in the Adirondacks, where he set up a primitive laboratory in his home and taught himself the new science of bacteriology. The first tubercular cases came to him in 1884, and in the following year he opened the first sanitarium on the American continent, the Adirondack Cottage Sanitarium.[31]

By the time Frederic Coolidge's tuberculosis was diagnosed Trudeau's work was already widely recognized. And certainly Fred would have been aware that the regimen of treatment at Saranac was not for the faint of heart. Through his own experience Trudeau now understood that the illness could not be conquered by keeping the patient confined to stuffy and overheated rooms—as was the earlier practice—but that, on the contrary, the patient improved with exposure to fresh air, even in the coldest weather. Wide-open windows and cots on balconies completely exposed to the elements were the mainstay of Trudeau's therapy. Fred willingly submitted to the regimen, at first lying perfectly still on his back and eating abundantly while being attended by a nurse whom Albert had procured for him, and coming indoors only for meals and to wrap himself in layers of blankets and furs to prepare to sleep outside.

The sense of isolation that the years in Saranac imposed upon Elizabeth can be appreciated only when viewed in the context of the preceding five years. During that period she had experienced the loss of two children, faced the specter of her worsening deafness, accepted the tragedy of her husband's syphilis and the prospect of no more children, and finally suffered the abandonment of a new home and her dreams of cultivating the extended social and intellectual circle of friends such as she had enjoyed in Chicago. Some sense of her emotional state is revealed in a letter to her mother written shortly after the move to Saranac. "I fear my letters have troubled you lately but I feel that I must have someone to talk to. . . . You know how hard it is to rely upon quivering nerves and some of the shock of six weeks ago has left its reaction. . . . I am still unnerved and that will disappear in time. They all go through it here. It is sad to see all these young wives whose husbands are battling for life. I sometimes think it harder to stand and wait, than to do the fighting."[32] Her letters tellingly refer to this period as her "Saranac exile."

What Fred's mental state was throughout all this is nowhere recorded but is hinted at in Elizabeth's letter to her parents written almost exactly one year after their installation in the Adirondacks:

> *I know what you say about optimism is true and valuable, but I think that occasionally one's physical makeup is responsible for a state of blues*

> *which has no support in logic. I am ashamed that my conscience and common sense are not always equal to the task of subduing my "nerves" for I know how much I have to be grateful for. I think if I could feel sure of F's support I should mind this upheaval very little; but when a cyclone comes and there is no storm cellar one naturally falls to trembling. Doubtless I exaggerate the possibilities of the future, for certainly at present F seems brave and stronger than I; and that is all I need.*[33]

In April of 1903 Amelia died. Nan and Albert could only "rejoice that she is at rest (for) she has been mentally dead for long."[34] Amelia's body was brought back to Chicago and interred next to that of Thomas Atwood, as she had wished. By summer Fred was visibly improved, able to hunt, fish, and travel, so by the end of August he and Elizabeth made a trip to Canada. But as always, during periods of improved health and renewed energy Fred tended to overexert himself, making Elizabeth both apprehensive and nervous over what she considered his absolute carelessness.[35]

The influence of this disruption of the family upon Sprague at age eight can be only partially ascertained by Nan's faithful chronicle of events. After the precipitous departure of his parents, Sprague remained with Nan and Albert. Elizabeth had returned home briefly in August and when her leave-taking again made Nan "weepy," little Sprague became her comforter. In October Nan took him to join his parents at Saranac, where he entered wholeheartedly into school, began singing and violin lessons, learned to use snow shoes, and sometimes even went camping with his father. Nonetheless the experience left him with a lifelong fear of germs and an extreme concern for cleanliness.[36]

By December of 1904 Fred's condition had improved so markedly that he was able to leave Saranac, though his doctors advised against returning to Chicago and the contaminated air of the big city and urged instead a move to the healthy climate of the mountains. But he and Elizabeth were eager to leave that place of sickness, death, and desolation and begin life over again. In August they went to Pittsfield in the Berkshire Mountains to look over the town with a view to settling there, and by October they had moved.

Perhaps it was the remembrance of that moonlit sleigh ride in Pittsfield some fifteen years earlier that drew them back to a happier time when, in the bloom of their first love, Fred had proposed to Elizabeth. Bravely they went off to begin again, attempting a return to the perhaps irrecoverable past. Did they possibly recall the lines that Elizabeth had so recently set to music:

When our two souls stand up, erect and strong . . .
What bitter wrong can earth do to us
That we should not long be here contented?[37]

CHAPTER SIX

Châtelaine of a Great Estate

On the mountain there is freedom! The world is perfect everywhere, save where man comes with his torment.

– JOHANN CHRISTOPH FRIEDRICH VON SCHILLER, *THE BRIDE FROM MESSINA*, IV, VII.

THE INDIANS WHO originally called it *Pon-toos-uc* on the *Housaton-uck*, the "place beyond the mountains," divined the very essence of this lovely spot, where the streams that form the source of the Housatonic River meet and begin their course southward to Long Island Sound. The town of Pittsfield itself lies in the beautiful valley between the Taconic and Berkshire mountain ranges, under the timbered slopes of Mt. Greylock. The town is situated at an altitude of 1,000 feet above sea level, and its clean, dry air promised an ideal location for the treatment of tuberculosis. But quite apart from its physical beauty and healthful climate, Pittsfield had already attained a degree of notoriety for the list of distinguished people associated with it in one way or another, beginning with William Pitt, who was prime minister of England at the time the town was incorporated in 1761.

The first land grant given was to Colonel Jacob Wendell, the great-grandfather of Oliver Wendell Holmes, and Holmes himself often passed his summers there. It was in Pittsfield too, on his "Arrowhead Farm," that Herman Melville wrote the great American classic *Moby Dick* in 1851.[1] Streets, squares, and other landmarks of the city still today bear the names of its famous residents. More contemporaneous with the arrival of the Coolidges in Pittsfield was the appearance on the scene of a young glove salesman by the name of Samuel Goldfish, who became the future movie mogul Samuel Goldwyn.[2]

Pittsfield's location on the river and at the junction of the Boston and Albany Railroad with the far-flung New York Central line was an important factor in its transformation from an agricultural to an industrial center in the period between 1820 and 1890.[3] By the time the Coolidges moved there it was already heavily industrial, noted especially for its mills. The change in the mills themselves is a commentary on the town's metamorphosis, for what had begun as gristmills next became sawmills, and by 1904 they were largely paper and textile mills.

For Fred and Elizabeth the move was much more than nostalgia for the halcyon days that led them to attempt to recapture the romance of this memorable spot. The new location promised salutary health benefits for Fred and provided a fresh beginning for his medical practice, for the town boasted an already well established hospital, the House of Mercy.[4] Doctors at Saranac had already encouraged Fred to begin to practice medicine again, at least in a limited way. Soon after his establishment in Pittsfield he became associated with the House of Mercy and by 1906 had set up a successful orthopedic clinic in the hospital. Although his precarious health allowed only a limited practice, Fred entered into it with characteristic enthusiasm and a certain abandon.

Diary entries and letters of the period document his personal concern and care for his patients. He was a doctor who made house calls to distant places and kept his fees to a minimum in order to serve the needs of the poor.[5] Perhaps Fred envisioned the move as an opportunity to put into practice the high-minded ideals about service that he so often articulated in his letters to Elizabeth during their courtship years. Whatever his motives, the nature of his relationship with his patients is well summarized in the words of Dr. Henry Colt, who was both Fred's colleague and later one of his personal physicians. "To the very poor he was kindness personified, and to them he gave without hesitation the best of his time, strength, and ability. He inspired confidence in his patients, and they looked to him not only as a skillful surgeon, but as a kind and devoted friend."[6] Despite his disappointment over the abandonment of a medical career in Chicago Fred entered into Pittsfield life with as much spirit and enthusiasm as possible. George H. Tucker remembered Fred years later as one who "in his quiet way filled a unique place in the life of Pittsfield and endeared himself to all who came into contact with him. He did many deeds of love; he knew the burdens of others, and often made light hearts out of heavy ones."[7]

As Elizabeth once again began the task of turning a temporary dwelling into a gracious home, she channeled her energies into musicales that served as opportunities for her to perform and to begin to create her own extended circle of friends. There is evidence that she had done this in a limited way even in Saranac, but now Pittsfield allowed a broader scope and permitted her to bring in members of the Boston Symphony to play chamber music in which she usually participated as pianist. She spent many hours each day practicing for these soirées, which were financed with the help of her mother. But the music-making by no means depended solely upon paid professional help, for in Pittsfield Elizabeth soon found a musical partner in the very capable Gertrude Watson, who would in time become one of her few intimate woman friends and ultimately her constant companion. Of all the surviving recollections of Gertrude Watson, that which best captures her personality and her spirit is one short sentence of Daniel Gregory Mason: "Everything about Gertrude was large—her house, her garden, her car, her person, and above all her heart."[8] Her magnanimous and warm-hearted nature responded at once to the difficult experience that her new friend had just been through, and she welcomed Elizabeth enthusiastically into her home, her music-making, and her friendship.

Gertrude had studied piano in Vienna with Leschetizky, Paderewski's last teacher, and was an accomplished performer. Although she never became famous—or perhaps never chose to—she did tour for a time with such distinguished performers as the English cellist May Mukle, as well as violist-composer Rebecca Clarke.[9] It was inevitable that Gertrude and Elizabeth should seek each other out. Although they were much alike in many ways, they were nonetheless strikingly different in others. Mason, who knew both women well, perceived that Gertrude Watson was as "ample natured as her friend Elizabeth Coolidge was strong-willed. . . . Both (were) large, strong women, both passionately devoted to music, both in later years afflicted with deafness; they were different enough in nearly all other ways; Mrs. Coolidge so ambitious, strong-willed and efficient; Miss Watson so large-hearted, so fond of beautiful things from quartets to tea doilies, and so loving and kind to her innumerable friends."[10]

Watson's home had several large rooms that functioned as salons for evening musicales, and in pleasant weather post-recital entertainment spilled out onto the expansive lawn with its flower gardens and arbors. The occasions on which Elizabeth performed there served as a dim reminder of the unattainable career that quite clearly she had once dreamed of. Her thoughts on this matter are frankly revealed in a letter to her parents written on her fortieth birthday, only weeks after settling in Pittsfield.

> *My dearest Papa and Mamma,*
>
> *Your sweet birthday letters were waiting for me here yesterday when I returned from Boston. I wish I could rejoice more over my anniversaries, as I should if they seemed to me to mark off the years of a satisfactory life. But I started out with such impossible ambitions that I cannot help feeling the forty-year milestone to mark a very insignificant career, whose highest powers are already gone. I suppose this is only egotism, for my "career" matters so little. Still, it was dear to me. . . . In the meantime, the symphonies are still dumb, the pictures still unpainted, the radiant family of children unborn (save for the one dear exception), the home, center of hospitality to all that is happiest and most brilliant—a shifting, rented affair! Oh, well, doubtless the effort is the chief joy.*[11]

In a matter of months Fred and Elizabeth had decided to make Pittsfield their permanent home. They purchased a plot of sixty acres, engaged Charlie Coolidge to design the house, and Fred's other brother, David—a landscape artist in the firm of Frederick Olmsted (designer of New York's Central Park)—to create the gardens with their large flower beds, benches, arbors, and pergola.[12] The property lay to the north of the highway leading from Pittsfield westward to New Lebanon in New York. To the west lay Gertrude Watson's land, which overlooked beautiful Lake Onata, the "Lake of the Wild Doe."[13]

Elizabeth with Gertrude Watson, one of her closest friends, circa 1913
Jeffrey Coolidge Photography, Boston

The deed for the Coolidge land is dated 10 April 1905, and exactly one month later, when Nan came to Pittsfield to visit, Elizabeth took her to see the building site. Nan's reaction as noted in the diary is telling. "I wish for her sake and her friends, she had fewer nerves."[14] Elizabeth was understandably apprehensive over a venture of such magnitude, undertaken at a time when Fred's health was still so uncertain and stability as a family so precarious. Despite the prospect of their beautiful new home, Nan could see that all was not well with her children. "They are not happy as I wish—nor as well. . . . I think E would have begged me to give up California and stay with her. My heart is torn. I want to stay with her, but feel my duty to be otherwise."[15] Otho was not well, so Nan and Albert prepared to make their annual pilgrimage to Pasadena to visit him in November instead of waiting until February.

It is evident that through the years a gradual transformation of the mother-daughter relationship had been taking place. The experience of Fred's illness and the open-hearted, open-handed moral and financial support of her parents caused Elizabeth to perceive her mother now in an entirely different light. She had begun to comprehend the importance of family and no longer regarded her mother's presence as interference in her affairs. She had always been close to her thoughtful, gentle, soft-spoken father, but the sharp words and ill feelings that had sometimes scarred her relationship with Nan were now largely a thing of the past. Where formerly Elizabeth had frequently retreated into a brooding silence that left Nan perplexed, now her exchanges with her mother were characterized by a richness of emotion frankly expressed. The buggy rides, teas, and shopping excursions of earlier times gave way to shared confidences on a much deeper level. Elizabeth often spoke of her fears for the future and her many frustrations with the present. The tenderness of this more mature love for her mother is expressed in a letter penned many years later in which she says simply, "There is no loss like that of a mother."

Elizabeth was acutely aware of her parents' sacrifices on her behalf and knew very well that in every crisis both Nan and Albert, who were now nearly seventy years old, were ready at a moment's notice to be at her side. Even in later years the Spragues shuttled—always unquestioningly—from coast to coast as they divided their ministrations between the declining Otho in California and Fred and Elizabeth, who might be anywhere from Boston to New York to Pittsfield, or wherever the course of Fred's illness directed their migration in search of the latest treatment.

The interim before the completion of the house was brightened by the singular recognition paid to Elizabeth by the Musical Club of Chicago, which presented a complete program of her songs, including the *After Supper Songs,* the Browning Cycle, and what appears to be a new creation, *The Mother Goose Songs.*[16] It was probably the success of her earlier set of children's songs that encouraged Elizabeth to allow her singer-friend, Francis Rogers, to present the Mother Goose manuscript to Gustave Schirmer for consideration.[17] On 15 February 1902 Schirmer wrote to say, "I will soon submit them (the songs) to the judgment of my infant son. He is a connoisseur and has a large library on this subject."[18] Apparently his son approved, for they were published by G. Schirmer in 1904.

A few years later when Elizabeth was finally able to study with Percy Goetschius, she took the *Mother Goose Songs* to her first lesson for his criticism. His written response is revealing. "Had I seen your 'Mother Goose' before our meeting, it would not have changed my opinion, but only strengthened it—in regard to your talent and your possible studies. . . . Anyone who sees the 'Mother Goose' would exclaim, 'the person who wrote that series does not need to study the rudiments.'"[19]

For the time being, however, composition had to take a back seat to her preoccupation with the more immediate concerns of moving, selecting furniture and carpets, and above all making plans for a housewarming fit to inaugurate a home in which she could re-create the kind of rich cultural and social ambiance that she had known back in her days on Prairie Avenue. But fate intervened again, and Elizabeth's plans and preparations for moving into her new home were interrupted in January of 1906 when Fred had a sudden relapse and had to be taken immediately to Dr. Pfaff in Boston, who predicted that Fred "was losing ground and would continue to do so."[20] Elizabeth rushed to Chicago to seek a second opinion from Dr. Sanger Brown. Throughout the course of Fred's illness it was always Elizabeth who took the initiative in searching for specialists and new treatments.

Fred's letters from this period were so cheerful as to suggest that Pfaff must surely have been mistaken in his diagnosis. They are filled with expressions of his gratitude for her dedication and support and the realization that his illness has been a difficult ordeal for her. In one of the most touching of the letters he shares with her the response he made to Dr. Frank Billings when his old Chicago friend and colleague sympathized with him for "no longer being in the ring with the medical men of Chicago." Fred explains, "I told him that I have a rich life with you darling, that I would not have had in Chicago. . . . Thank you dear Puss for being so good and lovable, and for loving me. It seems important that such love has been able to last through these fifteen years, but it has, and it shines more and more as the years go by."[21]

It was at this time that Elizabeth began to study piano with Harold Bauer.[22] These lessons were very likely not only therapeutic but were a conscious part of her preparation for the move into the new house and its official inauguration. Many of the more practical matters were being managed by Nan, who was by now back in Chicago overseeing the dismantling of Elizabeth's house there and packing her furniture to go to Pittsfield.[23] Elizabeth was thus freed to make preparations for the official housewarming of the new home, which was christened Upway Fields, after the little town of Upway, England, from which the Spragues had originated. The official inauguration in November was an elegant affair, with much music supplied by instrumentalists from the Boston Symphony and Elizabeth herself doing the honors at the piano.

Upway Fields, which is still standing, has the character of a gracious manor house, its strong classical elements of design softened by the muted yellow tint of the stucco exterior and the striped awnings.[24] The broad southern façade was pierced by triple arches that welcomed the visitor onto a palm-bedecked porch leading to the foyer. An expansive two-story structure, the house had colonnaded porches at either end, providing an unobstructed view across the rolling lawn with the purple hills as a distant backdrop. Inside, the most dominant feature, after the elegant stairway that graced the entrance, was the large music room at the eastern end of the house, which was actually a double room measuring more than forty feet from north to south. It was graced by twin fireplaces and opened at either end by large French doors with arched windows above the lintels. The house comprised more than thirty rooms, including servants' quarters and a special room at the west end of the second floor

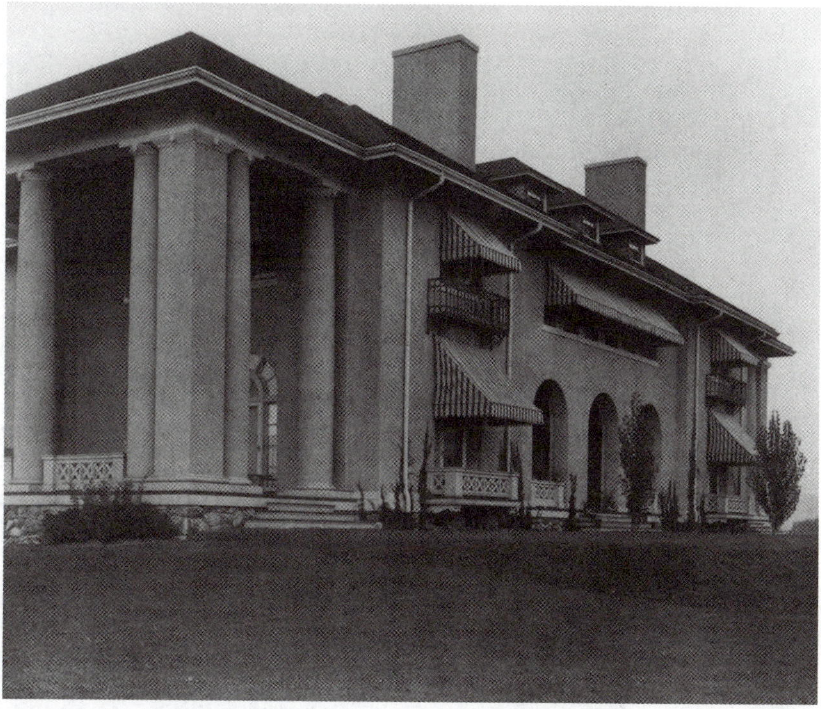

"Upway Fields," Fred and Elizabeth's home in Pittsfield, designed by Charles Allerton Coolidge in 1906 and named for the village in England from which the Spragues originated. In 1918 she gave the house to be used as the Berkshire County School for Crippled Children.

Shepley Bulfinch Richardson and Abbott, Boston

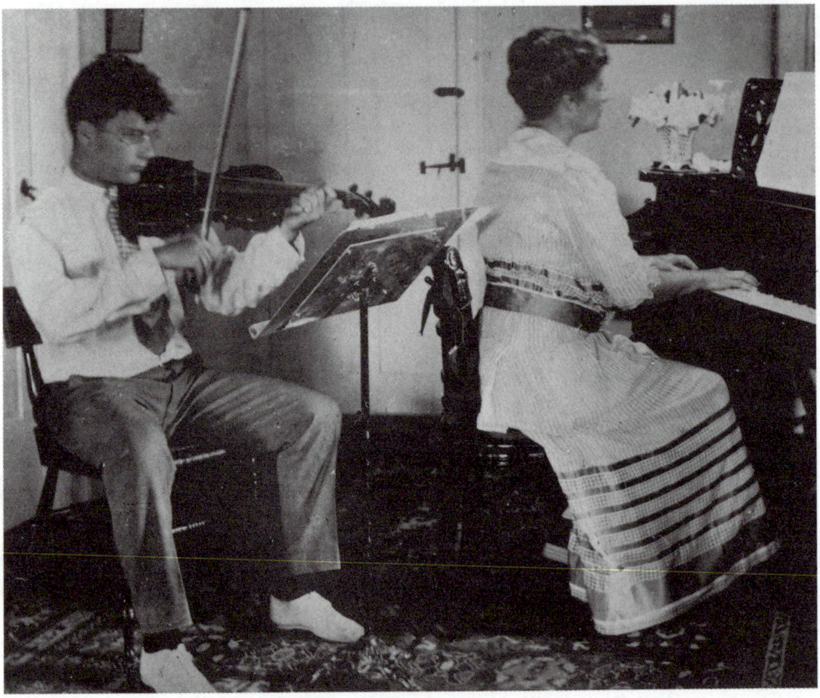

Elizabeth accompanying her son, Sprague, at Pittsfield

Jeffrey Coolidge Photography, Boston

designated on the architect's drawings as Mrs. Sprague's room. Among the accoutrements of the new household was the "machine"—Nan's description of an automobile—which was kept in the stable. It is not known just when the Sprague/Coolidge choice of locomotion changed from the horse and buggy to the auto, but it seems likely that it should have occurred well before this time. We know that shortly after the turn of the century Sprague Warner and Company began using trucks to transport merchandise. At whatever time the car arrived in the household, it effected the transformation of that favorite form of diversion—the joy ride—into what would ever after be Elizabeth's preferred relaxation, "motoring." Sprague, too, became an inveterate auto collector and aficionado and for many years, even after he was teaching at Harvard, he continued to drive an ancient Franklin and an electric car of 1914 vintage.[25]

By this time Sprague was twelve years old and was sent off in September to study at the Fessendon School in West Newton, Massachusetts, where the headmaster declared him "the brightest boy in school—two years ahead of his class."[26] Already he was showing a great interest in things electrical and had rigged up a homemade telegraph. Musical studies, too, were keeping pace; he now played the violin quite well, could follow a musical score accurately, and understood the elements of harmony and the formal construction of music. However proud Elizabeth was of his accomplishments she had to admit to Nan that "He is bitter and hard to train. Let us hope that, like a diamond's, the polish is difficult to impart, . . . meanwhile I am the over-worked polishing wheel."[27] It is not surprising that the precocious twelve-year-old who had for the greater part of his life been moved about, uprooted from one home and set of friends to another, sometimes tutored privately and at others thrust into a new school, should have problems. He had been shuttled by force of circumstances from one set of authority figures to another, all of whom attempted to compensate for these experiences by doting upon and even spoiling him. Elizabeth's decision to send him away to Fessendon may have been motivated by her recognition of the need for greater stability in his young life as much as it was by the desire for a solid education.

In his intermittent spurts of good health Fred was becoming more and more interested and involved in the Boys' Club of Pittsfield, where he served as physical instructor and member of the board of directors. The Boys' Club, founded by Zenas Crane in 1900,[28] became something of a family endeavor, with Albert making generous contributions to the work and Elizabeth beginning to teach there. To her already considerable musical activities she now added the role of pedagogue. As early as 1905 she had formed a children's class and trained them in singing with the help of a teacher named Miss Denny, and now she began to give piano lessons to the boys.

Next to his medical practice Fred's other humanitarian preoccupation was his determination to contribute to the eradication of tuberculosis. It was largely through his efforts that the Pittsfield Anti-Tuberculosis Society was formed in 1907.[29] The work began as a clinic for the care of tubercular patients by visiting nurses who treated them in their homes. Albert and Elizabeth both contributed generously as well, and the work endured long beyond Fred's lifetime, until the steady decline in the disease made it no longer necessary to keep the clinic open.[30]

Just days before Christmas, 1906, Fred became desperately ill. Nan's hurried entry in her diary on 22 December is testimony of the urgency with which she and Albert responded to their daughter's need. "News Fred no better and *E wants us.* We go at 5:30."[31] Her letter to Otho written on Christmas Day is a vivid account of what awaited them in Pittsfield. Fred had suffered a severe attack of some sort while making his daily rounds at the Boys' Club.

> *He felt himself getting very ill and knew he could not get home and went into the Club room. He was alone in the room when the complete collapse came—but a friend in an adjoining room heard him and went to find him desperately ill—he at once summoned doctors, who saw 'twas heart failure. They thought him already dead at first—but vigorous treatment revived him—a bed was sent for and a nurse and for four days he lay there, they fearing the move would bring on a relapse. Two doctors and two nurses were in constant attendance, day and night.*[32]

As if Fred's illness were not debilitating enough, the treatment of nitroglycerin hypodermics induced severe nausea and vertigo, and Dr.

Councilman believed that he would not live through this last bout. From this period dates the first slight chink in Fred's armor of optimism, his otherwise serene and cheerful acceptance of this dreadful illness. As a physician he must have realized his dismal prognosis, and Nan noted the change in his countenance in her diary. "We do not know if he knows how ill he has been! E and I see, or think we see, now and then a sad anxious expression in his face. I believe he knows perfectly well his condition and the seriousness of his case—but (he) hesitates on E's account to allude to it. The sweetest side of his always sweet nature comes out now."[33]

On the heels of this sad Christmas came an even sadder New Year's Day, for it marked a serious relapse that left Fred partially deaf. Elizabeth sent for specialists from New York, and Dr. Councilman was also called in. Both he and Dr. Pfaff believed it imperative that Fred be moved at once to Boston.[34] Albert procured a private coach to transport the patient, doctors, and family. Elizabeth took a suite of furnished rooms in Boston in order to be with Fred while he underwent a painful therapy of massive doses of iodides, which he could take for only eleven or twelve days at a time. There was no thought of her returning to Upway Fields while Fred remained in Boston alone. It was a repetition of sorts of the move to Saranac just four years earlier, as once again Elizabeth found it necessary to pull up stakes and leave a new house which, in this case, they had enjoyed for less than five months.

By mid-January 1907 Fred was able to leave the hospital. Though he was weak, could not focus his eyes, and experienced increasing deafness, he nonetheless moved into the Touraine Hotel.[35] Elizabeth remained with him in Boston, writing daily letters to her parents—letters that trace the tantalizing improvements and cruel declines in Fred's condition that followed in rapid succession. One of the most cryptic of Nan's diary entries reads, "E tells me what Dr. Blake tells her!"[36] We can only assume that like the dreaded word "syphilis," this latest prognosis was simply too painful, too awful to inscribe. All indications suggest that this may have been the first symptom of the decline of Fred's mental faculties.

By summer he was able to be back in Pittsfield but needed constant nursing care. On 7 December his father died in Boston, and Fred was at least well enough to be with his family in their bereavement, but as the year drew to an end Elizabeth found that Fred was becoming more and more difficult to care for, and it was apparent that she needed help. Although his physicians agreed, Elizabeth confided to her mother that "any such argument with Fred is worse than useless . . . as it makes him all the more opposed and is dangerous to his brain. . . . He cannot see why there is any 'responsibility' or 'care' from which I'd be free: he is an overwhelming care. If he . . . realized it, I think he might kill himself."[37]

At every critical point in Fred's illness Elizabeth's hearing loss seemed to be worse. After this particular bout she needed extensive treatment in New York and admitted to Nan that she was enjoying her freedom while there. Meanwhile, between his periodic hunting expeditions Fred was sitting for a portrait by Ernest Ipsen, who had already painted Albert and Nan.[38] Elizabeth was keeping up her contact with the Chicago clubs, and Sprague was sending home enthusiastic weekly reports from the Hill School, where his scholastic record was brilliant despite demerits for conduct. On closing day of the semester he reaped three first prizes: algebra, Latin, and German.[39]

The catalog of events for the year 1908 held its share of good news too. Over the years young Harmony Twichell, the daughter of Albert's old friend Joe Twichell, had been a frequent guest in the Sprague home and had become a kind of adopted daughter to Nan and Albert. Nan's diary entries during this time contain increasing references to Harmony, whose carefully preserved letters to the Spragues always address them as aunt and uncle. So it is not surprising that there was general rejoicing when Harmony wrote to say that she was engaged to a most wonderful man named Charlie Ives.[40] The Spragues and Coolidges were destined to become quite familiar with Ives, for there were many outings together after Harmony's marriage. One curious incident Nan found fit to preserve in the diary: "Charlie and Harmony Ives come to E's. . . . We have music in the evening. Sprague plays. Mr. Ives is quite musical and is composing but he can't play! He tried to play with (the) violin but did so badly that E couldn't stand it, and took the piano."[41]

But best of all, Fred was feeling well enough to resume his practice, and the orthopedic clinic that he had had to forsake at the time of his serious attack was now reopened. Elizabeth believed him to be the best

Harmony Twichell Ives, Joseph Twichell's daughter and wife of Charles Ives. Harmony was like a daughter to Albert and Nan.

Jeffrey Coolidge Photography, Boston

he had been in years, and Fred himself boasted, "I have forgotten all about bad health."[42] By the end of the year things appeared to be settling into a welcome calm. For only the second time since Fred and Elizabeth's marriage Nan and Albert were alone at Christmas without their children. Elizabeth's letter written on the last day of the year has an air of tranquility about it that is unusual for the period, yet it suggests a presentiment that perhaps this was only a quiet interlude. "We have settled with our routine again, . . . and 1908 (is) drawing within a few hours of its end. . . . I feel great satisfaction with the year. . . . Now what has 1909 in store?"[43]

CHAPTER SEVEN

The Eye of the Storm

My heart is widowed but it is well with my soul.

– ELIZABETH SPRAGUE COOLIDGE,

LETTER TO HER MOTHER, JANUARY 1912

THE YEAR 1909 brought newfound serenity and improved health that enabled the Coolidges to settle down from their medical wanderings and begin to piece together the fragments of their lives. With renewed vigor Fred returned to his medicine and Elizabeth to her music.

Fred was again drawing attention for his orthopedic work. In March Elizabeth shared with her mother the news that he had performed a brilliant operation. "Nine doctors, including all the prominent ones went to see it and some one wrote it up—not Fred. It was a great success and Fred was as happy as could be. Isn't it fine that he is doing his work at last."[1]

Sprague, too, was developing as he entered adolescence, becoming "more thoughtful of others and better mannered." He was receiving excellent reports from Hill School in Pottsdown, Pennsylvania, where teachers described him as "brilliant, a genius." He took first in Greek, and was showing great potential in the sciences. Latin and algebra, however, were so easy for him that he quickly became bored and was sometimes a nuisance in class.[2]

The only shadow cast upon this new tranquility was the death of Otho, who seemed to have waited to die until his brother and sister-in-law reached him in Pasadena on 18 February. He remained conscious briefly and in the early hours of 20 February his long battle with ill health ended quietly. There was a great outpouring of affection from friends in Chicago as well as those who knew him in California. Nan and Albert stayed there for a time to be with the children and to settle Otho's estate; finally on 6 April they returned with his remains to Chicago. Albert had procured a private coach for the family and an empty express wagon for the casket. The body was taken to Graceland Cemetery for a service and private burial.[3]

Elizabeth was by now devoting more and more time to the serious study of composition and to free her for this Nan sent her maid, Alice, to help out at Upway Fields. It was just at this time too that Daniel Gregory Mason and his wife began to spend summers in Pittsfield, and Elizabeth recognized his presence there as a unique opportunity to resume her composition studies while remaining at home with Fred. In view of the chronology of events as unfolded later in the summer, Mason's polite refusal to her request is particularly interesting.

> *DEAR MRS. COOLIDGE,*
>
> *On thinking further about the question of the lessons I have reached the conclusion that it really would be unwise for me to undertake them. Business engagements, however, interesting, have a sort of horror for me in summer, when it is so important to me to preserve my leisure quite intact. Trusting you will understand the point of view, I am with regret*
>
> *Sincerely yours,*
>
> *DANIEL GREGORY MASON*
>
> *PS I have written so formally that I fear I have not made it plain how much I appreciate what work of yours I have seen (particularly the charming children's songs) and how much I should enjoy working with a "pupil" of so much talent.*[4]

His later reflections on the event are a commentary on Elizabeth's single-minded persistence.

> *When we came to live in Pittsfield she asked me to give her lessons in composition. Fearing the distraction of any teaching in the only part of*

> *our year I could devote to my own composing, I declined; but it amuses me to discover in my journal, in the latter part of the summer: "corrected four chapters of proof and gave Mrs. Coolidge a lesson." I don't remember how my change of mind came about. In the long run people usually did what Mrs. Coolidge wanted.*[5]

Her resolve to improve her skills was part of a carefully laid plan—the boldest of her self-assertions to date. It was her determination to go to Berlin to study after completing another serious round of piano and composition lessons here at home. It may have been a kind of unconscious desire to rectify the great disappointment of not being able to remain in Berlin to study at the end of her first European tour in 1883. As yet she made no mention of it in letters to her mother, to Fred, or to Sprague, but circumstances suggest that she had discussed it with Gertrude Watson, who was to go with her.

From later correspondence and diary entries it is evident that she planned to take Sprague along in order to give him the benefit of the European training that she had been denied. She seems to have aimed for two years down the road, when he would have finished secondary school and before he entered college. To enhance his already fairly developed musical knowledge and prepare him for Berlin she arranged for violin lessons with Gustave Dannreuther, who agreed to tutor Sprague in the elements of harmony as well.[6] As for her own advancement, she intensified her quest for the best artist-teachers and composition tutors, and in the space of several months solicited numerous letters of introduction and recommendation from the likes of Daniel Gregory Mason, who suggested piano study with either Rafael Joseffy, Paolo Gallico, or Winifred Bauer (the sister of Harold), and also wrote a letter of introduction to Percy Goetschius for composition. Regina Watson, too, supplied a glowing letter for her to present to Joseffy.[7] On the other hand, Frederick Stock, who by this time had succeeded Theodore Thomas as conductor of the Chicago Symphony and become a good friend of the Spragues, recommended study with Joseph Lhevinne or Ossip Gabrilowitsch, both of whom were in Berlin. He was certain that Gabrilowitsch's assistant, Frances McElwee, was in touch with the circle of professional musicians in and around Berlin and would be able to find a proper violin teacher for Sprague too.[8]

On the strength of Amy Beach's recommendations of five years earlier, and encouraged by Mason as well, Elizabeth finally was able to begin study with Goetschius, who was in New York. His first letter to her indicates that although his contract did not allow him to give private lessons outside the Institute of Musical Art, he would quietly take her on as a pupil, telling her to say nothing to anyone but merely to come directly to his studio. Clearly Elizabeth had indicated to him the need to "go back to the beginning: and review the rudiments." His response to the compositions that she submitted to him says as much for his pedagogical method as it does for her musical skills. After perusing the Browning Cycle he wrote, "I find myself indebted to you for a very delightful and interesting hour or two. The songs are so full of musical beauty, true poetic significance and correct feeling that they might easily stand for finished products—were it not for evidences of occasional technical deficiency." It is obvious from his comments that he recognized the difficulty of instructing someone as gifted as Elizabeth who, by dint of great effort and determination and with only fragmentary tutoring undertaken in fits and starts between family crises, had managed to produce several significant works. In Goetschius's opinion, "It is hazardous for any outsider to impose his notion upon such a musical 'talent,' for any one of many possible errors in judgment (like reckless pruning) is likely to check or destroy the natural forces, which are destined to work in their own way and arrive at fullness along their own (possibly unusual) avenues. Hence my embarrassment. . . . A person who (by talent and intelligence) has reached the point in any *artistic* pursuit at which you now stand, should not, in my opinion, 'go back to the beginning.'"[9]

Like Amy Beach, Goetschius believed Elizabeth had found her métier in the simpler style of music that he believed to be "more successful and effective than the dramatic and elaborate songs you showed me in manuscript some months ago. . . . By this, however, I would not for the world discourage any inclination you may ever feel to express yourself in the elaborate style. Do *always* as you feel impelled to do."[10]

And she did. The lessons and correspondence with Goetschius extended through the next two years, the longest period in which she was able to work exclusively with one composition teacher. Despite his insistence that she need not go back over the rudiments, there are reams of manuscript paper densely filled with the most laboriously worked out exercises in modulation from each of the twenty-four keys to the other twenty-three. Although they are undated, it appears likely that they may have been in preparation for her next major composition essay.[11] Apparently Goetschius's admonitions to stay with the simple style neither dampened her enthusiasm nor intimidated her from attempting a large abstract form in purely instrumental music. Without the crutch of a text to lean on she began work on what she refers to at this time as her "sonata."[12]

Her father's birthday greeting for 1909 contained his perennial and tender assurance of love, encouragement, pride in her accomplishments and, as always, money. With Fred's limited practice, his medical bills, Sprague's education, and the expenses of maintaining Upway Fields with a staff of servants, her father's support was a godsend. Her letter of thanks reveals a quieter, more serene and philosophical Elizabeth than some of her previous angst-ridden epistles. "I thank you very lovingly for your kind words. Age serves its principal purpose, I think, in showing us the values of life, the chief of which is love, and the next best, work. I feel very rich in the first, from my family and my chosen friends; and I am learning, I hope, to appreciate more, as I grow older, the blessing of giving love as well as receiving it."[13]

Her "work" was not merely restricted to her own private pursuits as a skilled but amateur performer and composer, but included a genuine investment of time and industry in the school she had started. Yet she had the good sense to realize that she needed diversion and found it in frequent short trips to New York and Boston with Gertrude. She planned to go to Chicago in November but made it clear to her parents where her first priority lay. She could not remain with them for an extended holiday, for when she stayed away too long Fred became very lonely and depressed and felt neglected, so she must return to him for Thanksgiving.

The year 1909 ended much as it had begun, its twelve months constituting one of the least harried years of their life together since the onset of Fred's illness. There were minor worries and cares, but it was a blessedly calm interval. However, with the advent of 1910 Fred suffered "some sort of an attack" that necessitated a hasty return to Boston and

Dr. Pfaff.[14] This time his heart was affected—a condition his doctors believed was induced by taking too many barbiturates. But Fred responded well to treatment and soon returned to his activities at the Anti-Tuberculosis Association and the Boys' Club.

Elizabeth, too, broadened the scope of her work with the boys by enlarging the faculty of her school and diversifying the curriculum. At this time she formed an orchestra and sought out a violin teacher who was already on the faculty of the Settlement School in New York, hoping thereby to enlist his help in doing for the Boys' Club—though in a smaller way—what was being done in New York.[15] By the time she began this new addition to her school thirty-six boys had applied, forty-eight lessons were given in the first week, and there was already a waiting list.[16] She provided three pianos for practice purposes, allotted a budget of $1,500 a year for the project, and offered instruction to the boys at the rate of ten cents a lesson. Elizabeth had already begun to prove herself a capable businesswoman by renting out the cottages on the property to help with finances, and now she added to her considerable achievements as a teacher. The work stimulated much interest in the community too, and several of her boys continued their musical education and went on to become professionals.[17]

Although Elizabeth may seem to have used music to create a bulwark against her vulnerability, there is no question of it ever supplanting or even lessening her love for Fred. If anything, the short diversions she enjoyed and the escape she found in her work became the strength that fortified her and kept alive at least a glimmer of hope for their future. At all times she continued to seek out news of progress in the treatment of syphilis that might offer some prospect of cure for Fred and a more normal life together. The very nature of his illness made of their relationship a love that both united and separated them, one that fed on the strength of the will to love and reached new depths of devotion.

By late 1910, Elizabeth had heard of a new treatment for syphilis, a scientific breakthrough discovered by German immunologist Paul Ehrlich, whose experiments had resulted in the drug, salvorsan, which came to be known as "the magic bullet." Because it was the result of 606 experiments with an arsenic compound, it was popularly referred to simply as "the 606."[18] Salvorsan was actually an early experiment in the field of chemotherapy, and since it was an unproven treatment there were few American doctors who administered it. Elizabeth learned of one in Chicago and, full of hope, wrote to her parents in late December that Fred would be arriving there on the 3 January to submit to this new therapy. Between Nan's diary entries for the period and Fred's letters back to Elizabeth in Pittsfield, the nature of the treatment as well as its side effects are well documented. According to Nan, "Fred goes directly to the doctor who gives him the treatment—injecting in two places the stuff—whatever it is—the new discovery. He is ordered to bed to remain there for a few days. . . . He has to be carefully watched but the symptoms do occur."[19] Throughout the treatment Fred stayed with Nan and Albert and obviously confided to Nan something of the nature of the disease and the possible outcome of the treatment. Although he and Elizabeth had high hopes for this miracle drug, Nan's instincts led her to fear the terrible disappointment and discouragement that would result if the 606 failed to stop the disease. As a physician Fred certainly understood fully the nature of the risk involved, but his letters to his wife are full of hope and contain his insights into the working of the drug.

> *This is the third day I am in bed most of the time, feeling rather unmanly but not exactly sick. . . . I have a couple of sore places on my back between my shoulders where the injections are made. No bad symptoms whatever. I fancy I shall have to stay in the house about a week in all and be very careful for another week. You see the stuff is put into the muscles and remains there being absorbed gradually for at least a week or two. . . . My darling if this 606 is only a success, as it looks like so far, how deeply thankful I shall be my dear true darling little girl. It really has been hard, dear one, knowing that the blamed old disease was steadily and surely going on and that any time I might have another worse attack. But darling we will hope for the best, with good prospect of good results.*[20]

Fred responded well to the treatment, and just as he had done so often after a period of serious sickness, once again indulged in what seemed to Elizabeth like needless exertion. The experiment with the 606 had been a very anxious time for her, and she made no attempt to hide her disappointment from her mother when Fred, almost immediately after returning to Pittsfield, left on a hunting trip. "Fred left me again for two weeks, and if I hadn't the faculty for self employment I should be pretty forlorn, for it is raining outside and very lonely within. But I, fortunately, have had so much practice in adjusting my inner life that I am really lacking time for all the things I have to do. Just now it is your 'sonata': I believe I am writing something rather good."[21]

Such apparent insensitivity on the part of Fred must have seemed a rebuff in return for her efforts to search out treatment for him; at the same time it may also simply reflect the increasing deterioration of his mental faculties and emotional stability. Tertiary syphilis affects almost any part of the body, and its most important incapacitating or fatal manifestations are cardiovascular syphilis, neurosyphilis, and ocular syphilis. Fred had already experienced a weakening of his heart and a loss of hearing, and would soon suffer the dimming of his sight as well. The most dreaded of these complications was neurosyphilis, which causes mental changes and mood alterations, gradually resulting in a complete change of personality. Elizabeth had already observed early symptoms of such change in his behavior as his mood understandably fluctuated between depression and hope—invariably false hope. Only six weeks after the treatment in Chicago he was elated to report to Nan that the result of his latest blood test was negative, whereas in December it had been "strongly positive. . . . I shall test it again in 6 weeks, and in 6 months, hoping I can really believe it is so. But as it is I am very happy. . . . Oh how glad I am that I took the experiment and that you and Daddy were there to support me."[22]

The personal therapy that Elizabeth found in her work was rewarded by the prospering of her school. In just six months the enrollment had increased from thirty-six to sixty-eight pupils, with 129 lessons given weekly by an enlarged teaching staff.[23] With the program so well under control by summer 1911, she decided to pursue the Berlin trip, and this time confided the news to Nan, who obviously approved, referring to her scheme as "E's darling secret."[24] But the plans were hardly divulged when Fred suffered his most serious attack, on 15 August. Elizabeth, Sprague, and Gertrude all rallied around his bed, and Nan and Albert left for Pittsfield in haste, obviously intending to remain for a while since they ordered their car to be sent the following day.[25] They arrived to find that Fred had suffered a stroke; his left side was paralyzed and he was unable to speak or to swallow. Dr. Councilman came immediately, and Elizabeth moved into her parents' cottage in order to make room in the big house for Fred's medical staff. Only she and Sprague were permitted to see Fred, and then for but a few minutes; not even the Coolidges were allowed in. Nan describes Elizabeth as "miserable and hysterical" as she watched her husband's physical suffering and the deterioration of his mind. For two months he fluctuated between periods of delirium and lucidity, sometimes saying things that indicated he comprehended the seriousness of his symptoms. To his nurse he confided, "It would have been better had it ended a month ago."[26] By September Nan feared "for his mentality," and nurses confirmed that the degeneration of his mind was serious—which in Nan's diary translates as "imbecility." According to her, at those moments when he was able to speak his "talk was crazy" and he wept much of the time.[27] October brought another crisis and more consultation among physicians: at times there were as many as eight doctors involved in the case.

With winter approaching it became imperative to make some provisions for his care over the next few months. In the opinion of the Pittsfield doctors Fred was too sick to be moved to Boston as he would have liked. His lungs were involved now and he was losing ground quickly. In addition to his already critical condition he suffered a recurrence of tuberculosis. As both physician and family member, Dr. Councilman's concern now was for Elizabeth as much as for his brother-in-law, and he questioned the wisdom of attempting to care for Fred at home. To Elizabeth he wrote, "You cannot take care of him, particularly if the mental condition grows worse. . . . I think taking all conditions into consideration it would be impossible for you to take charge of this yourself. . . . It seems to me you must realize that while he can get better, he may get much worse. . . . I have thought much of you and have great sympathy for you in the great trials you have had to meet in the past years, and which you have met bravely."[28]

By now it had become painfully clear that Elizabeth's trip to Berlin would have to be postponed. By the end of August it had also been decided that Sprague would attend Harvard, as his father and grandfather Coolidge had. With Fred's condition so critical it fell to Nan, now seventy-four years old, to accompany Sprague to Cambridge, find suitable rooms, and buy the necessary furnishings and clothes for him. It was indeed a sad day when he left, for he had been a great consolation to his mother in this trying time. Nan's devotion and generosity through it all confirmed Elizabeth's realization that her relationship with her mother was now truly one of deep friendship. "Your love is very dear to me and the knowledge of how you are carrying me in your heart is a background which I need and love. No one can ever take your place in my life-long love and sympathy and companionship: and I count it my supreme blessing that my darling mother is alive to cherish me and help me."[29]

Sprague returned briefly to be with his mother on 12 November, his parents' twentieth wedding anniversary. Despite the circumstances it was not as sad a day as it might have been. Although Fred had grown "simple and slow minded" Elizabeth admitted she felt quite happy as she sat by his bed and read to him. "I have grown to face the tragedy of losing him by inches, but I cannot accustom myself nor reconcile myself to his pain and sorrow."[30]

The doctors had repeatedly advised Elizabeth, for her own health, to get away, so in November she left for Chicago for a visit and in early December went with Gertrude to Boston. She returned to find that Fred "had had another distinct stroke . . . which completely paralyzed his throat. He could swallow nothing and had another high fever." Plans to take him south in early 1912 had to be abandoned, so Elizabeth decided that "we shall stay where we are. . . . On Christmas day he came downstairs for the first time in four months, but was pretty blue, wept and longed for the health that will never be his—but is still hoping against hope."[31]

Throughout the ordeal Gertrude was with Elizabeth almost constantly. She moved into the cottage with her and lovingly attempted to relieve her friend's burden by thoughtfully planning little diversions—but most of all by simply being a quiet, comforting presence. Her devotion to Elizabeth was a great consolation to Albert and Nan, to whose expressions of gratitude Gertrude responded, "Please realize that I have chosen the thing I want most to do when I am devoting my time and thought to helping E over her hard winter, that nothing could begin to give me such true happiness; so the word sacrifice must be eliminated from your mind for it never enters mine."[32]

An added sorrow occurred when on 1 August 1912 Elizabeth lost her oldest and dearest friend, Regina Watson. Fred's condition made it impossible for her to return to Chicago for the funeral as she desperately wanted to. To his pain and weakness were added severe depression, dependence on morphine, and a "little jealous streak" that led him to feel neglected if she went away for too long.

Elizabeth felt the loss of her beloved teacher and friend very deeply, for Regina Watson was one of the few people with whom the true nature of Fred's illness was fully shared. Watson's unfailing devotion to her former student is tenderly conveyed in the letter she wrote to Elizabeth just after hearing the news of Fred's most recent attack.

> *My heart is breaking over the news your mother told me on the telephone last evening. . . . My poor child—what anguish you are going through! Poor Fred—whom I learned to love . . . for his sweetness, his gentleness and unfailing courtesy—that he should be thus smitten! When I thought of you this summer it was always with unfailing delight, that you were at last to have the long coveted year abroad; . . . I cannot write much now today—my heart is too sore and also, all details are lacking. But you will know, dearest, that every fiber of my being is with you now and always.*[33]

Shored up by the love of such friends and the devotion of her parents, Elizabeth was beginning to plumb the unknown depths of her strength and became conscious of a new "inner poise" that seems to have been given her to endure this latest trial. To her mother she confided, "I do not understand it myself, for as you well know my love for Fred has been my life's love, and my heart is widowed; but it is well with my soul that it is still in tune and that I can say 'Thy will be done' without losing faith in life. I am glad that my own sorrow and even dear Fred's undeserved and horrible fate, do not embitter me, and so you may know what is best in me is not succumbing but is really victorious in the knowledge of what my husband's life has stood for. In that I am rich—a wealth that the future cannot alter."[34]

The knowledge of Fred's dedication to his profession was a consolation to Elizabeth and an inspiration to others as well. Before Fred was stricken in 1911, Albert had already spoken to him of making a contribution to the work of the Anti-Tuberculosis Society, and now, wishing to make good his promise, he approached Elizabeth and asked, "[F]or what shall the money be used? I had thought if the institution became a permanent sanitarium, like the Saranac or the one in Pasadena, and adopted the cottage system, I would like to build a Fred Coolidge Cottage as a testimonial of his skill and unselfish devotion."[35] Elizabeth immediately consulted with Dr. Colt and enthusiastically related to her father that the most pressing need of the Society was for a cottage that would provide sleeping space for women patients."[36] It was to be given in Fred's name and would be based upon the model of Trudeau's, but with the most modern improvements.

Albert Sprague had always been generous, and in his later years his philanthropy reached out beyond the circle of family and friends to embrace more and more expansive humanitarian causes. At about the time of his bequest to the Anti-Tuberculosis Society, he gave the final $10,000 necessary to complete the $100,000 raised by friends of Otho in order to create the Sprague Home for Nurses, which was given to Presbyterian Hospital in Chicago as a memorial to his brother and in time to Albert as well.[37]

Although Fred remained physically weak, he was spiritually uplifted by his father-in-law's contribution to the cause of eradicating tuberculosis and reacted with as much enthusiasm as his strength permitted. On pleasant days he was able to be outside in a wheelchair and even attempted to walk a bit, tottering along on the arm of Frank, his attendant. Yet even now vestiges of his sweet disposition still surfaced. Daniel Gregory Mason recalled years later, "I can still see him, sitting with his nurse on an upper piazza as the rest of us started out for a day's motoring, waving his hand to us with a cheerfulness that seemed heroic. [His] retiring manners hid what only those who knew his story realized to be a heroic nature."[38] In May 1912 he again took the 606, and three times more in July. His letter to Elizabeth on their twenty-first wedding anniversary that year, written in a faint, shaky, and sometimes almost indecipherable hand—so different from the fine and beautiful handwriting of the early letters—is a graphic and sad reminder of the powerful toll the disease had taken. Yet among the scrawls the message that can be made out is clearly one of loving gratitude. "You are the most precious girl in the world darling, and have made me a wonderful wife. . . . You are a truly great woman and I thank my stars that you have belonged to me dearest."[39]

Amid the trials and turmoil of 1912, the one truly pleasurable highlight was an elaborate golden wedding celebration that Elizabeth staged for her parents in Gertrude's home on Lake Onata. The esteem with which the Spragues were held back in their home town is reflected by the number of friends who came all the way from Chicago to Pittsfield for the occasion. Among them were such prominent members of the community as the Hutchinsons, Ryersons, Bartletts, Byrons, Smiths, Ayers, Johnsons, Fullers, and their nephew, A. A. Sprague II.[40] Together with the Glessners, who were unable to attend, they gave the couple a dozen solid gold plates to which Elizabeth added a complete coffee service in gold. Their offerings seem symbolic of the course of Nan and Albert's life together since that day fifty years earlier when their wedding reception occurred on the platform of a small train station in Vermont and the gift of two precious salt spoons constituted their entire silver service.

August 1913 marked the second anniversary of Fred's most debilitating attack, and he had neither walked nor gotten out of bed alone since then. In his lucid moments he understood fully the hopelessness of his case, longed for the end to come, and on one occasion even "commanded Dr. Paddock to order an overdose of morphine."[41] His state of despair impelled Elizabeth to seek out additional specialists who, in consultation, advised taking Fred to the Rockefeller Institute for some new treatment being administered there by Dr. Draper. Nan, Elizabeth, and the maid left immediately for New York, where they settled on two units in a building on 59th Street overlooking Central Park.[42] A few days later Fred was brought by his two nurses and a male attendant, was installed in his new quarters, and underwent his first treatment, to which he reacted rather violently. After a short time, however, he began to show some improvement, and again recognizing what Elizabeth had done for him, wrote, "You took me from the jaws of certain death, dearest, and have given me a chance."[43]

On Elizabeth's forty-ninth birthday Nan's secret wish for her, inscribed in the diary, was: "I hope for her betterment she is not to see Fred at all for a number of months."[44] She was undoubtedly echoing Dr.

Draper's advice that Elizabeth should simply get away from Fred, for her own sake as well as for his. This complete separation was difficult for Elizabeth to accept and created serious financial problems which, once again, were quietly resolved by Albert.[45]

In accordance with the doctor's orders, Elizabeth removed herself from the scene by traveling, and when she was home she lost herself in her music. The major composition to result from this period is a very significant achievement, her String Quartet in E Minor.[46] There is no documentation to indicate exactly with whom she was studying at the time, but a reference in an earlier letter from Goetschius suggests that she may have still been with him when she wrote the work. "I am truly curious to see your Sonata movement, and expect to find it very interesting. But we shall see—perhaps the Dirge will follow as a natural consequence."[47] That "the dirge to follow" was the second movement of her quartet (which in its final form is marked *Largo lamentoso*) is confirmed at a later date when the Manhattan String Quartet was preparing to record the work. Elizabeth wrote, "I am going to take the liberty of asking you to . . . play the funeral march a good deal more slowly than I have ever heard you do it. It should have the real character of a dirge and should be full of the elegiac spirit at a very slow tempo."[48]

This movement was written just at the time when Fred had his second stroke, and its somber character seems to suggest that for Elizabeth it may have been a catharsis of sorts, in somewhat the same way that the Browning Cycle of songs had been autobiographical. But no sadder commentary could be found than her description of the transformation in the man she loved so dearly. "Poor, poor Beadie. From a modest, self-effacing, unmercenary, refined gentleman, he has become a vain egoist; self-centered, indecent, and money-loving. What could so speak more decisively for the change that the awful disease has wrought in my dear lovable boy?"[49]

CHAPTER EIGHT

Severed Moorings

Let me not beg for the stilling of my pain but for the heart to conquer it. Let me not look for allies in life's battlefield but to my own strength.

– RABINDRANATH TAGORE, *FRUIT GATHERINGS*

IN THE CAST of characters of Elizabeth's life-drama, the quiet hero was always Albert Arnold Sprague, paterfamilias. He seemed at times to recede into the silent background, more or less upstaged by his garrulous wife, while the drama of his daughter's life unfolded with the intensity of a verismo opera. Yet, his was a kind of sacred presence, the deus ex machina who seemed to set all things right.

His devotion to Nancy Atwood, so tenderly expressed in the one surviving love letter from their courtship days, grew unfalteringly throughout their long marriage. The message that accompanied his gift to her on her seventy-fifth birthday is a simple but eloquent expression: "Let this circle of diamonds be a reminder of my unbounded love for you—my faithful companion and dearest friend."[1] Nancy, despite her sometimes excessive emotional displays, could always say, "I feel more and more that my anchorage is in your love which is and always will remain so sweet and strong."[2]

Still a vigorous man at age seventy-nine, Albert remained vitally interested in the arts, politics, his business, and above all his family. Throughout his son-in-law's illness he had continued his quiet support, and now as Fred's condition grew more critical he watched with a loving father's solicitude as his daughter struggled through this painful trial and did what he could to alleviate it. Elizabeth lived on a generous allowance from her parents, and A. A.'s checks came unfailingly.

Whether she realized it or not, she was learning something of her father's equanimity in the day-to-day battle, and also of his management skills. As financial considerations became more pressing she sought means of supplementing her income by teaching, selling Sprague's old violin, renting out the cottages on her property, and even leasing Upway Fields during the periods when she could not be there.

Although her parents suggested spending the summer of 1914 in Pittsfield, Elizabeth's disagreement with them over the matter revealed the degree to which her nerves and endurance had been tested during the course of Fred's illness, and instead she proposed not keeping house anywhere at all, simply "motoring around" for the summer. Though her wishes were contrary to those of her parents, they were completely in compliance with Dr. Draper's orders for separation from Fred. Pittsfield and Upway Fields had come to represent pain and disappointment to Elizabeth. Her beautiful home there, in which she and Fred had shared only a few untroubled months before the onset of his last illness, was becoming something of a millstone, a mockery of her quest for untroubled domesticity. Just this once she disagreed emphatically with her parents: "Although I realize that you're proposing it for my happiness, I do not want to live in Pittsfield again . . . for I have a real feeling against another summer there. . . . I must consider my nerves and Pittsfield is not what they need."[3]

By June, however, after several pleasant outings with Gertrude Watson, she had changed her mind. Nan and Albert did all that they could to ease the situation by literally transporting themselves and their entire staff—cook, waitress, maid, and chauffeur—to Pittsfield for the summer.[4]

To effect the separation prescribed by Dr. Draper, Fred and his nurse, Jane Cleary, were installed for the summer in a cottage at Sound Beach on Long Island. The Spragues continued to send things to them but, in compliance with the doctor's orders, there was no visiting. The summer was brightened somewhat by much music-making and poetry reading, and especially by a visit of the Carleton Spragues. But by summer's end Elizabeth was once again faced with the decision of how to provide for Fred's care throughout another fall and winter. She had to vacate her New York apartments, and after a tiring search selected a new one on 79th Street for Fred, and an unfurnished one for herself at 850 Park Avenue. The old familiar routine of closing down one home and moving furniture to another began all over again. Nan shopped for the necessities and kept the accounts, and by mid-November Fred and Elizabeth were finally settled in their respective new quarters.

In the autumn of this final move to New York a new personality entered the picture in the person of Margaret (Peg) Coit, a sophomore from Wellesley College who had obviously caught Sprague's fancy. Sprague, who was just beginning his senior year at Harvard, made Phi Beta Kappa, was becoming seriously interested in socialism, and had now fallen in love—apparently for the first time. All evidence from his letters suggests that up to now his greatest preoccupations had been science, music, and cars. Peg changed all that. It helped that she was a serious student of chemistry and enjoyed spirited debate with him on a wide variety of issues. Although Elizabeth and Nan both liked her very much, Sprague's sudden interest in her was the source of some consternation, prompting Nan to observe, "We hardly know what to think. He really seems very much interested and fond of her. S thinks her scholarly—which is what attracts him to her—anyhow he is attracted."[5]

As Christmas approached it became clear that this romance was maturing, and although Sprague and Peg announced their intentions to postpone marriage for two years until she had graduated and he had the opportunity to study abroad, Elizabeth still expressed concern about their immaturity. The family's reservations regarding early marriage were based mainly upon the fear that it would distract him from his work and derail what surely promised to be a brilliant career.

Sprague's response to this opposition bristled with exactly the kind of determination that he had inherited from his mother and is reiterated time and again in his candid rebuttals to their objections. "Your fears are entirely groundless. . . . It is exactly our great and common interest in our work, especially our chemistry, which has brought us together. We are not a distraction, but a stimulus to one another. . . . Peg is a very fine and sensible girl, to know whom is a great privilege, . . . and to be loved by whom is a great inspiration."[6]

Romance was on everyone's mind at Christmas 1914, and there is very little mention of Fred, who was still being so devotedly attended by

Jane Cleary. He appeared simple and happy as a child, with head full of wild dreams, but he was more docile than before. With the knowledge that he was so well cared for, Elizabeth felt justified in occupying herself more and more with her music, while Nan and Albert remained in Chicago, apparently well and happy.

When weather permitted Albert enjoyed his daily eighteen holes of golf, and when in Pittsfield he indulged in regular morning chats with his cronies at the bank. As the senior member of the Sprague Warner firm he kept regular office hours daily whenever he was in Chicago, and because of the firm grip he maintained on the affairs of his business, his associates somehow never perceived him to be advanced in years.

On Sunday, 10 January 1915, he and Nan motored to their nephew's home on Lake Shore Drive to lunch with him, and from there they went directly to the Fine Arts Theater to attend a concert by the Flonzaley Quartet. After the concert the Glessners ran into the Spragues in the lobby and chatted briefly. John Glessner, writing in his journal a few days later, indicated that A. A. seemed in the best of health and good spirits.[7] But on returning home Albert complained of feeling a bit unwell and went to bed early. A short time later as Nan sat reading at his bedside he suddenly gasped and was gone. Her diary entry for that day reads simply, "The End."

Elizabeth's immediate reaction is not recorded, but it could only have been devastating to lose her father at this difficult time. She came at once, as did her cousin, Albert Arnold II, who was a great comforter to all. Ever since the days when Elizabeth's parents had rescued him during his wild-oats period at Harvard, his relationship with his uncle had grown far beyond one consisting of merely avuncular good counsel and encouragement. And more than once Elizabeth acknowledged her special affection for him, for she thought of him as the brother that she never had. In the next months he would dutifully fulfill that role many times.

The business community of Chicago reeled under the shock of Albert Sprague's sudden death, and testimonials to his nobility of character and his honor as a businessman filled newspapers and trade journals in Chicago and across the country. By 1915, Sprague Warner had grown into one of the industrial monuments of Chicago and one of the

A. A. Sprague II, Elizabeth's cousin, of whom she said, "He had my father's name and as such, was doubly close to me, taking the place of the brother I never had."

Chicago Historical Society

largest and most successful wholesale grocery houses in the entire United States, with an annual volume of business exceeding $14 million.

After the death of Otho Sr., young Albert assumed his father's position as partner in the business, and he recalled at this time how his uncle Albert "had held daily councils in his office. At these councils he gave out homely advice and encouragement and consequently the atmosphere of the office was more that of a home than an office."[8] Even with the phenomenal growth of the company, something of that personal touch remained the hallmark of the firm. Albert Arnold Sprague's last official act created a monument that was a testimonial to the ideals by which he lived. Just days before his death he realized a long-cherished plan to establish a pension for his employees, one provided not by his will but by the Sprague Warner Corporation. In January 1914 a large sum of money was set aside for this purpose, and at the meeting of the Board of Directors just four days before his death, the plan was approved and Albert selected the first three recipients.

The *New York City American Grocer* trade journal characterized Sprague as "a man of marked executive abilities; big of brain; big of heart."[9] And the *Chicago Post* eulogized him as "perhaps the most finely generous man in the generation of large-minded men who lifted Chicago up from a village to a great city."[10] Newspapers reported the size of Albert's estate as over $4 million ($62 million in 1996 dollars). By the terms of his will he bequeathed significant sums to charity; $50,000 to Presbyterian Hospital, and the same amount to the Art Institute.[11] His personal bequests to his family included $400,000 to Nan, $100,000 to Elizabeth, $50,000 to Fred, and $5,000 to each of Otho's children. A second codicil to his original will raised his initial $200,000 trust for Elizabeth to $400,000, and a third codicil provided that in the case of total failure of dependents the balance of his residuary estate should be divided equally between the University of Chicago and Yale. Two other trusts were created; one for Sprague, who was to receive $100,000 when he reached the age of twenty-five, and a second of $50,000 for Joe Twichell.[12]

Elizabeth wasted no time in deciding upon a proper memorial to her father. The last time she had seen him alive he had told her he believed the most wonderful thing about Chicago was its orchestra. His long association with the Symphony as both guarantor and enthusiastic music lover, as well as his close friendship with the orchestra's conductors, were well known. As a tribute to Albert the Symphony played the Andante from Johann Sebastian Bach's Suite in F Major at two of its January concerts. It was undoubtedly her father's love of the orchestra and his recent creation of the pension plan for his employees that combined to inspire Elizabeth's memorial. Just days after his death she communicated her intent to Frederick Stock and the orchestra's board, and one week later Charles H. Hamill, second vice-president of the Orchestral Association, announced from the stage:

> *Last week we had the melancholy pleasure of hearing that beautiful Bach Andante, the noble tribute to a worthy citizen of Chicago, and a devoted friend of the Orchestra, Albert Arnold Sprague. Tonight the trustees make you sharers in the unalloyed pleasure that they have in a gift made this day to the Orchestra. Mrs. Elizabeth Sprague Coolidge . . . has given the generous sum of one hundred thousand dollars. This fund is to be kept separate and the income only employed under the direction of the trustees in payment of pensions and sick benefits to the men of the Orchestra.*[13]

Elizabeth's gift to the symphony represented a generous one-half of the personal fund that she had inherited only days before. It was an unprecedented event in the history of the American symphony orchestra and had the desirable effect of inducing others to follow suit—a motive that would become the distinctive trade-mark of Elizabeth's giving for the rest of her life. Newspapers acknowledged her action and its noble goal, and soon Hamill reported to her that Bryon Lathrop had just added $25,000 to the pension fund.[14] It pleased Elizabeth for, clearly, she had hoped and expected that the initial endowment would prompt others to follow her example. That she took some satisfaction in it is evident in her response to Lathrop's gift: "How nice it is that a fresh spirit has been infused into the musical public, assuring the ultimate completion of the fund and arousing new loyalty to the interests of the orchestra. I think that it is more valuable to music than the fund itself, and am correspondingly delighted, for it seems to vindicate my device."[15]

With this generous and visionary act, Elizabeth, in one magnificent gesture, initiated her life of philanthropy and removed the one weakness that threatened the continuance of Chicago's great orchestra. Its conductor, Frederick Stock, was deeply grateful, and in seeking a proper expression of gratitude for this wonderful gift, consulted with the Glessners, who agreed with him that

> *nothing could be more appropriate as to present on a program . . . several numbers in grateful recognition of you and your esteemed father's noble deed. For one of these I should like to ask you whether you would let me have your string quartet, the middle movements of which would lend themselves most favorably for augmentation, I mean in a rendition for the entire string choir of our orchestra. Provided this idea meets with your approval, kindly send your score and the set of parts which was used here, when the entire work was played in a "Musicale" in your father's house a few years ago.*[16]

Elizabeth, of course, was pleased to comply, and approximately one year after her initial gift, on the evening of 3 February 1916, the orchestra played her work, and a special reception was held in her honor. In making the necessary alterations in the music Stock had studied the score thoroughly and was impressed with her talent. He encouraged her to continue her composition studies and recommended working with Charles Martin Loeffler.[17] Accordingly he supplied her with a letter of introduction in which he describes her as having a "fine musical nature, . . . she comes to you desiring to further pursue her studies of musical composition. She has already written a few more or less pretentious works, but feels the need of somebody's advice whose authority on questions pertaining to the art of composition is unquestionable. I don't know of anybody in this country who could help Mrs. Coolidge as much as you can."[18]

Despite Stock's strong recommendation Loeffler did not wish to teach at this time, but his introduction to Coolidge marked the beginning of a warm friendship and an association that would soon be very important to both of them.

In the period immediately after Albert's death, Nan was faced with important decisions. Should she live with Elizabeth in New York, should she remain alone in the big house in Chicago, or should she take one of the cottages in Pittsfield? And what sort of memorial should she leave to her beloved husband of fifty-two years? Life alone in Chicago was out of the question, and besides, with Fred so ill, Elizabeth needed her mother near her. In April 1915 Nan had returned briefly to Chicago to close her house temporarily, and just as she was returning to the East Fred had another serious attack. He had been scheduled to be moved to his summer house at Sound Beach on 9 May, but he was far too sick to travel. Two days later doctors operated to remove a kidney, and it was clear that he could not live long. Charlie came, and Elizabeth kept watch at his bedside constantly until he died in the early hours of 15 May 1915. The cause of death as indicated on the death certificate was acute pyonephrosis complicated by postoperative bronchial pneumonia.[19]

In the chronicle of Fred's illness there is one more or less faceless presence who surfaces from time to time—his faithful nurse Jane F. Cleary, who cared for Fred so devotedly during the last years of his life and who did much to relieve the burden from Elizabeth's shoulders, especially after Dr. Draper prescribed her separation from Fred. Clearly Elizabeth and Fred meant to reward her, for the first item in Fred's will of 10 February 1913 bequeathed to her the sum of $3,000, and to Myra Prout, his other nurse, $2,000 ($46,500 in 1996 dollars).[20]

After Fred's death it was a sad and exhausted Elizabeth who now became the object of Cleary's ministrations. In the space of exactly four months Elizabeth had lost her father and her husband. The first death had been a painful wrenching from her life of one who was sound, vigorous, and a constant source of love and inspiration; the second had been a painfully slow and inexorable destruction before her eyes of the mind and body of the great love of her life. The final closure could only have been, for him, the freeing of his spirit from his broken body—and for her an exhausted calm after twenty years of sharing his sufferings.

Fred's funeral was held at Upway Fields, and his ashes were interred in the Pittsfield Cemetery. On her doctor's and Miss Cleary's recommendations Elizabeth submitted to a short rest cure in June but used the time to contemplate what sort of memorial she would make to Fred. Later that month she looked on with pride as Sprague graduated, summa cum laude, from Harvard, but she realized at the same time that he was leaving the nest. After Harvard she and Nan returned to her apartment at 850 Park Avenue where, predictably, Elizabeth lost herself in her music, and Nan, still grieving over Albert, was extremely lonely.

By July Elizabeth announced plans for her memorial to her husband. She sent a letter to Dr. Henry Colt, president of the Pittsfield Anti-Tuberculosis Association, a letter stating her intention to give to the group $100,000 to be held in trust for the benefit of a new building to be known as "The Frederic Shurtleff Coolidge Memorial Home."[21] It was the perfect monument to Fred, for, as she explained: "[T]o me his name is synonymous with loving service to mankind, and the Pittsfield Anti-Tuberculosis Association more than anything symbolizes . . . his personal endeavor toward such service."[22] She made it clear that her objective in specifying the use to which the income should be put was "to enlarge the scope and influence of the association's work; not to lessen the responsibility of the community in supporting what has already been undertaken."[23]

At about the same time Nan decided to make a major offering to Presbyterian Hospital in Chicago—though this would not be her main memorial to Albert. She contributed $110,000 to pay off the mortgage on the nurses' home built by friends of Otho and contributed to so generously by Albert. The building, begun in 1912, would hereafter be known as "The Sprague Home for Nurses of the Presbyterian Hospital of Chicago."[24]

In September mother and daughter, now both widows, found themselves reluctantly facing the fact that Sprague and Peg were about to be married, despite their earlier talk of waiting until Peg graduated. After the wedding at the Coit's home in Aurora, New York, on 22 September 1915, the newlyweds made their home in Cambridge. Peg transferred from Wellesley to Radcliffe, where she could be nearer Sprague, and she eventually received her degree in chemistry from that institution. Elizabeth was under great pressure as she attempted to reconcile her genuine concern for Sprague's happiness with her own disappointment over what she still considered his hasty decision. Moreover, it extinguished all hope of realizing her long-desired chance for the two of them to study in Berlin. She struggled with her own emotions as she saw her only child go off to begin a new life that would always include her but would never be quite the same again.

In something of a reversal of roles Nan now often felt that she was the child and that Elizabeth had become the mother. But both women were strong in the face of their losses. While Elizabeth busied herself with practice and composing she encouraged her mother to use this time to write the recollections of her early life in Vermont.[25] It was a time of healing for both. Their intense relationship as mother and daughter, teacher and student, and mentor and disciple, had weathered many a storm in earlier years, and now reached a new depth of maturity in the empathetic experience of grief. This new dimension of mutual love and devotion laid to rest once and for all even the memory of any early hostilities—hostilities that had arisen, after all, largely from the very similarity of their characters. They had been like flint striking flint, and now both utilized those same flinty attributes to save themselves from wallowing in anything remotely resembling self-pity. The letters that passed between Nan and Frances Glessner make that very clear.

At the time of Albert's death John Glessner wrote a beautiful memorial to his friend and sent a copy to Nan. After paying tribute to Albert's business acumen he ends with a remembrance that only one who knew him very well could have written:

> *I have eaten his bread, and he has eaten mine; I have visited in his home, and he has visited in mine; I have known him in joy and sorrow, in business reverses and in business prosperity. I have never heard from him a word of complaint or impatience. He did not parade his heart or his religion before the world, but he had both. He was of stainless honor, and abounding love for his fellow man. I lay my tribute of affection upon his grave. I would not bring him back: I mourn that he has gone. I knew him long and well. Truer friend no man ever had than Albert Sprague.*[26]

In response Nan wrote, "my eyes are full of tears—my heart is full of gratitude. Perhaps by and by I shall have more courage—and I want to have. I must not live a killjoy, and be ungrateful for all I have had and still have."[27]

It may have been the enthusiasm generated by Elizabeth's memorial to her father that determined once and for all what Nan's major monument to her husband should be. Albert had always loved music, and he cherished a deep affection for his alma mater, so no more appropriate memorial to him could have been chosen that that offered by Nan through Elizabeth's letter to Arthur T. Hadley, president of Yale University.

She pointed out that her father's "lifelong loyalty to, and interest in his college have made it seem to my mother a fitting object for her memorial gift. She has in mind a small building costing from one hundred and fifty to two hundred thousand dollars; and asked me to inquire of you whether there may be opportunity at Yale for such a building." Although the letter mentions several possibilities Elizabeth ventured her own suggestion of an art gallery or music hall "which would be very suitable, as my father did a great deal, always, towards the fostering of art and music in Chicago."[28]

All parties concerned agreed that a music hall would be most appropriate, and Nan and Elizabeth both made it clear that they wished Charlie Coolidge to be the architect of the new building, at the same time calling Hadley's attention to the academic buildings that Charlie had already designed at the University of Chicago, Harvard, Brown, and Wellesley. Unfortunately Nan did not live to see the completion of Sprague Hall. On 28 March 1916, after a few days of illness, she died at Lakewood, New Jersey. The diary that she had kept since 1854 contains only a few sparse entries in the last week, sometimes only the date, and an occasional reference to feeling unwell. Elizabeth, in company with her cousins Lucy and Albert, made yet another sad trip across the country in the private rail car that Albert had procured, and Nancy Ann Sprague was laid to rest in Graceland Cemetery beside the husband she adored.

With the kind of dispatch that was becoming her trademark, within two weeks of her mother's death Elizabeth made a gift of an additional $100,000 to the Chicago Symphony Orchestra pension fund established to memorialize her father. Once again Charles Hamill announced it from the stage and made the requisite change in the name of the fund which would hereafter be known as "The Albert and Nancy Sprague Memorial Fund."[29]

With her father, husband, and mother so lately deceased and Sprague now married and living in Cambridge, Elizabeth faced the loss of her support system. It was now unrealistic to continue the upkeep of two homes in Chicago, but to the end of her life she maintained a real affection for the city of her birth and continued to refer to it as her hometown. In a gesture honoring Fred and the medical profession, Elizabeth gave her parents' home at 2710 Prairie Avenue to Presbyterian Hospital to be used as a residence for nurses,[30] and her own home on the same street (at 2636) for the use of nurses from the Catholic hospital.[31]

It had been Nancy Sprague's wish that of the $200,000 that she gave to Yale, $150,000 should be spent for the construction of the building, $20,000 for equipment and furnishings, and $30,000 for maintenance. When bids for the building made it evident that it could not be constructed for less than $175,000 Elizabeth agreed to supply the remaining $25,000.[32] In addition, she gave portraits of her mother and father to the university that still today hang on the landings of the stairs in the foyer.[33]

With Sprague Hall scheduled for completion in time for the fall term of 1917, Elizabeth set about formulating plans for the official dedication on 25 November. The guest list for the occasion included such composers as Chadwick, Goldmark, Hill, Sessions, and Mason, as well as Chicago notables and personal friends, many of whom were transported from New York to New Haven in Elizabeth's private car.

Throughout the planning stages Elizabeth and Horatio Parker, who was then the dean of Yale's School of Music, remained in close contact, and Parker had a great deal to say about practical aspects of the building as well as the ceremony of dedication that included an address by John Haskell Hewitt, L.L.D., a classmate and friend of Albert Sprague. Unlike the windy rhetoric that often graces such formal occasions, Hewitt's address was a straightforward and heartfelt testimonial of one who knew A. A. Sprague well, loved him as a friend, and could speak not only of his achievements in the world of commerce, but could reflect more personally on his friend's character. Hewitt recalled that "probably no one in the class had a more lovable disposition or was held in higher esteem," adding that although Sprague was a handsome man "no one ever detected in him any feeling of pride, either because of his good looks or qualities of character or success in business. . . . Unlike many prosperous business men, Mr. Sprague did not grow more avaricious with years but rather more generous."[34]

Charlie Coolidge then presented the keys of the building to President Hadley, who in turn handed them over to Dr. Parker. It was on this occasion that the familiar emblem of the key first appeared on the pass for admission to Yale's concerts.

It had indeed been a season of memorials, but there were more to come. In 1916 a group of Pittsfield residents formed the Berkshire County Society for the Care of Crippled and Deformed Children, with Fred's former colleague, Dr. Henry Colt, as president. The following year Elizabeth and Mrs. Murray Crane funded a summer camp for crippled children near the Sprague cottage on West Avenue.[35] The success of the undertaking so encouraged Elizabeth that she made a more substantial gift and endowed the society permanently with a contribution of $50,000. The following year she began negotiations with a Boston physician, W. R. MacAusland, and offered an additional gift of $150,000. The planning, organization, and execution of a project of this magnitude required some months to complete, and Elizabeth became impatient. She could well understand the slow grinding of the wheels of creativity in the arts, but she was never noted for her patience when it involved business matters. Through some miscommunication or misinterpretation of MacAusland's plans, she wavered briefly and threatened to retract the offer. But she had tasted the satisfaction of giving to such worthy causes and through MacAusland's diplomatic handling of the situation went forward with the plan. His letters to her are a valuable commentary on her growing skills as both entrepreneur and patron: "I have quite a lot to do with business affairs and with people who support charities. I have never met any woman or man with a clearer vision of responsibility than you have. . . . Very few people part with their money the way you do. In fact I have never seen anyone who did it so beautifully."[36]

By 1918 she gave to the society not only the promised endowment but also her estate, Upway Fields, to use as a school for crippled children. It was a perfect memorial to Fred, who as a child had suffered from osteomyelitis and, perhaps as a result, had always had a particular interest in the orthopedic problems of the young.

There were yet two smaller but significant endowments to be made in Fred's name. The first was a gift of $2,400 made to Columbia University annually from 1915 to 1920 for the support of two research fellowships in medicine.[37] And at Harvard, Elizabeth endowed a room in the new dormitory in the name of her husband and provided for a student-loan fund.[38]

Amid her larger and well-publicized philanthropic efforts there were also innumerable unobtrusive—though immensely helpful—small gifts. One was her contribution to Arthur Farwell and Bernet Tuthill to support their work at the Music Settlement School at 35 East 3rd Street in New York, money that enabled them to provide lessons and instruments for children.[39] Leo Sowerby and Eric DeLamarter struck a sympathetic note in Elizabeth's heart with their request for help to establish a chamber music series in Chicago, where there was great enthusiasm for the symphony but little interest in the more intimate medium of chamber music. Both men would continue to receive her support.[40]

Ever since Regina Watson's death in 1912 Elizabeth had cherished the idea of establishing a suitable memorial to her dear friend and teacher. Now that she was in a position to do so she began to solicit the assistance of other Chicago friends of Mrs. Watson in order to erect a cottage in her honor at the MacDowell Colony in Peterborough, New Hampshire.[41] It marked the beginning of Coolidge's long association with Marian MacDowell and her support of the Colony through its critical early years.

The last of the major philanthropic ventures before Elizabeth embarked upon her career as the great patron of chamber music was in behalf of her younger cousin, Lucy Sprague, who by now was married to the economist Wesley Clair Mitchell (Robin), who had studied at the University of Chicago under both Dewey and Veblen. Although Elizabeth was fourteen years older than her cousin there was a close bond between them, forged partly by Lucy's fondness for her Aunt Nan, and also by the fact that both she and her older cousin were independent thinkers who had developed a keen sense of social awareness. The two were different in that Lucy had a college education; after graduating from Radcliffe she went on to teach English and eventually became the first dean of women at the University of California.[42]

The Mitchells had moved to New York City in 1912, where Lucy began to "find herself," declaring that in New York "you can be anything you want to be except conspicuous." Her life's work centered on children, and with the help of her husband she established the New School for Social Research, which pioneered the psychological testing of children. Shortly after Nan's death Elizabeth dined one evening with the Mitchells in their house on Washington Square. Over dinner, Lucy shared with her cousin the plans she had for a new undertaking. She describes the occasion as "perhaps the most astounding of all the strokes of luck I have had in my life," for although Elizabeth knew that she wanted to use her money primarily to advance the cause of music, she needed time to formulate her plans, but in the meantime "she wanted to do something for education, which she said she knew little about but believed important. So important, that she would underwrite a plan if Robin and I could devise one that seemed good enough."[43] The next morning Lucy wrote: "In the wakeful hours of the night I turned over and over the problem you put up to us last night and I found my ideas sprouting at such a rate that I could hardly wait for morning to come to test them in a cold black and white statement. You brought this letter upon your own head so treat it indulgently. . . . I would like to suggest a plan of enormous scope which could be worked out bit by bit, as rapidly or as slowly as the occasion warranted. . . . I am still quite overwhelmed by your offer last night."[44]

Lucy's plan would include, among other things, a laboratory school for handicapped children. It would be associated with a neurological institute and would provide nature study for city children. Even at this preliminary stage Elizabeth initially agreed to underwrite the project to the extent of $10,000 a year, and a few weeks later she raised the offer to $50,000 per annum for ten years. More remarkable even than the financial generosity were the conditions that she attached—namely, that she should not be pressured to understand or even be interested in the group's work, for she would be engrossed in her own plans for music. It was an arrangement probably unprecedented in the annals of patronage.[45]

In the years immediately following the death of her parents and her husband Elizabeth had dispensed an unusually generous amount of her inheritance in what might at first appear to have been a kind of reckless abandon—perhaps an impulsive emotional release after the losses she had just sustained. Not so! It is very apparent that she always was convinced that the object of her major patronage should be music in some fashion but she needed to buy time in order to formulate her plans. In the interim she was at one and the same time learning the ways of philanthropy, designing her own unique style of giving, and providing noble memorials to the parents, husband, and friend she loved so deeply—memorials that were not mere vagaries, but were calculated to serve the needs of others.

In the short space of fifteen months she had lost her entire support system. From her role as the long-suffering wife who, though afflicted, always enjoyed the love, moral support, and financial security of her remarkable parents, she had become more or less a solitary figure suddenly cut adrift from her moorings. The fact that she was now the heiress of a sizable fortune could not compensate the pain of loss. Moreover, with the fortune she also inherited the burden of conscience, the Sprague sense of accountability to society and morality in the stewardship of wealth. It was at once a legacy of riches and responsibility, and Elizabeth now faced the task of how best to fulfill her mission.

PART TWO

[W]omen are well beyond youth when they begin, often unconsciously, to create another story.

– CAROLYN G. HEILBRUN

CHAPTER NINE

Interlude: Testing the Waters

Grow old along with me
The best is yet to be;
The last of life
For which the first was made.
– ROBERT BROWNING, *RABBI BEN EZRA*

There was never any doubt in Elizabeth's mind that music would be the object of her philanthropic efforts. No better appraisal of the role of music in her life could be found than in comments she made when her string quartet was performed in 1936 as part of an NBC broadcast entitled "Music Is My Hobby." She explained that she perceived her own life to be divided into periods differentiated from each other by the manner in which music served her:

> *First, stands the character discipline of a long course of piano study. My teacher's exaction from me, throughout my girlhood, of reverence for duty; of coordinated self-control; of uncompromising fidelity to standards. This laid the foundation of whatever mental and moral strength may be mine, and as an influence of lasting force was second only to that of my Mother.*
>
> *During the second period of my musical life, this habit of wrestling with impersonal difficulties stood me in life-saving stead as I found many painful and insoluble personal problems. Without the mechanical stabilizer of hard piano practice and its concomitant sense of power and balance, my emotional equilibrium must have been wrecked.*

> *The third and still present period includes my amateur efforts at composition. The need thus ministered to is that of self-expression, as a spiritual refuge from my increasing deafness. This, if anything, I must consider my "hobby," and as such I modestly share it with the radio audience as a suggestion that making music, by either playing or writing it, is not the exclusive pleasure of professional musicians.*[1]

Elizabeth was about to begin to repay her debt to the art that had sustained her so faithfully all her life. As she left behind the role of wife and daughter and moved gradually into the arena of patron it is important to view this transformation within the context of developments in the larger musical world of the period.

It may have been a desire to escape the grandiose gestures of late romanticism, or simply a reaction to the gargantuan dimensions of much late-nineteenth-century music, that caused a resurgence of interest in chamber music around the turn of the century that lasted well into the 1900s. Elizabeth's interests and motives, however, were more personal. Although there is much evidence that she loved opera and symphonic music, her taste had gradually turned to the more intimate genre of chamber music—undoubtedly by virtue of the fact that it was the most practical form of music-making for her during her married life because it could be performed at home while she remained near Fred. At the same time it offered her the opportunity to sit in as a participant whenever she wished. Quite apart from the sense of intimacy that chamber music provided there was also the practical aspect of the economic advantage of patronizing small ensembles. And it allowed her a degree of control that larger performing organizations could simply not afford to extend.

At precisely the same time that Coolidge was questioning what form her patronage should take, Walter Wilson Cobbett (1847–1937),[2] an English businessman and amateur violinist with a passion for chamber music, was underwriting scholarly work on the subject, offering prizes for chamber music compositions, and publishing a series of articles that would lead ultimately to his monumental *Cyclopaedia of Chamber Music.*[3] Coolidge was well acquainted with his work, and in time the two became good friends.

The decision to devote her energy and her money to the cause of chamber music was greatly influenced by a timely confluence of people and events just at this juncture in her personal life: the disbanding of the Kneisel Quartet, the death of Edward de Coppet, a letter from the young Austrian violinist, Hugo Kortschak, a surprise visit from Frederick Stock, and her friendship with Edwin T. Rice.

Beyond the example of Cobbett, Coolidge was probably most influenced by Franz Kneisel (1865–1926) and Edward de Coppet (1855–1916), the founders of the Kneisel and the Flonzaley Quartets, both of whom she knew intimately.

Kneisel had been concertmaster of the Bilse Orchestra in Berlin before being recruited by Henry Lee Higginson and the conductor, Wilhelm Gericke, to fulfill that position in the Boston Symphony Orchestra, where his desk-mate was Charles Martin Loeffler. Shortly after joining the Boston Symphony, Kneisel formed a quartet from the principals of the orchestra, and by December 1885 the Kneisel Quartet had already made its debut in New York.[4] By 1903 all the members had resigned from the orchestra in order to devote themselves exclusively to quartet playing. Two years later they moved to New York, where they joined the faculty of the Institute of Musical Art, established in 1903 by Frank Damrosch with support from James Loeb.[5] The ensemble went on to become pioneers for the cause of the quartet in the United States and also enthusiastic advocates of much new music.[6]

Elizabeth knew Franz and his family personally, spent a good deal of time at their home at Blue Hills, Maine, and continued her association with the next generation after their father's death.[7]

The second, and undoubtedly even greater, influence was Edward de Coppet, the son of a Swiss financier who had established offices in the United States, where Edward was born. He began his profession as a broker in the New York office of his father's firm, but his first love was music. After some years at a job that he did not particularly enjoy he sold his stocks and bonds and invested wisely enough to amass a fortune that enabled him to retire from business and devote himself exclusively to the support of chamber music.[8] He became quite proficient at the keyboard, and his American wife, Pauline Bonis, was an accomplished pianist who frequently played informally with the groups sponsored by her husband. While living in New York Elizabeth had on many occasions joined them for these chamber music evenings in their home. She and Edward de Coppet actually had much in common besides their love of chamber music: both suffered severe hearing loss but despite the handicap and the necessity of cumbersome hearing devices, continued to perform from time to time.

The first rehearsals of the Flonzaley Quartet were held in the privacy of de Coppet's estate on Lake Geneva, and later in his New York home, with Edward always in attendance, score in hand, and even sometimes coaching the artists.[9] By 1904 the quartet was ready to perform publicly in Europe, and the following year began concertizing in the United States. Although critics hailed the ensemble for its elegance and refinement of tone, they pointed out a certain lack of power and dynamism in their playing. Nonetheless, the Flonzaley Quartet is recognized in the annals of chamber music history as one of the finest. It was certainly a great influence upon the development of quartet playing and quartet literature in America for the first quarter of this century.

On 30 April 1916, barely six weeks after Nan's death, de Coppet died suddenly, just as he was about to entertain guests (including the Glessners) at dinner.[10] Although his son, André, assumed his father's role as patron and generously supported the quartet until its disbanding in 1928, in retrospect the elder de Coppet's death seems almost a portent of things to come in Elizabeth's life, for it was only a few days later that she received a letter that would, once and for all, influence the form and the character of her own patronage. It was from Hugo Kortschak, a young Austrian violinist who had recently resigned from the Chicago Symphony Orchestra in order to devote himself to performing chamber music. With three other musicians who were still members of the orchestra he had formed a quartet that was already receiving very favorable criticism. The demands of the orchestra's schedule, however, allowed little time for rehearsal, so he appealed to Coolidge for help, assuring her that "We are all in love with quartet-playing and want to devote our whole existence to this art. . . . What we need now is the possibility to give all our time and strength to the quartet work and to make it our exclusive vocation. . . . This can be done only through the financial help of people who love art sufficiently to lend this help for art's sake. In no other way has ever a great organization succeeded to overcome the initial difficulties!"[11]

It was a bold gesture on the part of Kortschak, but the high-minded ideal that his letter expressed, the notion of exclusive dedication to the cause of the quartet, and the concept of a patron lending support "for art's sake," obviously struck a harmonious note with Elizabeth. The fact that she responded immediately, apparently needing no time to reflect, confirms that she had been thinking along these same lines. Indeed, she later admitted that she had often envied de Coppet the privilege of intimate association with his own ensemble and later had even consulted him about such a responsibility. Kortschak could not possibly have known how crucial the timing of his letter was. By return mail she wrote: "I was very much interested in your letter, received this morning. . . . It is a strange thing that your proposition is exactly what I had been having in mind for some years. . . . Ever since I have known the late Mr. E. J. de Coppet, and have had the wonderful privilege of listening to the Flonzaley Quartette both at his house and in public, I have wished that the time might some time arrive when I, too, might foster and develop a string quartet of finest quality."[12]

By this time she had already had the pleasure of playing with several quartets from Boston as well as with artists like David Mannes and Georges Longy, and she felt quite competent to perform for private audiences. It is apparent from the very outset that whatever form her musical work took, she intended to be personally involved in it at all levels. But this posed a serious problem. Realizing that the distance between these musicians in Chicago and herself in New York would make her participation impossible, she pointed out to Kortschak that "practicing with you myself would be out of the question. . . . I have always thought that if I decided to foster a quartette like this, I should wish them to reside in Pittsfield, my summer home, for at least six or eight weeks in the summer, during which time they could practice arduously and decide on plans for the coming winters, and that those winters should be spent in New York, where I am living."[13]

Her friendship with Frederick Stock and her loyalty to the Chicago Symphony Orchestra caused her some hesitation in recruiting her quartet from his best players. She recognized, however, that since the idea had originated with Kortschak, not with her, the musicians had already determined to leave the orchestra, so she placed the responsibility squarely on them.[14] She indicated her interest and offered support but on the condition that the men move to New York for at least three years, after which she envisioned placing them with a manager. It was their decision, but she requested to know from them what kind of salary they would require in order to support their families and still be able to devote themselves exclusively to this venture.

Kortschak's proposal resonated with her desire to found a quartet just as de Coppet had done, which is clear from the closing words of her letter: "Your artistic ideal and mine are the same, and I hope that we can work together, even though it should be in a smaller way than we should both desire."[15]

Only a few weeks later, while in Chicago to attend to her mother's estate, Elizabeth heard the artists and was so impressed with their rendition of the Franck Quartet that before she left they signed a three-year contract, the terms of which guaranteed the possibility of her attending rehearsals and even playing with them in the literature that required piano. She chose to call her newly acquired ensemble the Berkshire Quartet, but privately referred to the members affectionately as her "Berkshire Boys." Wisely, she made it part of their agreement that "they should not play publicly until, by their concentrated practice, they should have reached a satisfactory level of excellence."

The violist, Dash, was not willing to relocate in New York, but by early summer of 1916 Kortschak was able to engage Clarence Evans in his place. The first members of the quartet were Kortschak (first violin), Hermann Felber (second violin), Clarence Evans (viola), and Emmerin Stoeber (cello).[16] With their move to New York, Elizabeth was concerned about providing suitable living quarters for the artists and their families and saw to it that Kortschak, as leader of the group, was installed in the apartment adjacent to her own—the apartment that had been Nan's up to the time of her death. Such proximity allowed the musicians easy access to Elizabeth's apartment and provided for some pleasant surprises, such as the early morning birthday serenade by the quartet playing outside her window. Years later she confessed "delightful as was this early serenade, I had a few misgivings as to the reaction of my surrounding neighbor cliff-dwellers. What was my relief, at its close, to hear from the windows the sound of spontaneous applause."[17]

The quartet arrived in Pittsfield in June, only one month after the initial exchange of letters and, as Elizabeth desired, moved on to New York for the winter. Their first performances were limited to an audience of friends and chamber music enthusiasts, but by 1918 the quartet was ready to appear publicly in New York City. It was fortuitous that their debut occurred only a few months after the dissolution of the Kneisel ensemble. That fact was not lost on the critic of the *New York Times* who predicted that the Berkshire Quartet might well be the heir to the position left vacant by the recently disbanded Kneisel ensemble.[18] It was an auspicious beginning.

In the course of the summer before the Berkshire Quartet's debut there occurred another event of profound and lasting import. Frederick Stock was in New England in 1917 to take part in the Litchfield County Festival in Norfolk, Connecticut, organized by his friend and fellow countryman, Gustave J. Stoeckel.[19] If Elizabeth had felt any concern over robbing Stock of two of his best players in the Chicago Symphony, surely Stock felt no resentment. He was, in fact, entirely supportive of her endeavors for the cause of chamber music and seems to have been the one to plant in her head the notion of establishing a quartet-in-residence and building a permanent performing space in which to present them. For this reason he urged her to go with him to Norfolk to see the music shed that Stoeckel had built there.[20]

When at dinner one evening Stock expressed the wish that her quartet might be heard at Stoeckel's festival she responded: "Why go so far? Why not have our own festival at our own home?" It seemed a casual remark at the time, but it is clear that she had already considered such a possibility. Though she had spoken privately about it to the members of the quartet, she later admitted, "I secretly pondered the idea and elaborated it in my imagination until I had secured the permission of my son to build a music hall and some artists' bungalows on South Mountain, his property."[21]

There is yet one key figure to consider in this crucial interval of Elizabeth's life. He is Edwin T. Rice, a Wall Street attorney who had studied music seriously before becoming a lawyer and continued to do so as an avid amateur.[22] With his legal and musical knowledge Rice was an invaluable counsel to many musical organizations and had been intimately connected with the affairs of both the Kneisel and Flonzaley Quartets. He was a close personal friend of de Coppet and assisted him with the legal aspects of the formation of his quartet. In 1907, when the cellist of the Kneisel Quartet resigned just at the same time that Kneisel himself was offered the conductorship of the then relatively unimportant Philadelphia Orchestra, it was Rice who averted the premature dissolution of the quartet by encouraging Kneisel to go abroad to look for another cellist.[23] As a result of the search he engaged the solo cellist of the Vienna State Opera Orchestra, Willem Willeke, who soon became a major figure in Elizabeth's plans as well.

Through his association with de Coppet, Rice became a close friend of Elizabeth and a frequent participant in her house-music evenings, eventually becoming also her financial and legal advisor in matters relating to the establishment of her ensembles and the incorporation of her South Mountain endeavors.[24] He brought to his legal work energy and enthusiasm born of an intimate knowledge of chamber music repertoire, which he acquired by actually performing it.[25] In time he even formed his own quartet with Edouard and Gaston Déthier and David Sanders, who had been a pupil of Joachim.

Rice's knowledge was far greater than that of the ordinary dilettante, for although he was a walking encyclopedia of information about chamber music, he was responsible for the first performance in this country of a number of major contemporary compositions. In addition to his interest in performance he was counsel for the Society for the Publishing of American Music and had assisted Cobbett in obtaining some contributions from the United States for his *Cyclopaedia.* For his outstanding service Elizabeth chose to award him the Coolidge Medal in 1936. He is distinguished as the only nonprofessional musician (composer or performer) besides Cobbett to receive that award.

The coincidence of these events and the cast of characters thus gathered together more or less serendipitously enabled Coolidge to begin in a serious way the major philanthropic work of her life. Neither she nor any one of the individuals concerned could possibly have foreseen the consequences of this action. Looking back upon this period many years later, Elizabeth described it as "the prelude" to the main section of her magnum opus, which was about to begin.[26]

CHAPTER TEN

Grand Lady of the Berkshires

Thou large-brained woman and large-hearted man.

– ELIZABETH BARRETT BROWNING TO GEORGE SAND

WITH NAN'S DEATH in 1916 the door to the private world of Elizabeth's emotional state, so faithfully recorded in her mother's diary, was effectively closed. Consequently, there is little in the way of personal disclosure at this point in her life to reveal whatever misgivings or uncertainties may have assailed her as she entered a realm of philanthropy so dominated by men with far more money and experience than she had.

In a relatively short time her patronage would generate a voluminous correspondence, but what has survived from these first critical years of her professional life are mainly formal business letters—for the most part only those addressed to her, for she had not yet begun to keep copies of her own half of the correspondence. Soon, however, certain of these professional relationships would blossom into close personal friendships, and the intimate exchanges and forthright opinions expressed in them often resemble Nan's insightful observations.

By 1917 there was already material evidence of the degree of Coolidge's dedication to her mission, for while the newly formed Berkshire Quartet was practicing and building its repertoire, Coolidge was, quite literally, engaged in her own kind of building. From the outset her vision of a music colony included a physical home for her quartet, and Stock's suggestion of a festival was merely the catalyst that set in motion the plans that had been germinating in her mind for several years.

Up to this time Elizabeth's life had been governed largely by the exigencies of her husband's ill health. But now, after a brief period of searching—not so much for her self-determination but rather for the refinement of form that her work should take—she quickly and efficiently assumed command of her own life. And it cannot be denied that to some extent she attempted to control the lives of others as well. In this connection it should be remembered, however, that many of the key personalities in her master plan were very young when they came to her, and when she spoke of her "Berkshire Boys" it is likely that although she recognized their artistry and maturity as musicians, they were truly still boys to her. Hugo Kortschak was a young man of thirty-two when he wrote the letter proposing the notion of a quartet, William Kroll was twenty-two when he came to the Elshuco Trio, and Jacques Gordon was a mere nineteen years of age when he joined the quartet.

Even before her Berkshire Quartet had matured beyond private musicales, Elizabeth was making plans to create a music colony that would not only offer adequate performance space to present her quartet to the public but would also provide comfortable housing for her musicians. Since she had just given away her estate at Upway Fields, she no longer owned property in Pittsfield, so she tactfully involved Sprague in her endeavor by suggesting that the colony be established on the edge of his property just outside the city, at South Mountain.[1] With his approval she moved quickly, and in the summer of 1917 her cottage, the auditorium, and the bungalows for the musicians were completed.[2] Her designation of the auditorium as "the Temple" is more than a mere sobriquet, for on more than one occasion Elizabeth had made it quite clear that music was her religion.[3]

In design the building was simplicity itself: a wooden structure with painted walls, exposed crossbeams, and heavy supporting timbers. Seating was provided by pews bought from a church in New Hampshire. Daniel Gregory Mason believed that it was the predominance of wooden structural elements that gave to the Temple its wonderful acoustics, which he found far superior to many modern buildings made of steel and concrete.[4] Critics differed in their reaction to the spartan simplicity of the auditorium, but Alfredo Casella seems to have come closest to Elizabeth's intent when he described it as like a little Protestant chapel "where nothing distracts the listener from the deepest communion with the art of sound." He credited "this almost religious correlation between music and nature [as] an idea which could originate only in the mind of such an artistic, generous, and noble-spirited lady as Mrs. Coolidge."[5]

The cottages furnished for the musicians were simple but comfortable homes that allowed the artists easy access to each other for practice but at the same time provided the essential element of privacy. Each little house had its fanciful name and even a logo that Elizabeth had designed for it.

In the autumn of 1917 Elizabeth formally announced the first Berkshire Festival, which would take place the following September, and she unveiled her Berkshire Competition to encourage the composition of chamber music. At the time of the festival she would award a prize of $1,000 for the best string quartet manuscript submitted, and the winning piece was guaranteed a performance. All submissions were to be blind entries identified only by a number and a code name; the identity of the composer was contained in a sealed envelope marked on the outside with the code name only. These are preserved among the Coolidge memorabilia at the Library of Congress and attest to the fact that some outstanding talents competed unsuccessfully—among them Hindemith, Zemlinsky, Krenek, Webern, Badings, and Tansman to name but a few.

The response was overwhelming. By the beginning of April Kortschak reported, "Today came the 61st quartet." Probably not since the days of Haydn and Mozart had so much creative energy been channeled into the quartet genre at one time, and Kortschak was quick to give credit, noting that "it is really remarkable what your idea has done—this concentration of so many minds on the point of a quartet must have a most beneficial influence."[6] In all, eighty-two manuscripts were submitted. The panel of judges selected by Elizabeth consisted of Ossip Gabrilowitsch, Franz Kneisel, Hugo Kortschak, Georges Longy, Kurt Schindler, and Frederick Stock; the first Berkshire Prize winner was a young Polish composer, Tadeusz Iarecki (1888–1954), who had been trained under Taniev at the Moscow Conservatory.

The Berkshire Colony was officially dedicated on 4 May 1918 with a flag-raising celebration and a festive luncheon, and the initial festival the following September set the pattern to be followed for succeeding ones: five programs spread over a period of three weekdays beginning with a 4:00 P.M. concert on the first day and performances at 11:00 A.M. and 4:00 P.M. on the two following days. At the conclusion of each festival Coolidge would announce the requirements for the next year's composition. After 1922 the competition became biennial, alternating with a commission.

Not even the rainy weather at the inaugural concert could dampen the enthusiasm with which the event was greeted. Surprisingly, though, the only major newspaper to send a critic to cover the event was the *Christian Science Monitor.* Several music journals were represented however, and the local critic, Alfred Human, left a vivid account describing the long trail of automobiles winding up the mountain road to deposit an impressive assembly of notables of the musical world: Kneisel, Svenčenski, Gabrilowitsch, three members of the Flonzaley Quartet (Betti, Bailly, and Archambeau), Olive Mead and her ensemble, Efrem Zimbalist, Kurt Schindler, Rebecca Clarke, Susan Metcalfe Casals, Frederick Stock, Daniel Gregory Mason, Oscar Sonneck, Louise Homer, and more than 400 others. By the critic's account the arrival that stirred the greatest excitement was that of Fritz Kreisler.[7]

Many years later Elizabeth reflected on the wonderfully international character of this group assembled just two months before the armistice, even as some of the nations represented were actually still locked in deadly combat. It included "the Italian Ugo Ara and Austrian Fritz Kreisler, each of whom had fought against the other's country. German Emmeran Stoeber and French Georges Longy, listening in appreciation each to the other's music; Hungarian Harmati playing Russian music; Austrian Kortschak leading his Quartet in a prize-winning Polish composition."[8]

Before this assembly of some of the most distinguished musicians of the world Elizabeth proudly led her "Berkshire Boys" onto the stage and officially opened the festival with a quintet arrangement of the Star Spangled Banner. The first composition ever to be performed in the Temple was Beethoven's Quartet in E-flat, op. 127, which was followed by the second place entry in the competition, Alois Reiser's Quartet in E Minor. The final work again found Elizabeth on stage, this time to perform the Thuille Quintet for Piano and String Quartet, op. 21.

A very special event of this first festival was the inauguration of a new ensemble called the Elshuco Trio, comprised of Samuel Gardner, violin, Richard Epstein, piano, and Willem Willeke, cello. The origin of the unusual name of the ensemble quickly became the subject of speculation, and it seems that even Elizabeth herself was in the dark until Willeke shared with her the joke that Gardner, Horatio Parker, and Henry Krehbiel all thought it an Indian name. "It seems to me that no one knows what Elshuco (a peach of a name) really means! You, my dear Mrs. Coolidge, came very near, and here it is. El-shu-co, *El*izabeth *Shu*rtleff *Co*olidge."[9]

The formation of the Elshuco Trio marks the entrance into Elizabeth's life of one of the most important musical partners of her career, Willem Willeke (1880–1950), cellist of the recently disbanded Kneisel Quartet. At age thirty-eight Willeke brought to his work the background and experience of one easily twice his age. He was born in The Hague and as a child came to the attention of playwrights Ibsen and Bjornsen, with whom he often spent his holidays. While still a boy he impressed audiences by appearing with orchestras as soloist in the Schumann Piano Concerto in the first half of a concert and then taking up his cello to play a Haydn concerto in the second half. His musical training included the study of conducting with Gustav Mahler, Arthur Nikisch, and Hans Richter. At age fourteen he played the Brahms violoncello sonatas and other Brahms chamber works with the composer himself at the piano. But the musical world was very nearly deprived of his talents when he took up the study of medicine and received degrees from the universities of Bonn and Vienna. It was Joseph Joachim who enlisted Willeke to play with the Joachim String Quartet at the Bonn Beethoven Festival and then persuaded him to abandon medicine altogether for a career in music.

Willeke then toured Scandinavia with Edvard Grieg and later concertized in Europe and the United States with Richard Strauss—in both instances playing their sonatas for the cello, with the composers at the keyboard. It was a great coup for Elizabeth to obtain the services of so fine an artist.[10] As cellist he brought to the Elshuco Trio, and still later to the Festival Quartet of South Mountain, not only a wealth of experience and artistry but also the richness of tone of his 1641 Amati instrument, one of only four known to have been made by that master.[11]

The other stalwart colleague who was so important to her for both his musical and his organizational talents was the young man who originally proposed the idea of the quartet, Hugo Kortschak. Born in Graz, Austria, in 1884, Kortschak studied violin with the famous pedagogue, Otakar Sevčik, and after immigrating to the United States in the early 1900s went on to become a distinguished teacher himself, heading the violin department at Yale for twenty-eight years. The comedian Jack Benny studied with him at one time.

Although the Berkshire Quartet ceased to exist as an ongoing organization after the third festival in 1920, Kortschak continued to work for Coolidge in various capacities—on juries for competitions, as secretary of the Berkshire Music Colony, and as manager of her 1931 European tour. She thought highly of him, and clearly the feeling was mutual. Writing to her from New York after leaving the quartet, he admitted, "I miss my playing with you immensely; you have been the greatest and best artistic influence that I have ever had and our exchange of opinions has been a wonderful education for me."[12]

With the Berkshire enterprise in the capable hands of Kortschak, Elizabeth was free to pursue other significant philanthropic works that are less well known but nonetheless important. She began just at this time her seemingly endless efforts to assist immigrant composers and performers to establish themselves in America. The first, and one of the most notable, was Ernest Bloch (1880–1959). At age thirty-six Bloch came to the United States to conduct for the Maud Allan Dance Company and decided to stay in America. His arrival in New York coincided with the opening of the music school established by David Mannes and his wife, the former Clara Damrosch. It is not surprising that Mannes, the son of poor Jewish immigrants from Poland, and his wife, the daughter of a Jewish father, should rise to the occasion and attempt to hire Bloch to teach for them.[13] Not surprisingly, they looked to Elizabeth for help.

It was inevitable that the lives of Elizabeth Coolidge and the Damrosch clan should intersect at some point. Elizabeth corresponded with Clara and David Mannes and frequently enjoyed informal sessions playing sonatas with David when she was living in New York during the last years of Fred's illness. Mannes was undoubtedly well aware of Coolidge's generous support of her cousin Lucy's educational ventures, which were roughly contemporary with his work at the Third Street Settlement Music School. He was deeply devoted to assisting the immigrants on the Lower East Side and by 1910 became the music director of the School, the very institution upon which Elizabeth had attempted to model her more modest efforts for the boys at Upway Fields. Their backgrounds could not have been more dissimilar, but they were at one in their vision of the power of music to influence the souls of men.

Elizabeth had offered Clara some financial assistance in 1916,[14] and in the following year came to her aid by providing money to hire Ernest Bloch. Clara's letter of 8 May 1917 refers to Elizabeth's initial gift of $2,000 toward Bloch's salary: "You should be the first to know that we have concluded arrangements with Mr. Bloch to work with us for the next two years. . . . We feel that we are more than fortunate to have this man's influence in our school. I need not say how grateful we are to you for wanting to help us the first year and we hope to see you here working with Mr. Bloch."[15]

There is no evidence that Elizabeth had as yet met Ernest Bloch personally, but she surely knew of his reputation and, ever on the lookout for composition teachers, must have expressed to Clara her interest in studying with him. In gratitude for her help Clara responded by reserving a private hour with Mr. Bloch without charge since "you said last spring you would love to work with him, so we do hope that you will feel like doing this."[16]

Her studies with Bloch never came to pass. Instead, from 1919 to 1921 she worked with Rubin Goldmark, who had succeeded Percy Goetschius at the Institute of Musical Art.[17] She did, however, come to know Bloch very well, and it was he who introduced Elizabeth to his friend Carl Engel, a man who more than any other influenced the course of her philanthropic work.[18]

Over the years Elizabeth's association with Bloch would ripen into a close friendship. From the allusions in the half of their correspondence that has survived, it is apparent that their relationship was characterized by an intimate sharing of their respective trials. The fact that Bloch's angst-ridden letters to her never really identify the cause of his depression and despair suggest that these were confidences shared in private conversation. He apparently found in Elizabeth—a woman sixteen years his senior, who had so recently experienced illness, suffering, and the loss of loved ones in her own life—a trusted confidant. And it appears from his letters that she too must have confided in him. "The talk we had together, in your little car, on the last day in Pittsfield has come back to me more and more, into my thoughts and feelings. . . . You were so sad and discouraged . . . and I have known so well *that* sadness and *that* discouragement."[19] It is clear from the remainder of the letter that Elizabeth took him to visit the School for Crippled Children while he was in Pittsfield, and what he found there touched him deeply.

In a letter written just at the time that Bloch announced his resignation from the Cleveland Institute of Music, he reminded Elizabeth that "you asked me to write to you when I was in distress. . . . I am . . . now, my dear Mrs. Coolidge—and one day I will explain to you all that great tragedy."[20] There is much talk of death and despair, of being hated and wasted. Again he appealed to Coolidge for help, this time requesting that she assist him in obtaining the conductorship of the Rochester Eastman Symphony Orchestra. She did in fact write to Eastman, but the position never materialized.[21]

At the same time she was trying to get a conducting appointment for Ossip Gabrilowitsch. Her old friend and teacher, Daniel Gregory Mason, was a close friend of Gabrilowitsch and his wife, Clara Clemens, the daughter of Mark Twain. Mason held Gabrilowitsch in high esteem as a conductor and began a campaign to obtain a position for him with one of the New York orchestras, especially since he thought little of the "resident time beaters," Walter Damrosch and Joseph Stransky. But they were too firmly established with their orchestras, so Mason directed his efforts to raising money to engage an ad hoc orchestra for Gabrilowitsch to conduct for three concerts in Aeolian Hall in December 1917. The high artistic quality of these concerts encouraged Mason to present his friend in a series of orchestra concerts in Carnegie Hall. Elizabeth contributed $2,000 to the cause, which was also supported by André de Coppet, among others. Although the effort did not bring about exactly the wished-for result, it was very likely a factor in Gabrilowitsch's appointment as conductor of the Detroit Symphony in 1918, where he remained until his death in 1936, building that orchestra into a fine ensemble.[22]

With the successful conclusion of the first festival, Elizabeth announced plans for the next. The competition in 1919 would be for an original chamber work featuring the viola, her favorite instrument. The scope of the second festival was to be even grander. In addition to showcasing the Berkshire Quartet in the opening and closing concerts, the program included the Flonzaley Quartet and a concert of vocal chamber music arranged and conducted by Frederick Stock.

The festival of 1919 was marred by a crisis of sorts, though at the time it could hardly have been known to anyone other than Elizabeth's most intimate friends and the jury assembled for that year, whose members were Richard Aldrich, Louis Bailly, Harold Bauer, Rubin Goldmark, Georges Longy, and Frederick Stock. After examining the seventy-two manuscripts entered in the competition, the balloting resulted in a tie between two of Elizabeth's personal friends, Ernest Bloch and Rebecca Clarke. Coolidge was called upon to cast the deciding vote, and did so in favor of Bloch, whose winning composition was the Suite for Viola and Piano. Clarke's Sonata for Viola and Piano was awarded second prize, and both works were performed at the festival by Louis Bailly of the Berkshire Quartet with pianist Harold Bauer. Thereafter, every jury was made up of an uneven number of adjudicators.

As an intimate friend of Elizabeth and a judge in the competition, Stock was fully aware of the painful dilemma that the tie had caused for Elizabeth. In a letter written before the official announcement of the decision, Stock provided a deeper insight into the matter, reminding her that "we, you and I, at least, may reflect upon the outcome of the contest with one weeping eye and one laughing eye." He obviously believed that Bloch's work deserved the prize but at the same time found much in Clarke's sonata to recommend her. "Her Sonata has much charm; the first movement is very fine, but the scherzo is so freakish and has no thematic substance of any consequence; the last movement is too rhapsodic." It is also evident from Stock's letter that gender was a consideration—at least in his mind. "What the wise-acres would have said, had a 'Woman Composer' and one of your personal friends in Pittsfield won the prize, I do not dare to contemplate." That Stock clearly found it convenient to ignore the obvious fact that Bloch was also a close friend of Elizabeth only validates his fears that in choosing a woman there would have been "suspicions of a 'frame-up' between you and the judges . . . and . . . we might have had a great deal of other trouble besides. All things considered, we were most fortunate in our choice."[23]

Even before the results of the competition were publicly announced, Coolidge wrote a personal letter to Clarke in which she not only admitted her distress over the situation, but at the same time assured Clarke that she had based her decision strictly upon "ethical and not personal lines." By return mail Rebecca assured her friend, "I was most deeply touched when I got your letter this morning, and can't tell you how much I admire you for your absolute directness to me, and towards the whole of this affair. . . . I am only so very sorry that you have had all the worry in connection with me. But I shall always remember our talk and keep your letter and (if you will let me say it) look upon you as a great friend."[24]

Clarke's demeanor throughout the whole episode was admirable. She had high praise for Bloch's composition and took great pleasure in having her piece performed in the same festival. "As far as my own place on the program goes, I would like to tell you that . . . through your competition this year you have given me the greatest impetus to further work that anything possibly could."[25]

The festivals, though they involved a great deal of administrative work, were so well under control that Elizabeth again devoted time to other endeavors that were not quite so well publicized. One of the most important of these was her little-known support of the MacDowell Colony. Her association with the work of the colony dated to 1915, when, with the help of some of her Chicago friends, she created the Regina Watson Memorial honoring her friend and teacher. *Reports of the Edward MacDowell Memorial Association* reveal that from 1916 to 1935 Coolidge was not only an annual contributor, but was for most of those years the largest single donor.[26]

Founded in 1907, the colony was in its infancy when Edward MacDowell died the following year and his widow, Marian, assumed its direction. She guided it through difficult years during which she and Elizabeth became close friends. The letters they exchanged not only document that relationship but also reveal the high esteem with which Elizabeth viewed the work of the MacDowell Colony. Even when she was deeply involved in her endowment of the Library of Congress she still continued her annual contributions to the colony. Such largesse, not only of gift but also of attitude and spirit, was not lost on Marian MacDowell: "It has always been to me a sort of a beautiful miracle, the wonderful help you have given us through all these years. Most people, with such a big interest of work of their own, could never have even thought of helping along so splendidly another scheme. It first shows how big you are—without your help we could never have accomplished what we have."[27]

Coolidge's efforts for the colony were publicly acknowledged and honored at a testimonial dinner in her honor at the MacDowell Club House in New York City on 5 January 1929, at which the English Singers, the Elshuco Trio, the London String Quartet, and Martha Graham all performed. In his address on that occasion, Dr. Louis Anspacher characterized Coolidge's mode of patronage as "aristocratic munificence" that motivated her to relinquish the license to "impose her ideas, or utilize art arrogantly to express herself. [S]he has, with a true creator's humility, helped the artist to realize his own vision . . . [and] with a sanctified and committed altruism, has devoted her fortune making it possible for great music to survive in a rather deaf and un-heeding world, and to be brought to people all over the world. . . . [She] has been immovable and dogmatic only in her sense of mission and vocation."[28]

The third Berkshire Festival in 1920 was at once a beginning and an end, for it marked the first appearance of the London String Quartet in the United States and the last performance of the Berkshire Quartet as an ongoing organization. Although the three-year contract that they had signed in 1917 was due to expire, rumor had it that the dissolution of the ensemble was precipitated by a problem that Kortschak was having with his arm. However, letters that passed between him and Coolidge indicate that there was considerable tension within the ensemble, and that it was actually Coolidge's suggestion to end the quartet. In retrospect, Kortschak reflected, "What a difficult thing cooperation in art is!

Even greatest sincerity and unity of purpose provided, there still remains the fact that artistic expression is different in every artist's mind—there is no absolute and indisputable truth about it. In face of this, chamber music seems almost an absurdity, an illusion impossible to realize."[29]

The Berkshire Quartet chose to open this, its last festival, with what is arguably one of Beethoven's most profound works, the Quartet in C-sharp Minor, op. 131, and to close the concert with a performance of the prize-winning composition for that year, Gian Francesco Malipiero's *Rispetti e Strambotti* for string quartet. Out of the 136 manuscripts from eighteen countries that were entered in the competition that year, the jury of five (Ara, Bloch, Borowski, Stoeber, and Svenčenski) cast four votes solidly for the Malipiero work.

As the scope of the festivals enlarged, more and more European artists hitherto unheard in the United States were introduced through the Pittsfield concerts. Elizabeth's reputation as a patron was being spread far and wide. Her various philanthropic efforts were likewise becoming more far-reaching, and with the festival of 1920 began her romance with Italy and her association with Malipiero. She had known Ugo Ara from the time he was violist with the Flonzaley Quartet. Ara, who had left the quartet to go back to Italy and fight in World War I, was an intimate friend of Malipiero. He was, by good fortune, able to attend one of the early Berkshire Festivals and wrote to Elizabeth his enthusiastic impressions of it as well as his hopes for the future. The very international character of the festivals from the outset prompted Ara to recommend that after the war Elizabeth should extend their scope and take her ensembles and her prize-winning works to Europe. His suggestion was the seed of the successful European festivals that she would mount between the two world wars, beginning in Ara's homeland, Italy, where he worked with Alfredo Casella.

More immediately, however, Ara became the intermediary in a most ambitious undertaking that would expand Elizabeth's scope of patronage even wider. During the summer preceding the festival of 1920 the New York concert manager, Loudon Charlton, announced his plan to bring the Toscanini–La Scala Orchestra to the United States for a ten-week tour. The main sponsor of this ambitious undertaking was André de Coppet, who engaged Ara to go to Italy to secure the complicated arrangements with Toscanini. Coolidge, along with ten other patrons, pledged to underwrite the cost of the project, which was a grueling schedule that took the orchestra to thirty cities for a total of fifty-four concerts in ten weeks, the first week of which was to be devoted to recording sessions. In December of 1920 Elizabeth gave to Ara a check for $10,000, representing half of her pledge.

The venture was plagued with more than its share of complications, which are detailed in Charlton's memo to the guarantors. To begin with, "the Orchestra was compelled to sail from Italy two weeks earlier than scheduled, which situation was met by devoting the first two weeks after arrival to making of Victor records." At the end of these twelve weeks, "the American quarantine on all Mediterranean shipping necessitated the Orchestra remaining in this country an additional four weeks at our expense." The time was taken up by making more recordings which "because of Maestro Toscanini's unshakable artistic principles, threatened to be an almost insurmountable difficulty."[30]

When all expenditures were tallied the balance sheet showed a deficit of $65,882, of which the subscribers had already paid $28,750. Confident that royalties from the Victor records would make up the shortfall, de Coppet personally advanced the remaining $37,132.12 and expected that in time he could repay the underwriters as well.[31] However, just at this time the recording industry was sustaining severe losses—generally attributed to the advent of radio—and as a result royalties for 1923 amounted to just over $4,000. In an effort to recoup, the Victor Company developed in 1924 a completely new recording process that greatly improved the quality of its sound recordings but at the same time rendered the Toscanini–La Scala records unsalable. All of the unsold records that Victor dealers had in stock were returned to the company and charged against the Toscanini–La Scala account, with the result that royalties for 1924 fell to a disastrous $64.75.

In all, thirty-two recordings had been made and, since the Italian orchestra had been brought over by the underwriters, these records could not be remade because Toscanini was by this time under contract with the New York Philharmonic. In Charlton's opinion, "These old-process Toscanini records, being practically obsolete because of the superiority of all the different orchestral records that have been made under the new process, there seems to be practically no hope that any considerable sale . . . will ever be possible, except perhaps as curiosities."[32]

Despite the financial losses of the Toscanini–La Scala debacle, the one redeeming feature of the venture was the recruitment of Ugo Ara into Coolidge's task force. News of her festivals was appearing in the Italian press, and with Malipiero's winning of the 1920 competition the time was right to press Elizabeth to extend the scope of her work and take her ensembles and her prize-winning works to Europe. With a sense of timing as delicate as any called upon in his many years of ensemble playing with the Flonzaley Quartet, Ara chose a strategic moment to propose his idea. Elizabeth's plans for the 1921 festival were being besieged by an uncommon assortment of problems, chief among them the cancellation of the Rosé Quartet, which had been engaged to play five concerts. Ara wrote, saying, "I am distressed to hear of all the difficulties you are having with the Rosé Quartet, distressed but not surprised. I wonder if there has ever been a greater chasm between the European and American spirit than at the present moment."[33] At the same time he emphasized his belief that the Temple of South Mountain was part of Elizabeth's mission to reconcile the Old and the New World of music. By autumn he was back in Italy and able to report firsthand the impact that Coolidge's work was having in his own country. "I am so pleased to see how well your work is understood and appreciated in Italy. It is such a joy to think that my country, better, perhaps, than any other one, has grasped the boldness of your enterprise and the grandeur of your efforts."[34]

Although it would be two more years before her first European festival in Rome, the correspondence between Coolidge and Ara kept the idea alive, and Elizabeth began formulating plans even while she was deeply involved in the more pressing issue of salvaging her fourth Berkshire Festival. The Letz Quartet and the Quartet of the Detroit Symphony were engaged to replace the Rosé Quartet, and Gabrilowitsch came to the rescue by joining the Detroit ensemble as pianist, along with double bassist Gaston Brohan, in a performance of Schubert's "Trout Quintet."

Kortschak, who was by now the secretary of the Berkshire Music Colony, found it necessary in 1921 to publish some specific directives regarding the competition. Each year a certain number of manuscripts had to be disqualified because of failure to meet the requirements and/or deadlines for submission. Hereafter no transcriptions, adaptations, or works previously published or performed would be accepted. Moreover, it was necessary to establish some regulation of performance rights. It was agreed that for four months after the date of award, Coolidge would have full control over both the publication and the private performance of works chosen. After that the manuscript would be transferred to her while the copyright remained with the composer.

The prize that year was to be awarded for a composition featuring piano, violin, and cello. Of the sixty-four manuscripts submitted, one-third were by American composers. However, Oscar Sonneck, who was on the jury, found the overall quality of the compositions disappointing. In his letter written to Coolidge after the fact, he left an invaluable account of the arduous procedure involved in selecting a winner in these competitions. Before the committee assembled each of the jurors examined all of the compositions submitted and rated each on a scale of one to one hundred. At the first meeting of the panel, those manuscripts rated less than a seventy-five were eliminated from further consideration, and those above seventy-five were then played by artists on the jury, who were always selected especially for their ability to sight-read well enough to give a fair evaluation of the works. This sometimes required several days. Each judge then cast his vote: A work rated less than seventy-five was automatically given a zero, and anything above seventy-five got an exact numerical rating. The scores were averaged and the five highest were then given another performance before the final vote was taken. At that time each judge ranked the five in order of preference and deposited his vote in the ballot box, which was then opened by Coolidge and the votes recorded by her. When the winning entry had been determined Elizabeth ceremoniously broke open the sealed envelope and revealed the identity of the winner.[35] All seemed pleased to learn that H. Waldo Warner, violist of the London String Quartet, had captured the first prize. His Suite for Piano, Violin and Cello was given its premiere performance by the Elshuco Trio, which now had two new members. Elias Breeskin had replaced Samuel Gardner and Aurelio Giorni, pianist, took the position left vacant by the death of Richard Epstein. Of the original members, only Willem Willeke remained. Despite the earlier problems the festival was a success and at its conclusion Elizabeth announced that the prize for the 1922 Berkshire Chamber Music Competition would be awarded for a string quartet.

Following her usual pattern of interspersing festivals with independent works of patronage, Elizabeth's major undertaking between the fourth and fifth festivals was a substantial contribution of over $4,000 to help assemble an orchestra of eighty-six members for a New York concert conducted by Pablo Casals, with whom she was already well acquainted.

The fifth Berkshire Festival brought in seventy manuscripts from eleven countries. In the opinion of Charles Martin Loeffler and Henry Eichheim, who were judges, many of the works were of very poor quality. (Other members of the jury were Pablo Casals, Lawrence Gilman, and Hans Letz.) This may have been a factor in Elizabeth's decision not to hold a competition for the sixth festival in 1923 but instead to offer two commissions, one to Rebecca Clarke and the other to Eugene Goossens. Clarke was an accomplished violist who had studied at the Royal College of Music with Lionel Tertis and also was a composition student of Charles Stanford. Elizabeth had come to know her through her old friend Gertrude Watson, who had made extensive concert tours for war relief playing with Clarke and the famous English cellist May Mukle.[36]

Both women had participated in earlier festivals. Elizabeth's decision not to have a competition in 1922 but instead to commission two works may have been in part her gesture to Rebecca Clarke who, by Coolidge's decisive vote, had lost out to Bloch in 1919. A respectable period of time had passed so that she could with impunity offer Clarke a commission. It seems significant, however, that this was the first time Coolidge had ever commissioned two works for the same event, and the fact that the other commission went to Goossens, who was as yet completely unknown to her, tempts one to speculate that she was playing it safe, hedging any lingering accusations of favoritism such as Stock had feared in 1919.

The work stipulated for 1922 was to feature the cello. Goossens's *Phantasy Sextet in One Movement* for three violins, viola, and two cellos was premiered by a stunning assembly of artists: Albert Spalding,

Elizabeth Sprague Coolidge. Charcoal sketch by John Singer Sargent, 1923.

Library of Congress

Edouard Déthier, Hugo Kortschak, Lionel Tertis, May Mukle, and Emmeran Stoeber.

Coolidge had already determined that Myra Hess should be the pianist for Clarke's piece but apparently indicated to her that she was undecided about the choice of a cellist. Well aware that Coolidge was always the final arbiter in all decisions relating to the choice of soloists for her festivals, Clarke summoned the courage to make a suggestion: "[T]here is one thing I am simply longing to say to you, but I hardly dare to, because it is awfully presumptuous of me to offer an opinion. . . . I have been wondering if . . . you had ever thought of the possibility of having a *woman!* I can't help feeling, and I believe you do too, that a great cause is served in putting the work of women executants on an equal footing with that of men." Worried for fear that Coolidge might think May Mukle had put her up to it, Clarke assured her, "I am doing it absolutely off my own bat, so that if you do not like my having spoken of it, please be offended with *me* only."[37] In the end, Mukle did perform Clarke's work but her name does not appear on the program, only that of Hess as pianist.

The year 1923 was a watershed in Elizabeth's career as a patron. In many respects it was one of the most satisfying personally, for it marked the beginning of some of her deepest and most enduring friendships. The strong English presence at the Berkshire Festival resulted in her intimate relationship with the Bridges, and her visit to Rome that summer marked her first association with the Pro Arte Quartet, as well as the beginning of her many musical pilgrimages to Italy. Ugo Ara's suggestion made two years earlier was about to become a reality as Elizabeth made plans to sponsor a festival in Italy to present some of her Berkshire music, for by now she had accumulated a significant cache of original modern compositions. She engaged Ara to act as her European contact and he, with the help of Alfredo Casella, arranged her historic first European festival, which was held at the American Academy in Rome. It was by all accounts a very successful venture, and Coolidge herself loved to reflect years later on the pleasant hours she spent socially with her new friends Malipiero, Respighi, Casella, and de Falla, as well as the young resident Fellows of the Academy: Howard Hanson, Randall Thompson, and her protégé Leo Sowerby. She had also brought along her New York friends, Lillian Littlehales, Gladys North, and Kurt Schindler. Coolidge loved to recall how "on a grand piano in my pleasant parlor, they would sometimes play over for me their recent compositions. I particularly remember de Falla, rendering with his little short hands, a very effective version of his 'Nights in the Gardens of Spain,' recently composed for piano and orchestra. Or, between rehearsals, we would drive to Frascati for lunch; or, at midnight, visit the Colosseum by moonlight. De Falla, however, was more apt to seek a church, to pray while we others amused ourselves."[38]

After the Italian festival she presented two concerts of Berkshire music in London in July and then returned home to Pittsfield to prepare for the sixth festival there, which inaugurated her newly formed Festival Quartet of South Mountain. The group included Willem Willeke as cellist and introduced into the picture another personality who would become a major figure in the Coolidge circle—William Kroll, the quartet's first violinist, and violinist of the Elshuco Trio.

The roster of artists assembled for 1923 was indeed impressive, with Great Britain being unusually well represented. In addition to Clarke and Goossens, whose works had been commissioned for the occasion, the London String Quartet was on hand to play the opening concert. The added presence of such notable Britons as Myra Hess, May Mukle, Lionel Tertis, Frank Bridge, Arnold Bax, Catherine Goodsen, and B. J. Dale elicited Coolidge's famous description of the festival as simply "too much of Albion."[39]

The participation of so many artists from abroad actually gave impetus to another of Coolidge's forward-looking undertakings—her outreach to institutions of higher learning. The expenses involved in bringing artists from distant places were great and in many cases Elizabeth, through her countless contacts in the music world, was responsible for obtaining additional engagements for them in colleges and universities. For the time being these were usually entrusted to concert managements, but the idea and the initial impulse came from Coolidge herself.

The year 1924 marked the seventh and the last of the annually scheduled Berkshire Festivals, though there would be others in 1928, 1934, and 1938. The competition for 1924 was to be for a chamber work that included one or more vocal parts. There were 109 manuscripts entered from twelve countries, and for the first time the prize went to an American, Wallingford Riegger, for his *La belle dame sans merçi.* Honorable mention was awarded to Frederick Jacobi for his *Two Assyrian Prayers.*

Despite the success of the Berkshire Festivals, Elizabeth began to fear for the perpetuation of her work, and soon came to realize that if her activities at South Mountain were to survive beyond her lifetime they must be institutionalized and impersonalized. In her words, "they were sufficiently important . . . not to be dependent upon the life, the good will or the bank account of any individual."[40] She had already approached Yale University and the American Academy of Arts and Letters with the notion of an alliance. Although Robert Underwood Johnson, president of the Academy at the time, was much interested, neither of these institutions felt able to assume the responsibility.

The initial idea for the solution of this problem may be traced to what began as a social event, a relaxation after her 1923 festival when she invited Frank Bridge and his wife, Ethel, to remain in America for a while and to vacation with her as she motored down the East Coast. After their excursion to southern Virginia the group stopped in Washington, D.C. and visited, among other places, the Library of Congress. Coolidge and her friends were invited to lunch with the chiefs of the various divisions of the Library, which at the time was presided over by Herbert Putnam, Librarian of Congress. The conversation naturally turned to her Berkshire Festivals and some consideration of her possibly sending performances to the hallowed halls of the Library. Though she could not have known at this time the full import of this new contact, the protagonist in the next phase of her philanthropic effort had been waiting in the wings since her second Berkshire Festival, when Bloch requested tickets for his friend Carl Engel.

CHAPTER ELEVEN

Enter the Archangel

The meeting of two personalities is like the contact of two chemical substances: If there is any reaction both are transformed.

– CARL GUSTAV JUNG,

MODERN MAN IN SEARCH OF A SOUL

WHILE ELIZABETH'S LUNCHEON at the Library of Congress may at first appear to have been just one more fortuitous occasion in the sequence of events leading up to her largest philanthropic endeavor, there is considerable evidence that the notion of such an association and its consequences for the Library had actually been on the minds of others for some time. Of the gifted men who sat at table with her that day, Herbert Putnam and Carl Engel were soon to become main players in the action, and although Oscar Sonneck (1873–1928), the third member of the triumvirate, was absent, it would soon become apparent that he had skillfully prepared the way for what was about to transpire.

The efforts of these three men should not be perceived as a kind of bloodless, self-serving "cultivation" of a possible patron. It was their sense of dedication to the mission of the Library of Congress and its potential to become the major musical research facility of the nation that prompted them to undertake the often difficult task of facilitating this unprecedented relationship with a strong-willed, apolitical, and frequently impatient patron who undertook to involve the United States government in the unlikely business of art. Forging a relationship required vision, patience, tact, and commitment on the part of all concerned.

Of the three men mentioned it was Carl Engel who would bear the greatest responsibility. Brilliant, urbane, witty, and meticulous, Engel seemed gifted by nature to be the one to work out the details of this new partnership and maintain an amicable relationship with a patron who could sometimes be imperious in her demands.

Engel was nearly twenty years Elizabeth's junior and was by birth, breeding, and education as different from her Yankee background as imaginable. He was born in Paris in 1883 of German parents and was educated in Strasbourg and Munich before coming to the United States in 1905. He worked for a time in the music publishing business and as a free-lance critic, editor, and composer. It was at the urging of Oscar Sonneck that Herbert Putnam hired Engel in 1922 to succeed Sonneck as chief of the Music Division of the Library of Congress. Over a period of several years Sonneck had deftly prepared all the parties concerned for the role that each would assume in the emerging scenario.[1]

Elizabeth knew all three of the men, particularly Sonneck, who had begun corresponding with her in early 1920. Perhaps even more important than his polite and rather businesslike early letters to Elizabeth are the more candid ones that he was exchanging at the same time with Herbert Putnam—letters that reflect his prescient conviction that Coolidge was warming to the thought of an association with the Library and that he had, in fact, been cautiously nurturing the idea.[2] This is quite clear from a sequence of memos dating from December 1921—well before the famous luncheon of 1923. By this time Sonneck had left the Library of Congress to assume a position in New York with the publishing house of Schirmer, but his heart remained at the Library. He had come there in 1902 and in the space of fifteen years had forged what can best be described as a mere accumulation of music and books amassed by reason of the copyright deposit into a major research collection.[3]

Although he was an American citizen, Sonneck was perceived by many to be German, because his German mother had taken him back to her country as an infant shortly after the death of his father. Despite his European training and experience, he became an ardent promoter of American music and felt a deep affection for the United States. Yet this apparent German connection became a serious problem for him during World War I, when he was placed under government surveillance. He was

Carl Engel, Chief of the Music Division of the Library of Congress at the time of Coolidge's endowment, and her intimate friend

Library of Congress

deeply offended by the discovery of this lack of confidence in him personally, particularly on the part of those who should have known better.[4]

In a lengthy letter to Carl Engel written in 1921, Sonneck encouraged Engel to accept the position as his successor at the Library of Congress, a position that Putnam had actually held "open for the prodigal son to return should the Schirmer experiment prove unbearable for him."[5] Even though Sonneck was not happy in his new position with Schirmer, the thought of returning to the $3,000 salary of the chief of the Music Division kept him from going back to the job he so loved. Moreover, his dedication to the cause of the American composer prompted him to remain with the publishing house that he believed was becoming too purely commercial. He felt compelled to stay there, where he could be an advocate for the American composer, whose standard he had ardently taken up.

In Sonneck's opinion, Otto Kinkeldey and Carl Engel were the only two candidates capable of continuing to build on the groundwork he had carefully laid at the Library of Congress. But with Kinkeldey's appointment as head of the Music Division of the New York Public Library in 1915, Engel remained alone in the running. Sonneck's ultimate word of encouragement to Engel is a mark of his high esteem for Engel's abilities and a testimony of his genuine respect for Herbert Putnam, whom he characterized as "a 'boss' who never lets you feel that he is a boss. A man who will back you up every time, if you by your ability and industry and judgment have gained his confidence. It would be a relief and a pleasure, as it was for me, to work under an administrative genius, a diplomat, a gentleman of culture like Herbert Putnam."[6] Similarly, Putnam's high esteem for Sonneck and respect for his opinion did much to pave the way for Engel's entry into the arena as chief of the Music Division in 1922.[7]

Sonneck's departure from the Library of Congress in no way effected an end to his association with that institution, as his correspondence with Putnam and Engel testifies. It is clear from his letter to Putnam as early as 1921 that he was privy to Coolidge's concern over institutionalizing the work that she had begun in the Berkshires as well as her growing interest in an affiliation with the Library of Congress. That he was aware of certain difficulties inherent in the realization of such an unprecedented partnership is apparent in his correspondence with Putnam: "Of course I do not know at this end precisely what your difficulties are, but this I do know that Mrs. Coolidge has set her heart and ambition on this affair and . . . is fully prepared to spend thousands of dollars to see it go through with some éclat. . . . [S]he is in such a frame of mind that there is no telling where a successful carrying out of the scheme will lead to in the interest of the Library. I have already paved the way for the future and with proper strategy the generosity of Mrs. Coolidge will respond."[8]

By this time Sonneck had had sufficient experience with Coolidge to realize that she could be something of a benevolent dictator—and he was aware that her single-minded pursuit could easily be led off course by a careless hand. At the same time he recognized her susceptibility to diplomatically presented suggestions, and in his opinion one with just the right combination of breeding, wit, and an unfailing sense of timing might bring this delicate mission to a successful completion. Clearly he saw his friend and protégé, Engel, as the ideal choice and pressed his cause with Putnam: "My recommendation, in view of what may become of the whole matter later on, is, not to disappoint Mrs. Coolidge so that her generosity will benefit some other institution. Keep her in line by accepting definitely with a suitable letter of appreciation, her gift with all the ribbons. Do not let her ardor and ambition cool off. Accept middle of February and make Engel work his head off to arrange matters. . . . If Mrs. Coolidge can be made happy now, I am morally certain that the Library of Congress and the U.S. government will not regret it later on, awkward as may be this particular project for certain reasons."[9]

In the five years since Elizabeth had inaugurated her Berkshire Festival she had weathered some serious trials of her own. She had observed the disbanding of her Berkshire Quartet, had seen power struggles among musicians, and had dispensed many thousands of dollars in the hope of ensuring the continuity of her work. At the same time she had already experienced the heady satisfaction of extending her mission beyond South Mountain and into more far-flung places.

Coolidge believed passionately that "the activities begun on South Mountain ought to be perpetuated and that the best—perhaps the only—way to do that would be to institutionalize and impersonalize them."[10] The degree of stability that Elizabeth perceived as essential if her mission was to be fulfilled was likely to be found only in some agency of the federal government, and the most obvious choice was the Library of Congress, where she had already begun to feel at home through her association with the Sonneck, Putnam, and Engel.

The boldness of the proposal that she was about to make to the U.S. government is all the more remarkable considering that her scheme of a federal partnership was coming from a citizen who, until only a few years before, had been disenfranchised by reason of gender. This unprecedented plan, which was entirely her invention, presented obstacles of such proportion that anyone with less of what Engel would later dub her "enlightened obstinacy" would never have dared consider it. Undaunted by the complexity of it, she pressed on. The ultimate success of the venture, however, owes much to the combination of Putnam's wisdom and patience and Engel's diplomacy and hard work.

Elizabeth's relationship with Engel traversed a course from polite diplomacy to genuine friendship based upon a mutual respect and love that seemed to thrive on the conquering of obstacles as well as the shared exultation in their achievements. The earliest surviving correspondence between Coolidge and Engel is a brief and proper thank-you note from Engel after the fifth Berkshire Festival in 1922, when he had been her guest and she had shared with him her collection of scores and letters. He ventured to ask if she had "given any thought to the ultimate disposal of [her] autographs," adding that "it would seem but fitting that your fine collection be someday placed with our National Library as a permanent testimony to the ideals and munificence of a remarkable American woman. Please advise me whether I may entertain a hope that you will thus enrich, in time, what is already one of the most important musical collections in the world."[11]

Nearly two months elapsed before Engel received her response. She admitted that she found his proposal "an interesting suggestion," but explained, "I have another plan in view for them; but as this plan is vague and uncertain, it may seem more fitting to will them to the Congressional Library; and of this, if I ultimately decided upon it, I will let you know."[12] Her long delay in responding to Engel is quite uncharacteristic and perhaps calculated—as was her noncommittal answer to his inquiry about the manuscripts. It is possible that she was simply buying time that would allow her to consider other options, and it was almost certainly calculated to provide an opportunity to observe Engel at work, for the letter goes on to invite him to serve as a juror for her 1924 competition. If this was a test of Engel's mettle and determination she must surely have been favorably impressed by his answer. Far from being cowed or even mildly discouraged he dared to remind her (diplomatically enough), "You are a part of the musical history of our country, therefore, the record of your achievement should be lifted from out the personal or local sphere, and placed among the national archives."[13] This early show of his resolve that so appealed to Coolidge presaged the characteristically animated exchanges of their later correspondence.

At the time Engel could not have known of her previous offer to Yale and the Academy of Arts and Letters. The fact that neither had agreed to the idea did not dampen her enthusiasm but may have served to confirm the wisdom of opting for the government affiliation. Within months she sent the manuscripts to the Library of Congress, at the same time expressing her desire to bring these Berkshire compositions to life by sending her Festival Quartet and Elshuco Trio to the Library to give a series of performances. She obviously could not have known that the Library's facilities for performance of any kind were limited to an ancient piano in the basement. Engel shared her letter with Putnam, and both agreed that so stimulating an opportunity was one that Washington could not afford to miss. However, Engel pointed out, "to Mr. Putnam's keen regret, your suggestion that the library, in a way sponsor your concerts can not be followed for the simple reason that there is no suitable auditorium in the library building. Nor does there seem to be any other branch of the government service that could adequately present your players." It is tempting to speculate that Engel was taking a calculated risk when he recommended that she look elsewhere for a place to perform. In a brilliant tactical move he quoted her own words with which she had once expressed the desire "to remove art from" what she so aptly called "those fields of rivalry and maneuver—society and business." He may have been playing his ace card when he ended with Putnam's suggestion that "perhaps the most effective and dignified course would be to approach the Washington Society of the Fine Arts (which is) absolutely uncommercial."[14]

In the end a home for Elizabeth's first festival in Washington was found in the auditorium of the Freer Gallery, which was itself the product of an enlightened bequest by an earlier patron, Charles L. Freer, who made the donation through the Smithsonian Institution, backed by the urging of President Theodore Roosevelt. It is the opinion of some that Elizabeth was not as fortunate in Calvin Coolidge as Freer had been in Roosevelt, who made it known that if the regents of the Smithsonian failed to accept Freer's gift, he, as president, would find other ways "to prevent the loss to the United States Government, and therefore to the people of the United States, of one of the most valuable collections which any private individual has ever given to any people."[15]

But for the intervention of Mary Howe, composer and close friend of Engel, the whole endeavor might have been scuttled. At about this time Howe and her house guest, Olga Samaroff, were invited to luncheon with Engel and Putnam at the Library of Congress, and in the course of conversation Mary ventured to ask Putnam if he had accepted Coolidge's offer of a concert in Washington. Engel attempted to hush her and said, "It's all up the spout." But Mary Howe did not give up easily and pursued the matter with Putnam then and there. He admitted that there were two problems, the lack of a place for the concert, and the creation of an invitation list. Howe then asked, "If you had a place in which to have the concert, would you have it?" He answered, "Yes, but there is still the list to prevent." Mary convinced him that that was not a problem, and forthwith set about preparing the invitation list and finding a hall. It was Howe who made the first overture to the Freer officials and took "Clengel" (her children's nickname for Carl Engel) to meet with John Lodge, curator of the Freer Gallery. All was nearly lost when Engel and Lodge reacted very badly to one another—mainly because Lodge demanded to see the manuscripts of the pieces to be performed before he would give permission. Engel found his request insulting and reacted accordingly. This mutual offense resulted largely from ignorance. Engel was unaware that Lodge was a competent musician and was ruffled by his demands, while Lodge, on the other hand, apparently had no knowledge of the esteem with which Elizabeth's Berkshire Festivals were held in the musical world. In the end Howe was able to mediate and Lodge guaranteed permission, though he admitted that he did not like all of the works performed. He was silenced, however, by Mary's reminder that after all "he had the Peacock Room to explain . . . so he could hardly do less than be honest and open-minded as to the pieces being played."[16]

The use of the Freer Gallery was a brilliant compromise that seems to have satisfied all parties concerned, and with the concerts on 7, 8, and 9 February 1924, Coolidge's formal association with the Library of Congress became a reality. The event brought national attention to Elizabeth's new affiliation, increased her determination to carry her plans forward, and effected a much-needed injection of musical life into the city of Washington.

Plans for the Freer Gallery concerts are well documented, since Coolidge spent the preceding months in Cambridge near her son and communicated her every wish to Engel, who soon found himself in the position of general factotum, attending to all manner of details, many of which were concerned with the purely social aspects of the occasion. Elizabeth directed him to engage rooms at the Willard Hotel for twenty guests for three days, at her expense. In addition she required "a small pleasant private dining room [for] an informal Bohemian supper . . . after the festivities are finished . . . a room to accommodate twenty-five to fifty people."[17] She had initiated the custom of parties after her festivals in Pittsfield and these postconcert celebrations in time became de rigueur—not always appreciated by tired, and perhaps less socially inclined, musicians.

Throughout the planning of the concerts Elizabeth insisted that the weight of the programs be devoted to contemporary compositions. Accordingly, out of the nine works performed over three evenings, the classics were represented solely by one Haydn String Quartet (op. 20, no. 4) and one Beethoven Piano Trio (op. 70, no. 1). The lion's share of the programs was given to the performance of compositions associated with the Berkshire Festivals either as winners of the competition, commissions, or dedications. It was a special joy to Elizabeth that four of the seven modern composers represented on the program were present in the audience.[18]

The concerts were a triumph for Elizabeth. The first-night audience was made up of just the right mix of government officials, diplomats,

Washington socialites, and genuine music lovers. With each successive evening the audience grew significantly, so that by the third night "it not merely exhausted the chairs, [it] even packed into the corridor beyond."[19] The lavish program printed for the occasion contains reviews of each of the works performed as well as a reproduction of the opening page of the holograph and a listing of all the manuscripts that Coolidge was donating to the Library. The opening night was graced by speeches both before the after the music, by Putnam, Engel, and Coolidge herself. In her remarks Elizabeth thanked a long list of those with whom she had worked over the years and reserved the final expressions of gratitude for Putnam and Engel. The last word, however was granted to Putnam, whose comments are a testimony to his nobility of character: "In coupling me with Mr. Engel in her appreciations (and especially in putting my name first) she has been too liberal to my office and its pretensions. The vitality of the work of the Government is not due to the administrator. It is due to the men associated with him, who, from the spark within them, light the flame, and with their devotion nurse and guard it. Theirs is the art; it is they who are the artists; it is they who create and achieve. . . . We administrators, in contrast, are but part of the mechanism of the Government."[20]

Among the many favorable reactions to the Freer concerts, Engel received a complaint from one enthusiast who lamented the lack of notice in the press. The indignant auditor demanded, "What is the matter with the Washington papers? Why should I have to go to Baltimore or New York to get a real notice of these recitals?"[21] It was a legitimate complaint, but as Engel sagely noted, "Observance by the outside press is of more concern to us than dereliction by the press of Washington need be. But in the final expression the press of Washington has certainly risen to its duty (I do not say to its 'opportunity,' for that would imply critical competence not to be expected.)"[22] The musical education of Washington—still considered something of a cultural backwater—would not take place overnight, as is evident from a letter written just two years later in which Engel deplored the fact that a performance of Bach's *St. Matthew Passion* had left a deficit of nearly $5,000. "This town is not ripe for things like that. It has neither the money nor the understanding. What an appalling situation for our Capital! And now our own worth seems only a drop in the bucket—But it is a drop of the right stuff!"[23]

It was a pattern throughout Coolidge's life as a philanthropist that before one good work was accomplished, the idea of the next was already well formulated in her mind. So it is no surprise that before the flush of satisfaction and pride over the Freer concerts had even begun to fade, Elizabeth was at the drawing board with another project. Within days she wrote to say "I am thinking a great deal about our next step, and before I sail for Europe, I shall outline to you some of the plans which had occurred to me desirable and feasible."[24] Engel responded by return mail and two days later joined her in New York to discuss plans for the future. It is evident that the Freer Gallery concerts had unleashed in Elizabeth an enthusiasm about to be manifested in what would be her largest and unquestionably most far-reaching plan.

It was Elizabeth's unswerving conviction that her association with the Library of Congress should ensure that the works contained in its collection of manuscripts and printed music should not merely lie mutely on the shelves but be brought to life in performance. It very quickly became evident that this was also a long-cherished desire of Engel's as well. By late 1923 his correspondence with her began to take on a more personal and "unofficial" character in a series of handwritten letters in which he confided his thoughts on the subject. "I prefer to answer your last letter unofficially, chiefly because I want to confess that your suggestion to have the Music Division sponsor musical concerts of an especially fine and dignified character, has been my wish ever since I came to Washington two years ago."[25] It is a mark of Engel's confidence in Putnam's wisdom that, despite his eagerness to promote the performance of this music, he accepted the librarian's opinion that "this is still beyond the scope of the Library. His (Putnam's) judgment in matters of policy is so excellent that I have unhesitatingly, although regretfully, accepted the wisdom of his reasons. Nevertheless, he is an ardent lover of music and I know him to be most anxious that your suggestion should be acted on in some way or other."[26]

Her ideas for the "next step" to which she referred in her letter of 19 February were shared in private conversation with Engel. By autumn, however, she was ready to communicate her plan in writing to Herbert

Putnam. Her letter of 23 October 1924 contained the initial expression of her intent to endow the Library of Congress by the donation of an auditorium for the performance of chamber music as well as a trust fund to ensure the promotion of it. Such an offer to the government from a private citizen was unprecedented, and it created innumerable problems involving bureaucratic red tape never before encountered. It required two weeks of intensive study and negotiation on the part of Elizabeth's attorney, Richard Hale, and officials of the Library before the letter of intent was reworded in a fashion that permitted Putnam to present it to the Congress of the United States on 4 December.

> *My dear Mr. Putnam:*
>
> *Confirming the intentions expressed in my letter of October 23, 1924, and welcomed by you, I ask you to submit to Congress the following offer, to wit: In pursuance of my desire to increase the resources of the Music Division of the Library of Congress, especially in the promotion of chamber music, for which I am making an additional provision in the nature of an endowment, I offer to the Congress of the United States, the sum of $60,000 for the construction and equipment, in connection with the Library, of an auditorium, which shall also be available (at the discretion of the Librarian and the Chief of the Music Division) for any other suitable purpose, secondary to the needs of the Music Division.*[27]

Throughout the delicate negotiations Putnam again displayed his administrative genius with his patient and clear-headed sorting out of the problems. At issue was the fundamental question of the government's inability to accept the trust fund. While there was no impediment to accepting material gifts like the auditorium and the manuscripts, there was no legislation in place to permit the Library of Congress to accept and hold in trust the principal of a fund, the income of which might be used for operational expenses and the increase of its collections. On Putnam's recommendation and the advice of her attorney, Elizabeth agreed to a recasting of the offer that clearly separated the gift of the auditorium from the endowment of the trust, and the two were submitted to Congress as separate proposals. Despite the complexity of the issue, the whole transaction for the gift of the auditorium and the manuscripts was completed in the short space of just three months. Elizabeth's letter of intent is dated 23 October 1924; the revised version is from 12 November, and on that same day she met Engel in Boston to present him with a check for $60,000 (more than $538,000 in 1996 dollars) for the construction of the auditorium.[28] However, Putnam's formal letter of thanks, which was written three days later, explains that he could only hold the check pending the action of Congress, "since if I were to deposit it, I must deposit it with the United States Treasurer, and in that case it would cease to draw interest, while by holding it, the $60,000, remaining as it does in your account in the Northern Trust Company, will continue to draw interest."[29]

By separating the endowment from the auditorium Putnam was now able to transmit Coolidge' s offer to Congress on 4 December, and six days later Senator George W. Pepper of Pennsylvania introduced the bill in the Senate. After discussion in the Committee on the Library, the bill went to the House of Representatives, where it was introduced by Representative Robert Luce of Massachusetts, passed, and was signed into law by President Coolidge on 23 January 1925.[30]

Providing the mechanism for the trust to be accepted was more complicated, and several possible options were proposed by Hale, who expressed concern over the possibility that Elizabeth might be financially overextended. Harold Rockwell, her advisor from the Northern Trust Company in Chicago, expressed similar concerns, stressing the transitory character of the personal element involved: "We wonder if you have given full consideration to the question as to whether or not your plans will be carried out in the way that you wish after your original associates die or retire, and particularly when your personal inspiration is not behind the work."[31]

She appreciated the advice of her counselors but manifested no fear or hesitation either at their suggestions of possible failure or at the various convoluted procedures suggested by Hale for circumventing the government's lack of ability to accept bequests of money. The most complicated of these was his recommendation of making the gift of the trust through the Smithsonian Institution, which had already established a precedent in its acceptance of such bequests and whose charter appeared to permit it for, unlike the Library of Congress, the Smithsonian was a corporation.

With some alteration in language the bill to establish the trust was introduced into the Senate on 9 January 1925, again by Senator Pepper. Ten days later Elizabeth executed the deed of trust transferring to the Library of Congress the principal of over $400,000 (over $35.6 million in 1996 dollars). It was estimated that this money would generate an income of more than $28,000 ($249,000 in 1996 dollars) annually. The Senate passed the bill on 18 February. The House approved it with some minor amendments on 27 February, and on 3 March the Coolidge Foundation became a reality when President Calvin Coolidge signed it into law (Public Law 541, 68th Cong. S.3899). The entire legal procedure for the donation of both the auditorium and the trust was accomplished in a period of less than five months from the time of Elizabeth's first letter of intent.

Putnam's delight in the arrangement is succinctly stated in his official report for that year. In his opinion the real significance of using the Freer auditorium lay in the fact that the first concerts were given "in a governmental building devoted to the fine arts and under governmental auspices, the first notable recognition by our Government (apart from its maintenance of the collection in the Library) of music as one of the finer arts—entitled to its concern and encouragement."[32] It now required very little to convince Putnam of the value of bringing the Library's holdings to life through performance, and in retrospect he recalled the wisdom of Coolidge as well as Engel's insistence. "He (Engel) could not bear that all that melody should remain imprisoned within inarticulate covers. He yearned to release it in utterance, to see it go forth on its proper mission: to arouse, to refresh, to solace, to delight."[33]

The fact that the gift of the auditorium and the Foundation occurred during the administration of Calvin Coolidge inevitably gave rise to a spate of amusing mistaken identifications of Elizabeth as the wife of the president. She enjoyed referring to herself as "the other Mrs. Coolidge," and Frank Bridge made a hobby of collecting and sending to her such howlers as this one from the *London Daily Mirror:* "I wonder how many people present at the opening of the Diaghileff season at His Majesty's Theatre knew that Stravinsky's *Apollon Musagète* which is included in the program, was commissioned by Mrs. Calvin Coolidge, wife of the American President. Mrs. Coolidge has always been tremendously fond of music, but the 'silent' President lives up to his name by choosing the movies as his favorite form of entertainment."[34]

By this time Elizabeth and Engel had worked together through the planning and preparation of the Freer Gallery concerts, had endured what seemed to them like endless technicalities in the drafting of the document establishing the trust, and had waited impatiently for Congress to act. These experiences had only served to deepen their growing friendship, the first of several such valued relationships that Elizabeth enjoyed with men whose company and devotion to her were real and sincere but not romantic. In every case the difference in their ages, their status as married men, her fondness for their wives, and her propriety—coupled with a rather maternal attitude—placed them outside the pale of sentimental attachment and beyond possible accusations of a gossiping public. Although Elizabeth seemed genuinely to enjoy the attention shown to her by the many composers and artists with whom she dealt over the years—most of them men—the notion of her having romantic relationships with any of them is unimaginable. Moreover, Fred was still very much a presence in her memory. It was only in 1925, ten years after his death, that she began to use her feminine signature rather than Mrs. Frederic Shurtleff Coolidge.

It cannot be denied that Elizabeth manifested a predilection for gentlemen with a healthy sense of humor (which certainly Engel had), and despite the fact that her figure had reached somewhat amazonian proportions, she still appreciated the occasional flattering turn of phrase at which Engel excelled. His letters to her had grown longer and more personal since the time of the Freer Gallery concerts and were almost always handwritten now. Even those purely business communications that were typewritten lack a formal salutation, for he had instructed his secretary to leave it blank so that he could write in his own personal, often intimate, salutation and also add postscripts of a private nature after the letter had passed through the hands of his office staff. These nearly always address Elizabeth by his favorite sobriquet, "Faerie Queen." The earliest surviving letter to contain that title dates from 16 November 1924, just after the announcement of her gift to the Library. Only with the "inner court" of her friends did Elizabeth ever exchange nicknames and it was a mark of genuine affection when she permitted such familiarity and began to indulge in a pun on Engel's name, addressing him as *du lieber Engel* or sometimes promoting him to the rank of archangel, calling him Mike or Michel. This latter nickname is of a somewhat more obscure origin and can only be understood when paired with his other favored name for her, "Line." He had at one time suggested that her initials, ESC, should signify *Ecellentissima Santa Cecilia* and now explained: "If I had not affectionately dubbed you already with one set of initials, I should have called you P.M.—which does not stand for Post Meridian. I should want it to stand for *Pneu Michelin*. You who have motored through France know that excellent tire's much advertised virtue, *il boit l'obstacle*."[35] He rightly predicted that in their association Michel and Line would have many opportunities to devour obstacles, and his letters begin to be threaded with references to this and even sometimes illustrations as well.[36]

Coolidge relished this playful kind of intimacy and must have complained once of a particular letter from him that seemed too formal, for he assured her that if she ever received from him another letter that sounded "officially distant" it was only because offices are full of files into which letters are put "for apparently no other reason than to make them handier for the curious." He confessed that he kept her letters "locked up in my inner sanctum with some other private correspondence which (when I am no more) will bear witness that, if I had no other merit, at least I had some marvelous friends. And the most marvelous among them stand out well—queenlike."[37]

On the same day that Herbert Putnam delivered Elizabeth's offer of the gift to the Congress, Engel penned an unusually long letter to her from the hospital where he was recuperating from surgery. It marks a new phase in their relationship, characterized by the growing ability to disagree amiably and by his frank admission of her importance in his life:

> *I have once before in my life—some fifteen years ago—come in contact with a personality almost as strong and extraordinary as is yours. It was my privilege to learn a lot through that contact. I propose to learn from you. In matters of selecting the programs I want to follow your lead. But I know that you will respect me only the more if—while submitting to your*

judgment—I candidly tell you whenever things present themselves to my view in a different light. Yours is the right to call the tune—and the Berkshire Festivals have amply demonstrated that you do the calling as no one else has ever done. But precisely because you are an exception, I think that it would be a mistake to include you among what someone somewhere called the 99 people out of a 100 to whom intelligence in others means no more than the discovery of a person who is in intellectual acquiescence with themselves. Therefore, I humbly claim the right to register intellectual divergences, should they occur, not because I wish to differ with you for the sake of argument, but because I want to remain true to my conception of you as one of the most exceptional beings I know, and as not belonging to the 99 out of 100.[38]

With the next phase of their association they would all too soon encounter a rather steady diet of obstacles to be devoured.

CHAPTER TWELVE

The Eagle Sings

Make no little plans; they have no magic to stir men's souls.

– ATTRIBUTED TO DANIEL BURNHAM

ON THE OCCASION of the first Library of Congress Festival, Carl Engel wrote, "All the world knows that the American Eagle has a voice, and that occasionally, his scream can make itself heard with an excellent effect over a fairly wide range. What will be news to most people, is that the Eagle's voice has of late acquired suaver and more melodious accents."[1] He was, of course, referring to the newly created logo that would hereafter appear on the programs of performances in the Coolidge Auditorium. The familiar ornithological emblem of the eagle, with the destructive bolts of Jupiter clutched in its talons, now exchanged the implements of war for Apollo's lyre.

Engel well knew that the impetus for Coolidge's recent gift to the Library could be traced to that moment in 1922 when he dropped into the mail a simple thank-you note after the fifth Berkshire Festival. That such a simple gesture should lead to a $500,000 gift to the American public seemed nothing short of a miracle.

The degree of Coolidge's trust in Engel's judgment is attested by her letter to him written even before the transaction of the trust was accomplished. "As I told you, I have a strong feeling of preference for remaining out of the contracts or signatures beyond which I have already given."[2] It is a further measure of her confidence in him that she sailed for Europe in the summer of 1925, leaving him to superintend the building project as well as to plan the dedication concerts of the first festival. However deprived of her companionship he may have felt, posterity can only be grateful for the distance separating them, for it occasioned an outpouring of letters that document every detail of progress in the building as well as preparations for the festival. By May Engel could report that: "The building is growing visibly. The wooden structure for the ramp is erected; the outline for the stage is discernible. Four steel girders rise to heaven like the legs of a huge up-turned animal. The conduits for the lights are laid, the pouring of the concrete has begun. The outer wall is up to the height of the lobby. . . . The contractor in person is here every day and all day long, to supervise the whole."[3]

Within days of Elizabeth's letter of intent Engel penned a long and ebullient response describing his dream of an auditorium, from the most practical aspects of construction down to the finest detail of ornament. It was his idea that the hall should be constructed in an existing courtyard, thus utilizing in part already standing walls and also conserving heat. He envisioned a hall larger than the Freer Auditorium, seating about 600, beautifully appointed and opening onto a courtyard with topiary trees and flowering plants supplied by the nearby botanical gardens. The stage would be circular in shape, the interior walls would be painted by none other than John Singer Sargent, and the foyer should be adorned by a bas-relief of Elizabeth.[4]

While the building project moved rapidly forward, details for the festival performances weighed heavily on Engel. He was well aware that the notoriety of the occasion demanded a well-oiled performance, and no detail of the preparations was too minute to escape his meticulous attention. Quite apart from the business of selecting the repertoire to be performed there were serious concerns that some of the works commissioned for the occasion would possibly not be finished on time, that the organ installation would not be completed, and that certain composers' requirements for a larger instrumentation would exceed the budget for the festival. It fell to him to prod or to cajole—whatever the circumstances required. That he did so with great tact and sensitivity is suggested when Elizabeth remarked, "I . . . greatly admire the *politesse* with which you can utter a firm 'NO' and feel more and more glad that I can put part of this disagreeable duty on to your shoulders."[5]

There were also housekeeping-type concerns that required Engel's attention: the delicate matter of the guest list in a city where both diplomatic protocol and social register dictated decorum, the selection of the

Bas-relief in the foyer of the Coolidge Auditorium at the Library of Congress, executed by Brenda Putnam, daughter of Herbert Putnam, Librarian of Congress

Library of Congress

right furniture for the stage, and the training and rehearsing of stage-hands and ushers—to all of which he attended personally. Despite the demands on his time and energy, he sent nearly daily reports to Elizabeth in Italy and she, not surprisingly, responded gratefully but in her candid way continued to issue long-distance demands that did not make his life any easier.

One of the most valuable by-products of their correspondence is the revelation of his perspicacity as a critic, and the genteel, yet fearlessly accurate, way that he could lay the scalpel to the flesh of a swollen ego. John Erskine once said of him "I know of no other musical criticism written in America today which is so thoughtful or so scholarly, or which implies a taste so discriminating."[6] Engel was too much the gentleman ever to offend in his published critical essays, but his judgments of talent and/or temperament, shared with Elizabeth in the privacy of their letters, were vivid—sometimes verging on mordent—and were communicated with a freshness suggesting that they may have been penned in the wake of altercations with performers. The freedom with which he shared (and Elizabeth received) these often unvarnished and sharp-witted observations is one more sign of their growing mutual trust.

Engel had the enviable ability to separate his appraisal of genius from his personal feelings and reactions to the temperamental behavior of some of the artists with whom he worked. The creation of harmless nicknames for such individuals, shared only with Elizabeth, appears to have been the buffer that enabled him to carry on. Thus William Kroll, whom he admired greatly but at first found prickly to deal with, becomes in their correspondence, "artful William" or sometimes "Prince William of Orange."

Engel's tolerance was stretched to the limit when, despite his misgivings about working with the ultrasensitive Ernest Bloch, he wrote to Coolidge suggesting that Bloch conduct his own concerto for the Festival of 1926: "I have in mind that it would please Bloch very much to be thus distinguished by an invitation (while the distinction would really be all on our side if he accepts)." That he was fully aware of the possible consequences is clear from his reminder that "You and I know his genius and his shortcomings. The latter, however, are as nothing compared with the first."[7]

Coolidge agreed with the proposal, and in March Engel wrote to say that he had just sent off to Bloch the Marcello and Mozart scores that would be included on the program, adding, "I am quite prepared to have him tell me all sorts of dreadful things about either of them. It would not be natural if he didn't. But I'm prepared to stand my ground."[8] By June, however, his patience was wearing thin when he reported to her: "Imagine that just about a week ago I received one of those characteristic telegrams from Bloch throwing over the whole concert, skidding out from under his agreement, pleading depression, 'artistic conscience,' and what not. I was truly infuriated and almost beside myself. I shall not bore you. . . . You know Bloch as well as I do. He can't stand the Malipiero number and had faults to find with Marcello and Mozart. In short he is more Catholic than the Pope."[9] Engel's sharing of such frustrations with Coolidge seems to have been something of a safety valve, for at least in this case the performance did go through without incident.

Not all of his criticisms were negative, however. He was constantly on the lookout for young talent and was usually unerring in his perception of it. This is born out by his enthusiastic predictions of a brilliant career for a young pianist whose technique he found brilliant and pedaling masterful. He reported to Elizabeth, "probably as he grows older and riper, that certain indefinable something will get into his playing which will make him truly great."[10] That young artist was the twenty-three-year-old Vladimir Horowitz. Nor did he shrink from criticizing such a seasoned and respected performer as Paderewski, whom he heard at the White House in 1928. To Coolidge he commented, "[H]e still plays louder than any other pianist alive."[11]

His uncanny discernment of character sometimes rescued Elizabeth from employing artists that he knew would not work well together. When Coolidge suggested hiring Wanda Landowska for one of her festivals in which cellist Guglierma Suggia was also to play, Engel responded that "it would have whetted my appetite to the keenest edge to see what two such remarkable women like Landowska and Suggia would have done if left on stage to fight it out among themselves."[12] But undoubtedly his most heartfelt warning of possible disaster came in 1926 in response to Coolidge's suggestion to employ Ravel, who had proven temperamental in their dealings the previous year. The urgency of Engel's entreaty rings loud and clear despite the elaborate wordplay: "Hear my cry and attend unto my prayer. Do not at this late and critical hour ravel up matters with Ravel! I have still a good deal of unraveling to do before we can attack the ravelin." He facetiously suggested that if she wished to spend the extra money on Ravel they might as well have Gauthier too. "That would make a three ring circus; we could probably get even some of the New York critics to come over for the occasion and watch 'em do the 'death-leap.' But no Ravel at the Festival."[13]

Elizabeth, too, was refining her critical skills. When Engel suggested a completely English program for the second concert of the opening festival she hesitated, reminding him of the strong English presence at her sixth Berkshire Festival, which she described as "too much of Albion at Pittsfield."[14] And when Ernest Bloch began to compose music intended to pay homage to his adopted country she wrote: "I like him best when he is himself, a Jewish Prophet (the last of the Old Testament line) and feel that his inspiration from David and Solomon is more vital and inevitable than that which he has adopted from Abraham Lincoln and Walt Whitman."[15]

The selection of artists and repertoire for the festivals involved a comfortable give-and-take and letters reveal some prejudices on the part of both. Engel, an acknowledged gourmet, sometimes likened program planning to menu-making, noting that "our ears and our stomachs have physical limitations. They must be wooed by contrasts and blends and we all know that while we enjoy a substantial one course meal . . . better than anything else, the nicely planned dinner consisting of several courses should be so devised that morsels exquisitely prepared give us the same satisfaction we would have from simpler and more substantial fare."[16]

The question of selecting repertoire for the dedication concert became a sensitive issue, for Elizabeth's choices were undeniably influenced by family alliances and personal attachments to certain friends whose merits and suitability Engel had the temerity to challenge. He voiced his objections. "I cannot say that the first program standing, Casella, Jacobi, Stock strikes me as an ideal one. . . . I understand and appreciate the reasons that prompted you to put Jacobi and Stock on the first program. Moreover, you had already promised them to produce their works on this occasion."[17]

Engel had no argument with her commissioning of Loeffler to write his *Cantico del frate sole,* for Loeffler was a major talent and a close friend of his as well. But he had serious reservations about Jacobi's *Two Assyrian Prayers,* which had won honorable mention in the seventh Berkshire Competition in 1924. His reason had to do more with his belief that the work was not fully suited to chamber music; that "the music would stand a full orchestration . . . and [its] oriental or barbaric splendor would be expressed more convincingly by all the resources of the modern orchestra."[18]

He argued instead for a greater American presence on the program, pressing for inclusion of one of Chadwick's quartets. "I believe that our first program would gain by the inclusion of at least one good Anglo-Saxon name; and if that happens to belong to . . . the dean of native American composers, we can hardly lay ourselves open to criticism."[19] In the end Elizabeth prevailed and Jacobi and Stock remained on the program. The official dedication of the auditorium with the first Library of Congress Festival consisted of five concerts, beginning on 28 October 1925 and ending on her birthday, 30 October, thus establishing the tradition of Founder's Day.

Inevitably there arose the question of whether to open the festival with an invocation by the chaplain of Congress. Coolidge summarily settled the matter saying that she felt Loeffler's beautiful setting of St. Francis's "Canticle of the Sun" was "surely a more exultant hymn of praise and devotion than would be likely to issue from the Senate or the House of Representatives."[20] So the first concert opened with a Bach chorale played by organist Lynwood Farnam at the new Skinner organ, followed without break by the Loeffler piece sung by Madame Povla Frijsh. The Stock and Jacobi works followed, and the concert was rounded off by the Handel Organ Concerto in F, op. 4, no. 4.

The second concert was devoted entirely to music of Beethoven, and the third was a program by the English Singers performing mainly classic madrigal repertoire spiced by a few folk song arrangements of Vaughn Williams and Holst. The third day opened with a varied but all-Italian program featuring works of Caldara, Boccherini, and one of

Elizabeth's new Italian friends, Pizzetti. The last of the five concerts included quartets of Howard Hanson and Debussy and ended with Schubert's monumental Quintet in C, op. 163. The concerts were attended by many notables of the musical world, as well as by Grace Coolidge, the wife of the president who, on this occasion at least, might have been designated "the other Mrs. Coolidge."

The Library of Congress programs are in sharp contrast to those of the Freer Gallery the preceding year, which were much more heavily weighted in favor of twentieth-century works. It would appear that Coolidge and Engel took to heart Putnam's advice, especially regarding the first evening. Engel conveyed to her the Librarian's belief that "it would be dangerous to let modern music occupy too large a place on it. Our audience that first night will be necessarily more 'official' than at the other concerts."[21]

So the three contemporary works performed the first evening were safely framed by Bach at the head and Handel at the conclusion. It is not surprising that some critics still found too great a "left-wing" presence on the concert. Even Richard Aldrich, writing for the *New York Times,* found the Handel concerto at the end "like a soothing balm after too much modernity."[22] As expected, it was the contemporary compositions that provoked the severest criticism. The reviewer for the *Washington Herald* declared Howard Hanson's quartet "devoid of form and harmony . . . [having] passages of some beauty which but emphasized the many measures of riotous noises," whereas the Debussy quartet which followed showed "only a little chaos."[23] Aldrich at least made some allowance for Pizzetti's trio, which showed that "he has not sold his Italian birthright of melody for a mess of modern pottage in the shape of atonality, polytonality, and haughty disdain of tunefulness."[24] At least some progress had been made since the recent review that identified the composer as Mr. Pizzicato.

Boston music lovers reacted with an understandable tinge of regret at the migration of the Coolidge festivals from Pittsfield to Washington—from the austere simplicity of the Temple at South Mountain in its sylvan setting, to what Henry Taylor Parker described as Washington's "insatiable maw of bureaucracy." This may explain why Loeffler, who was a great favorite among Bostonians, was on this occasion sharply criticized by Parker, who found his scores more interesting "when he was pagan and decadent" than when "he practices tonal pieties."[25] The reference is to Loeffler's earlier and very successful *Pagan Poems* and *The Devil's Villanella.*

Although the venue of the festival would be moved to Washington, Pittsfield was hardly dispossessed. Elizabeth appointed Willem Willeke to assume the direction of music activities at South Mountain, and there were already rumors that a festival was planned for there the following year. This, in fact, did not occur until 1928, but in the meantime under Willeke's able management South Mountain remained, for the time being, a vital musical establishment.

The reactions of the critics and public alike must have served to remind Engel of Sonneck's warning that "Washington is not Boston, artistically or musically." Although Sonneck believed that Washington had improved musically since he went there in 1902, Engel was painfully aware that the capital city was not yet entirely out of the swamp. As he set about planning for the next festival, Engel penned a note to Elizabeth that clearly reflects his awareness of the delicate balance required to navigate a course between genuine audience education on the one hand and capitulation to popular taste on the other. To complicate matters, the demand for employing more local performers also arose. His response was unequivocal. "I am the last one to suggest that the Library act as a musical incubator for unripe talent or engage in charity to second-rate musicians. Nor have I the least intention of waxing unduly warm over faint lights merely because they are 'local.'" Then reverting to his favorite gastronomic metaphors, he defended his position with regard to programming. "I have no fear that to pass out occasionally a few slices of coarse but wholesome bread—*entre caviar et perdrix*—will necessarily misrepresent our aims!" Clearly he perceived the musical community of Washington to be "still in a formative stage, like stomachs that would be better nourished by bread than by delicacies."[26]

However uncomprehending the musical public of Washington must have seemed to Engel at the time, Elizabeth was never discouraged by reviews. Her only reaction to the newspaper clippings that Engel sent to her was amusement at the lack of perception on the part of people who should know better, and determination to continue to provide the best in chamber music—not only to the capital city—but to the entire nation through the efforts of the Coolidge Foundation.

Within its first season the Coolidge Auditorium at the Library of Congress hosted twenty-five programs of chamber music, and the Foundation began its outreach program by sponsoring performances in New York, Boston, Cleveland, Chicago, San Francisco, and Los Angeles. Without a doubt one of the most important early innovations of the Foundation was its introduction of broadcast concerts. At the time of the first festival Washington newspapers announced that the Arlington Navy Radio Station, NAA, would go on the air with entertainment for the first time. "[M]arking an innovation in their work of this kind, [it] will broadcast the fall festival inaugurating the Chamber Music Auditorium at the Library of Congress in Washington. . . . Both the Radio Corporation of America and American Telephone and Telegraph Co. are endeavoring to share the broadcasting privileges."[27] However, the Navy station was simply not equipped to undertake work of this character, and although the attempt was commendable, the results were disappointing. Nevertheless, when newspapers announced the following year that the festival would not be broadcast, music lovers loudly expressed their disappointment.

Meanwhile the work of the Foundation was gathering momentum, adding to its activities scholarly lectures presented by such first-rate musicologists as Dom Anselm Hughes, Charles Sanford Terry, and Edmund Fellowes. It was Engel's wish to publish these lectures, for he believed that "it is through the printed word—no matter how small the word—so long as it is the right word, that the Elizabeth Sprague Coolidge Foundation can reach into every nook and corner of the country and make itself felt abroad."[28] He mused that over the course of the years a modest accumulation of fine papers that would result from such a program might be published in a collection. Although this never came to fruition, Coolidge did contribute generously to other substantial musicological endeavors, and the work of the Foundation unquestionably became a major factor in the general music education of the American public.

In 1928 Elizabeth turned her efforts to Pittsfield and offered another Berkshire Festival, the eighth, which featured a newly re-formed Berkshire Quartet as well as the South Mountain Quartet and Elshuco

Trio.[29] In 1929 the venue returned to the Library of Congress with a varied program highlighted by an evening of Americana, including Negro spirituals and folk music arrangements of John Jacob Niles. No festival was held in either Pittsfield or Washington in 1930. Instead, Coolidge mounted a truly memorable festival in her hometown of Chicago.[30]

In the period following the establishment of the Foundation, Elizabeth traveled a great deal, spending several months of each year in Cambridge near her son and his family, several in California where she claimed her hearing improved, and also returning nearly every summer to Europe, where she was not only scouting for talent and sponsoring festivals, but was also adding to the ever growing circle of musical friends. She always traveled with a maid, who frequently had to double as secretary and nurse, and she sometimes took her car and her chauffeur. When her grandchildren were old enough to appreciate the experience, each of them was given an opportunity to go with Gram.[31] Her grandson, Dr. John C. Coolidge, recalls that immediately upon boarding ship Gram went straight to bed and remained there for the entire voyage, managing things from her stateroom. Though she loved motoring, she never learned to drive, and also resisted Engel's attempts to convince her of the merits of air travel.

On his frequent trips to Europe, Engel too was on the alert for talent. One of his most significant contacts occurred during the summer of 1927, when he met with Stravinsky and offered him a commission to compose a ballet for the next festival. The terms of the agreement as spelled out in Engel's letter to Elizabeth are representative of the standard procedure followed for her commissions. The contract established performance rights—in this case providing for exclusive performance (for North America only) during a period of six months from the date of the first performance and without payment for the use of the orchestral material. In addition it stipulated that the Library of Congress was to have the world premiere of the work. Certain parameters were laid out in order to control length and instrumentation, and the subject of the ballet was to be a story of the composer's choice. As always, the autograph manuscript was to remain in the collection of the Library of Congress, with the understanding that it should not be copied. The result was Stravinsky's *Apollon Musagète*.[32]

Although the agreement specified that the piano score was to be ready by mid-February of 1928 and the full score one month later, when February came and Engel still did not know even the title of the work, and had not heard from Paris in reply to his cable asking for the scenario and costume requirements, his patience was running out. The situation was exacerbated by the fact that he had to learn the title of the ballet by reading it in the *Musical Standard*, from which he also discovered that the instrumentation of the piece was for strings only. He complained to Elizabeth, "It is rather strange that this intelligence should reach us through a British magazine rather than directly through the composer or the composer's man of affairs."[33] Although Stravinsky was neither the first nor the last to be dilatory in fulfilling a commission, his delays contributed to a collection of problems that prompted Engel to describe the 1928 festival as "the most Michelinesque yet."[34]

This first Coolidge Festival to include dance music was conducted by Hans Kindler, with musicians from the Philadelphia Orchestra. Despite a fine performance the piece was not well received, and critics were harsh in their assessment of the Stravinsky work. Lawrence Gilman, writing for the *New York Tribune*, found it "a preposterous medley of styles, a tonal *olla podrida* without substance or flavor, lukewarm, thin, unnourishing. Bits of Handel, Gounod, Wagner, Bellini, Delibes, Johann Strauss and fragments of a dozen other of Stravinsky's predecessors out of different centuries, float to the surface, disappear, reappear. The music is without coherence, without integrity of style. Trite, feeble, amorphous, it is the most vapid and pointless utterance we have ever had from this unpredictable genius." In short, he questioned, "Is it a thing to resent as an affront or to weep over as the maundering of a once fecund and vigorous musical brain, which only last year gave us so superb a thing as the *Oedipus Rex?*"[35]

If it proved anything, the Stravinsky performance demonstrated that the Coolidge Auditorium lent itself well to small-scale staged musical productions. From the very beginning artists and audiences alike commented on the excellent acoustics and sight lines of the Coolidge Auditorium. Its size—just over 500 seats—and the rake of the auditorium floor were perfect for chamber music, but the audiences clamoring for entrance often exceeded the capacity of the hall. Although the concerts were free, tickets were required to help control the crowds. These were at first handed out at the Library but in June of 1928 the *Daily News* announced that beginning with that season tickets would be distributed by the T. Arthur Smith Concert Bureau at a nominal service charge of twenty-five cents.

In response to Elizabeth's vehement objection to even this insignificant charge, Engel attempted to explain that "the constant demands for preferential treatment, the wrangling with disappointed applicants and the nervous strain of coping with these conditions made the work a nuisance rather than a pleasure." He believed that the procedure "would not deter the real music lovers from among 'our swells' who now clamor for admission because they think the concerts 'fashionable.'"[36] The idea of tickets, even at such a modest fee, was contrary to Elizabeth's original insistence that the concerts she supported should always be free. Engel, on the other hand, had to deal with the reality of complaining clientele. His overriding concern, however, had more to do with the danger that with the concerts the Foundation might be catering to an elitist group. He wrote strongly of this to Elizabeth: "The longer I watch the purely social influence of the work of the Foundation, the more I am impressed that it is not commensurate with the aims we have set ourselves. . . . [A]s a means of providing 500 Washingtonians (and always more or less the same group) with a few free concerts of chamber music during the winter, the Foundation is not really functioning as it should. . . . Our public consists of many most appreciative listeners; but not a few of them do not require philanthropy or free concerts. . . . I am not satisfied that . . . this is the best we can do."[37]

He likened the role of the Foundation to that of the U.S. Bureau of Standards—a kind of experimental laboratory that "can justify such attempts as may involve (perhaps not always successfully) encouragement of native composers."[38]

This issue of promoting American composers had come up repeatedly in the earliest years of the Foundation, with the foreign-born Engel championing American talent, and the American-born Coolidge steadfastly adhering to a policy that promoted the *best* talent available, which to her usually meant European. The matter came to a head in 1926 in the exchange of letters stating their respective viewpoints. They document not only the disagreement, but also the degree of mutual respect that allowed for such frank dissent and argument. Each asked the other to destroy the letter but, luckily for posterity, neither did. Elizabeth's manifesto came first and clearly was prompted by an earlier conversation on the subject of Americanism: "I should feel as you do about 'America first' in any government undertaking . . . were it not that my idea of service to America does not fully embrace the Monroe Doctrine. In other words, it seems to me that one of our highest needs in this country is of an honest reverence for quality; the only way to know and revere musical quality is to hear it. So, it seems to me a more patriotic thing to supply the best than to protect the national 'infant industry,' and really, in the end, the *only* way to develop Art."[39]

Engel's response was written within a half hour of receiving her letter, which he called an inspired document: "From the heart it came and to the heart it has gone. . . . I knew you would understand and always will. . . . The Library is part of America's machinery [and] as such it has certain special responsibilities towards America, but *not* in an exclusive sense." He was fond of reminding her that he was born and bred European. "But my sense of loyalty to the country that has given me an opportunity to serve what I love best in the world, is stronger than any congenital affinities of taste, culture and art." He harbored a deep-seated skepticism that too much internationalism might be a decidedly weakening influence. "Nothing will further the ideal brotherhood of men—and women—as will a kinship of ideals. And of all the ideals that I know, none has the universality of appeal that belongs to the arts, particularly to the art of music." Although as a government official he was keenly aware of his obligation to American music, he was quick to warn that it did not "mean necessarily 'Hear America First, foremost, and solely!' That is the motto of cheap and superficial . . . agitators who live by advocating a false brand of patriotism."[40]

In time each of them mellowed to some extent, and Elizabeth acknowledged that she was "learning to see around the corner" a bit more. She had, by her own admission, come to recognize the Library for what it was intended to be, not specifically a musical agent, but part of America's machinery. Indeed, she became indignant when Alma Wertheim spoke out in the *New York Times,* criticizing the Coolidge competition for neglecting American composers and talent. The tone of Elizabeth's reaction suggests the degree to which the accusation rankled her: "I wonder if Miss Wertheim realizes how I have almost at the point of the bayonet insisted upon American works in Boston and in Europe. The only quartet which refused me this favor in Boston was an American one—the Curtis from Philadelphia. . . . Yes, I should like to say with her 'Here in this Congressional Library at least an American work.' And to this I should like to add, 'which has been able to stand competition with the music of the world and has been selected because it is great music, needing no protective tariff, nor other American propaganda to place it on its deserved pedestal.'"[41]

In 1928 the cause of American music lost a champion when Oscar Sonneck died, and to those who knew him and worked with him it was the personal loss of a stalwart friend and advocate as well. Engel, in particular, was profoundly affected by this tragedy and confided in Elizabeth, "Sonneck's death has been a severe shock to me. I am thankful that by a providential chance I was permitted to accompany him in the ambulance to the hospital and spend the hours before his operation at his bedside. . . . We can serve Sonneck's memory in no better way than by carrying on as he would have us do. I shall miss him terribly."[42]

Elizabeth's respect for Sonneck and her concern for the cause of American music were to meet in her establishment of the Sonneck scholarship for research in American music, an eminently appropriate memorial but unfortunately a dream born before its time. It is a sad testimony to the lack of interest in American music that Otto Kinkeldey, to whom she had entrusted the dispersal of the scholarship funds, was literally unable to give the money away. Finally after three years Coolidge regretfully announced that she would plan no further budget for the project.[43]

In every other respect, however, the work of the Foundation was flourishing. As it reached out to an ever-widening clientele and gained international renown, the thought occurred to Elizabeth to establish some kind of award to recognize distinguished service in the field of chamber music. Her action clearly owes much to the example of Cobbett who had honored her with the conferral of the award that he had established in 1924. She tested the idea on Engel and suggested that the medal should contain the Library's new emblem, the "Singing

Eagle."[44] Appropriately enough, the first award was given to Cobbett on Founder's Day, 1932, with the ambassador of Great Britain accepting the medal for the eighty-five-year-old Cobbett, who was unable to attend.[45]

With the Foundation now firmly established Engel joined Elizabeth in her dreams for further collaboration with the government, completing his speech before the first festival audience in Washington with the statement that "Eventually the efforts will be realized to create here a national conservatory of music. The first step has been taken; the Eagle has been made to sing!"[46]

CHAPTER THIRTEEN

Peripatetic Patron

Where we love is home, home that our feet may leave,
but not our hearts.
– OLIVER WENDELL HOLMES, *HOMESICK IN HEAVEN*

ONE OF ELIZABETH COOLIDGE'S most remarkable talents was her ability to devise and execute more than one large and complex plan at a time. Her success had much to do with her ability and willingness to delegate authority to trustworthy colleagues. No less amazing was Elizabeth's mobility. Beginning in the early twenties she was, paradoxically, at home in two worlds and at the same time at home nowhere. There were periods of time when home simply represented the state to which she paid income tax. Tracking her movements by defining her legal residence provides only the barest outline of her movements, for the greater part of her time seems to have been spent in hotels and in transit. From 1914 until 1923 she maintained the New York apartment at 850 Park Avenue that she had taken in 1914, when Fred moved there for treatment in his last illness. By 1923 she moved to the Colony Club at 62nd Street and Park Avenue—the elegant Women's' club conceived by a group of Newport ladies in the summer of 1900.

For Coolidge the Colony Club was a convenience. It is difficult to imagine her participating in roller skating or mah-jongg, recreations that were popular with the club members of the day. She very likely felt more at home with such singular personalities among contemporary Colony members as Ethel Barrymore and the cigar-smoking poetess Amy Lowell. And her ideals would certainly have been more in keeping with the interests of Mrs. August Belmont and Mrs. John De Witt Peltz, who are credited with rescuing the Metropolitan Opera during the Depression.

During her frequent and prolonged absences from New York, Elizabeth often employed the services of the Colony Club to procure tickets, forward mail, and to purchase items that she was unable to obtain elsewhere. But with the increasing demands of her travel schedule she found it necessary to change to nonresident status in 1930—which resulted in her being removed from the social register since now she neither owned nor rented a house. If she felt any regret over this action she left no record of it, only some letters registering complaints of inefficiency in taking care of mail and not sending notices of dues. She continued nonresident status until 1933, when she moved to the Meridian Mansion, a luxury apartment at 2400 16th Street, N.W., in the District of Columbia. Here she occupied a large unit that permitted her to seat as many as 200 guests at a private musicale.[1] Nonetheless, she usually referred to it as "my sweet little apartment," and she frequently offered it gratis to musician-friends who had little money and need of a quiet place to work.

Tracking Coolidge's movements in the decade of the 1920s (her mid-fifties to mid-sixties) reveals a rigorous schedule, demanding enough to tax the energies of a much younger woman. She regularly shuttled across the continent by train and sailed to Europe for several months of the year. Thanksgiving and Christmas were usually spent in Cambridge with Sprague and his family, and January found her on her way to California. Here she most frequently took a suite in the Biltmore Hotel in Los Angeles, but she also enjoyed staying in the private homes of various friends in Oakland, Santa Barbara, San Francisco, Pomona, Palo Alto, and Ojai. In late spring or early summer she sailed for Europe, often spending extra time in Italy, and by fall she returned to America, sometimes going directly to Cambridge, but often stopping in New York for various medical treatments.

Elizabeth's robust stature and phenomenal endurance belied her often fragile physical condition, the extent of which she seldom revealed. She suffered the usual ailments related to aging—digestive problems, anemia, and arthritis—and was often lonely and sometimes even suicidal.[2] Although those who worked with Coolidge were usually impressed by her stamina, it was only in private and with her family and closest friends that she revealed her vulnerability—emotional as well as physical. To Sprague she confided, "I do not wish to whine about it, but when I tell you that every day for the past three months I have had a sore throat and more or less an insistent inconvenience under my teeth, I think you will know that I am under a real nervous strain and that when the weather is bad and I am alone I am—to say the least—pretty much bored. I have at least nine weekly appointments with doctors and am beginning to wonder whether they are what ails me."[3]

Her increasing deafness drove her to seek more treatment from specialists in New York and Boston and led her on a seemingly endless search for an improved hearing apparatus. In later years her increasingly cumbersome hearing aids were never hidden from view under her voluminous scarves and sweaters but were displayed as prominently as her pearls. One of Coolidge's most endearing qualities was the open and often witty manner with which she dealt with her deafness. Of her many eminently quotable utterances perhaps the best-known is her response to a young artist who queried, "Mrs. Coolidge, why is it that you do so much for the cause of modern music and you do nothing for modern art?" She quickly responded, "Young man, I may be deaf but I'm not blind!" Despite the resolute courage that she showed in accepting the burden of her deafness, to her friends she sometimes admitted the difficulty of it. Margaret Deneke, an organist from Oxford who lectured at the Library of Congress in the late 1920s, recalled being invited to Elizabeth's apartment, where she "collected a lovely bouquet of red roses from the table and gave them to me . . . and confided in me how painful it was to be physically debarred from much conversation and from enjoying lectures. Tears came to my eyes and [she] kissed me."[4] Her letters are likewise threaded with admissions that listening to music was at times almost intolerable. Even more so, the pleasure that she derived from performing chamber music sometimes became instead a veritable torture. This is evident from her admission to Hans Kindler: "You have no idea how difficult it is to concentrate on Brahms when there is an entirely different composition roaring inside one's head, without rhythm or harmony but simply incessant noises."[5] Nevertheless, she continued to play the piano even in her last years, when she could do so only with the help of a wire that connected her hearing aid to the soundboard of the piano.

However trying the loss of hearing was for Coolidge, it was offset to some degree by the advent of grandchildren, who were a great joy to her. Letters to her closest friends are filled with news of the twin boys born in 1918 and named for their two grandfathers, Frederic Shurtleff Coolidge and John C. Coit. The arrival of baby Elizabeth in 1921 was a special joy to her, and in 1929 the family was complete with the birth of Margaret, who it seems was frightened by her grandmother, "not thoroughly realizing how harmless her ancestress can be. . . . I'm hoping that her fright at my unwonted appearance may soon calm itself."[6]

During World War I Sprague took a position in the Chemical Warfare Service in Washington, D. C. and served as an enlisted man, working on the chemical properties of activated charcoal used in gas masks. While his profession was that of scientist, his ardent avocation was that of musician. In his student days at Harvard he had been an active member of the Pierian Musical Sodality and continued throughout his life to play both the viola and the oboe, often joining in the ensembles that his mother supported whenever an added viola was needed. By 1924 Sprague had completed his doctorate in chemistry and was teaching at Harvard. Elizabeth was now sixty years old, in the throes of her plans for the Freer Gallery concerts, and experiencing not only anxiety and fatigue but also a sense of insecurity that she speaks of frankly in her letters to Sprague and Peg: "I do want . . . to keep the assurances which you both gave me when I was with you, that you would be willing, even at a sacrifice, to take your old mother away sometimes, for which I think that there is no alternative between staying here, even during bad weather, or poking off somewhere alone. I get into panics of dread which frighten away sleep and peace of mind."[7]

Such admissions of fear and weakness would probably have surprised most of her professional colleagues, who knew her only as one thoroughly in control. But these expressions of uncertainty and weakness provide some rare glimpses into the growing difficulty of balancing personal needs with her increasing professional activities. Clearly both were essential to her mental and physical health, and sometimes her choice of one over the other resulted in strained relations with her family, which had obviously been discussed in a visit to Cambridge. It was an exchange that precipitated her hasty departure for New York, from

Elizabeth reading The Wind in the Willows *to her grandchildren, the joy of her old age*

Jeffrey Coolidge Photography, Boston

where she wrote: "As I told you in Cambridge, the interest which I have in keeping well and that which I have in being near you alternate with each other in seeming the more important to me according to the keenness with which I am missing one or the other." Yet she assured him that her priority would always be devotion to family. "The interest which I have in my musical work is quite secondary to the other two, for I feel that wherever I am I can accomplish a certain amount of it even by myself, as I did at Saranac Lake." Such a frankly emotional letter seems obviously to have been prompted by some disagreement during her recent visit with her son, when the question of their separation was discussed. She admitted, "I feel rather heart broken at the conviction that it is best for us to live apart during so many months of the year, but . . . as I have always said, your career . . . should not be thwarted by the comparatively short and unimportant needs of my health and state of mind. When I am ready to give up health considerations for the sake of being near you, I know that I shall always be cherished and welcome in your family, and so shall keep that knowledge as a last resort."[8]

The periodic absence of family companionship would, in the next few years, be somewhat assuaged by the addition of a whole new circle of friends. The Berkshire Festivals had brought Elizabeth in contact with a great number of European composers and performers, many of whom remained lifelong friends. Among these one of the earliest and most cherished was Frank Bridge who, like Engel, created a nickname for her. Because Coolidge's maiden name was Elizabeth Penn Sprague, some friends called her Penny. She explained that "Bridge metamorphosed this nickname into *deux sous,* which is the French equivalent to an English penny, and I was always called 'Soucie.'"[9] Actually Bridge usually Anglicized it to Suzy and created a rhyme by signing himself variously as 2 Zee, 2ZZ, or Twosie, or sometimes writing a musical monogram, on a grand staff, with a quarter note F below the staff and a dotted half note B-flat five lines above the staff.

Coolidge was a true Anglophile, by predilection and by blood. She had already established close ties with various British performers and composers, especially Rebecca Clarke and May Mukle, and she undoubtedly knew Frank Bridge at least by reputation. It is likely that her first hearing of his music was at her own third Berkshire Festival, when Bridge's First Quartet in E Minor was performed. Their first meeting occurred in May of 1922 at a tea party at the home of Mrs. Winthrop Rogers, whose husband owned the London branch of the Schirmer publishing house.

Elizabeth seems to have responded to Bridge favorably at once, and his letters to her contained in the Library of Congress collection suggest that the attraction was reciprocated. His correspondence—almost entirely handwritten—is voluminous and often illustrated with amusing drawings, for Bridge was a gifted caricaturist. His garrulous wit reaches full throttle in his South Mountain Gazette—many pages of nonsense and drawings that are almost meaningless unless studied with the Bridge-Fass correspondence at the Britten-Pears Library in Aldeburgh, England. From that correspondence it also becomes quite clear that Bridge, and especially his wife Ethel, found Elizabeth's attentions stifling, her manner domineering, and the whole South Mountain experience draining. It is in the Bridges' letters to their friend Marjorie Fass, back in England that they revealed their real feelings, which propriety required them to restrain while they were Elizabeth's guests. Ethel's letters in particular provide the unvarnished version of their reactions to Coolidge at this early stage. In the light of later developments it is important to recognize the letters for what they were, a safe sounding board deflecting the impact of sudden encounter with so commanding—and sometimes overpowering—a personality as Coolidge.

At the Rogers tea party in 1922 Bridge shared with Elizabeth his concern that his heavy load of teaching allowed too little time to compose. She responded at once by inviting him to come and spend time composing in the quiet retreat at Pittsfield. None of her letters to him from this early period survive in the Library of Congress collection, but their content is easily discerned from his frank responses. Bridge hesitated to accept the Pittsfield invitation, giving various reasons why it was not a good idea: He would miss out on some professional opportunities at home if he were gone too long, and although the quiet of Pittsfield would provide time to write, he admitted that "new places interest me so much that I should be making holiday the whole time. . . . I know it would take me more than three months to acclimatize my brain cells to the new surroundings." However, remembering her admonition "to take tarts while they are passing them," he ventured to suggest an alternative. Would she arrange with various conductors in the United States to have some of his works performed with him conducting?[10]

She apparently had no problem with the suggestion and immediately cabled money for him and Ethel to come to the Berkshire Festival and remain as her guests for three months of touring and conducting. Her appeals to Stock, Gabrilovitsch, Stokowski, Damrosch, Monteux, and Sokoloff resulted in Bridge's conducting his own works with the Cleveland, Boston, Detroit, and New York orchestras. In addition she made a serious but unsuccessful attempt to procure a position for him at the Eastman School of Music.

Ethel Bridge's epistles to Marjorie Fass during this period are a valuable commentary on the goings-on at South Mountain as well as the course of their rocky relationship with Coolidge. She found Sprague "to be very nice. He is very abrupt, tells his mother off wonderfully and yet is so polite all the time."[11] Peg is described as "one of the nicest girls I ever met, just as free and natural and open hearted as Sprague is quiet and detached."[12] And Gertrude Watson was, in her opinion, "a perfect old pet" in contrast to "the Dowager Empress of South Mountain."[13] Frank was amused by the designation of the auditorium as the Temple and attested that "that there temple that one talks so much about is a CHAPEL!!! Believe me."[14] He wryly observed, "I foresee it is well understood by the inner and outside circle of the South Mountain habitués that there is a most careful attitude maintained about not treading on the Templar's toes."[15] The "Empressina" reigned supreme.

Elizabeth, like her mother before her, was a great believer in the therapeutic value of a ride in the country and frequently took Frank with her in her electric car, doing her best to convince him to accept her help. It seems quite evident that much of Ethel's animosity stems from her feeling of being left out on these occasions. "She doesn't ask me, rude old thing—although there's room for four easily. [T]he Dowager Empress with her imperial T-M C-T smile, [sits] high up on her leather rostrum in her seven passenger chariot."[16] From her throne she pontificates; "Susie had . . . a 'heart to hearter.' . . . She took him out for a drive and on (the matter of) François refusing everything in the way of help or patronage, it has been decided that the subject is not to be mentioned again. Of course she means it all most kindly and it is tremendously generous of her but Margot—one couldn't ever bear to feel that we'd accepted such things from anyone."[17]

Clearly Elizabeth's autocratic ways, her ordering of events for the day and then often changing at a whim, wore on the Bridges, but with the success of Frank's conducting tour—entirely arranged and paid for by Coolidge—their attitude gradually changed, and they were able to see past her imperial bearing and into the sincerity of her heart. By the time the Bridges returned to England, Frank had come to recognize the importance and value of what Elizabeth had done for them. In December he wrote, "[A]t this moment I see only your decision to help me out of the rut of my gray-haired professional existence, because you wanted to do this for me. I say only 'thank you'—you know how much this really means."[18] In the following years he was able to discontinue his burdensome teaching thanks to Elizabeth's annual birthday checks of $2,000, which he gratefully acknowledged. "I can't refrain any longer from telling you how I shall never be able to describe that sense of release or that mental freedom that has resulted from the cessation of instrumental teaching. Even now I have to pinch myself to make sure that I am not drowning."[19]

Although the Coolidge-Bridge friendship had begun a bit one-sided, it matured into an enduring relationship that resulted in some of Bridge's finest efforts, all dedicated to Elizabeth: the Second Violin Sonata, the Third and Fourth String Quartets, the Second Piano Trio, several shorter works, and an amusing homage to her "Michelinesque" endeavors with Engel, entitled "The Pneu World," a work for violoncello and piano based upon the opening bars of the Star-Spangled Banner. Eventually, Ethel too found in Elizabeth a faithful and loving friend, especially during the difficult days of World War II and at the time of Frank's death.

Elizabeth had returned to Europe in the summer of 1922 for the first time since she and Fred had gone there twenty-nine years earlier. The trip marked what would become almost an annual pilgrimage until the outbreak of World War II, and was the beginning of her love affair with Italy. There was a strong French connection among Elizabeth's new Italian friends that undoubtedly had much to do with the extension of her activities in that country as well. Casella had studied at the Paris Conservatoire and for years lived in Paris, where he became an intimate friend of Ravel and Enesco and was associated with the progressive French Independent Music Society founded by Ravel. Both Casella and Malipiero were friendly with Henry Prunières, a French musicologist and champion of new music who did much to promote the music of the new Italian school in the concerts sponsored by the *Revue Musicale*, of which he was editor. So when Elizabeth wrote to Anna Malipiero that she would be returning to Italy in March 1924 "mainly to renew friendship," she was, whether she realized it or not, adding a whole new dimension to her work, for the Casella-Malipiero-Prunières trinity of disciples would soon become facilitators of her mission.

This was the same period during which she was consciously maturing her plans for the Library of Congress. Engel remained in Washington superintending the building, managing the infant Foundation, and playing foreign correspondent for Elizabeth while she sponsored a festival in Venice, spent much time with her Italian friends, and laid plans for a larger festival in 1926. It is significant that her first thoughts of possibly dissolving the Berkshire Colony come from this year of accelerated activity both in Europe and at the Library of Congress.[20]

The sojourns of 1926 and 1927 were the occasion of many memorable events: a dinner honoring Toscanini, a meeting with Gabriele D'Annunzio, and, in 1927 alone, nine invitational concerts in six countries. Her efforts were described by the *Musical Times* of London as "an international musical crusade, one of the romances of modern music."[21] The degree of notoriety that these festivals were achieving in the foreign press is reflected in Anna Malipiero's enthusiastic announcement that the distaff side of the cognoscenti would be represented the following year, for both Alma Mahler and the Princesse de Polignac (herself an important music patron) had written of their plans to attend the next festival.

The European festival of 1927 was by far Elizabeth's most ambitious yet, involving concerts in Oxford, Amsterdam, Rotterdam, Brussels, Paris, Vienna, Prague, Berlin, and Venice. Although in the early stages of her work Coolidge sometimes employed the services of commercial concert managers, she had very little faith in them and preferred to entrust her far-flung undertakings in Europe to friends who shared her

Elizabeth enjoying her favorite pastime, "motoring," with Alphonse Onnou and Germain Prévost, first violinist and violist, respectively, of the Pro Arte Quartet

Library of Congress

ideals and had already proven their musical and entrepreneurial skills. Moreover, common sense dictated the desirability of choosing someone with established European connections and facility with languages. Much credit for the success of the 1927 tour went to the man she chose as manager and general factotum, the brilliant young Dutch cellist Hans Kindler.

Elizabeth's first association with Kindler was in 1917 when she attended a Carnegie Hall concert organized by the Society of the Friends of Music to present the works of Ernest Bloch to the American public for the first time. On that occasion Kindler gave the world premiere of Bloch's rhapsody for cello, *Schelomo.* Casals had been scheduled to perform it but had to leave the country suddenly, and Kindler, who was at the time the principal cellist of the Philadelphia Orchestra, was called upon to replace him.[22]

After six seasons with the Philadelphia Orchestra, Kindler resigned in order to establish an international career as soloist, and for the next ten years (ca. 1920–30) kept a hectic schedule of concertizing in North America, Europe, and the Far East that earned him the title "The Flying Dutchman." During one of his returns to the United States, Elizabeth was able to engage him to play at the 1924 Berkshire Festival, and the following year he made his American debut on the podium when he conducted Riegger's prize-winning *La belle dame sans merçi* at Pittsfield.[23]

Thanks to Kindler's tidy mind and meticulous bookkeeping, details of the 1927 festival tour (11 September–16 October) are the best-preserved accounts of any of her European exploits and offer an inside look at workings on the grass-roots level. Not only did the manager's responsibilities begin with the planning of the event, but they included a thorough report after the completion of the tour—not to mention sundry purely personal obligations such as meeting Elizabeth and her maid at Le Havre and helping her through customs and onto the train for Paris.

Coolidge usually preferred to dispense a lump sum of money to her manager, who was then responsible for disbursements. The initial amount to Kindler for this trip was $6,000, to which she later added substantially. From that amount he was to budget travel, artist's fees, housing, and incidental expenses. It was his responsibility to procure the performance spaces, make all of the local arrangements, and see to the printing of the programs.[24] The care with which he attended to these matters is attested by the surviving drafts of programs and even ledgers indicating artists' fees and rentals, all in Kindler's hand. Elizabeth maintained a certain amount of control over the selection of repertoire and performers, but her correspondence with Kindler contains much evidence that he often gave excellent advice on both these counts. The fact that she usually accepted his judgment speaks highly of her confidence in him. One of his greatest assets in this respect was his sensitivity to the predilection of certain ensembles for certain types of music, not to mention his acute perception of the tastes of local audiences. His skill in combining the right repertoire on a program also saved her from more than one disaster.

Another of Kindler's services to Coolidge was his recommendation that she should seek out some prominent European composers to commission. He believed that in doing so she would not only be rendering them an incalculable service but would also obviate certain inevitable risks where juries were involved, thus ensuring a consistently high quality in the works that she commissioned.[25] Bridge, too, was of the opinion that some of the dedications were not worthy of her, and Engel likewise wished that "we might learn the lesson of not buying any more cats—not even Italian ones—in the bag."[26]

So with her permission, Kindler approached one of the most notable composers of the time with an offer of 10,000 francs (about $550) for a chamber work in any form, with the usual performance rights spelled out. The result was Ravel's *Chansons Madécasses.* But there were troubles with Ravel, who was very tardy in fulfilling his commission, and when Elizabeth became irritated by his dilatory performance she enlisted the help of Prunières. "May I ask your intercession in this matter, namely, that you would represent to Mr. Ravel that I am greatly disappointed as the time goes by and he does not fulfill his promise of sending me the other two (songs) which were positively promised by the first of January and for all three of which I paid him."[27] Eventually the piece was premiered by Jane Bathori with Ravel at the piano—but only after some temperamental haggling over an additional fee for his performance. For a subsequent performance in the Netherlands he attempted to raise his fee to 1,000 guilders ($400, nearly the amount of the original commission). At that point Kindler engaged Casella to play it instead.[28]

Kindler's value as a contact with European artists and composers at this particular time cannot be exaggerated. One notable example suffices to demonstrate how his good advice resulted in one of Coolidge's most prestigious commissions. When Elizabeth suggested opening the Berlin concert with works of Bliss and Bridge, Kindler cautioned against it: "I see your point of wanting to encourage the young ones and always have loved that part of your activities especially well. At the same time, when one tackles a city of the musical importance of Berlin, it seems to me, especially for the first time there, hazardous to put in a composition as yet unwritten by a young man (Bliss) who until now has not produced a first class work, especially to start the program . . . and then to be followed by the problematical Bridge."[29]

In his opinion this would have been musical suicide. Instead he suggested asking Schönberg for a work. "[A] quartet by him would be a trump card for the concerts and a tremendous attraction."[30] At first Schönberg hesitated. He had heard that Coolidge's usual commission was $1,000 and believed he should have more. Moreover, because of his contract with his publisher, he could not fulfill her usual demand that the manuscript be turned over to her and ultimately to the Library of Congress. Unintimidated by Schönberg's reputation, Elizabeth's response to his request for more money remained a firm no: "I do not feel that we should pay an extravagant price to Mr. Schönberg unless he gives us more privileges than merely presenting him with a first class performance of his work. By this I mean that I think a souvenir copy of the work with some kind of inscription upon it, should belong to me and also that I should have the rights to first performances at least in America for a few months after receiving it. I agree with you that it would be a great addition to our programs to have his quartet, but I cannot see why we should pay him a large fee unless we have a few special privileges."[31]

Kindler agreed emphatically, "[W]here anyone ever so much as hesitates when an offer from you is concerned I feel like slamming the door on them and calling them 'you damned fool.'"[32] However, he diplomatically curbed his impulses and in a matter of weeks was able to report that Schönberg agreed to her conditions and suggested that the Kolisch Quartet should premiere the work, which he believed would require a minimum of twelve rehearsals with him in attendance. The result was his Quartet no. 3, op. 30.

It was undoubtedly Kindler's yeoman service and the skill that he manifested in interpreting contemporary music that caused Coolidge to select him to conduct the premiere of Stravinsky's *Apollon Musagète* in 1928. The degree of his gratitude and affection for her is expressed in a letter to her secretary when in December of 1928 he was unable to attend the testimonial dinner for her sponsored by the MacDowell Club in New York City. He was performing in Indianapolis that night and wrote to her secretary to say, "I regret [my absence] all the more as I love her; with no one in the musical world have I had such marvelous, stimulating, exciting and satisfying experiences as an artist, as with her—I'd cheerfully go through a fire for her, if it would be necessary, for one of her wonderful plans—and that is not just a phrase."[33] Elizabeth's response is touching: "Dear old Hans. I almost wept last night at reading the letter which you wrote to Miss Lawton instead of being present at the dinner which the MacDowell Club gave me. I missed you there but when I read that letter I [was] almost glad that you could not come for I suppose you would not have written it if you had been there in person. . . . Do you know what was the note in it which struck me first and most deeply? It was that of your affection. . . . As I told you before, Hans, you are almost like a son to me and I thank you for your willingness to play that role."[34]

Over the next few years Kindler appeared frequently at the Library both as soloist and conductor, and when Coolidge moved to Washington and Kindler became conductor of the National Symphony Orchestra, their association was even more frequent.

Coolidge's expansion of activities at this time appears almost reckless, her appetite for involvement, Lucullan. Even so, she found time and energy to devote to her personal intellectual pursuits. Wherever she stayed, even briefly, she required a piano in her room and often practiced as much as six hours a day. In the late 1920s she was performing a good deal with William Kroll, Rudolph Kolisch, and the Kolisch and the Stradivari Quartets, and during her stays in California she continued her composition studies with Domenico Brescia at Mills College. Always an avid reader, she regularly ordered books from Brentano's in New York. Her wide-ranging interests can be seen in an order of 1928 that includes such diverse titles as Henry Laidler's *Historical and Socialist Thought,* Louis Martin Sears's *History of American Foreign Relations,* Cone's *Self Mastery through Conscious Autosuggestion,* the *Fine Arts Gazette* of London, and Lady Pamela Glenconnor's biography of her son.

Through the experience of her bicoastal living Elizabeth grew very fond of wintering in California, where the climate agreed with her, her health improved, and she began to cultivate some close friendships. It is not surprising that she extended her benefactions to various colleges, universities and public libraries there, particularly in Los Angeles and the San Francisco Bay area. She was especially fond of Oakland and had strong ties with Mills College through the head of its Music Department, Luther Marchant. Mills had originated in 1852 and quickly became known for its strong music program. In 1928 the college erected a much-needed music building. Distinctly Mediterranean in design, the structure includes a 600-seat concert hall that separates the teaching rooms in the right wing from the practice rooms in the left.[35] Elizabeth's gift of a series of four gala concerts for the dedication marks the beginning of her long and fruitful association with Mills. The first concert opened with a sextet for winds and piano by Domenico Brescia, Elizabeth doing the honors at the keyboard. The piece begins with several measures for the piano alone, hence the first sounds in the new hall were hers. She admitted later what a great thrill this was to her.

At the onset of the Great Depression in 1929, Elizabeth's income was diminished, and in her efforts to retrench she curtailed the social aspects of the festivals and moved her concerts from expensive theaters and salons into the homes offered for use by her many musical friends: Toscanini, Malipiero, Casella and D'Annunzio. She reminded Sprague, "I am trying in every way to make up for the drastic reduction of my resources during the present year and anything extra on the other side of the balance is undertaken with a good deal of thought. . . . I am temporarily depriving myself of a good many of the things to which I am accustomed in order that I may not have to disappoint the people to whom I have pledged my help in the various undertakings."[36] When eventually it became necessary to cut back on her annual subsidies to Bridge, Willeke, Mills College, and the MacDowell Association, she did so only reluctantly, and set the example by first cutting her own personal budget twenty-five percent and that of her son ten percent. She undoubtedly recalled the words she had once written to Sprague: "No one should live as you and I do without devoting a part of our opportunities to the world."[37] Now she was prepared to demonstrate the sincerity of such an utterance. "I am not sorry to do my part in bringing about a general reformation, even though it involves much sacrifice. As I wrote to you before, it is not the personal sacrifice, but I did not know how deeply I cared about the musical projects which I have been able to assist."[38]

The end of the decade marked the fifth anniversary of her association with the Library of Congress and a great diversification in the work of the Coolidge Foundation. She had commissioned some outstanding compositions, had begun her pioneer work in radio, and was contemplating the establishment of a resident quartet at the Library. She believed it "would be a splendid foundation for teaching which might lead to a conservatory."[39] With that in mind she approached Alfred Pochon, second violinist of the Flonzaley Quartet, just at the time that the ensemble was disbanding and asked if he would be interested in forming a quartet that would divide its residency between the Library of Congress and Mills College and would not only perform but would also teach. This arrangement, like her desire for a national conservatory in the capital city, was one of her few dreams that would remain unfulfilled.

In many respects 1930 turned out to be a banner year. In February Engel completed arrangements with NBC to air four half-hour programs of chamber music on successive Sunday afternoons beginning in March. On the debit side, however, was the change in Engel's job at the Library of Congress that was brought about by his acceptance of the position of president of the publishing firm of G. Schirmer in New York City. Although he continued to work at the Library with an increased staff, it meant that he had to divide his time between the two places. It is clear from their correspondence that Elizabeth strongly supported his decision to accept Schirmer's offer of the position left vacant by Sonneck's death, but she was anxious at the thought of his necessary absences from the Library. Engel, however, was quick to remind her of the advantages of his presence in New York City, which had made possible his dealings with NBC and enabled him to offer a commission to Prokofiev on one of the composer's frequent visits to New York.

By midsummer of 1930 Elizabeth announced her intention to postpone her trip to Europe until after the next festival, and she bade goodbye to Engel, who was off to attend the festival of the International Society of Contemporary Music in Liège and to scout for talent. While in Paris he had the opportunity to meet Prokofiev, who played for him the quartet she had commissioned. Engel reported to Coolidge, "I must confess that it strongly appealed to me. . . . One or two little scruples that I ventured to express to Prokofiev he accepted in the kindest spirit and was apparently glad to have my frank opinion, which he seemed ready to accept. I believe we shall have a very fine work to present to the world. As you remember, it is the first string quartet that Prokofiev has written."[40]

From Los Angeles Elizabeth exchanged letters of a more personal nature with Prokofiev in which the two commiserated over their respective dental problems. On that subject she wrote more forthrightly to Engel, "I have not a single tooth left in my upper jaw. A marvelously handsome set is being manufactured for me."[41] Although her toothless condition kept her from going out, she had no hesitation in inviting the Pro Arte Quartet to come and play for her. "I am sure that such good friends as you . . . have always been to me, will not mind seeing me under this great disadvantage—for I simply cannot bear to have you leave Los Angeles without seeing you and hearing you."[42] There is plenty of evidence that friendship and musical considerations always prevailed over vanity.

She once broke her earphone and badly bruised her ear when she tripped over a double bass, and the side of her head had to be shaved. In response to Bridge's concern she wrote, "I am touched by your inquiries about my head and hair. I have now accumulated a 'fringe' which is neither one thing nor the other. It is too long and bristly to be successfully hidden, and too short to be caught in with the rest and made to know its place. However, as you know, I do not base my friendships or affection upon my beauty, and feel that you will be just as glad to see me as though I had a perfectly satisfactory permanent wave."[43]

It seems appropriate that the two major events that marked the beginning of the new decade should symbolize the poles of her heightened activity on both sides of the Atlantic. From Europe came the news that Paul Claudel had nominated Elizabeth to be named a Chevalier of the National Order of the Legion of Honor of France.[44] The news thrilled her, for this was indeed a great distinction. Riding on the crest of the announcement she mounted on the home front her most ambitious American festival to date.

Although Coolidge had become something of a musical gypsy in the 1920s she always and emphatically acknowledged Chicago as her hometown. So it is not surprising that when she decided to produce a festival in the place of her birth, no expense or effort was spared to make it special. Chicago papers heralded the event as the greatest gathering of musical celebrities that the city had ever seen. The red carpet was rolled out for its illustrious daughter and The Cliff Dwellers, Onwentsia, and Arts Club vied with one another in honoring her at sumptuous dinners and receptions.

Elizabeth reserved an entire floor of the Stevens Hotel for thirty-three guests—all of them eminent musicians—who had gathered at her request (and her expense) from both coasts of America and various parts of Europe as well. Although she had assembled some of the world's finest artists for the occasion, she was disappointed not to be able to present the Cortot-Thibaud-Casals Trio, as she had planned. And because of scheduling conflicts her efforts to obtain the service of Fritz Kreisler also came to naught. He was, in fact, appearing at Orchestra Hall in Chicago on the very day that her festival began. Nonetheless, she could feel justifiably pleased that out of the five concerts given in Simpson Auditorium of the Field Museum, fifteen of the twenty-four works performed were composed for her. In addition, a number of the performers on the program were making their first American appearances. Among them were the Brosa Quartet of London, the German pianist Emma Lübbecke-Job, and the English pianist Harriet Cohen, who brought along her Bechstein concert grand piano.

Coolidge scheduled a performance of Malipiero's *Ritrovari* in the hope that she could lure the composer and his wife to attend the festival, for this would be the first American performance of the composition and the Malipieros had never been in the United States. She did her best to convince him to leave Asolo, where he lived like an oyster attached to its rock. She wired $1,000 for transportation and offered to meet them in New York with tickets for Chicago, but to no avail. It was typical of Malipiero who, according to his wife, "wants to travel . . . but it is a nervous condition that he cannot overcome when he is face to face with a journey or any change."[45] Despite the fact that they did not come, Elizabeth instructed them to keep $500 of the sum she had sent.

Disappointments notwithstanding, the festival was a grand occasion highlighted by the performance of a work by Paul Hindemith commissioned for the event. For one nervous moment, that too nearly went awry. Elizabeth had first of all invited Hindemith to participate in the festival, and he had politely but firmly declined, claiming that his concert schedule would not permit it, though it is possible that he may still have harbored strong feelings about the failure of his entries in the Berkshire competitions of 1920 and 1922. So Coolidge then made him an offer of a commission so tempting that he could hardly refuse: She invited him to compose a concerto for piano and chamber orchestra. He warmed to the prospect but replied that her usual offer of $1,000 was not sufficient. He would do it only if paid 10,000 marks (about $2,385). She agreed, and sweetened the deal by suggesting that Hindemith's good friend Emma Lübbecke-Job should be the soloist. The piece would be conducted by the very able Hugo Kortschak, who was dispatched to Frankfurt in the summer to confer with composer and soloist.[46]

Hindemith did not come to the festival but he was well represented by Lübbecke-Job, who received high praise for her artistry. The concerto and two of Hindemith's other works were performed on the opening program, alternated with three works by Bach. The juxtaposition of these two German contrapuntists on the same program was a brilliant idea and was not lost on the Chicago critics. But by and large the response to Hindemith's works was cool, and Felix Borowski, writing in the *Christian Science Monitor,* observed, "It cannot be said . . . that Bach's fame has been materially dimmed by the three compositions of his modern rival that were set forth at this music making."[47] *Musical America*'s Arthur Goldberg believed the experiment "left both gentlemen about where they were before."[48]

The contemporary works in general were not well received. Malipiero's *Ritrovari* was dubbed "obscure," and Glenn Dillard Gunn of the *Chicago Herald Examiner* found these new works like those of the modernist painters "busy with squares, angles, dividers and other instruments of geometric precision, working out new patterns." And as if to excuse the lack of the public's comprehension (not to mention his own) he compared the affair to a recent blunder at the Art Institute, where a modern picture had mistakenly been hung upside down. "They thought they had it right. . . . So it is . . . with modern music of the polytonal school."[49]

Although the opinions of critics never bothered Elizabeth, she had taken care in this case to provide informed coverage by someone eminently well qualified to review her work. Not long before the festival Henry Prunières had written to her asking help for his beleaguered *Revue Musicale.* Because she was already financially stretched by her commitment to the Chicago festival, she was not able to help him with an outright donation. It was typical of Elizabeth, however, not to capitulate to circumstances easily, and so she found an ingenious solution. From the money already budgeted for the festival she could pay Prunières to come as music critic, thus helping him and his journal and at the same time obtaining international publicity for her festival. She was richly rewarded by his intelligent reviews in *Le Figaro, Journal des Débats, Candide, Le Temps, La Revue Musicale,* and the *Frankfurter Zeitung.*[50]

Her hometown had welcomed her warmly, and she in turn had given graciously to it. The critic of the *Chicago Post* perhaps summed it up best. "What she is so freely giving, our people are joyously accepting, spirit meeting spirit with sympathetic understanding. Such things actually do happen in this world."[51] It had been a grueling schedule and at the same time a kind of love feast with the city she called home. And now it was time to rest—but only briefly.

CHAPTER FOURTEEN

Donna Elizabetta

Open my heart, and you will see
Graved inside it, Italy.
– ROBERT BROWNING, *DE GUSTIBUS*

FRANK BRIDGE ONCE quipped that he should address his letters to Elizabeth "ESC—the earth," for by her patronage she had truly become a citizen of the world. That she was American by birth and English by blood, there is no contesting, but it could surely be said that she was Italian by adoption, for she loved Italy and spent some of her happiest and healthiest times there. It is possible that this romance with Italy was engendered as early as her first trip to Europe with her parents in 1882, for her diary is filled with exuberant descriptions: from Carnival in Rome—where bands paraded and people pelted one another with flowers—to romantic scenes of Venice with music wafting out over the lagoon as musicians played from gondolas illumined by lanterns.

Whether consciously or not, Italy had made a deep impression on her as a girl, and it was now fast becoming the lodestone of her European existence. Here she cultivated a circle of close friends to whom she was drawn for rest and relaxation after her strenuous tours. The warm weather and sense of well-being that she enjoyed there made her contemplate wintering in Italy, and although her letters make frequent reference to it she never did so, mainly because of the worsening political situation there.

The major expansion of Coolidge's efforts in Europe occurred during the 1920s and early 1930s, coinciding exactly with the rising tide of Fascism and Nazism. It is tempting to speculate to what extent she was aware of the political turmoil brewing in Europe. Her interest in politics sometimes surfaced in her letters to friends, and we know that she was an avid reader of works on history, diplomacy, socialism, and democratic ideals. She was fiercely democratic in her thinking if not in party alliance, for the Spragues had always been staunch Republicans. So it comes as something of a surprise that when asked in later years if she would vote Republican, she responded emphatically, "No, I am not a republican and, in fact, many years of living in Washington (which as you know, has no franchise) have got me into the habit of watching other people vote; but if I ever should cast another vote, it would not be for the GOP."[1]

It was in 1922, the very year that Coolidge returned to Europe after an absence of nearly three decades, that Mussolini formed his Fascist government. Elizabeth could certainly be forgiven if she failed to see the direction in which things were developing in these early years. So did many of the more politically enlightened. It had much to do with what has been described as Mussolini's chameleonlike ability to "adapt his act to the audience of the moment."[2] For the time being Il Duce's dreams of building another Roman Empire had succeeded in bringing a degree of prosperity to the country. It was only later when Italy's aggression became apparent that Elizabeth reacted and spoke out unequivocally against the situation. She had often voiced her opposition to war and arms, and when her attorney sought means to lessen her income tax in order to free more money for her philanthropic work, she was delighted and responded, "I feel that every dollar that is so diverted will be like converting battle ships into good concerts and thereby adding to our nation's resources in, what seems to me, a more desirable manner."[3] She perceived her artistic endeavors as helping to build a marvelous common bond between nations and cultures, in her words, a kind of "Musical League of Nations."

There is a certain grim irony in the concurrence of events that mark Coolidge's efforts for the cause of musical brotherhood as they move apace with the steady and ominous advance of totalitarianism. Only weeks after her first European festival in Rome in 1923, Hitler attempted his famous Beer-Hall Putsch in Munich. Two years later, as the finishing touches were being made on the Coolidge Auditorium, he published the first volume of *Mein Kampf*, and in the year of her Oxford and Venice festivals (1926) the youth movements—*Ballilla* in Italy and *Hitlerjugend* in Germany—were formed.

Her gravitation toward Italy at this time should not be thought of as a turning away from Belgium, Germany, and Austria, where she continued to sponsor many wonderful concerts: It had more to do with friendship. Of the treasured memories of her time in Italy, one that stands out above all others is her meeting with the poet, playwright, novelist, and expatriate Gabriele D'Annunzio. Although she did not actually meet him until 1928, their association dates from the Roman festival of 1923, when it may be said that they became partners of sorts in an endeavor that was bound to speak to Elizabeth's heart—the cause of contemporary music.

Alfredo Casella was actually the facilitator in this relationship. While living in Paris from 1896 to 1915 he made friends with such progressive French intellectuals as Jean Cocteau and *Les Six*. He was present at the riotous premiere of Stravinsky's *Rite of Spring* in 1913, and when Ravel founded a dissident group of musicians in opposition to what he saw as the exclusivity of the Schola Cantorum, Casella joined. One of the most enthusiastic members of the group was his compatriot, D'Annunzio, who had come to France in 1910 as a "voluntary exile." He had, in fact, fled to escape his many creditors, for he was a riotous spendthrift.

When Casella returned to Italy in 1915, full of enthusiasm for the avant-garde, it was with the avowed intention of being a "Trojan horse" to introduce similar action in his own country, which he considered to be still backward and provincial in its taste, and too bound to nineteenth-century melodrama. He found like-minded enthusiasts in Malipiero, Respighi, Castelnuovo, and Pizzetti. With their cooperation, and the patronage of Count San Martino, Casella made several attempts to create an Italian National Music Society.[4] The venture was shortlived, but the flame was rekindled in 1923. At that time he spent the summer with Malipiero, who was able to gain entrée into the reclusive D'Annunzio's company. It is a mark of the poet's regard for the idea of such an association that when Casella and Malipiero requested an appointment, D'Annunzio—who did not usually receive callers or even open his mail—granted an immediate audience. His response to

Casella's plans was enthusiastic, but being habitually poor, he could give little more than his name and some completely unrealistic suggestions for raising money by exacting contributions from the Italian Merchant Marines, of whom he was nominally the head. The sailors, not surprisingly, showed little interest. An angel was needed.

Casella's account of Elizabeth's involvement in the scheme implies that by some marvelous clairvoyant communication she knew of their needs and miraculously sent money, like manna in the desert. The actual story is much more pedestrian. Casella simply wrote to Coolidge to tell her of the formation of the Società Italiana per la Musica Moderna (SIMM) and asked to subscribe her as a patron.[5] She accepted and immediately sent a check for $1,000 with no strings attached, thus enabling the fledgling society to sponsor in its first year ten performances of Schönberg's *Pierrot Lunaire* in seven Italian cities, with the composer conducting. For three years she supported the group which later changed its name to Corporazione delle Nuove Musiche (a name devised by D'Annunzio). In time it became the Italian arm of the International Society for Contemporary Music, which had been instituted in 1922. In the course of the following seasons her contributions helped to support concerts featuring Stravinsky's Octet and *L'Histoire du Soldat,* as well as music of Bartók, *Les Six,* and significant revivals of seventeenth-century Italian opera.[6] D'Annunzio eventually withdrew from the association but he always remained interested and in touch.

In October 1927 D'Annunzio wrote an effusive letter of thanks to Elizabeth, one of two missives from him that she always cherished. Both are flattering, cast in the rather unctuous style of which he was quite capable. Even long before that, Coolidge had expressed to Malipiero her desire to meet D'Annunzio. The sycophantic deference that Comandante D'Annunzio exacted from those who sought his favors—or even an audience—is attested by the fact that it took Malipiero several years to arrange the meeting. It was finally during her visit to Italy in the summer of 1928 that Elizabeth and the Malipieros were invited to D'Annunzio's villa, "La Vittoriale," on Lake Garda. Charmed and intrigued by D'Annunzio, Coolidge suggested that the next summer she might sponsor a concert for him at his villa, to which she would invite various friends and public figures, among them Mussolini.

Francesco assured Elizabeth that he would exert all diplomacy in carrying out her request so as not to ruffle D'Annunzio "because of all the bonds that unite me to him. It is such a delicate and difficult question that I could not approach him by letter, I must go in person and see how he feels about the matter, and I assure you that it is only for YOU and no one else that I would ever interrupt the work and go off to Gardone on the chance and hope that the door is open to me."[7]

In the same letter, Anna Malipiero expressed real enthusiasm for the idea but tactfully reminded Elizabeth that although D'Annunzio adored music, he always wanted it for himself alone. And regarding the guests, she advised, "your list is all right except in two instances: Mussolini and Respighi. Mussolini, owing to the . . . political relations existing between him and D'Annunzio, would have to be asked in a very official manner and it would be complicated. Respighi, for certain reasons relating directly to D'Annunzio (nothing to do with me or music) could not be included in any invitation to the Vittoriale. I cannot write you what these reasons are, but when I see you, I will tell you. . . . It is too delicate a question to explain more by letter."[8]

Malipiero made all the necessary arrangements, and the concert was set for 26 October 1929. The program was made up entirely of works of Monteverdi, Casella, and Malipiero. Kindler was invited to play Casella's Sonata for Cello and Piano, and he was joined by violinist William Kroll in Malipiero's Sonata *à tre.* The guest list, which had originally included (besides Mussolini) Toscanini, Alfano, Lualdi, Betti, Castelnuovo, Respighi, Pizzetti, Corti, Santoliquido, Tommasini, and Scalero, had to be abandoned. Only Elizabeth, the composers whose works were performed, the performers and their wives are mentioned as present in the two surviving accounts of the event. Both tales are valuable, for they permit a rare glimpse into D'Annunzio's reclusive existence and document not only his musical interests, but his outrageous ostentation. Elizabeth recalled years later, "After receiving us cordially D'Annunzio led us out to his garden; there, mounted on a cement foundation, was the forward half of the ship, 'Puglia,' of Fiume fame. This half was manned by one or two sailors; D'Annunzio himself was in full naval uniform. The small, totally bald *Comandante* presently gave the order '*Fuoco,*' whereupon were fired seven earsplitting blasts from a cannon mounted on the deck. Turning to me he said, deferentially, 'Madame, seven salutes; one for each note of the diatonic scale!'"[9]

In his account of the same episode, Kindler relates that he suggested to the poet that since each blast of the cannon cost 3,000 lire, he might consider using the pentatonic scale, which would cost only 15,000 instead of 21,000 lire. From Kindler we also learn the reason for the curious mutilation of the vessel. D'Annunzio believed passionately that Dalmatia should belong to Italy, and when the Treaty of Versailles denied the port of Fiume (Rijeka) to Italy, proposing instead to incorporate it into the newly formed Yugoslavia, he commandeered a battleship, recruited 300 volunteers, and occupied the city for three months until Italian government forces bombarded his headquarters and forced him to surrender. The ship, *Puglia,* is a remnant of this escapade. It appears that D'Annunzio had actually demanded the battleship from the government, and it had been sent to him dismantled on 200 oxcarts, but when it arrived it was found that there was room for only half of it—whereupon the *Comandante* announced that he would put up the rest when Dalmatia became Italy's.[10]

To render him harmless, the state kept D'Annunzio in a kind of solitary splendor and supplied him with anything he wanted, although he never had any money for himself. So when he said he needed sailors to keep the ship clean, the government sent him sailors. And when he needed cannon to announce visitors his request was granted, much to the distress of the villagers who would say, upon hearing the cannon fired, "The butcher is being paid today."[11]

Both Coolidge and Kindler comment on the strange collection of knickknacks that cluttered the *Comandante*'s house: The lower half of all statues was painted red, and his bedroom contained a cast of his right ear made of gold—for it was the organ through which the marvelous sounds of music came to him. But for Elizabeth, the pièce de résistance was "his own funeral catafalque . . . whereupon to take his last siesta—which I rather suppose, he did."[12] Upon their departure each of the honored guests received a special memento made by D'Annunzio's personal jeweler. To Kindler he gave a fine sapphire ring, to Elizabeth, a cigarette case adorned with an opal carved in cameo with the head of an American Indian. It remains today at the Library of Congress, with cigarettes still inside.

Still savoring the delight of the Gardone experience Elizabeth returned home faced with the task of mounting her ambitious festival in Chicago in the autumn of 1930 and another at the Library of Congress in the spring of 1931. Before she had closed the book on either of them she was already making plans for an extensive European festival in the fall of 1931. Although it would take her and her musicians to seven different countries, it would end with a glorious finale in Italy, to which she returned with all the instincts of a homing pigeon. The festival occurred in the year of her sixty-seventh birthday. Her old friend, Frances Glessner, once wrote, "I am 67 today. It is unpleasant to be 67: but it would be unpleasanter not to be, having got started."[13] Elizabeth had no time for such considerations as aging and no intention of slowing her pace, for this tour was one of marathon proportions—fourteen concerts in approximately six weeks, in eleven cities and seven countries. She sailed from New York on 24 September, accompanied by Gladys Caldwell and a maid, and arrived at Cuxhaven, Germany on 2 October. From here she went to Hamburg by train and then on to Berlin. The itinerary reads: 3–4 October, Berlin; 4–5 October, sleeper to Moscow; 6 October, arrive Moscow; 10 October, two concerts in Moscow; 11 October, leave Moscow; 12 October, arrive Warsaw; 13 October, arrive Vienna; 16–17 October, Budapest; 20 October, Graz; 24 October, Frankfurt; 26 October, arrive Paris (three concerts Paris). The pace slowed significantly when she reached Italy, with time for rest and socializing. There were concerts on 31 October at Malipiero's villa in Asolo, on 12 November in Rome, and on 18 November in Naples.[14]

Except for some time built into the schedule for rest at Malipiero's villa at Asolo near the end of the trip, the hectic travel schedule hardly left time for the actual concerts, let alone the many receptions, teas, testimonial dinners, and civic functions scheduled wherever they went. In Frankfurt she was presented with a bronze medal and made an honorary citizen, her name inscribed in the *Goldenes Buch* along with that of Charlemagne. The smooth running of this trip, as well as the advance arrangements with civic officials, was a result of the able management of Hugo Kortschak, who fulfilled his mission much as Kindler had done four years earlier. Like Kindler, Kortschak was European-born and educated and had the advantage of many contacts.

In April of 1931 Elizabeth had written to ask him to undertake this responsibility, which he eagerly agreed to do but with the request that he should be allowed to arrange a testimonial concert for her in his home town of Graz. She agreed and invited him to be her guest on a boat trip on the Danube from Vienna to Budapest, the only part of the tour that was not made by train. Between mid-July and mid-October Kortschak received checks totaling $11,000, from which sum he was to make the necessary expenditures. He showed great concern for Coolidge's well-being throughout the trip and even before. It is apparent that the exhausting itinerary she had set up was a matter of concern to him, for he wrote to alert her to the reality of the long hours that she would be required to spend on trains. He cautioned her that from Berlin to Moscow alone was a thirty-six-hour ride; from Bremen to Frankfurt, ten hours; Frankfurt to Vienna, twelve to fifteen hours; and Moscow to Vienna, a grueling forty-three hours. Kortschak agreed to meet her in Bremen and accompany her and her party the rest of the way. Despite the schedule she never missed a concert or reception. He was impressed with her resilience and good sportsmanship and at the close of the tour wrote from Paris: "You have been most marvelous to brave the inconveniences of the long railroad journeys and to inspire the audiences as well as the artists by your presence; it meant so much to everyone. . . . In all these cities you left behind a deep personal impression as well as an incalculably fine influence on both the arts of composition and of performance."[15]

Coolidge and Kortschak had carefully selected artists and composers to suit the particular locale. In Budapest the local Róth Quartet was chosen to play a concert that featured a composition of the Hungarian, Laszló Lajtha. Lübbecke-Job, a Frankfurt artist, was chosen to give in that city a repeat performance of the Hindemith Piano Concerto that she had premiered the previous year in Chicago. Not surprisingly, Hindemith's works were much better received in Germany than they had been in the United States. Nearly all of the concerts, regardless of locale, contained works of Coolidge's Italian friends Casella, Respighi, Malipiero, and Pizzetti.

As might be expected, national loyalties are reflected in the various reviews. The *Kölnisches Zeitung* struck a note close to Elizabeth's heart when it referred to her work as "an unpolitical, international gathering [where] Music acts . . . as the peacemaker of nations."[16] In view of what was happening in Germany at the time, there is a distinct irony in this observation—in 1931 the Nazi party was a dominant force in politics.

Not all the reviews were complimentary. The *Neues Politisches Volksblatt* found the music of Malipiero, Beck, and Lajtha "composed with too much intelligence and too little sentiment," and the *Nepazfa* declared that "beyond the borders of their country, in international relations Martinů's music has no progressive effect. The Czech composers are somehow cut off from general musical evolution, their railway-car seems to have been lost by the train and stands motionless somewhere near the station 'Richard Strauss.'"[17] Despite the sometimes uncomprehending appraisal of the critics, the reviews provide valuable and even amusing insights into the ceremonies surrounding the events and also reveal a definite curiosity on the part of the local inhabitants about this American woman who gratuitously spent so lavishly on the sponsorship of free concerts for them.

News of Coolidge's arrival with her musicians was usually announced in advance, and she was met at the train by distinguished musicians and civic officials, not to mention curious onlookers. In Budapest she was ceremoniously welcomed by composers Dohnányi and Hubay, and the *Magyarság* printed its notice under the caption "Mrs. Coolidge, the globe trotter mecaenas [*sic*] of chamber music has arrived with the Róth Quartet."[18] In general wherever Elizabeth went she attracted a good deal of attention. She was hailed as "the Prima Donna before whom the whole city does honor" by Vienna's *Neue Freie Presse,* which also made special note of her appearance and behavior. "The prima donna sits in the third row, in the center [of the] audience. We know she is sixty-seven years old, but we can scarcely believe it. Her head is that of a beautiful mature woman, her dark-blond natural-colored hair, entwined at the neck in a little knot, shows hardly any silver strands. Her cheeks are high-boned—Slavic? or perhaps Indian?—and her eyes hardly at all shaded by age, sparkle and flash, take everything in, appraising everything."[19]

Her entourage included not only her performers and their wives, but national and/or local celebrities and critics cleverly chosen to ensure the most informed and far-reaching coverage possible. Included were Prunières, Rosenfeld, and Labroca among others. She engaged the best hotels, and sometimes traveled on the Orient Express. Her usual approach to Venice is representative of her style. She always engaged rooms for herself and her entourage at the luxurious Danieli Hotel overlooking the lagoon, and ordered the Danieli launch to meet her and her party at Mestre, whence they made their way down the Grand Canal to the hotel. From within the intimate circle of her own performers comes Casella's description of what it was really like to travel with this indefatigable lady: "The arrival at the hotel of that tall, spectacled lady, followed by a retinue of twenty or thirty persons, most of them armed with musical instruments, was impossibly funny. The hotel was thus taken by assault by the cosmopolitan company, which was looked on with a certain amazement by other travelers who were not part of it." He had to admit, however, that "life with Mrs. Coolidge was not easy. Her guests were supposed to hold themselves at her disposal all day long and even late at night if she so desired. Around her there were organized a great number of official and unofficial receptions, teas, garden parties, and banquets. She is a woman of really phenomenal physical constitution; although she herself was never tired, her guests were often completely exhausted."[20]

A distinct change in the program occurred when the tour reached Paris, where the last of three concerts was devoted entirely to works of Monteverdi and Lully. This departure from the contemporary was not a whim but reflects a little-known interest of Coolidge, her love of early music that led her to subsidize several very significant musicological undertakings.

The inspiration for the most extensive of these works originated at Asolo, the charming and historic Veneto hill town near Venice, where in 1489 Caterina Cornaro, Queen of Cypress, Jerusalem, and Armenia, held court in her ancient stone house "La Mura." The town figures in Browning's *Pippa Passes* and perhaps is best known today as the final resting place of Eleanora Duse, the most famous tragedienne of her age and the one great love of D'Annunzio's hectic love life. Here in picturesque Asolo, Malipiero maintained a modest villa where Coolidge loved to spend time after her tours. During one of these visits Malipiero shared with her his dream of editing the complete works of his idol, Monteverdi. Although Elizabeth's concept of musicology was somewhat idiosyncratic, she recognized the importance of such an undertaking. Her view, which went beyond scholarly research to include performance, was actually very enlightened. So when Malipiero proposed the idea she listened.

It cannot be denied that her decision to help him was strongly motivated by her genuine friendship with him and his wife Anna. Considered by many to be the most original voice of the progressive Italian group, Malipiero was a moody hypochondriac who nursed a persistent persecution complex. But he was as doggedly single-minded in his work as Elizabeth was in hers, so his fanatic dedication to whatever he undertook appealed to her. He was at this time teaching composition at the Conservatory in Parma and had neither the time nor the money to undertake so comprehensive a work as the Opera Omnia of the prolific Monteverdi. Elizabeth's method of endowment is one of her more brilliant solutions to a problem, adroitly calculated to serve both the recipient and the donor and at the same time preserve Malipiero's fragile ego. She devised a plan whereby she would advance the necessary money to him by subscribing to thirty-three complete sets of the Monteverdi work, which were to be sent to thirty-two libraries of her choice. Of the thirty-third, which was of course reserved for her, she said, "I regard [it] as my own and have nothing more precious."[21]

Malipiero labored intensely at the project, and the six volumes comprising Series One were completed in only two years. By June of 1939 volume fifteen was finished but worsening conditions in Italy threatened to prevent the completion of the two remaining volumes. It was only under the most difficult circumstances that the Monteverdi work was finally realized in 1942. Work on the project is thoroughly documented in the Coolidge/Malipiero correspondence at the Library of Congress and at Fondazione Cini in Venice.[22] From their letters it is clear that Elizabeth found a soul mate in Francesco who, like Engel and Bridge, bequeathed her yet another nickname, Santa Elizabetta. She in turn elevated him to her own private pantheon, calling him "the saint." Besides the money designated for the Monteverdi work, beginning in 1932 Elizabeth sent him each year a check for $1,000 on 4 October, the feast of his patron saint, Francis of Assisi, and another (usually for $750) on 17 November, the feast of St. Elizabeth. It was always specified that the money should be used for him and Anna. In addition Elizabeth enabled him to build a little music hall at his villa, which he appropriately christened Sala Coolidge. And partly for her own convenience and comfort during her holidays there, she financed the addition of "that Anglo-Saxon convenience," a modern bathroom.

In the meantime, Henry Prunières approached Elizabeth with a similar plan to edit the complete works of Lully. She likewise assisted him, though not to the same extent. Unfortunately Prunières died after completing only a few volumes.[23] But there was yet one other cooperation with Malipiero. After the war she undertook to support his complete edition of the works of Vivaldi. Sadly, neither patron nor editor lived to see the completion of this ambitious work.

Despite her genuine love for the Malipieros Elizabeth eventually cut off all financial support. Her birthday check to Francesco in 1935 was sent with a strong warning that was prompted by her opposition to Italy's aggression in Abyssinia. She cautioned that the money "was to celebrate . . . the fact of your arriving on this planet to enrich the world. It is for you and Anna and you must promise that no part of it shall in any way be given to assist your government in any war, for my conscience would not allow me to further anything of this kind."[24] By 1940, friendship notwithstanding, she ceased support altogether, saying "[I] could not send any money into Italy while the country was pursuing a policy which so distresses an American democrat like myself, for I do not wish even by a small coin any contribution to available Italian funds."[25] It was a decision probably as difficult for her to make as it was for him to accept, and she attempted to soften the blow with the reminder that "no political strife between our ideologies can alter my affection for you and Anna, for well I know that our spiritual relationship and understanding lie deeper than the political loyalties which at present alienate us physically."[26]

The Paris performance of Lully's *Cadmus* and the Monteverdi concert were the visible and audible fruit of her cooperation with Malipiero and Prunières and a perfect prelude to the ceremony in which the French government awarded her the medal of the Legion of Honor.

Monsieur Painlevé, representing the French Ministry of Foreign Affairs, gave a speech honoring Coolidge and then, with tears in his eyes, pinned the Cross of the Legion of Honor upon her shoulder and kissed both her cheeks. Frank Bridge, speaking not only for himself, but also for Elizabeth's many friends gathered there, said "You were simply wonderful. It is probably the most thrilling . . . of all your experiences. . . . That we all appeared to share the curious mixture of nervousness, pleasure and pride and honour, was not at all a figment of the imagination. We were intensely proud of you. . . . How you did not collapse under the strain I cannot think, I can only repeat to you what we all felt—how marvelously you kept up and that your gracious acknowledgment of the honours could not have been bettered by anyone."[27]

After the Paris festivities Coolidge and company headed south to repeat the Lully/Monteverdi concert in Rome. Elizabeth was always sentimental about anniversaries and had scheduled the Roman concert on 12 November, which would have been her fortieth wedding anniversary, and the last concert in Naples on the feast of her patron saint. In Rome as in Paris the affair ended splendidly with the French ambassador giving a *déjeuner d'honneur* for Elizabeth at the French embassy and the Italian government doing the same at the Casino Valadier on the Pincio, where she received yet another medal.

The last stop of the tour was in Naples, from which Coolidge would sail for home. By now the pace of things had slackened and there was time to rest, to savor the successes of the tour, and to share these last pleasant days with her friends. By the time she reached Naples her party had grown to include not only the regulars whose works were being performed—Alfano, Casella, Castelnuovo, Malipiero, Respighi, and Pizzetti—but also Prunières and his wife, Warick and Mrs. Evans, Signor Napolitano (her local manager), the young composer Mario Pilati, her California friends Gladys Caldwell and Luther Marchant, and her ever faithful Ugo Ara. All were her guests at the hotel and for meals, which were sometimes taken on a rooftop terrace. Here, at lunch on the last day, they looked out over the beautiful Bay of Naples, where the ship that was to carry Coolidge and her American friends home lay at anchor, and they watched as a column of smoke rose lazily from Vesuvius, arching high above them. One of the composers suggested that as a fitting farewell they should collaborate on a little composition in Coolidge's honor. Casella dashed to his room for manuscript paper and it was agreed that each composer, in alphabetical order, should write four bars of music in the key of C, 4/4 meter, without knowing what the others had written. "Alfano led off, using sixteenth notes; Casella followed, crowding his four bars with thirty-second notes; then Castelnuovo; Malipiero, very modernistic; and, finally Respighi, with an ecclesiastical cadence pronounced the Amen. But how to hear it?"[28]

The ship was due to sail at 4:00 P.M., so Elizabeth invited her composer friends to tea in the ship's lounge, where Casella did the honors at the piano and serenaded her with this curious polyglot piece that she always referred to as her Round Robin. After the last farewells, as the ship steamed out of the harbor and she watched the familiar figures on the pier gradually disappear, she could not have anticipated the hard times that lay ahead for her composer-friends, whose hastily written farewell she carried home as a treasured memento of what had been a truly memorable experience. There would be two more trips to Italy after this, but no more gala tours of this scope, for within the next year her income would decrease by twenty percent.

There is a sense of restlessness conveyed in the letters of this period, which record many changes of plan necessitated by forces beyond her control. She had intended a trip to Italy in 1932 but had to postpone it because of the shortfall in her income. She did return in 1933, and planned to do so in 1934 as well. Instead she had to postpone again to the following year. But when 1935 came, she canceled her visits to Italy, Brussels, and Paris and decided instead to provide some concerts there but not to attend. She wired $3,500 to Bridge to cover expenses, and then suddenly changed her mind and did go after all. This last-minute change of plans was brought about by the notification that she was to receive the coveted Décoration d'Officier de l'Ordre de la Couronne, Léopold, Roi des Belges in recognition of her extensive work in Belgium. She had already been presented to the queen of the Belgians in 1931, when she was escorted to court by Alexandre Tansman. This time Bridge met her in Brussels to do the honors. She admitted to him that she was growing tired of "auspicing" other people's work and was frightened at the prospect of war, but returned to London with him to make the most of the opportunity to spend some weeks with friends there, taking her diversion "all in a lump" as she put it. It would be her last visit to Europe.

Back home her musical activity intensified, much of it under the auspices of the Coolidge Foundation. In 1933 alone there were contracts for eighteen radio broadcasts, and at the Library of Congress the festivals continued in 1933, 1935, and 1937. In between the Washington events she presented the last of her Berkshire festivals in 1934 and 1938. She was hardly idle and complained occasionally of needing some breathing space, which she usually sought in California, a place where she could rest, practice, and compose "without regard for the people I have asked to do things for me." But thoughts of impending war and the danger to her many friends in Europe weighed on her heavily, and she confessed to Bridge, "It tears my heart with apprehension for you all."[29]

From Europe the migration of intellectuals had begun, and many of the composers with whom Elizabeth had worked were now in the United States. Schönberg had come in 1934, Hindemith in 1937, Stravinsky in 1939, and Bartók in 1940. Of her close Italian friends only Castelnuovo, who was Jewish, had fled his country in 1939, and Toscanini, who fearlessly and outspokenly opposed Fascism, spent the war years in New York, conducting and also assisting refugees to obtain American entry visas and jobs in the United States. To those who appealed to her for help she responded as best she could, usually helping to find employment here. Meanwhile, she took some consolation that at least these awful developments occurred near the end of her life, and she could enjoy the happy memories of the wonderful work that she had undertaken with her European friends. Her sensibilities and high-minded ideal of a Musical League of Nations would have been deeply offended at the manner in which music was being utilized in Axis propaganda. To be sure, Hitler had some appreciation of music and championed the work of Wagner, whose nationalistic ideals and concept of a superior race bore frightening resemblance to his own. And Fascist propaganda had made a great effort to present Mussolini as the violin-playing humanist who made much show of patronizing music. In 1938 the two dictators, along with Ribbentrop and Hess, attended the *Maggio Musicale* in Florence, where solidarity of the Axis powers was symbolized in the stage decorations consisting of flowers and swastikas.[30]

One cannot help wondering whether Coolidge was aware of the extent to which her Italian friends found that survival sometimes meant compromise with Fascism. "Most Italian musicians lived through the twenty-year fraud [of Fascism] in much the same way as other citizens, by trying to carry on their daily lives without becoming involved in the pros and cons of the regime."[31] Italy's posture—at least initially—seemed more liberal than that of Germany, where Schönberg's music was decreed decadent and Hindemith was accused of "cultural Bolshevism." In Italy Il Duce's racial thinking began to manifest itself in 1936, and by 1938 he published the ten-point "Manifesto of the Race," declaring Italians to be Aryans and forbidding marriage with non-Aryans.[32]

At the same time that Elizabeth was intensifying her work in Italy, some of the composers that she was supporting attempted to ingratiate themselves with Mussolini by dedicating works to him, sending him manuscripts, and inviting him to attend performances of their compositions. Because of D'Annunzio's love of music and his accessibility to Il Duce, composers often appealed to him to intercede for them. His entreaties are preserved in numerous letters and telegrams addressed to Mussolini in behalf of these "poor cinderellas." It is clear that D'Annunzio was comfortable enough with Mussolini to address him as *charo chompagno,* and to jog his memory with regard to certain promises made. In May of 1929 he ventured to inquire "if you have forgotten your promise with regard to the three academicians, Ildebrando Pizzetti, Gian Francesco Malipiero, Giuseppe Brunati. . . . Since you, a lover of music, . . . have employed at the Accademia (Santa Cecilia) the good offices of Giordano and Mascagni, do not exclude the two who are the richest in artistic genius but poorest in good fortune, Pizzetti and Malipiero. With regard to the last, the title he has earned in undertaking with such love and such wisdom the publication of the complete works of the most divine Claudio Monteverdi, should be recommendation enough."[33]

Malipiero did in time hold an office in the Fascist Union of Musicians and became the director of the conservatory in Venice, but he never felt that he received the recognition in his homeland that had been accorded to him elsewhere. The knowledge of his various obsequious overtures to Mussolini might well call into question the sincerity of his devotion to Elizabeth. He approached Mussolini often with requests for audiences; when he was finally granted one in 1930, he offered Il Duce "in homage" six portfolios of his works, many of which he had previously dedicated to Elizabeth, including the prize-winning *Rispetti e Strambotti*.[34] It is doubtful that he viewed this action as any betrayal of their friendship. In some of her personal, handwritten letters to Malipiero, Elizabeth reveals her most vulnerable side when she makes rare protestations of her feelings. Whereas she usually kept copies of her letters and passed them on to the Library of Congress, these seem purposely to have been expunged from that collection by her and are preserved only in Malipiero's personal papers at Fondazione Cini in Venice. In view of Malipiero's frequent attempts to ingratiate himself with the Fascist regime—to which he knew she was so categorically opposed—this letter is especially poignant:

> *My beloved Francesco, Because you have asked it, and because I too, want it, I am writing to you in freedom from shyness, deafness, and the handicap of a foreign tongue, to try to tell you how much your spiritual friendship means to me.*
>
> *My life—my inner life—is a lonely one, set in a surrounding of materialism and mechanical "efficiency" such as you can hardly visualize in Asolo. From preoccupation with "things" (though beautiful and interesting they are) it is nourishing to heart and soul to turn to the thought of you. . . . To know that you find in me a sister . . .dispels some of the spiritual loneliness.*
>
> *To work for Truth and Beauty shall continue to be our happy destiny, as we are both able; with this purpose in our hearts, let us go forward together though separated by many thousands of miles. You must write me of your work (which is your heart) and continue to love me. Though we should never meet again (which may God forbid!) our spirits are permanently in touch through our common fidelity to a cause. . . . Please know that I am always lovingly and faithfully yours.*[35]

Malipiero's behavior, which when taken at face value might appear to be an outright betrayal of Coolidge's good will, was more likely just another manifestation of his neurotic conviction that he was constantly the target of vicious plots contrived by jealous rivals. He should probably not be judged too harshly for the equivocal posture that led him to choose compromise instead of the kind of inflexible ideological opposition shown by Hindemith and Bartók, for whom there was no dissembling. Malipiero's personality is aptly characterized by Harvey Sachs, who believes that "a clinical psychologist might have a better chance than a music historian at explaining Malipiero's dealings with the fascists."[36] In the end his comportment under the Fascist regime is somewhat vindicated by Anna's reports that until after September of 1943 she remained in Asolo, and while German and Italian officers occupied their villa she courageously hid a British soldier in her bathroom. In the meantime "Francesco, in Venice, was working as only he knows how, working at his wonderful music but also working for the liberation. They were strenuous and nerve wracking days, and we got intimate knowledge of bombing, shooting, and hanging—also having our houses burnt down in reprisals."[37]

By 1945 the Malipiero correspondence was renewed, and Elizabeth did what she could to help them in the difficult postwar period of adjustment. Malipiero was certainly not the only Italian composer to take an ambiguous stance during the Fascist regime. Perhaps the most Janus-faced of them all was Francesco Santoliquido, a composer of lesser stature than Casella or Malipiero who throughout the 1920s published vitriolic anti-Semitic articles in the Fascist daily *Il Tevere.* At the same time he was unashamedly attempting to cultivate Coolidge's favor. He wrote to her in 1928 to say that he was composing a trio for her. Later he did write two pieces for wind instruments which he dedicated to her with the request that she have them published in the United States. Still later he wrote from Tunisia, where he had gone to finish an opera, asking her to send money. She neither commissioned anything nor assisted him financially.[38] His pathetic and mean-spirited retaliation is contained in an article entitled "*La piovra musicale ebraica*" (The Blood-Sucking Musical Jew), in which he suggests that the only reason that Coolidge supported Casella and his circle is that she was deaf and probably could not hear their cacophony.[39]

Coolidge was gifted with a remarkable ability to perceive when people's motives were self-serving. Casella believed it was a learned asset that came through years of being the target of all those who wished to impose on her generosity. "She learned to distinguish her few really unmercenary friends from the innumerable ones who sought to obtain her money for their various schemes."[40] A strange and amusing catalog of curios offered to her for sale could be compiled from the letters addressed to her. They include, among other things, a shirt that once belonged to Beethoven, a lock of Brahms's hair, and the pen with which Meyerbeer composed *Le Prophète.* She steadfastly ignored such solicitations but reacted generously to entreaties of real worth. One of the most notable examples came in 1934 when she wrote to Engel: "Schönberg is trying to sell [the score of] Wozzeck for his pupil [Berg] and like all the rest of the world he has turned to me to produce the cash."[41] She was not able to supply the entire sum at that time but in the end she helped the Library of Congress to acquire the manuscript for the asking price of 6,000 Austrian schillings, about $1,040.[42]

In her culling of the musical wheat from the chaff Elizabeth chose to reward talent and services not only with money and commissions but with the honor of the Coolidge Medal. She bestowed it upon Casella in 1934, Malipiero in 1937, and Bridge in 1938. And for their services as performers and managers of her European festivals she honored Kortschak in 1938 and Kindler in 1939—twelve years after his successful tour. Though pleased and honored, Kindler obviously thought the distinction was a bit slow in coming. When Coolidge repeated her thanks to him backstage after the formal presentation, he quipped, "But you know, Elizabeth, it is a little like declaring Jeanne d'Arc a virgin after four hundred years."[43]

Coolidge's largesse has prompted many comparisons with other patrons over the years. Domenico Brescia once reflected that "in all the epochs there have been this enlightened people, like the Bardi family of Florence. In our age the blessings do not pour so often or so freely, except in unusual and therefore doubly admired instances, like in the case of our Lady who is doing now what great patrons of the Renaissance did."[44] If she had done no other good in her life she would still deserve the laurels bestowed on her by Prunières when he christened her "an American Maecenas."[45]

CHAPTER FIFTEEN

An American Maecenas at Home

Time and trouble will tame an advanced young woman, but an advanced old woman is uncontrollable by any earthly force.

– DOROTHY L. SAYERS

THE PLUCKY ENGLISH would respond to their country's declaration of war on Germany in 1939 by singing "We're gonna hang out the washing on the Siegfried line . . . if the Siegfried line's still there." If it is true that popular music is often the index of a nation's collective morale, then the tune that Coolidge heard soon after her triumphant return from her tour in 1931 was an ominous portent of the troubles ahead: America was singing, "Brother can you spare a dime?"

Elizabeth was brought up short by the alarming news that the income from the Coolidge Foundation Trust was expected to be at least $7,500 less than the preceding year. Her letters of this period are full of references to the shortfall, and they make no secret of the fact that she blamed the city of Chicago in large measure. She had already been asked to provide music for the Chicago World's Fair in 1933 and had planned to do so. But this latest development caused her to reconsider. In an unusually candid letter to Frank Bridge she admitted that she had changed her mind about sending music to the fair for two reasons: "The first is that I cannot afford the risk of a good deal of financial loss, and the second (perhaps unworthily) is a feeling of resentment against the city itself, which is to blame for the drastic reduction of my income. Of course, I am not saying this publicly." At issue was the fact that the city of Chicago had defaulted on bonds in which she was heavily invested, and she placed much of the blame upon the city's "inefficient and muddled" handling of its affairs. As a result she felt keenly that "until they can hold up their heads in honorable payment of their just obligations, they should not expect much interest in their undertaking of this expensive World's Fair. Still, if I could afford it otherwise, I should do it notwithstanding these somewhat spiteful reflections, but I cannot—so that's that."[1]

The distress over her reduced income contributed to a general sense of disquietude about conditions in the United States, where, in her opinion, incessant crime, scandals, and "universal muddle-headedness . . . seem to inflict our government." She blamed much of this upon sensational journalism, especially as it related to the kidnapping of the Lindbergh baby. The subject appears often in her letters, and it is apparent that the safety of her grandchildren was a matter of serious concern to her. Her usual patriotism was uncharacteristically dimmed by the attitude she expressed to Sprague about the Lindbergh case. "It makes me ashamed of my country to realize that such things can happen unpunished here, and I really think that if you were not so firmly established as American citizens, I should like to live in England or Italy where, at least the word 'law' has some meaning and importance."[2] Half in jest—but with a genuine hint of worry—she wrote to Bridge, "The thought has even occurred to me as I take my daily constitutional promenades through the streets of Los Angeles, that by some strange chance they might wish to kidnap me! In that case will you come forward with a new composition as ransom?"[3]

Plans during this period seldom could be made more than three months in advance, until she knew what her quarterly income would be. But with Stock's tactful intervention she did, in fact, supply some music for the Chicago World's Fair.

Coolidge's general sense of unrest was undoubtedly exacerbated by Engel's final resignation from the Library of Congress. Since 1930 he had served the Library and G. Schirmer, trying to meet the demands of both. After three difficult years of shuttling between Washington and New York, he made the decision to settle once and for all in New York to become president of Schirmer Publishing Company, effective 1 July 1934.

It was a difficult decision for Engel, who admitted: "I need not tell you how reluctantly I came to a final—and inevitable—decision. Nor need I say here how keenly I have appreciated the distinctive and unique privilege of collaborating with you in the establishment of the Coolidge Foundation." Realizing that this would be difficult for Coolidge as well, he reminded her that it might be in the best interest of the Foundation "if it is not left to depend too greatly on the influence of any particular individual . . . or of any group of individuals, but is allowed to develop impersonally though in the spirit that conceived and shaped it."[4]

It is clear from her response that Engel had already discussed the offer with her. Nevertheless she admitted: "I do not know exactly how to answer your letter which arrived today and which, though in no way surprising, was still just a little of a shock. . . . I know it is all for the good and I was quite truly sincere in saying that I hoped you would make the decision as you have, nevertheless, it leaves me with a certain feeling of bereavement." Her respect and affection for Engel had grown immensely and she admitted that the existence of the Foundation and the wonderful accomplishments already to its credit were due in large measure to him. "I can never put into words my gratitude and sense of obligation."[5]

Engel was succeeded by the youthful Oliver Strunk, who had been trained at Cornell under Kinkeldey and had studied in Berlin with Johannes Wolf, Curt Sachs, and Arnold Schering. Strunk was eager to please Coolidge, whose reputation was undoubtedly well-known to him, for he had been on the staff of the Library since 1928. Soon after his appointment he wrote, "Let *me* as your new chief assure *you* of my eagerness to make myself as useful as possible and of my determination to live up to the magnificent record of my predecessor. These things I cannot accomplish without your confidence and his assistance."[6]

She welcomed him cordially but formally, addressing him as Oliver Strunk, Esquire, for nearly half a year before inquiring when she might begin to call him simply Oliver, noting that "You are much younger than my own son, and I have so long been in the habit of addressing the Chief of the Music Division as Mike . . . but my reverence for your office does not let me call you by your first name without asking your permission."[7]

Despite efforts on the part of both, things did not go smoothly. After only one month on the job Strunk was having difficulty answering her queries about the upcoming festival, yet by September he was courageous enough to disagree with her wish to give the entire broadcast season to the Pro Arte Quartet for the complete Beethoven cycle. Surprisingly, she agreed. Nevertheless, in the course of the next year she began to register complaints about publicity materials being too late, and when Strunk spent six weeks in Europe and failed to notify Engel that he was to receive the Coolidge Medal in October, Elizabeth was understandably annoyed. It is apparent that by 1936 relations were becoming seriously strained. There was an unfortunate misunderstanding over his decision to allow the Kolisch Quartet to perform the Dvořák quartet in a radio broadcast that contained no modern works. Coolidge was of the opinion that Strunk had allowed himself to be swayed by Mr. Lang of the broadcasting company and wrote to remind him that the programs should be approved by the committee, or at least by him in consultation with her. "I really feel that it is those who pay the bill who should have the deciding vote—in order to accomplish their main purpose, which, after all, is not to please the National Broadcasting Company, but to serve the musical interest of the country."[8]

To his credit, Strunk accepted full responsibility for the decision and stood his ground, reminding her that the Foundation had offered many programs in the past that consisted entirely of modern works and made a case for an occasional all-classical program, "especially when these are not hackneyed classics. In any case, I should like you to know that the programs you complain of are not due to my having submitted to the judgment of the broadcasting companies."[9]

Coolidge's insistence upon punctilious attention to financial matters was seriously violated when certain checks that she had sent did not promptly appear in the financial statement. As a result, she began to send her communications and her money directly to Herbert Putnam. She had kept Engel apprised of her dissatisfaction and indicated that the situation in Washington was a matter of grave concern to her. He was aware of the problem and tried to mollify her with the assurance that between the two of them they could "easily overcome any little difficulty." But, never known for her patience in these situations, Elizabeth took matters into her own hands and in November of 1936 altered the original trust deed, thus removing the chief of the Music Division (Strunk) as chairman of the Foundation and naming Engel in his place. She assured Engel, "My main objective in making the alteration in the Deed of Trust was to accomplish more efficiently the original purpose of the Coolidge Foundation and, after more than two years of fluctuating under the present administration, it seems to me that this can better be done by transferring a considerable part of the authority from Mr. Strunk's shoulders to yours." It is clear that these conditions were to apply only to Strunk's administration, for she was quite willing "to maintain (or even increase) the amount of salary appropriated for Chief of Music Division if, by so doing, I could again secure the service of a first rate man." In her opinion a simple solution would be "either to accept a mediocre salary for mediocre work, . . . or to find again a Chief of Music Division who would carry forward the distinguished mission of the Coolidge Foundation with an adequate reimbursement."[10]

It came as no surprise when Engel wrote in May to inform her that the librarian had asked for Strunk's resignation, and he would be leaving by the end of September 1937. Strunk, understandably, was deeply hurt and sped to New York, where he spent twelve consecutive hours with Engel trying to sort out his feelings. Engel was genuinely concerned and had hoped that a resolution could be found, but finally he had to agree to the librarian's decision. He hoped that Putnam would not rush to fill the office, and believed Strunk's assistant, Harold Spivacke, would be the best person for the job.

It was an unfortunate incident and a difficult situation for all parties concerned. For the thirty-three-year-old Strunk, it could not have been easy to follow a man of Engel's experience and stature who, moreover, was such a trusted advisor, friend, and confidant of Elizabeth. For Engel, who from a distance played the role of pacificator, this new turn of events created a real dilemma, for just at this time the Schirmer board was considering the extension of his contract, which was due to expire in May of 1940, and had asked him to sign for another ten years. His heart was still at the Library of Congress, and although the Schirmer job was financially much more advantageous to him, now that the position of chief was open again, he felt as if he were signing his life away to renew his contract with Schirmer. He frankly admitted to Elizabeth that "As long as I felt there was a future for Strunk in Washington, I had rather given up all thought of returning there. But now I am very much in a quandary."[11] And for Elizabeth at age seventy-three it was a difficult move too. Engel would have been the first to admit that she could be very demanding at times, but it should be understood that the decision to replace Strunk was not based upon her dissatisfaction alone, nor was she lacking in genuine compassion for him. Spivacke did become acting chief of the division, but from New York Engel continued to handle all of the Coolidge business, as he had promised her he would. By October he was able to report great satisfaction with the changes in the division.

Despite the Depression, the 1930s had been a decade of expansion and notable achievements for the Coolidge Foundation. In the last months of Engel's administration several important composers were commissioned to write quartets, among them Roy Harris, Edward Burlingame Hill, Henry Eichheim, and Béla Bartók. Casella's trio was brought over from Italy for a series of performances, including one at the White House for which Elizabeth and the trio members were invited to a state dinner with the Roosevelts. Several distinguished artists were given their first hearing in America, including the Adolph Busch Quartet and Busch's son-in-law, the young Rudolph Serkin, as well as the renowned Kolisch Quartet, which would in time premiere the Bartók commission, his Fifth String Quartet.

In speaking confidentially to Kolisch's wife, Engel told her that the Foundation had offered a commission to Alban Berg. She assured him that her husband was an intimate friend of Berg, who very likely would let Kolisch see the work as it developed and certainly would want the Kolisch Quartet to premiere it. Over the years Elizabeth was becoming identified as a patron of the modern Viennese school of twelve-tone composition. She had already commissioned Schönberg's Third Quartet in 1927, and would commission his Fourth in 1936, as well as Webern's Fourth Quartet in 1938. Now with Berg the triumvirate would be complete. The emergence of the Kolisch Quartet in her affairs at this time was a genuine boon to Elizabeth in this new association with the Viennese atonal composers, for the ensemble was well known for its performance of this music. Kolisch had studied with Schönberg, who considered the Kolisch Quartet to be the finest in existence. Certainly their predilection for contemporary music made them the superlative interpreters of the Viennese twelve-tone school. Schönberg, being Jewish, had fled from Europe earlier and the Kolisch ensemble settled in the United States in 1935, playing a most important role in introducing this new music to America. But they were versatile as well. Engel was enthusiastic over their performance of Beethoven's Quartet, op. 130, in New York and wrote to Elizabeth, "I cannot speak too highly of the extraordinary accomplishments of the quartet, of the superlative understanding and taste they show in everything that they do. . . . I wish that every quartet player in town would seize the opportunity of hearing them."[12]

Kolisch had been pleased with his reception in New York and was impressed by the number of people in the audience who followed the music, score in hand, many of them identified by Engel as expatriate Germans. This German presence had been noticeable already the previous year when Hindemith came to the United States for concerts of his works in Washington, New York, Boston, and Buffalo. The Coolidge Foundation must receive credit for this achievement, which alone would be sufficient to distinguish the eighth Library of Congress Festival in 1937 as a benchmark. The festival was significant for the Library but also for American music in general, for the experience appears to have been a turning point in Hindemith's life, and from it date his first thoughts of possibly settling in this country.

The Festival was Strunk's last achievement before leaving the Library in the fall. He had carried on most of the communications with the composer and when Hindemith finally met him he genuinely liked the young man. Ironically, at one time Strunk had applied for admission to the Berlin Hochschule, and Hindemith had denied him entrance. The fact seemed to provide a common ground of interest for them. Their first correspondence had been devoted largely to the selection of repertoire for the festival. Strunk had suggested some early works, but Hindemith steadfastly insisted upon more recent compositions that were in accordance with his theories of composition as contained in his *Unterweisung im Tonsatz*,[13] which he was just then in the process of writing. His one exception was the Sonata for Solo Viola (composed in 1922), for he was to perform it himself and realized that it was an ideal vehicle to display his virtuosity.

Hindemith's arrival in New York was purposely kept from the press in an effort not to steal Coolidge's thunder, for it had been a great achievement for her to obtain his services. There was little danger that the German press would leak the information for by this time Hindemith was persona non grata in his own country, accused of the sin of "spiritual non-Aryanism." In Washington, however, the press capitalized on the event and made special note of the fact that this festival would mark the fifth American premiere of a Hindemith work under the auspices of Elizabeth Coolidge.[14]

On the whole, Hindemith was well-impressed with the quality of the performers engaged for the Festival. He had great praise for flutist George Barrère and the young Puerto Rican pianist Jésus Marie Sanroma for their splendid performance of his Flute Sonata, and for the Madrigal Singers of the Dessoff Choir for their rendition of his *Four Songs on Old Texts.* But privately, in his letters to his wife, he had harsh words for Carlos Chávez, who conducted the orchestra for *Der Schwanendreher* and apparently had not done his homework. At the rehearsal he found the musicians good but Chávez unable to control them, so a second rehearsal was scheduled, more for the conductor's sake than the instrumentalists. It was Hindemith's impression that Chávez "thinks he is as good as Toscanini and Furtwängler combined."[15] The New York performance with Lange conducting had been less than satisfactory too, sounding "more like a herd of wild sea lions being turned than a swan."[16] The composer's dissatisfaction with the performance of this new work is reflected in the fact that although the Victor Company had planned to record the concerto, he declined.

Hindemith's private journal contains some wonderfully refreshing and insightful observations about American life—musical and otherwise—as seen through the eyes of a foreigner gifted with keen wit and an eye quick to perceive incongruities in the conventions of much social discourse. His first glimpse of the New York skyline with its skyscrapers reminded him of a castle gone berserk "with countless sharp and narrow turrets trying to outdo each other." When Mrs. Morgenthau gave a reception for him he identified her as "the lady whose husband signs all the dollar bills."[17] And the view from atop the Empire State Building at night with "a million lights and swarms of humanity in the streets" he found unbelievably beautiful, but reflected, "That people can accomplish all this for purely commercial purposes is shocking when you realize it was their religious faith that moved the Egyptians to their great achievements."[18] Strunk and his wife provided many opportunities for Hindemith to experience American social life and even arranged an evening in New York's Cotton Club and a Harlem dance hall, after which they settled into some serious beer-drinking together. He seemed genuinely to like the Strunks.

More to the point here are Hindemith's private reactions to Coolidge, the festival, and the social aspects of his Washington visit, which took place during the Cherry Blossom Festival. He found the socializing taxing. On the day of his performance Mrs. Meyer hosted a luncheon at which Nadia Boulanger was one of the guests. Her effusive greeting seems to have overwhelmed him. "[S]he welcomed me like a blissful piano teacher greeting one of her students who had just made his debut—with embraces and kisses in front of the assembled company. I was afraid that was the general custom when I was presented to Mrs. Coolidge." At the luncheon that followed he was seated in the place of honor "next to Minerva [Coolidge], . . . and I talked with her a long time. Like all the others, she said I should move here and that all kinds of arrangements could be made which would be satisfactory to me. . . . I told her I would think about it."[19]

He was rescued from "the polyp-like arms" of the rest of the company by Strunk's wife, who spirited him away to see the cherry blossoms. In its springtime loveliness Washington impressed him as more beautiful than the stone masses of New York, and the government buildings reminded him of Athens or Ephesus.[20] He was much more interested in the beauty of nature than in the constant round of parties in his honor, and when Mrs. Robert Wood Bliss gave a reception at Dumbarton Oaks, where the walls were hung with great paintings, he complained that the "energetic and lusty" guests who wanted to shake his hand did not allow time for him to enjoy the art works. On the day of the concert, between the rehearsal and performance, Elizabeth gave a large luncheon party at which she presided from the head of the table "all booted and spurred, as impressive as an armed robber baron." At the end of the luncheon she sat on a small chair near the door to receive the compliments of the guests. It reminded Hindemith "very much of Polyphemus' Hell, in which all of the escaping sheep are examined in the stomach."[21]

Before leaving Washington Hindemith made a solitary early-morning trip to the Tidal Basin for a last quiet look at the cherry blossoms, and then was off to New York, Boston, and Buffalo for more performances of his music. Finally, on board the SS *Europa* on his way home, he had the time and solitude to sort out his feelings and wrote a long letter to Coolidge: "I have had a tour which was for me interesting and instructive to the highest degree. As far as I can judge, my music did not make a bad impression at the Washington Festival or in the other cities, so I leave the country wherein I was so warmly received with a feeling of artistic satisfaction." Despite his initial reactions to Coolidge it is clear that he recognized the sincerity of her efforts in his behalf. "That all this was possible is due entirely to you; I thank you sincerely and with all my heart for the honor of the invitation and for the recognition you let me share. . . . You were so kind . . . to urge me to stay a longer time in the U.S.A. I answered you then somewhat vaguely, since I had no idea what the reaction would be to me and my music. Now that I know it is positive, I have meanwhile been thinking a great deal about it and have come to believe that your proposal is right."[22]

Hindemith returned to America in 1938 and again in 1939, and finally emigrated in 1940 to join the faculty at Yale. Through his work there and in summer sessions at the Berkshire Music Center at Tanglewood, he exerted a strong influence upon the younger generation of American composers who studied with him. Although his ostracization by his own country may have in time caused him to choose to come to America anyway, Coolidge's role in inviting him and providing such generous exposure of his music in this country ultimately played an important part in both his own career and the course of American music of the twentieth century.

With her move to Washington in 1933 Coolidge began to cultivate a whole new circle of friends. One of the closest of these was the composer Mary Howe, whose association with Coolidge began with the Freer Gallery concerts in 1924 and continued over the years as Howe offered her home for receptions and parties after the Library of Congress affairs. One of the most memorable of these occurred after the initial festival in 1925, when the English Singers offered to entertain Elizabeth's guests somewhere after the concert, gratis. Since Coolidge was staying in a hotel, Mary offered her home, and all were treated to an evening of madrigals. Another of Howe's early interventions occurred in 1925, when Brenda Putnam had completed her lovely bas-relief of Elizabeth that now graces the foyer of the Coolidge Auditorium. Engel admitted to Mary that money had been budgeted to pay the artist but that he had no funds to pay for the installation of the piece. Howe immediately responded "[S]hucks give it as the three Howe children's contribution." Unofficially, it was thus arranged and so recorded.[23]

Together with Carl Engel, Howe took an active role in establishing the Chamber Music Society of Washington, which later became the Friends of Music of the Library of Congress. For one of their programs Engel invited Mary, who was a fine pianist, to play the Fauré Piano Quartet with an ensemble in which the cellist was Hans Kindler. It was the beginning of a warm friendship of great significance for the city of Washington, for Mary and her husband believed firmly that the nation's capital should have a symphony orchestra and helped to promote Kindler's cause as conductor.

As early as the 1890s Washington had hosted traveling orchestras from Chicago, Cleveland, Philadelphia, Cincinnati, and New York—which seems to have satisfied the local demand for such entertainment. This may have had something to do with the peculiar constituency of the city whose major "industry" was government and whose population was therefore in some measure transient. The first local effort came in 1900 when Captain William H. Santelman, leader of the U.S. Marine Band, created an orchestra of his enlisted men augmented by some local musicians. His efforts were impressive but short-lived. A second attempt was made by the composer Reginald de Koven who invested a good deal of his own money in the Washington Symphony Orchestra (1902–1905); in its short history it boasted such soloists as Paderewski, Louise Homer, and Jacques Thibaud. Unfortunately it too was a financial failure. There were other attempts by a local musician named Herman Rakeman and a Swedish immigrant conductor, Heinrich Hammer, who eventually collaborated between 1910 and 1912. Still later Kurt Hetzel attempted to re-form the Washington Symphony Orchestra in 1926.[24] It was not for lack of talent that these ventures failed, for Washington had its share of fine instrumentalists, many of whom were well-trained performers employed in theater orchestras before the days of the talkies. Substantial financial backing was needed.

This arrived in the person of Frank Frost, an oil magnate and music enthusiast who moved to Washington from California in 1930. Frost and Coolidge had already met and had collaborated in sponsoring one of her festivals in Ojai Valley, California in 1926, where Hans Kindler performed as soloist. Soon after arriving in Washington, Frost evolved a plan to gather eighty instrumentalists to do three concerts, each with a different conductor, to determine if Washington could and would support an orchestra—and to select a possible director. Rudolf Schueller from the Cleveland Institute of Music conducted the first performance, which was not entirely satisfactory. The dissatisfied element then approached Walter Damrosch for help, and it was he who recommended Kindler. Kindler was then engaged to conduct the second concert (except for one selection by Gustav Strube, who conducted his own piece) and was an immediate success—not only because of his musical skills, but his "blonde good looks, delft blue eyes" and charming manner helped considerably. It was unanimously agreed that he should conduct the third concert as well.

In the heat of the enthusiasm a National Symphony Society was organized and held its first meeting at the home of Mary and Walter Howe. Frank Frost was elected chairman and George Gaul chosen as secretary of the new organization. However, with the worsening of the Depression, plans had to be temporarily abandoned and the orchestra disbanded. Kindler left for a European tour but the interest was kept alive by the press and by Kindler's intermittent visits to the city.[25] A new campaign was launched in 1931 and Kindler, recognizing the importance of his presence there, returned to Washington and took up residence at the Mayflower Hotel, where he devoted himself energetically to collecting the more than 20,000 pledges of the previous year that had been unfulfilled and to obtaining several large donations from well-heeled friends. It was only after there was sufficient money to guarantee the first season that he left in May for another European tour. The Howes worked diligently for the cause of the National Symphony and, as might be expected, approached Elizabeth for help. Letters exchanged throughout this period indicate that she and the Howes had by this time become very close friends, and in view of Mary's generous assistance to Elizabeth it was logical that she might expect Coolidge to come to their aid now in behalf of the symphony. But when Mary approached her she responded with a letter to Walter Howe, in his capacity as chairman of the Orchestra Committee, saying that while she agreed in principle and supported the idea wholeheartedly, she could not give any financial assistance: "I need no arguments to convince me of the great value of Hans's work or of the splendid scheme of a Washington orchestra. For many years I have wished that such an orchestra might not only be local and national in name but in fact might be supported by the government, as it certainly should be." It was not for any lack of interest in Hans, or music, or in Washington that she failed to contribute, but because "I want to adhere to my plan of doing it through chamber music, believing that in so concentrating I can best carry on the work which I have already begun in these directions." The shortfall in her income at this time unquestionably was a factor in her decision, and she even admitted, "If I were not obliged to consider the limitation of my resources I should not wish all this but should gladly and probably voluntarily join you in your endeavors for the orchestra. . . . I simply cannot do it all—which I regret deeply—and it is with the earnest hope that you will understand and respect my decision."[26]

Year after year came the requests from Mary and just as regularly came the refusals from Elizabeth. To their credit Kindler, the Howes, and Coolidge managed to maintain their friendship despite their difference of opinion on this one score. Undoubtedly the ability of both women to preserve their objectivity throughout this prolonged debate owed much to their mutually forthright modes of operation. Mary Howe could be just as direct as Coolidge, and in 1936 when Elizabeth failed to renew even her $25 membership in the Orchestra Association, Mary wrote very frankly: "I must confess I was very much disappointed to have your letter from Los Angeles this morning. Not that I was looking for a large subscription or pledge because I know and thoroughly understand your allegiance and responsibility towards chamber music. But as we have had you on our membership list for a year or two it is of course a chagrin no longer to list a name of such distinction especially when we are beginning to feel we have won our spurs." Finally Mary reminded her: "I had hoped you might squeeze out the $25, just as I was able to squeeze out $100 for the Quartet at the Library of Congress."[27]

Still the answer was no. Elizabeth did remind Mary, however, that she had offered the orchestra four $1,000 engagements and would probably continue to do so. Nonetheless, Howe's determination won through. By 1939 Mary pointed out very plainly: "What I think you do not realize yourself is that the fact that we do not have you even as a member of the Orchestra Association at $25 tacitly expresses a disapproval which I am entirely convinced you do not feel. . . . Your opinion is of enormous weight and for that very reason I realize you do not give your approval lightly. I am not asking you to approve the Orchestra musically. . . . I am asking you, so to speak, to let the light of your countenance shine upon a civic project. . . . I think it is a sort of black eye for us from a civic point of view not to have you listed as a member of the Orchestra Association in a town where you are par excellence, the most distinguished and beneficent music patron."[28]

Finally Coolidge contributed $100, hoping that this would "heal the 'black eye' as which the absence of my name on the membership list has been interpreted, for I assure you that nothing of the kind was in my mind." Mary was pleased and responded simply "you are a swell girl!"[29]

As tightfisted as Coolidge appeared to be throughout this exchange with Mrs. Howe, her determination to maintain chamber music as the primary object of her patronage was not the only reason for her seemingly stubborn refusal of any significant financial support to the fledgling National Symphony Orchestra. She did in time engage a chamber orchestra made up of instrumentalists from the symphony to perform at the Coolidge Auditorium under Kindler's direction, and perhaps more importantly, she lent the prestige of her name to the cause of the orchestra when some controversy over Kindler's policies became widely publicized. She had already won one battle with federal bureaucracy when she created the Library of Congress Trust Fund, and she had become an outspoken proponent of government support for the arts. Nowhere is this more clearly and publicly stated than in this letter to the *Washington Post:* "I believe that the citizens of Washington themselves, and the cause of music in general would gain by the numerous secondary results which follow the establishment of a leading symphony orchestra in any community. . . . Is it too much to hope that one day the National Orchestra may become so in fact as well as in name, and that, like other imperative needs of our country, the best music should be guaranteed to its citizens by the government, and exemplified by its maintenance at the governmental center of the Nation?"[30]

It is symbolic of the survival of their friendship that in 1940 Mary Howe dedicated her recently completed string quartet to Elizabeth, who graciously received it and added it to her collection at the Library of Congress. Although the piece was performed privately by the Coolidge Quartet at the home of Edwin T. Rice that same year, there is no record that Coolidge ever programmed it publicly. Later, however, she did sponsor the Albeneri Trio in a performance of Howe's *Suite Mélancolique.*[31]

Over the years various women composers sent their manuscripts to Elizabeth, but Rebecca Clarke would remain the only woman ever commissioned. Unlike most of the men composers who frequently sent dedications to Coolidge in the (often not-too-subtle) hope of receiving a commission, the women usually simply made gifts of their works, or at least first asked permission to dedicate them to her. In the case of friends like Howe and Mabel Daniels, she always graciously accepted—but almost never performed them publicly. The ladies were perhaps just as ambitious as the men but were not quite so overt. A case in point is Mabel Daniels, who wrote to Elizabeth to tell her that she was working on a chamber piece "in modern style," three sketches for oboe, clarinet, and bassoon, for which she was providing an alternate viola part in place of the bassoon—"in case all the bassoons go to war."[32] Not a bad idea, since everyone knew that the viola was Coolidge's favorite instrument.

Helen Hopekirk wrote affectionate notes but was especially shy about approaching Elizabeth with anything even remotely suggestive of a hoped-for commission. The case of Amy Beach is unique. Years earlier Elizabeth had sent her works to Beach for criticism, and now Beach resurfaced in a different capacity, sending her manuscripts to Coolidge—not for critique, certainly. Beach was sufficiently established and self-assured by this time to express her hopes openly, but when she sent her Variations for Flute and String Quartet to Elizabeth, she wrote,

"It is seldom that I have cared so much for anything of mine as for this composition, and I cannot help hoping that it may appeal sufficiently to you to lead you to suggest it for a Festival performance at Pittsfield. . . . I realize fully that you have *tons* of music sent you, and that you can only have a small proportion of it performed there! So please do not let my wish as a 'fond parent' stand in your way in your great task of selection."[33]

Apparently Coolidge took her at her word and felt no compulsion to perform the work. This failure to encourage female composers with commissions, along with the notable absence of women's works from Coolidge-sponsored performances and from the roster of Coolidge medalists, raises the question of her attitude toward women's role in the world of professional music. She seems to have had no problem accepting women performers and, in fact, employed such artists as Myra Hess, Harriet Cohen, May Mukle, Katherine Goodson, and Kathleen Parlow; and she herself frequently performed with the ensembles that she sponsored. However, the reasons for her failure to support women composers are difficult to assess. As she herself made very clear, her own efforts at composition stemmed from very personal motives, and although she approached composition with the same kind of dedication that she brought to any of her work, she never seriously thought of herself as a composer. That is humorously brought home in a letter to her investment broker, who at the time of the Library of Congress endowment feared that she might be financially overextended. She wrote to tell him that she had just received a check for $9.99 royalties and assured him, "You see, I shall never have to worry about money."[34]

She must have been aware of how difficult it was for women composers to obtain a hearing of their works. If she had not perceived it on her own she was certainly apprised of it in no uncertain terms by the women themselves. Mary Howe was more fortunate than most because Kindler took a real interest in her work. He performed her *Dirge* and her tone poem *Stars* with both the National Symphony and the Robin Hood Dell Orchestra. Others were not so lucky. As early as 1926, Ethyl Smyth wrote to say that "Oxford is finally making me a music doctor, . . . but except for Sir Henry Wood none of our conductors take my work to America—nor will they 'til the grave has done away with the petticoat element."[35] And when Coolidge's friend, Mabel Daniels, sent the score of her *Deep Forest* (for chamber orchestra) to Elizabeth, she complained that "when a woman undertakes to write seriously for orchestra she is looked at rather askance by conductors. . . . I'm just starting to launch a piece for full orchestra and the final question I was asked was '*Do you do your own orchestration?*' which makes me *furious*."[36]

It is difficult to determine if Coolidge's apparent indifference to the cause of the woman composer sprang from deep-seated Victorian prejudice or from the same rather elitist attitude that caused her to spurn homegrown American works in her early programs at the Library of Congress. Her argument at that time was based upon the assumption—not actually verbalized but strongly suggested—that there were no American works of sufficient stature to compare with the European classics, and in her opinion the goals of the Foundation would be best served by recognized quality. By implication "quality" was equated in her mind with "European." Although there is no record in any of her letters or other writings that she may have consciously applied this kind of reasoning in her comparison of women's compositions with those of men, there is undeniable evidence of a certain elitism in her determination to eschew any association with the vernacular tradition in her activities.

Although Charles Martin Loeffler dedicated his Partita for Violin and Piano to Elizabeth, she allegedly took offense at the third movement (the *Divertissement*, subtitled *La Petite Princesse Nègre*), which showed decided jazz influences. She did, however, permit the movement to be played at the Library of Congress concert in 1934.[37] On another occasion Engel's suggestion of using Benny Goodman—whose performance of the Mozart Quintet for Clarinet and Strings, K. 581, had so impressed him—fell on an unsympathetic ear. She admitted, "I am perfectly delighted that Benny Goodman, and his public, are led into paths of Mozart's music, and consider it a wonderful thing for the course of chamber music," but added, "I do not wish the Coolidge Foundation to be credited with any cooperation with Benny Goodman."[38] If she objected to Benny Goodman one cannot help wondering how she must have felt when Handy's *St. Louis Blues* managed to find its way onto the program of the fourth Library of Congress Festival in 1929.

A new character entered the Library of Congress scene in 1936 in the person of Gertrude Clarke Whittall. It was during Strunk's administration that Whittall donated to the Library a quartet of Stradivari instruments. Upon hearing the news Elizabeth wrote enthusiastically: "I have just learned through Oliver Strunk of your magnificent offer to the Trust fund of the Library of Congress of the four superb instruments and I want to write you of how deeply I am impressed. Such a contribution should add enormously to the cultural effectiveness of the Music Department there, and, of course you know that the project is one which is dearest to my heart. May I offer you my sincerest congratulations for having made such a splendid gesture, and thank you for my share of the pleasure which I am sure will result."[39]

It seemed the ideal marriage of two unique gifts—the shrine to chamber music that Coolidge had provided and now the magnificent instruments that were to be used there. Elizabeth subsequently wrote to compliment Whittall on the wisdom of creating a trust fund that would provide for the instruments to be played by visiting artists. The aims of the two women were similar in many respects: Elizabeth sought to bring the musical repository of the Library alive in performance, and Whittall believed that fine instruments should be heard, not kept as museum pieces. She expressed this attitude clearly in response to Coolidge's letter: "You and I are *d'accord* in regard to the mission of music. . . . It should be futile for composers to write scores destined never to be heard. It would have been unfair to the rare instrument[s] . . . if they had been locked in glass cases and left mute forever. . . . I also—like you—believe that the Government will prove faithful to the trust placed in its hands."[40]

Letters exchanged between the two ladies are very cordial and suggest a feeling of mutual respect and admiration. That was dimmed somewhat when, in 1937, the concerts sponsored by the Whittall Foundation took over the NBC slot formerly occupied by the Coolidge Foundation concerts. Engel informed Elizabeth of it and, hoping to head off the objections that were sure to result, hastened to assure her that "Columbia will give us six Saturdays beginning 13 November. Best spot yet—40 minutes between 5:45 and 6:25."[41] Nevertheless, Coolidge was not happy about what she perceived as an incursion into her territory and responded: "I am sorry that the Whittall Foundation has got into our place with the National Broadcasting Company—not really because I am jealous of their work, but because I feel that their standards are so much lower than those which we have maintained that it may exert an unconscious influence upon the prestige which we have established for the Library of Congress broadcasts." She chose this opportunity to voice her opinion that there was "misinformation and misunderstanding about the relationship of the two Foundations, and while I welcome any extension of our pioneer work in behalf of the best music, I am sorry to have others lessen . . . the confidence with which the Coolidge Foundation has inspired the radio public under the auspices of the Library of Congress. . . . Please don't misunderstand this jealousy for our standards as any personal rivalry, but merely a desire to defend what has cost us so much effort to establish."[42]

The two ladies maintained a cordial relationship in their work, but for all her forswearing of any personal jealousy, Coolidge never really warmed to Whittall in the way that she had to other women friends. The two were very different in personality and style. Whittall was not of the same blue-blood stock as Elizabeth and had acquired her wealth by marriage to a man who dealt in fine carpets. Moreover, her entrance into the picture came at a time when Coolidge's fortune had been seriously diminished by the Depression, which may have made her more sensitive to this new rival. Nonetheless, the two foundations have endured and become pillars of the music program at the Library of Congress. The decorative grille that separates the Whittall Pavilion from the foyer of the Coolidge Auditorium is said to be a remnant of the "non-feud" and stands as a reminder of the separation of the two foundations that in actuality complement each other so beautifully.

There was one other slight disappointment for Elizabeth at the Library of Congress involving a bronze bust of herself that she had commissioned from the artist Jo Davidson. She intended it to be unveiled at the Founder's Day festivities in 1934, which would be her seventieth birthday. Because she was somewhat embarrassed at the thought of offering it to the Library herself, she wrote to Engel to suggest that although she paid for it ($3,000) it should come from Sprague as a gift to the Library of Congress Music Division held in trust for the Coolidge Foundation. However, the Library had a strict policy of not exhibiting likenesses of living persons. Engel's explanation is a masterful example of his ability to anticipate her objections and preclude them by appealing to her vanity:

> *That Mr. Davidson should have perpetuated (if he could) in drab and rigid bronze your bright and mobile countenance, is interesting. But frankly speaking, I think that however "tactfully" . . . we might go about it, we should not ask the Library of Congress to break a long and undeviating record of not accepting busts or paintings of living subjects—offered, in most cases, for no palpable purpose other than that of self-aggrandizement.*[43]

With a perfect checkmate, Engel gracefully sidestepped any counter from her by pointing out that while "such a purpose should be most remote from your own mind or intention, [that] does not void the chances of a wrong interpretation. And a misunderstanding would be doubly cruel, considering that your prime motive so often is love or charity."[44]

Before she could point out the disparity in this policy by reminding him of the bas-relief of her that already graced the foyer, he added, "If the tablet in our lobby—the only one of its kind in a United States building—was suggested and adopted, blame only me. . . . It was conceived as an architectural detail merely, and represents an appropriate statement of fact. Busts and portraits are in a different class."[45] He undoubtedly realized that the thought of hers being the only face of a living person displayed in a government building would forestall any further argument, and he was right. She accepted the decree very graciously and wrote to her friend Henry Eichheim, whose idea it was in the first place: "I have just heard from Carl Engel that it will not be in accordance with the precedent of the Library of Congress to accept portraits of living people and therefore, I see no way in which we can carry out our plan for the bronze bust next October—unless I should shuffle off before that, in which case please let me appoint you as the trustee of this work and ask you to offer it to them."[46]

Elizabeth was not only not about to "shuffle off," but she was still maintaining a hectic schedule. At the age of seventy-six she wrote to a friend, "At present I have seven engagements for Saturday, and am wondering how I shall have time even to wash my hands, much more to change my gown, from 9 o'clock in the morning until midnight."[47] She had her own methods of dealing with these time constraints, and they were often just as creative as her larger endeavors. On one occasion when she arrived in Washington for a festival, just off the train in time for a quick bite and then off at once to the concert, Mary Howe was concerned about her being able to change her dress. Howe's son, Bruce, recalls how "Mrs. C. just went to the little downstairs washroom next to the closet under the stairs and disappeared into it in her train dress. In a very few minutes she emerged in a long, black evening dress with gilt and gunmetal beads, she'd had it on under her day dress and kept right on schedule, every hair in place."[48]

Clearly, time had not tamed this advanced old lady.

CHAPTER SIXTEEN

Slings and Arrows

To remain aloof from silly provincial quarrels is the most dignified attitude for those who sincerely love art.

– ELIZABETH SPRAGUE COOLIDGE TO EDWIN T. RICE, 15 AUGUST 1937

IN THE DECADE of the 1930s Elizabeth reaped a bountiful crop of honors and triumphs, but not even the excitement of the tours or the recognition by foreign governments could dispel completely the shadows cast by problems that she encountered at Pittsfield and at Mills College. Sensitive friends who were privy to the circumstances did their best to divert her attention from the problems, even if only for a brief spell. Despite the delightful motoring trips to Lourdes and Barcelona with the Respighis and through Devonshire and Cornwall with the Bridges, Coolidge frequently found herself doing battle during these years. The contradictory aspects of her personality have, to some extent, obscured her motives as she faced these various problems.

In the 1930s Coolidge's association with the organization that she had created at South Mountain began to sour. There is a special poignancy about the blight on this relationship that had occupied such a special place in her heart, not only by reason of its birthright as her first major musical philanthropy but also because of the memories of her life in Massachusetts with Fred.

As early as 1925 some Pittsfield residents felt that Coolidge had abandoned them when she moved her venue to the Library of Congress. With the gradually expanding range of her activities both in the United States and abroad, and with her energy and her money now diffused over a wide geographic area, she remarked that she sometimes felt like the old woman in the shoe who had so many children she didn't know what to do. She was well aware that she had become something of an absentee landlord and needed a strong administrator to assume direction of the activities in the Berkshires. So with her son's approval, she filed incorporation papers in 1935 establishing the South Mountain Association, formed for the purpose of continuing the educational and cultural activities that she had inaugurated some eighteen years earlier.[1]

Inevitably, business and artistic considerations came into conflict from time to time, and although Elizabeth had (theoretically at least) given over the administration of the colony, she still attempted to maintain a certain amount of control—interference, some would call it. A major bone of contention was her unswerving commitment to providing free concerts, an issue over which she had already differed with Carl Engel. In 1935 she wrote to Willeke, who had begun charging admission in an effort to support the maintenance of South Mountain, that she wanted to revert to her old plan of giving free concerts, "which is part of my musical creed, and for which I feel I am devoting many thousands of dollars in Pittsfield; namely, that the music which I engage to be given from my Temple should be for the benefit of the community and the musical public at large by making it available to everyone."[2]

Willeke replied in a long and frank letter reminding her that by charging a modest one-dollar admission he had been able to hire soloists, rent pianos, pay printing and electric bills, and take care of various other expenses. He ventured to remind her that she once had said to him, "My God, Willem, I hate to be bothered with all these small details on the Mountain—water pump, septic tank, cesspool and other unpleasant items," so he had never bothered her with them. He pointed out also that with the money earned by charging for the use of the cottages on the property (that she had wanted given free) he had been able to tar the roads leading to the Temple and tend to other maintenance. Moreover, three years earlier she had also decreased his salary and he was, in a word, "broke, but not sad."[3]

By return mail Coolidge answered with equal frankness and a distinctively canny approach—for she had over the years developed a tidy legal mind—pointing out that he had confused the issue by introducing four topics instead of the one that she wished to discuss, namely, the tickets. While it is true that at an earlier time she had, in fact, consented to a small admission fee, she explained that it was "because you requested it, and, although I felt that the cause of chamber music suffered by it, I continued to allow it because I knew that Sprague preferred and approved it. I have not said all this to you before, because I knew that he believed that people better appreciate what they pay for."[4]

She finally addressed the other issues that Willeke had raised, pointing out, albeit somewhat grudgingly, that they were not really the subjects of her first communication, and her willingness to discuss them at all was, therefore, a concession to him. On the touchy question of Willeke's salary she reminded him: "I never bound myself to a permanent amount of salary, to you or anyone else. . . . My only promise to you was the management of the summer music on South Mountain for as long as you might wish it. . . . When the depression came, I felt it not only right, but obligatory, to reduce this disproportionate expense, as you know. With much less money, and more and more obligations, how could I do otherwise?"[5]

In her opinion, the best way to handle this "tangle of interests and misunderstandings about Pittsfield" was for her to reassume the entire musical responsibility of the summer season on the Mountain, leaving to Willem and Sprague all matters relating to the upkeep of the estate and use of buildings. Although it seemed a logical and clear-cut division of responsibility, she could not refrain from time to time from speaking out on matters that by her own definition were now outside her hands. Clearly, she found this to be one of those instances when the objective handling of administrative matters was complicated by friendship, and her closing remarks seem obviously intended to assuage any injured feelings on Willeke's part. "I cannot tell you how I appreciate the splendid work which you have done for me and for music; if the depression had not put a stop to it, I should have enjoyed continuing to do as a friend what it is quite out of the question for me to do as a business manager."[6]

It was largely these differences that prompted Elizabeth the following year to deed the South Mountain property to the South Mountain Association, thereby placing the maintenance and administration squarely in the hands of the president and the board of directors. The document is a forthright exposition of her motivation for this latest move. Although technically not an official of the board, she spoke as one having "the moral right . . . and artistic duty" to clarify her motive in incorporating the South Mountain creation into a state institution with a state charter. She perceived Willeke's occupancy of Mountain House, formerly Sprague's home, to be a clear violation of tax-exempt status, and made her position quite clear. "Until true educational purposes (such as class-rooms, studios, dormitories, practice rooms or other equipment) are served by Mountain House, I think therefore, that income for its taxes should be raised by renting or selling it."[7] It was her desire that with the assistance of the Association, the community might rally and the whole estate could be developed and enlarged into a far-reaching educational agency. If these projects were not realized she recommended closing the property temporarily and selling enough of it to pay the taxes and insurance on the remainder.

The transition did not go smoothly, and less than a year later Elizabeth wrote to Rice, as president of the South Mountain Association, that she had learned of "an undercurrent of unfriendliness and factionalism, which, of course, I deplore. I am resolved to take no further part in any pettiness, [and] I hope that you will do as I have done, namely withdraw from any official connection with this sordid affair, and leave to those who have seized control such petty tactics as they may see fit to adopt."[8] This treatment of Rice was a sore spot that she admitted "has resulted in an enormous diminution of my interest and sympathy in what I now consider to be their affair, and no longer mine."[9]

Relief from this anxiety came in the form of the preparations for her tenth Berkshire Festival in 1938. She left her imprint on the plans down to the last detail, so it is significant that she chose Hugo Kortschak, who by now was teaching at Yale, to be the music director rather than Willeke, who was relegated (along with the Association) to preparation of the Temple. Nor was the South Mountain Quartet featured in a prominent way. They did perform but so did five other ensembles—the Coolidge, Berkshire, Kolisch, Gordon, and Roth Quartets.

Even the musical aspects of the festival suffered some reverses when the special finale that Coolidge had planned was marred by a power struggle between two performers. She had decided to end with a gala performance of Bach's Fourth Brandenburg Concerto, which would be played by the combined quartets of that year—in her words a real "musical jollification." In rehearsal however it proved to be a nightmare for Kortschak when certain prima-donna attitudes surfaced over the selection of Feri Roth as soloist. When Kortschak reported this to Coolidge she responded, "I can never understand what seems to me the foolishness of everybody wanting to play first violin, feeling that in this way they are showing much more interest in themselves than in the music of the composers or the general success of the musical undertaking."[10] It is a tribute to Kortschak's tactful handling of the situation that the concert eventually went off smoothly. On a happier note, the festival was highlighted by two important premiere performances: Webern's Quartet, op. 28, and Bridge's Fourth Quartet, both dedicated to Coolidge.

Willeke's somewhat minimized role in the festival may have had something to do with Charles W. Power's report that the Willekes were gone so much of the time that the Association was required to take over more responsibility. To this Coolidge responded, "I am, of course, disappointed that they spend so little time in the home on South Mountain, as the principal idea of deeding my son's house and securing exemption from taxation for it, was that Mr. Willeke should fulfill his intention and desire to expand and prolong the work, and it was upon this assumption that the exemption was procured and the building was given to the South Mountain Association instead of to Harvard University, who were eager to use it for their summer school."[11]

Believing that no one who is employed by a board or a committee should be a member of that board or committee, she asked Willem and Sally Willeke to resign. On the same day she wrote to Willeke, "I must confess . . . that I fear I should not be at ease in Pittsfield as long as is missing the old cordial relationship between South Mountain and my very dear friend and helper, Mr. Edwin Rice. This would cause such an unnatural and, to me, unsympathetic atmosphere, that I should prefer to remain aloof in the hope that the future might bring a more equitable condition."[12]

A new voice was added to the discord in 1936 when Kathleen Parlow, one of Leopold Auer's outstanding students, became the first violinist of the South Mountain Quartet. She was already well known to Elizabeth for the fine work she had done at Mills College. At first things went very well, but over the years tensions grew between her and Willeke. Parlow claimed that he no longer practiced, and his playing had become "scratchy, woolly and out of tune."[13] With partisans from both sides of the controversy reporting to Coolidge, it was difficult to distance herself from the dissension, and although she could say she had "tried to remain outside the unfortunate bickering which has taken place among the South Mountain people for I suppose there are always two sides to every question," she nonetheless had to admit "in this instance my sympathies are very much with Miss Parlow."[14] The warm personal letters they exchanged indicate that Parlow felt comfortable confiding in Coolidge.

Sally Willeke obviously was aware that Parlow had Elizabeth's ear and appealed instead to Sprague, who responded in his usual candid manner in a letter that is a model of clarity. His comments are prefixed by the assurance that they are based solely upon his own observations and experience and not upon gossip. He admitted that he had perceived some deficiencies in Parlow's performance as an ensemble player, but noted that she had a legitimate reason to complain that rehearsals of the quartet were too few and too brief, and that the other three members of the quartet actually found it necessary to practice without Willeke. "It was not until two years ago that I learned that the other players were in the habit of holding regular rehearsals without Willem, in order to put the final edge on the program and to clear up points among themselves which they did not find opportunity to work on during the regular rehearsals. Since I found out about these rehearsals and participated in them, I can testify to their value."[15]

Another problem, in his opinion, was the "teacher and pupil" attitude that prevailed in rehearsals, an attitude that frowned upon independent or original ideas from the other members of the quartet. Finally, he raises the issue of disparity, which he believed to be at the bottom of all the criticisms. "Consider the facts. Willem lives in a palace, the others in shanties in various stages of ruin, for all the world like master and slave in the old South. Willem's students appear alone in the student recitals. After the concert, Willem has a reception at which the other artists are frequently not seen. No matter what may be the causes of these facts, I think they are deplorable for the morale of the mountain."[16]

Finally, after six years of service, Parlow left the South Mountain Quartet to return to her native Canada. Her decision to do so was motivated largely by what she identified as "intense jealousy . . . growing more and more out of bounds every day."[17] Obviously both sides had their staunch supporters, and people like Parlow and Mary Bristol, who had worked so many years for Elizabeth in Pittsfield, could relate just how the adversaries had aligned themselves.

Through it all Coolidge continued to support the musicals in the Temple, but in 1940, when she sent a check for $3,000 stipulating that it be for certain quartets of her choice, Samuel Colt, the new president, objected, pointing out that this violated Willeke's right as music director to select the performers.[18] It is clear that Colt was in the Willeke camp and felt a genuine concern to set the record straight in behalf of his friend, who had been the butt of so much criticism and who appears to have said almost nothing in his own defense. In 1949 Colt risked Coolidge's ire when he ventured the opinion that it was a mistake to continue to use the entire amount of her annual contribution to pay artists when Willeke was not only doing much of the maintenance work himself but was also paying for a good bit of it out of his own pocket. Colt enumerated the many expenses in preparation for last summer's season, reminding her also that Willem had received no salary. "It is characteristic of Willem's devotion to the institution which you established that since 1940 he has always insisted that all money contributed to the Association be used for repairs and maintenance for its future use."[19] In fact, "all expenses of keeping up the Mountain House, including a new steam boiler and oil burner, just completed, he (Willeke) has paid for out of his own pocket. . . . The Association has no money to give to Willem Willeke for a salary. It is true he pays no rent, but he gives all his chamber music and instructions free to pupils who study with him during the season, and that keeps the property tax exempt."[20]

It is evident that the dissension was wearing on Elizabeth, who privately confided to Mary Bristol, "The death of this enterprise would be merely one more event in what seems to be the dissolution of our world, from which most of my dearest friends have already left me, and which can only be compensated for by making new and constructive efforts for the future generations. This is a sad reflection, but I feel it is universal, as our old age accompanies that of the civilized world."[21]

Despite her disappointments and occasional hard feelings toward Pittsfield, there were still many there to whom she felt deeply committed in friendship, like Mary Bristol, Jay Rosenfeld, and the Kitsons. When she learned that Henry Kitson, the English sculptor who made his home in Pittsfield and who had done so much work for her at South Mountain, was in dire financial need, she quietly came to his rescue. It was Kitson who executed the bronze relief of Elizabeth that was placed in the Temple in 1933.

It seems symbolic of the survival of their friendship that when Willeke reopened the South Mountain Festival in 1949 Elizabeth sent him a check for $5,000—not from the Foundation but from her personally. He was obviously pleased and wrote, "I was happy to receive your nice letter because for many years I had thought your friendship for me was entirely destroyed forever, due to misrepresentations planted in your mind by people whom I rightly mistrust."[22]

The following year Willem Willeke died. His wife Sally, a cellist who had been his pupil at Juilliard and for years was his right hand in administering musical affairs of South Mountain, offered to carry on her husband's work there. Elizabeth responded warmly, accepting Sally's offer and agreeing to her idea of Sunday afternoon concerts at the Temple after the Tanglewood season closed. Despite accusations to the contrary, Elizabeth never lost interest in South Mountain, but as she told Samuel Colt, neither was she ever reconciled to the collapse of her original purpose, "which I had hoped to continue with the cooperation of what was once an interested and sympathetic public. Perhaps now that the war is ended, we may still find some way to re-establish the music, under a competent direction and contented artists, thus recapturing the support of a satisfied Berkshire audience, and reviving the prestige of South Mountain."[23]

The Willekes had many loyal friends in Pittsfield, and when Sally died in 1987 at the age of eighty she was eulogized as "South Mountain's driving force." Although South Mountain continues to exist—chamber music concerts are still held there—when the old cottages that Elizabeth had so long wished to have demolished were finally pulled down in 1973, it seemed symbolic of the end of an era.

Meanwhile, on the other side of the continent storms of another sort were brewing. Elizabeth had often admitted "California has half my heart." By now she was involved in musical activities up and down the West Coast, concentrated especially in the San Francisco Bay Area and in southern California where she sponsored concerts at the Los Angeles Public Library, UCLA, USC, Santa Barbara, Claremont College, Ojai, and Occidental College. But it was above all at Mills College in Oakland that she found her niche. Her affiliation with the school began in the late 1920s, with the dedication of the music building. Later Coolidge actually lived on the campus during the summer months while she studied composition with Brescia. By 1932 she began her annual sponsorship of the Pro Arte Quartet at Mills for summer sessions during which they not only performed two concerts weekly, but lived on campus, taught privately, and coached ensembles.

While living in Washington, Elizabeth was occasionally invited to the White House for teas and luncheons, and it was here that she became acquainted with Lou Henry Hoover, herself an enthusiastic music lover. When the Hoovers left the White House in 1933 they moved to Palo Alto, California, near Stanford University, and Coolidge was frequently their guest. Mrs. Hoover was a graduate of Stanford and had campaigned actively for the establishment of a music department for the university, which up to that time had no music program but merely employed an organist. In the same year that the Hoovers took up residence in California, Elizabeth announced her intention to send concerts to Stanford and Berkeley.

It is apparent from Elizabeth's correspondence with Aurelia Henry Reinhardt, the president of Mills College, and Luther Marchant, its dean of music, that they viewed these new affiliations as a threat to Mills, if not actually a betrayal. Mills was a small college that was proud of its long and distinguished tradition of music. So when Coolidge announced her intention to offer two free courses at much larger and well-endowed institutions, Reinhardt made haste to remind her of the likely consequences for Mills. In addition to free courses, it was part of Coolidge's plan to offer the Pro Arte Quartet in a series of concerts at Stanford and Berkeley that she would call "The Coolidge Series of California Students' Concerts." Reinhardt's letter emphatically underscores the fact that Mills College had achieved its stature as a pioneer in musical education in the Bay Area by supporting its activities from its own modest budget, without a music endowment. Her feelings about the two nearby universities are plainly stated. "For reasons inherent in their educational purpose, the two neighboring universities have frankly discouraged the arts—corporately through regents and trustees and officially through the faculty. For them it was never a matter of money, but rather an acknowledged educational policy." In her opinion, by installing an organ and developing a glee club, Stanford was sending a message "that engineers, chemists, and biologists did not need an education which recognized the place of music in civilization or in the life of a cultured human being."[24]

Coolidge responded politely but with determination to carry out her plans, citing her satisfaction in the fact that other educational institutions were longing to imitate the fine example of the summer institutes at Mills. "I am so glad to be one of those who can point the way! and I believe that we shall live to see every influential university and college taking this attitude toward a most important branch of culture."[25]

Coolidge carried out her intentions with regard to the larger rival universities, and through her cooperation with Hoover the activities at Stanford developed into what in time was called the Stanford Summer School of Music. The Pro Arte continued its resident program at Mills but also concertized at the neighboring institutions. Encouraged by the success of the Stanford venture, Mrs. Hoover gathered some interested people in her home in the summer of 1937 to discuss with Coolidge the possibility of the community bearing part of the financial burden of further concerts. From this meeting grew the rather loosely woven association of the "Friends of Music" and a fruitful continuation of the cooperation with Coolidge, who proposed a summer series that would feature a performance of all six of Bach's Brandenburg Concerti, with the Roth Quartet in residence forming the backbone of the ensemble. She estimated a price tag of $4,000 for six or eight weeks and promised half that amount if the Friends of Music could raise the other half.[26] It was an arrangement that pleased her, for Coolidge never believed in the dole.

Wisely, she determined that this affiliation with Stanford should be different from that of the Pro Arte at Mills, which was always solidly academic, emphasizing private lessons, coaching, and ensemble work along with the concerts. At Stanford, on the contrary, there would be no technical training (applied music) offered, only concerts and music appreciation lectures, because "there are already so many opportunities of learning to play or sing a solo."[27]

By 1939 Elizabeth was again having quartet problems, this time with the Roth ensemble. The unpleasant experience with the Brandenburg Concerto performance at the Berkshire Festival just a few months before was undoubtedly still fresh in her mind. Her strategy this time was to avoid being drawn into the problem that had arisen between Feri Roth and Molnar, the violist of the Roth quartet. She explained to Mrs. Hoover, "It might be wise to have a series of concerts which should not require the services of a string quartet." and suggested rather some trio concerts with violinist Sylvia Lent (Mrs. Alfred Frankenstein), pianist Gunnar Johansen, and a cellist of their choice.[28] The degree of her disgust with such bickering within ensembles can be measured from her resolve that "if they (the Friends of Music) should decide to continue next summer with the Roth Quartet, I should feel obliged to withdraw my cooperation during the summer quarter and do what I can for Stanford at some other time."[29] Hoover agreed and the problem was avoided for the moment.

Luther Marchant was one of Coolidge's favorite people and had long been a part of her coterie. He and his wife traveled in her entourage in the famous European tour of 1931, and Elizabeth spent a good deal of time with them when she was on campus at Mills. The misunderstanding with Mills was for him not only an academic concern but a personal one, for he was very fond of Elizabeth. Over the years Marchant had often pointed out to her that her contributions to Mills would be more far-reaching if they were during the academic year and not confined to summer, when fewer students were on campus. Now Mrs. Hoover and the Friends of Music were of the same mind. At an informal meeting of the organizing committee of the Friends (Coolidge was absent), Hoover reported her lack of success in convincing Elizabeth of this viewpoint and cited the difference in their attitudes. "Sometimes our plans are just diametrically opposed. We think if we could get music here when there are four thousand students attending the University instead of in the summer when there are nine hundred, or less than a quarter of the usual number, our contribution would be of much greater value."[30]

At issue was the practical question of the Friends of Music investing money and effort in a series limited to the summer. Hoover went on to explain how difficult it could be to change Coolidge's mind once she had it made up, describing her as "cunning." Even after Mr. Frankenstein pointed out to her that there had been forty concerts within the six weeks of the summer and only eight in ten months during the winter, Coolidge replied, "Yes, but you know I like the forty in the summer."[31]

With this latest expansion of her activities Elizabeth was caught up in scheduling difficulties, particularly with the Pro Arte Quartet. The added concerts made for an extremely taxing schedule for the quartet, and in her concern for the members (especially Onnou) she suggested cutting back on the amount of teaching the quartet would do at Mills. Marchant was understandably disappointed and said so: "Your stipulation regarding the teaching . . . is a grave disappointment to Mills College, as its summer sessions are periods of the highest type of musical instruction available."[32]

Elizabeth felt caught in this situation and described herself as trying "to make two and two make five, and in so doing, to please everybody." Once again the old bête noire of selling tickets raised its head and prompted what must have looked to Marchant like a threat. She wrote that in her opinion, "the problem of . . . giving large free concerts in the bay area region during the period of the Mills College Summer Session appears to be unreconcilable with that of the sale of tickets which you find necessary for continuing the Pro Arte work there; and leads me to the conclusion that after 1935 it will probably be better for us to go our own ways, you—with Mills College, and I, as best I can with the universities, not requiring the services of the same artists at the same period."[33]

To complicate matters, she had moved off-campus in 1936 and now was feeling isolated from Mills. Moreover, she was offended by Marchant's suggestion that she had grown "cool" in her love for the Pro Arte and "indifferent" toward Mills College. She protested that her love for the Pro Arte was never greater, and that if she appeared to be indifferent it was due partly to a lack of physical strength and the fact that her hearing was particularly bad at this time, but admitted that it was also "possibly due to an effort at self protection against home-sickness and jealousy at finding myself no longer included in the Mills College coterie and its friendly social gatherings. I know that this is a natural result of my having left the campus, and am ashamed of a weakness which I despise in others."[34]

She admitted to a waning interest in the summer school and the feeling that her role had slowly been reduced merely to paying bills instead of realizing her own wider projects. Moreover, it grieved her to realize that her activities at Berkeley were looked upon as being "hostile to Mills." In short she was feeling exploited, but perhaps fearing that her frank admissions would offend or bring an end to the work she had begun at Mills—of which she was justifiably proud—she appended to the letter a penciled note in her own hand: "Dear Luther, this letter is a testimony of the affection and regard for you which demand from me a fearless and honest reply to your frank and friendly letter. It is almost impersonal, and concerns not our mutual affection, but an unfortunate situation which I do not intend to allow to sever our deep friendship. Yours lovingly, Elizabeth."[35]

Marchant either accepted her terms or had by this time learned how to handle her. Both of them were aware that the existing conflict had more to do with the Mills music committee than with Marchant personally. Things came to a head when in 1938 Coolidge proposed sending her new Coolidge Quartet to play and teach during the next summer, when the Pro Arte could not be there. The committee rejected her offer and the $1,000 attached, and it fell to Marchant to explain the reasons. He must have felt himself a bit like the bearer of bad tidings in Greek tragedy who must die after delivering his message. Nonetheless he fulfilled his mission and wrote, "We are all very sorry not to be able to cooperate with you in bringing the Coolidge Quartet, but know that you will understand our position. With two large universities receiving your support in a series of concerts occurring at exactly the same time as ours and with each presenting free concerts by two of the best known quartets in America, we must have *first* a quartet that is known in the West and *second,* a quartet that will maintain the high musical standard of the Pro Arte."[36]

This last remark must have offended, but she saw his point. As an alternative, Marchant suggested engaging the Budapest String Quartet, which was already very popular in the area. Elizabeth agreed, allowing him to keep the $1,000 to obtain their services, adding that she admired them very much too. The following summer she announced that she assured the Pro Arte of $15,000 worth of engagements for 1940 (forty concerts) and was offering the usual summer residency at Mills, which Luther gratefully accepted—but with the condition that she not offer them at Stanford or Berkeley during the same summer.[37]

This arrangement would not come to pass, for reasons that neither of them could have dreamed of at the time. By fall of 1940 the Pro Arte would be half a quartet, its cellist stranded in Belgium and its first violinist fatally ill. For Elizabeth the personal sorrow of it was exacerbated by the unfortunate deterioration of her relationship with Mills, for the music committee had rejected her attempt to salvage the Pro Arte commitment for that summer. It seemed like the last straw to her.

The Mills-Coolidge cooperation had been a brilliant affiliation—not without its difficulties, admittedly, and although her ties with the college all but ceased in her later years, their association remained a happy memory. When in 1950 Spivacke wrote to say that the Coolidge Foundation was offering Walter Piston a commission to compose a work to celebrate the centennial of Mills College, she responded: "I am glad to agree with you with regard to the commissioned work for Mills College in 1952. I realize that this college has done much for Chamber Music on the West coast and I am proud and glad to remember that I initiated this work . . . and continued for years to sponsor the quartet programs given by the Stradivari, the Brosa and the Pro Arte Quartets."[38] Perhaps the ultimate proof of her continued affection lay in the bestowal of the Coolidge Medal upon Luther Marchant in 1947.

To isolate the difficulties at South Mountain and Mills College from the broader picture of Coolidge's life at this time may seem to emphasize unduly the debit side of the balance sheet and to ignore the fact of her advanced age. These were the years of her seventies, a time when most people have retired, yet she had chosen to swim upstream against the advancing years by accelerating her activities. To attempt to disentangle the complicated strands of Elizabeth Coolidge's complex personality is to begin to understand something of the exercise by which she seemed to be able to separate—with almost surgical precision—her personal feelings from her inviolable credo of "serving Art." But that in no way denies the pain involved on both sides. For now, at least, perhaps Lou Henry Hoover understood it best when she reduced into practical parlance Coolidge's unremitting resolve to put her art objectively above all other considerations: "We look at the students of the university, and what Mrs. Coolidge looks at is the development of Chamber Music in the United States."

CHAPTER SEVENTEEN

Digression: The Diaspora

The entire world has been so affected by the war. . . .
I hope that the artistic flame will not be extinguished and that
after the war we shall see a revival of activities in all directions,
creative as well as executive and educational.

– ELIZABETH SPRAGUE COOLIDGE TO ERNST TOCH,
23 SEPTEMBER 1942

ELIZABETH COOLIDGE SEEMS to have been endowed by nature with the ability to distinguish the blandishments of wheedling opportunists from the worthy appeals of those in genuine need. And when she responded to need, she responded with warmth. Hers was not a remote patronage, an antiseptic dispensing of humanitarian assistance from a clinical distance. Nowhere is that more evident than in her response to the victims of the diaspora at the time of World War II—it is one of the finest but least-known chapters of her life. Whether displaced for reasons of race, religion, or clash of political or artistic ideologies, the integrity of those composers and artists who had the courage to leave all rather than compromise their convictions evoked the noblest responses from her. Her assistance was both moral and financial and was, characteristically, designed to help not only the individual concerned but ultimately to enrich the musical public in general.

Many important compositions resulted from the commissions she offered to exiled composers at this time, and she used her influence in the musical world to help newly arrived refugees obtain teaching posts, positions in symphony orchestras, concert engagements, and lecture tours, many of which were quietly underwritten by her. Music history books are, understandably, silent on the subject of her involvement, for knowledge of this work could be had only from a detailed study of her letters and private papers. It is well known that the influx into the United States of some of Europe's greatest talents had a profound influence upon American musical life. It would be an exaggeration to suggest that Coolidge's role in this migration was in any respect causal, but her contribution to the sustenance of many of the displaced composers and artists deserves to be much better known.

The purging of Jews had begun earlier in Germany and Austria than in Italy, but by the fall of 1938 Jewish composers and performers had so effectively been eliminated in Italy that the Fascist newspaper *Il Telegrafo* boasted that in Florence "this year—thank God—soloists, conductors, interpreters, composers and directors of Jewish race have been excluded from both the symphonic season and the *Maggio Musicale.*"[1] One of the casualties of this purge was Mario Castelnuovo, who had served Elizabeth earlier and had accompanied her on part of the tour of 1931. He reenters her life and correspondence in 1938 in letters—now often written in fractured English—telling of fears for his future and the safety of his family. When his violin concerto "The Prophets" was scheduled for performance with the Turin Radio Orchestra and was suddenly and inexplicably withdrawn, he was concerned but believed it was because the conductor was a German and a Nazi.[2] But when the much-loved concerto of another Jewish composer, Mendelssohn, was also forbidden his concern changed to alarm, and he began surreptitiously to make plans to seek refuge in the United States.

It was an unfortunate coincidence that at about the same time the racial legislation was promulgated in Italy, Castelnuovo finally completed his *Aucassin et Nicolette,* a marionette fable that was scheduled for performance at the *Maggio Musicale Fiorentino.* With this new turn of events it had to be canceled, and he offered it to Coolidge for the Library of Congress. The withdrawal of his music and the new laws that forbade Jewish children to attend public schools brought him to the frightening realization that "if this is how they're beginning, anything is possible!

The only thing left is to leave!"[3] He describes in his autobiography the actual moment of departure from Italy. "It cannot be called sorrow, regret or spiritual suffering: it was almost physical torment, a tearing asunder, a mutilation. It seemed to be a dress rehearsal for Death; and indeed, since that time something in me has been absolutely dead: not Hope, but illusion. What has kept me alive has been love for those dear to me and for music."[4]

Recalling his earlier experiences with Elizabeth, especially her interest in and support of his work, he naturally turned to her for help and in 1938 wrote describing his situation, which "every day [is] worse for us. I hope to . . . stay here some time longer with my family; yet I have still the intention to go to America next autumn, at least for a concert tour, as you know I meant to do last autumn." Since his American manager, Coply, had suggested that he write a piano quartet for Coolidge, Castelnuovo now turned to her with the proposal. "[S]ince you seemed interested in it, . . . I wish to tell you that I would be extremely glad to write some chamber music work for you that could be performed next season."[5] There is no record that she gave any substantial financial assistance, which is likely because Castelnuovo had told her that Heifetz, Spalding, and Toscanini were helping him, and she preferred to give her money to those with no other source of aid. She did, however, take great pains to program his works, and when Castelnuovo moved to California in 1940 she arranged to have the reassembled London String Quartet perform the quartet that he had written for her 1930 Chicago festival. It seems a mark of his gratitude to Elizabeth and the Coolidge Foundation that he left to the Library of Congress a great number of his scores from his American period, many of which he himself regarded as crucial in his development.

In the case of another of her Jewish friends, Darius Milhaud, Coolidge's support was greater. When France fell in 1940 Milhaud quickly fled to America, leaving behind his parents and considerable wealth. It is common knowledge that upon arriving in the United States he was offered a teaching position at Mills College in Oakland, California. But history books tell us nothing of the influences at work behind the scenes. Milhaud wrote to Elizabeth from Lisbon on 23 June 1940 to say that he and his wife would be leaving on 18 July: "[W]e will be arriving in New York in the middle of summer and with far too little money. I hope to find work. I beg you to help me, dear Mrs. Coolidge. I thank you to find a master class in composition, a summer school course, or the direction of some conservatory—it does not matter which."[6]

Elizabeth must have acted with great dispatch, for upon his arrival Milhaud found waiting for him a letter offering not just summer employment but a full-time teaching position at Mills College in the fall. Since Coolidge's association with the school was one of long standing, she obviously felt secure in promoting Milhaud's cause with Luther Marchant. The timing was propitious, for with the death of Domenico Brescia, Mills had just lost its composition teacher, and Marchant jumped at the chance to procure for his faculty someone of the stature of Milhaud, especially since Coolidge offered to pay part of his salary. It was a happy arrangement from the beginning, and as early as the following November Marchant reported to her, "Mr. Milhaud is meeting with great success in every way. He has endeared himself to the faculty and students. His kindness, which is almost tenderness, his great knowledge and his ability as a teacher and his character as a man and a potential citizen have won for him a host of friends. . . . I want to make him a full professor and his position permanent." That all parties concerned seemed to be happy with the arrangement is evident from the remainder of Marchant's letter, for Milhaud had confided to him that "if he had to choose to live any place in the world, except France, he would want it to be Mills. . . . So you know how grateful I am for your suggesting him and for your help toward his salary. He is a great asset and compensates our loss of dear Brescia."[7]

Through her usual jaunts in California, Elizabeth kept in close touch with Milhaud, who confided to her that the Nazis had ransacked both his Paris apartment and his home in Aix. She shared his grief over his father's death in 1942 and his concern for his grievously ill mother, who was hidden in an unidentified French hospital while some ninety German soldiers occupied her house. The safety of his own manuscripts back in Paris was a great worry to Milhaud, so he was understandably relieved to learn that his publisher had hidden them securely. Nevertheless, he expressed grave concern for the safety of Satie's manuscripts, which he had brought with him to California, especially since after America's entry into war with Japan the West Coast was believed by many to be vulnerable to attack. Even Elizabeth curtailed her visits to California at this time, mainly for fear of being separated from her son and his family should the East Coast be attacked.[8]

Her support of Milhaud came in many forms. Immediately upon his arrival she commissioned a string quartet, his tenth, and programmed much of his music. There were lecture tours provided by her and still later other substantial commissions, most notably a ballet, *Jeux de printemps*, which was premiered in 1944. And Milhaud in turn dedicated no less than six works to her, all of which are deposited at the Library of Congress.

Her many connections in California were of considerable consequence for the immigrant musicians who settled there. With Schönberg's move to the United States in 1933, the teaching and performance of twelve-tone music literally came to a halt in Germany. And by the time of the Austrian Anschluss of 1935, the Nazis were promoting as part of their political propaganda a simpler art that would attract a wider popular base of support. With his transplantation to UCLA, Schönberg, as leader of the atonal school, was becoming a major influence on the course of American music.

By 1936 another Austrian-born Jew became the object of Elizabeth's beneficence. He was Ernst Toch, who had lived and taught in Berlin from 1929 to 1932. When Hitler came to power in 1933 Toch fled to England, where he lived in such desperate circumstances that within a period of two months Bruno Walter, Howard Hanson, Roger Sessions, Arnold Schönberg, Carlos Salzedo, and Serge Koussevitzky all wrote to Cowell and Kallen in the United States pleading his case. Kallen immediately turned to Elizabeth for money, and she responded at once with a contribution. In 1934 Toch arrived in New York, where he obtained a teaching position at the New School for Social Research. Coolidge met Toch in November of that year, but it was only after his move to California in 1936 that she came to know him and his wife Lily intimately, and her assistance became greater. Shortly after his arrival on the West Coast, Elizabeth offered him a generous commission of $1,000 in advance for a piano quintet, which he completed in 1938 and performed with the Roth Quartet that year in the last Berkshire Festival. In a letter written at about the same time Toch recounts a dream that he had—a dream that reveals something of Coolidge's importance in his life. After lying awake for some hours haunted by thoughts of injustice and violence in the world, Coolidge came to mind, "without any tangible connection, perhaps just by law of contrast. Presently all the anguish fell from my mind. I sent you a still greeting and fell asleep. This morning, in daylight, I thought you really should get this greeting—in all the privacy of thought."[9]

The degree to which Coolidge in turn opened her heart to the Tochs is evident from her correspondence as well. "Please let me say . . . I feel that the deep sympathy and understanding which exists between us, is founded on a much longer acquaintance than the date of our actual first meeting, and that we have merely resumed an interchange of friendship, which must have begun before we were born."[10]

When it was learned that Schönberg was retiring from UCLA, Toch asked Elizabeth to write to the university recommending him for the now-vacant post. She did so at once and some time later also arranged for his tone poem, *Pinocchio,* to be performed by the Boston Symphony Orchestra with Koussevitzky. There was one last offer of a commission for a piano trio in 1945, but failing health forced Toch to decline.

The case of Benjamin Britten is for several reasons unique among the exiles who sought Elizabeth's help. In view of Britten's relationship with the Bridges it was inevitable that he should come into Elizabeth's life sooner or later. To Frank and Ethel Bridge Britten was far more than a student: He was a son who came into their childless life as a precocious eleven-year-old composer. Bridge at first resisted accepting him as a student but soon came to recognize Britten's extraordinary gifts and agreed to teach him, often giving him lessons that went on for hours. Later, when Britten studied at the Royal College of Music he lived just across Kensington Gardens from the Bridges and often went with them to their home in Friston, near Eastbourne, on weekends and for holidays. Here he came to know also their musician-friend Marjorie Fass and took part in a good deal of very jolly music-making.

It is not surprising to find in the Bridge-Coolidge correspondence an enthusiastic letter introducing the young Britten to Elizabeth, for Bridge well knew that his generous and influential American friend was in a position to do a great deal for his protégé. So in 1939 when Britten went to the United States, Bridge wrote, "Our beloved Benjamin Britten, that young friend, pupil and quasi-adopted son of whom you have heard us talk very often, and who is probably *the* outstanding composer of the present young men here, has been in Canada and we now hear that he is going to New York. I am sure you would like him . . . and I do so hope a meeting materializes. I am so anxious that you should meet him through me, because he is a part of me!! How I wish I could have been present to personally introduce him. You will perhaps remember Peter Pears who sang with the English Singers. . . . He and Ben are together."[11]

In the fall of 1940 Elizabeth began discussing with Britten the possibility of his writing a work for her, and by 1941 she offered him a commission that resulted in his Quartet in D Major, op. 25, no. 1, which premiered at Occidental College and was repeated at the Library of Congress for Founder's Day in 1941—at which time Elizabeth presented him with the Coolidge Medal. He sent his sister a description of his patron and of the occasion. "It was quite an alarming ceremony, but Mrs. Coolidge, who is really a sweet old thing, made things easier by publicly referring to me as 'Benjy,' which made everyone smile sweetly. The Coolidge Quartet played my quartet with quite good success."[12]

Britten and Pears were pacifists, and it was their initial intention to seek émigré status in the States, but in order to find employment they needed to leave and reenter the country and were told that the recommendation of a prominent citizen would expedite receiving the necessary visa. Elizabeth, of course, was more than happy to assist with letters in their behalf. Britten had planned to go to Mexico or to Cuba briefly in order to comply with the immigration laws, but in the meantime news of the progress of the war at home and the Luftwaffe's nightly raids over London affected him so deeply that he determined to return home, despite the dangers of crossing the U-boat-infested waters of the North Atlantic. Britten and Pears left on 16 March 1942 on a Swedish cargo vessel that actually had to be abandoned by the convoy when its funnel caught fire. They finally reached home but not empty-handed, for once again Coolidge had been generous. It is quite evident that she liked "Benjy" immensely. Indeed, Britten's sister Beth indicates that the

Bridges, Marjorie Fass, and Wysten Auden were the only other people ever permitted to use that nickname.[13]

With Britten's return to England and the difficulty of censorship in communication, his correspondence with Coolidge ceased, but in the periodic letters that Ethel Bridge was able to get through, Elizabeth learned that Britten had been offered a job as conductor of the Royal Air Force Band and had refused because he would not wear a uniform. Among those asked to supply character references for him was Ethel Bridge (Frank by this time had died). Her letter makes it quite clear that Britten's feelings about war were deep-seated. "Even at the tender age of 13, his hatred of anything to do with war was extraordinary . . . and his passionate hatred has remained with him all through these years that I have known him. His whole outlook on life has been a living, genuine, and conscientious protest against war and all that it means. Knowing the very high opinion of his gifts and character which my husband held I consider that the gifts would be of greater value to the country if employed in an unmilitary way."[14] As pacifists Ben and Peter had to face a tribunal, which went very badly the first time. It was feared that they might have to go to prison, as Michael Tippett had, but they appealed, and Ethel was relieved to report to Elizabeth that in the end they were able to serve their country with their musical talents, going about and giving concerts.

There was one other dramatic and complicated effort on behalf of European artists caught in the maelstrom of the war: Elizabeth's efforts to rescue the Pro Arte Quartet represent perhaps her finest hour. The degree of her personal interest and involvement in this unique case was unquestionably influenced by her long and happy association with the quartet, dating from her first European tour in 1923, when Casella arranged for their performance in Rome and described their meeting as "love at first hearing." The Pro Arte Quartet was founded in Brussels in 1913, made its debut the following year (designated as the quartet to the Royal Crown), and first appeared in the United States at the second Library of Congress Festival in 1926. On that occasion the *Washington Star* noted that the official invitation came from the State Department through the Belgian ambassador—the first time that a personage connected with the fine arts was made a subject of diplomatic exchange. Between that time and their final settlement in America in 1940, the members of the quartet made thirty-three trips to the States, sponsored by Coolidge. She often referred to them as her favorite of all the ensembles that she supported, and she became personally attached to the members, especially Alphonse Onnou, first violinist, whose single-minded dedication to his art was so like her own. Henry Eichheim considered the ensemble "the perfect machine, the finest quartet I have ever heard."[15] And Gunnar Johansen—who in time became closely involved with the quartet—once described it as "the finest organization of its kind in existence . . . that perfect quadrangle that makes a perfect circle."[16]

The summer institutes that Coolidge funded at Mills College beginning in 1932 featured the Pro Arte in an eight-week residency during which the artists lived on campus, taught privately, coached student ensembles, held master classes, and gave two concerts weekly. It was a wonderfully successful venture and, with the exception of 1939, when the quartet represented Belgium in that country's pavilion at the New York World's Fair, these summer sessions continued through 1940. In addition, Coolidge presented them in tours of the United States from coast to coast, and in 1933 arranged their Town Hall debut, for which she anonymously guaranteed any deficit. That same summer she kept them with her for several weeks to explore repertoire with piano—with her, of course, at the keyboard. In 1934 she guaranteed them concerts totaling $27,000, and in the summer traveled with them "like family," in her words. In Europe, too, she sponsored them extensively and for the twenty-fifth anniversary of their founding presented a cycle of six concerts in Brussels that were repeated the following summer at Ravinia. The Pro Arte Quartet has the distinction of being the only ensemble for which she actually created a separate endowment. In 1938 she set aside $12,000 for a "Pro Arte-Coolidge Trust" with the clause that no more than $10,000 should be withdrawn in a given year. Two years later she guaranteed the quartet $15,000 worth of engagements in the United States.

In 1939 when the quartet's cellist, Robert Maas, became ill in Belgium, Elizabeth arranged to engage Warwick Evans, formerly cellist with the London String Quartet, in his place. Maas had to remain behind in Brussels when the Pro Arte came to America in the spring of 1940 for a series of concerts and its usual stint at Mills College in the summer. His illness was just the beginning of a series of misfortunes that dogged the quartet and threatened its dissolution, for with Hitler's invasion of Belgium the ensemble was literally stranded in America, minus one member. On 10 May 1940, the very day that radio wires carried the news that German paratroopers fell from the skies over Belgium and the Wehrmacht panzer divisions entered the lowlands, the Pro Arte Quartet was scheduled to perform an evening concert at the University of Wisconsin in Madison. Despite their anguish over the danger to their families left behind and their concern for Maas, the members insisted on performing and won praise and admiration for their courage. Johansen perhaps said it best: "If those three brave Belgians can play through the concert tonight while they know Brussels and their families are being destroyed, it is but another proof that music stands for something far greater than we are."[17]

Carl Bricken, an old friend with whom Elizabeth had long been acquainted through his work at the University of Chicago, had just become the head of the Music Department at the University of Wisconsin and was, like her, a great champion and admirer of the Pro Arte. As early as December of 1939 he and Elizabeth had already discussed the possibility of creating a residency for the quartet at the university, thus keeping them in this country, and ensuring the stability of a university appointment—always with the intention of bringing Maas to America when his health permitted. By spring Bricken was working furiously to raise enough money to offer the quartet a three-year contract, but just as the residency was secured Onnou became severely ill. With only half of the original Pro Arte remaining it seemed altogether likely that this great quartet had come to an end. Together Elizabeth and Bricken worked quickly to secure Evans's contract and to recruit the Spanish violinist, Antonio Brosa, to fill the first violin position. Bricken's letter informing Coolidge of the seriousness of Onnou's condition is testimony that his dilemma was more than that of an administrator faced with replacing a valued faculty member. It was that of a friend as well: "Yesterday, after the microscopic examination of the blood cells, it is now definitely established that the trouble is leukemia. It is fatal. . . . I have tried to bear up under this [ ] I can no longer deceive even myself. As you so wisely said before, we must face the facts. A difficult problem faces us. I don't know whether to tell Alphonse or not. It seems brutal to leave Mrs. Onnou at the sudden mercy of complete ignorance of the facts." The very existence of the Pro Arte Quartet was in the balance, and the question of a replacement had to be addressed immediately. It was no easy decision to make, for in Bricken's opinion "nobody can replace Onnou." It is a mark of his reliance upon Coolidge that he should share this difficult decision with her. "I have pulled no punches. The truth lies hard and bare on these pages as I read them over. My respect and affection for Alphonse has grown so that it makes it all the more difficult to see as clearly as I should. The Pro Arte must go on, and that is the objective that makes this load bearable."[18]

For Elizabeth, too, it was an emotional loss, and she was drawn into the situation in a particularly personal way when Onnou requested that she come to him as soon as possible. Much as her own parents had always gone to her in haste when she needed them, she too now left immediately for Madison, only to learn on arrival that she had been designated as the one to break the news to Onnou. To Marchant she wrote the following day, "We are of course trying to keep him from the complete knowledge of it, but it is my sad duty to go to him and tell him that the doctors have all pronounced that he must not expect to play for at least a year. This, I hope, will soften the blow for him, but for us it means . . . that he has not long to live. The night before last he had such paroxysms of pain and was so desperately ill that he has sent for me and, of course, I am hurrying to do what I can for my dearest friend."[19]

After a few days in Madison she made her farewells and returned to Cambridge. That her presence had been a great consolation is evident from Bricken's letter only days later. "I cannot tell you how much your visit meant and still means. I cannot tell you how much lasting affection all of us here have for you. You must know this and we send you, all together, our warmest love."[20] Elizabeth's intimate involvement in the personal lives of the members of the quartet and her high regard for their work simply would not permit her to assume a detached attitude. She paid for the services of two consulting physicians—one on the West Coast and the other a Nobel laureate in Boston—and she assumed all the hospital bills.

Only a few days later on 20 November Onnou died, surrounded by the members of the quartet, his wife, the doctor, a priest, and Bricken.

Elizabeth immediately offered to pay funeral expenses and promised to provide a monthly allowance for Onnou's wife, who was quite helpless, for she spoke no English and was herself not well. Elizabeth's actions through it all are a living testimony of the sincerity of words she wrote to Bricken just a few days before. "As I grow older I realize how incomparably more important human relationships are than anything else."[21] It was her most tender human side, but the drama was only beginning.

Despite the sense of personal loss there was little time for mourning. Bricken and Coolidge together quickly went about securing the services of Brosa and Evans as replacements for Onnou and Maas. The remaining original members of the ensemble, Laurent Halleux, second violinist, and Germaine Prévost, violist, were understandably distraught, isolated from their families and insecure for their future, and their feelings took the form of resentment toward the two newcomers who, in actuality, were attempting to rescue the Pro Arte from extinction. Elizabeth found herself in the middle of the controversy, with Halleux and Prévost appealing their cases to her on the one hand, and Brosa and Evans reporting the growing tensions and resentment toward them that threatened to disrupt the ensemble altogether. Both Prévost and Halleux asked her to help them find positions in symphony orchestras, and she promised to do so. However, she strongly urged them to "consider the advantage of a permanent engagement at so influential a central post as you would find at the University of Wisconsin."[22] In the meantime, the possible departure of Halleux and Prévost left Brosa and Evans in limbo, so in order to provide employment for them, Coolidge engaged her old friend Gunnar Johansen (who by this time was artist-in-residence at the University of Wisconsin) to form a trio, which only angered the two Belgians all the more. The tensions became so severe that Evans decided to leave the quartet. He explained to Bricken, "I cannot tell you how grieved I am to have to write to refuse your kind offer. I feel it would be impossible for me to be happy and work in harmony with the present personnel of the Quartet. You will remember Germain and Laurent did not speak to each other for over a month and now they have turned around as one man to vent their childishness on Tony [Brosa] because he was able to earn a few dollars with the trio which Mrs. Coolidge wanted."[23]

Elizabeth had never given up on the notion of securing passage out of Europe for Maas and had asked, "Do you think that there is the slightest possibility of our getting back Maas? Would money help in this matter, or the influence of the Library of Congress? This, of course, has been the understanding from the beginning, namely, that the original 'cellist would resume his place in the Quartet whenever possible."[24] Bricken responded, "It is my conviction that Maas's return to the two remaining members of the organization will save the Pro Arte Quartet. I am ready to do all in my power to support Maas here until such time as he will be able to join his colleagues."[25] With that assurance the two set about the task of negotiating an exit visa for Maas. Elizabeth always considered him to be the finest quartet cellist she knew, and her heart ached at the news that he was reduced to playing in cafés in Brussels to survive. She was determined to spare no effort in obtaining his safe passage.

Bricken and the university's attorneys carried on an extensive correspondence with Secretary of State Cordell Hull, and especially with Assistant Secretary of State Joseph E. Davies, who was a Wisconsin alumnus and who had already given generously to the fund to support the Pro Arte. Negotiations became even more complicated when it was learned that the surest route out of Belgium would be through Russia and Japan, which would require not only an exit visa but transit visas for passage through those countries. With America's entry into war with Japan in 1941 that possibility dissolved and Maas was forced to remain in Europe until the end of the war in 1945.

In the meantime the ensemble went through a succession of cellists. Evans left in 1941 and was replaced by Victor Gottlieb, who had just departed the feuding Coolidge Quartet. His place was taken one year later by George Sopkin, who was later drafted. The cellist position was finally stabilized with the addition of Ernst Friedlander in 1943. In the meantime, Bricken and Coolidge had been able to obtain passage for Halleux's wife and children in 1941, but Prévost's family did not join him until after the war.

Elizabeth's patience with the two Belgians was wearing thin. As harsh as their behavior toward Evans and Brosa appears, theirs was a difficult situation. The delicate relationship that exists within a performing ensemble is exceedingly fragile. Violinist Henri Temianka once told Elizabeth, "I have discovered that finding the right duo partner is almost as delicate a matter as finding the right partner in marriage."[26] A quartet, by analogy, would then be twice the problem. Privately she wrote to Bricken, "Needless to tell you that it is a grief to me to see so fine an organization disrupted by childish and unreasonable behavior on the part of the two for whose benefit all this effort has been made."[27] She threatened to withdraw completely and cast her lot and her money with the University Trio. Much credit is due Bricken, who with uncommon patience and diplomacy smoothed the matter and prevented her threatened action.

It is most unusual, even unique, in string quartet history that the original members of a group should stay together for as long as the Pro Arte had—nearly thirty years. Moreover, all who knew Alphonse Onnou agree that he was more than a fine violinist—he was a man of immense intellect and a charismatic artist. Bricken was right when he said no one could replace Onnou, particularly in the eyes and the affections of Halleux and Prévost. Brosa managed to steer a course through the tensions and changes of personnel until 1944, when he left the group to pursue a solo career. In 1943 Halleux left and was replaced by another Belgian, Albert Rahier. With Halleux's departure only Prévost of the original four remained. Brosa was replaced by a familiar friend and old associate of Elizabeth's, Rudolph Kolisch, whose own quartet was disbanded just at that time. There was some discussion as to whether it was appropriate to keep the name Pro Arte, but since the entire personnel of the quartet was not changed at the same time the name was retained and—much to the credit of Coolidge and Bricken—continues to this day at the University of Wisconsin, the longest surviving quartet to continue under one name.

Much of the original Pro Arte's greatness lay in its perfectionism. It is documented that they worked for fifteen years on a particular Beethoven quartet before performing it publicly. While they were noted for their interpretations of the classics, they were also outstanding proponents of new music. Milhaud summed it up well at the time of Onnou's death: "Contemporary composers have lost with Alphonse an incomparable interpreter."[28] It is undoubtedly this perfectionism that appealed so sincerely to Elizabeth and her "loyalty to standards."

There were, besides these individual cases, innumerable other Coolidge efforts for the cause of displaced musicians during the war years. A few examples are concerts to raise money for Jewish musicians and contributions to the Iron Curtain Refugee Fund, Operation Music for Israel, and the Committee for the Rescue of Jewish Refugee Children and their Rehabilitation in Palestine. It could certainly be said of her, as it was said of her father at the time of his death, that she did not parade her heart on her sleeve, but she had a large and tender heart.

CHAPTER EIGHTEEN

The Four Horsemen of the ApoCoolidge

A man lives not only his personal life, as an individual, but also, consciously or unconsciously, the life of his epoch and his contemporaries.

– THOMAS MANN, *THE MAGIC MOUNTAIN*

WHEN ELIZABETH CHRISTENED her newly formed Coolidge Quartet "the four horsemen of the ApoCoolidge," it was unlikely that she intended to convey the implication of that title as derived from the Book of Revelation, in which the fearsome equestrian four personified the evils of war. Her early references to the quartet are cavalier in character, more reminiscent of the adventures of Alexandre Dumas's *The Three Musketeers,* who went about dazzling all by their amazing exploits. She had put together a truly brilliant assemblage of talent, but one unfortunately susceptible to internal tensions.

On the occasion of its formal and official presentation to the public in a radio broadcast in 1936, the quartet was introduced by Elizabeth with a short speech in which she revealed her long-held wish to establish an official resident quartet at the Library of Congress that would be maintained by the Foundation. Now she announced that such a quartet had been assembled and would operate under contract with the government in behalf of the Coolidge Foundation. She concluded on a personal note: "My pleasure is augmented by pride in the fact that these four young artists have chosen to call themselves, 'the Coolidge Quartet.' No sweeter honor could befall me; because, to the high artistic esteem in which I hold them I feel a real family relationship—stronger, perhaps, than some of those of blood. In adopting my name they seem almost, to have become my adopted children."[1]

It was a financial arrangement unlike that of any other ensemble that she supported. She entrusted its leadership to first violinist William Kroll, who had already rendered yeoman service to her when at twenty-two he led the South Mountain Quartet and Elshuco Trio. The other members of the quartet were Nicolai Berezowsky (second violin), Nicolas Moldavan (viola), and Victor Gottlieb (cello). Kroll had been something of a child prodigy; he was accepted for study with Marteau at the Berlin Hochschule at the age of ten, and later worked with Franz Kneisel at the Institute of Musical Art in New York. Although he was a fine soloist, he made his name largely in chamber music, where it is said that "he led his quartet with authority, vigor, and much temperament."[2] In the opinion of some, it is this very "temperament" that had something to do with the frequent changes of personnel over the quartet's existence. In the span of six years the second violin chair would change five times, and in eight years, the viola twice and the cello three times.

It would be unfair to place the blame entirely on Kroll, however. Ideally a quartet must by its very nature be as fine-tuned in the blend of personalities as it is in talent and technique, but in an imperfect world this is a rare attainment. Martha Blum has aptly observed that "string quartets . . . are a bit like wildflowers. They are a source of beauty to some, indifference to others. They spring up in the strangest places and may scarcely last the season."[3] To this might be added that, like wildflowers, they bruise easily. Even a cursory look at the rosters of string quartets of this century will reveal the frequent movement of players from one ensemble to another. Squabbles within the performing organizations that she sponsored were not new to Elizabeth, who steadfastly and wisely did her best to distance herself from the fray when she was appealed to—usually by the dissenting figure. She was not always able to maintain a disinterested posture, however, and often became annoyed when she found herself drawn into the conflict by performers who came to her like schoolchildren to settle their differences. On these occasions she could be sharp in her admonitions. When, for example, the complaining violist attempted to gain her ear she replied, "I consider

William Kroll as the leader of the Coolidge Quartet, and must leave it to you both to decide whether you wish to play together. To me it is a matter of indifference. Please do not re-open this useless discussion."[4] In private she sagely summed up such internal struggles in the laconic observation that "they all want to play first violin."

It would be unfair to dwell on these problems and dismiss the many successes and brilliant performances of the Coolidge Quartet in its eight-year existence. In its first year alone the ensemble played eleven concerts at the Library of Congress, thirteen extension concerts in various other cities, and two radio broadcasts on CBS and NBC. Despite its employment by the government, Coolidge intended from the outset that the quartet's relationship with the Foundation should gradually decrease to the point that the ensemble would eventually become independent. Through the Foundation they played in colleges, universities, and libraries all over the country, and often Coolidge contributed anonymously whatever the host institution could not pay. At other times she contributed $100 to each concert if the ensemble agreed to accept a lower rate. On numerous occasions she admonished the members—Kroll especially—to seek other opportunities for performance besides the Library of Congress, and she encouraged them to engage a manager.

To help promote the quartet internationally, she sent them to perform at her festival in Mexico City in 1937. On the advice of her doctors, who believed that she could not tolerate the high altitude, Coolidge reluctantly remained at home but received enthusiastic reports of the success of her quartet. Two years later she featured them in another far-flung undertaking which she did attend, taking them with her to Hawaii for her gala Honolulu festival. In that same year she attempted, unsuccessfully, to create for them a residency at the University of Texas similar to the one that she established for the Pro Arte Quartet at the University of Wisconsin.

By 1941 tensions mounted to the point of threatening the dissolution of the quartet and, perhaps tired of the problem, she stood behind the decision to disband in 1943 and even encouraged Kroll to form a new ensemble under his own name. Although the Coolidge Quartet ceased to function as an ensemble, its members all continued in some way to be associated with Elizabeth in her quest to spread the gospel of chamber music.

As the four went their own ways, a new foursome emerged from the wings. They were not a quartet, but four unique individuals, each of whom brought into her life his own special gifts of friendship, a welcome measure of happiness, and a diversity of successes to brighten her declining years. They were Alexander Schneider, E. Power Biggs, Harold Spivacke, and Aaron Copland.

Even before the disbanding of the Coolidge Quartet, the Whittall Foundation initiated a series of concerts at the Library of Congress designed to bring in various quartets to perform on the Stradivari instruments that Gertrude Clarke Whittall had given to the Library in 1935. What seemed like a good idea was, however, an unsatisfactory arrangement, for string players understandably dislike performing on unfamiliar instruments. Rehearsal time was necessarily limited since Whittall had stipulated that the instruments could not be removed from the Library except for repair. She herself was well aware that string instruments deteriorate if not played, so with a little encouragement she increased the endowment of her Foundation to enable the Library to employ a quartet-in-residence. One of the ensembles that had performed on the Strads during the period of experimentation in 1938 was the Budapest String Quartet, which had only recently decided to make the United States its home.[5]

Commenting on the fact that the performances under the patronage of the Whittall Foundation took place in the Coolidge Auditorium, Mrs. Whittall is reported to have said that she felt "like a certain little bird who lays an egg in a nest built by another."[6] To add to the irony, the quartet chosen as residents functioned under a name that was at best misleading. Although in its origin the ensemble was truly all Hungarian, by the time they came to the Library of Congress the personnel was completely Russian, giving rise to a joke: What is one Russian? A thinker. Two Russians? Chess players. Three Russians? A conspiracy. Four Russians? The Budapest String Quartet, of course.[7]

Playing second violin in the quartet at the time was Alexander Schneider—Sasha to his friends—whose brother, Mischa, was cellist in the ensemble. Coolidge's correspondence with Sasha began in 1942,

Mrs. Coolidge at a luau given during her festival in Honolulu in 1939. At her right is William Kroll, first violinist of the Coolidge Quartet and the Elshuco Trio.

Library of Congress

when he was thirty-four and she a grandmotherly seventy-eight. Despite the difference in their ages, or maybe because of it, their relationship was a delight, unclouded by the kinds of problems that had sometimes plagued her other associations. They spent many hours together in her Washington apartment playing sonatas and afterward partaking of the gastronomic delights that Schneider was renowned for creating. These were wonderful times during which their friendship blossomed and Sasha felt comfortable enough with his elderly duet partner to confide his thoughts on possibly leaving the Budapest ensemble in order to pursue a career on his own. It was a difficult decision and a critical career move, one that Elizabeth supported probably with the knowledge that she had the money and influence to promote him in whatever path he chose. Schneider left the Budapest Quartet in 1944 just at the same time that Brosa left the Pro Arte, and he was invited to take the position of first violin in that organization. It was a tempting offer, and he indicated to Coolidge that he was very honored to be asked.

Despite the security that a permanent university appointment would mean for him, he declined. In February Elizabeth wrote to say that she was glad he had decided as he did and indicated that she had in mind "an idea, a plan" for him and harpsichordist Ralph Kirkpatrick—to promote them as a duo, with their debut performance under her auspices at the Library of Congress. She was also arranging a West Coast tour for them. They accepted, and during the time that they were away on tour, Schneider wrote faithfully to report their successes, even though he feared that "this may be boring to you, but I must say again, that it is only . . . your spirit in getting us started that has made all this possible."[8]

At the same time Sasha toyed with the idea of founding his own quartet but despaired of ever achieving that elusive alchemy that is the perfect ensemble. Coolidge understood, as perhaps few could, how difficult it was to achieve that goal. When he abandoned the idea, she approved and actually facilitated the formation of another ensemble, the Albeneri Trio. Its name, like that of the earlier Elshuco Trio, was an invention, a conjunction of the names of the three players: *Al*exander Schneider (violin), *Ben*ar Heifetz (cellist of the recently disbanded Kolisch Quartet), and *Eri*k Itor Kahn (pianist and husband of Franz

Kneisel's daughter, Marianne). Although it cannot be documented, it is likely that the name was Coolidge's invention. The newly created Albeneri Trio spent three weeks with Elizabeth in Pittsfield that summer, playing chamber music together, lingering pleasantly over Sasha's gourmet meals, enjoying long rides in the country, and just generally "making family" in much the same way that she had with the Pro Arte Quartet in 1934.

For Schneider 1947 was a banner year, a turning point in his career. With Coolidge's blessing and her money in his pocket, Sasha left to study with Pablo Casals in Prades, the little Catalan town near the Spanish border where the great cellist had gone as a gesture of opposition to the Franco regime in Spain. Casals had determined that he would never again perform in Spain as long as Franco ruled, nor would he play in those countries that recognized Spain's Fascist government and, true to his word, he stopped concertizing.

Sasha reported from Prades that he was practicing six to seven hours daily and spending two hours working with Casals, doing all six of the Bach Sonatas and Partitas for unaccompanied violin. His letters are filled with details about his work and of the high regard Casals had for Coolidge. "We talk a lot about you and he has the greatest admiration for you and your work." Casals undoubtedly remembered that as a much younger man he too had received of Coolidge's bounty when in 1921 she contributed $4,000 to provide an orchestra for him to conduct in New York. "When he heard that you made it possible for me to come here to study the Bach Suites, he was deeply moved."[9] In a touching letter to Elizabeth, Sasha professed his affection and indebtedness to his elderly patron and friend. "There are two people in my life who really help to shape all my decisions as a human being and as a musician: you and Pablo Casals."[10]

While Schneider was abroad perfecting his Bach, back home Elizabeth was making plans to present him in an all-Bach concert for her next birthday festival at the Library of Congress. Schneider astounded audiences by programming all six of the Bach Sonatas and Partitas in two recitals, a feat that Enesco, Heifetz, and even Casals himself thought was absolute insanity. Not only that—he was also playing the Bach unaccompanied Cello Suites on the viola.[11] There were intermittent attempts to form his own quartet, which he finally did in 1952. It lasted long enough to perform all of the more than eighty string quartets of Haydn. But for now Coolidge had even bigger plans to present Schneider in recitals commemorating the bicentennial of Bach's death in 1950. While the pieces of this large plan were more or less silently falling into place, another new personality was coming into focus.

Although Coolidge's decisions to embark upon large undertakings sometimes appeared spontaneous, they were never mere vagaries, but neither were they the result of interminable ruminations. Instead they moved swiftly along courses that had been logically plotted. Even in her old age her mind was a veritable hothouse of plans at different stages of germination, so that when presented with the right stimulus at the right time, her projects seemed to emerge suddenly in full-grown maturity. The key to the enigma of why she responded to some ideas or composers and not to others may usually be found in her correspondence. Those who were privy to her personal likes and prejudices knew well that she could be galvanized by a suggestion if it touched a favored subject—just as truly as cajolery could elicit her most trenchant responses. And timing was all-important.

In 1941, E. Power Biggs wrote to Coolidge asking if she might be interested in sponsoring him in a performance of a work for organ and harp by Marcel Grandjany, with whom she was already well acquainted through his work for her years before at Mills and Stanford, and more recently at the Library of Congress and the San Francisco Fair. She had often been the object of epistolary wooing, which usually left her unmoved, but Biggs was different. Whether it was his straightforward request or her previous association with Grandjany, she said yes at once, and the concert in effect became the prelude to another significant venture.

For years Coolidge had championed the potential of radio as a means of disseminating culture, often standing alone in her conviction. So when Biggs approached her after the concert with the idea of sponsoring him in a series of broadcasts of chamber music that included organ, she bought the idea with the enthusiasm of one who recognized that she had won another comrade to her crusade. Such allies had been few in the beginning. Even Engel had disagreed with her initially, fearing that radio would bring about a decline in attendance at concerts. Despite his early objections, she insisted that radio equipment be installed in the Coolidge Auditorium in 1925 so that "everything which goes on within it [can be] heard by as wide an audience as desires so to hear it."[12] Her initiative actually predates by two years the establishment of the Federal Radio Commission in 1927 (predecessor of the Federal Communications Commission, 1934).

The first essays in broadcasting were humble, but by 1934 her programs at the Library of Congress and elsewhere were being carried by the networks, who very quickly discovered that they had taken on a behemoth in Coolidge. Her broadsides arrived with regularity, chastising them for truncating performances to accommodate rigid time slots and for programming single movements of works, which she viewed as serious infractions of the inviolability of art. She made it clear what her priorities were—and by implication, what the networks' should be as well. "The music is more important to me than the broadcasting and should not be in any way mutilated or inartistically abbreviated for the sake of the National Broadcasting Company."[13] Not understanding—or possibly not wishing to understand—the constraints of commercial broadcasting, she complained to Howard Hinners, "I do hope that the time may come when our government will superintend this business as they do in England in order that the vast influence of the radio may sometimes be exercised in behalf of culture rather than a private profit."[14]

Her confidence in Biggs's proposal is attested to by the fact that when the Coolidge Foundation was unable to sponsor it, she did so personally. So the concerts began on 20 September 1942, broadcast by CBS on Sunday mornings from 9:15 to 9:45 at the headquarters of the U.S. Army School for Chaplains, located in the Germanic Museum of Harvard University (now the Busch-Reisinger). The programs were made up largely of baroque and classical music but also included some contemporary compositions of Poulenc, Piston, Sowerby, and Hindemith. All were chamber works for which Biggs was assisted by members of the Stradivari Quartet, the Bach Cantata Club of Boston, and the Fiedler Sinfonietta with Arthur Fiedler conducting.

The response was overwhelming and far surpassed even Elizabeth's expectations. Perhaps most rewarding of all were the letters from enthusiastic listeners in the military service, such as the young man who identified himself as an organist from Nottingham, England, now "out in Canada with the R[oyal] A[ir] F[orce]. Your programs reach us at 6:15 A.M. Sometimes . . . that hour finds me dressing at home, about twenty miles from work. Other times I am engaged, not too romantically, frying eggs and bacon by the hundreds over colossal hot stoves while your music drifts in like something from another world. Wherever I happen to be I rarely miss it."[15]

An anonymous letter from an Italian immigrant in California, who signed himself simply as "a gardener from Piedmont," proved how right she had been in her decision. "We do not know who is responsible for the fact that Mills College is on the air today. We have long wished the Music department would try . . . to share with us shut-ins your music. Do you realize that while a few fat ladies are probably crowding your new hall hundreds of us, if not thousands, who have music in their souls and never have the means to enjoy it are today having music from your school."[16]

The Biggs concerts continued through 1942, 1943, and 1944, sponsored by Elizabeth. For 1945 and 1946 they were broadcast in collaboration with her. Although the public's enthusiasm never waned, Coolidge had her problems with the networks and particularly with some of the local stations that did not wish to carry the programs. The failure of a station in Washington, D.C. to do so prompted her complaint, now couched in the majestic plural: "The radio companies have grown so commercial that they are selling almost every minute of their time, leaving the more altruistic and cultural broadcasting in favor of advertising rich sponsors. We have protested, especially in Washington where these organ recitals are tremendously appreciated, but to no avail."[17]

Despite her ongoing battle with the networks, Coolidge always regarded her radio work as among her most successful and gratifying endeavors. "I have never done anything that gave me more personal satisfaction and, of course, that is a hundred-fold greater (perhaps I might almost say a million-fold because they tell me that these broadcasts reach millions of listeners) on account of being able to share it so widely."[18] She was right and never missed an opportunity to remind those who had been her adversaries in the early years, as in her speech initiating one of her series when she said on the air to NBC, "I told you so." She did love being right.

In her evangelizing for the cause of chamber music through the use of radio she found a stalwart support in a third friend who, though he was certainly not new to her acquaintance, now assumed a major place in both her work and her friendship. Harold Spivacke had been employed at the Library of Congress ever since Engel left in 1934 and he was recruited to become the assistant to Engel's successor, Oliver Strunk. When Strunk left the Library just three years later, Spivacke—upon Engel's recommendation—became the Chief, retaining that position until his retirement in 1972. Spivacke brought to the job a unique combination of experience and skills. Before he took up the serious study of music in Berlin with Arnold Schering, Curt Sachs, and Karl Erik Schuman, he had been trained in economics and science, and after returning to the United States, studied library science at Columbia University while working a stint as research assistant to critic Olin Downes of the *New York Times.*

Spivacke was a man of vast intellectual interests and had a voracious appetite for work. He continued Engel's initiative but left the stamp of his own expansive views in the form of policies that greatly enhanced the copyright deposit, the Archive of American Folk Song, and the Recorded Sound Division.[19] Elizabeth liked him, and there is some evidence that she found his ideas to be a welcome contrast to Engel's. This was an unusual admission for her and, as her letter to Sprague notes, one that she had already discussed with her son. "I had a very pleasant evening at his (Spivacke's) home last night discussing plans for future activities of the Foundation. I am more and more pleased to have his sympathetic and intelligent cooperation in all these affairs, for as you know, I felt handicapped by the conservatism and what seemed to me almost contrariness of Mr. Engel."[20]

By 1944, Elizabeth was an octogenarian and, mindful of her age and declining health, Spivacke fulfilled his role as chief executive of the Coolidge Foundation with ever greater concern for her, assuming more and more responsibility for the everyday workings and decisions, seeking out composers to commission, and shielding her from unnecessary tensions that arose over budget and scheduling problems—while at the same time keeping her informed and happy. The classic example of Spivacke's style in handling Coolidge Foundation business may be seen in tracing the genesis of the commission that without a doubt is Coolidge's best known, Aaron Copland's *Appalachian Spring.* Copland's entry into her life at this time not only completes the quartet of friends and achievements, but brought with it some outstanding American talents, including Martha Graham, Erick Hawkins, and Merce Cunningham in an American classic that premiered on the occasion of Elizabeth's eightieth birthday. The coming together of these talents for that occasion was neither a happy accident nor a well-laid plan. On the contrary, it almost did not happen. Elizabeth's initial idea had been to commission a piece for Graham to mark the twenty-fifth anniversary of her Berkshire Festivals.[21] To Martha, Elizabeth wrote, "What I most hope for and intend is that the Coolidge Foundation should give a Festival in Pittsfield, thus linking the original Foundation with its highly developed successor."[22]

Elizabeth was already familiar with Martha Graham, for she had performed at the testimonial dinner for Coolidge sponsored by the MacDowell Colony at the clubhouse in New York in 1929, and Graham had more recently appeared in her Meridian Hill Park chamber music series in Washington in 1941. Coolidge must have been impressed and confidentially revealed to Graham her interest in commissioning Copland and Villa-Lobos to write some dance music for her. Martha was overjoyed and wrote, "When you told me of your plan I realized that this was not only a 'first' for me but for American Dance as well. To my knowledge this is the first time that a commissioning of works for the American Dance has ever happened. . . . It makes me feel that American dance has turned a corner, it has come of age. . . . I have dreamt of this happening—and now it has happened to me. . . . The two composers you have chosen are very exciting to me. I could not have asked for a more wonderful choice. I hope I can do something worthy of their music."[23]

Much of the credit must go to Erick Hawkins, whose role as dancer, collaborator, lover, and later husband of Graham was anything but disinterested. After the Meridian Park concert he had—apparently unknown to Martha—approached both Spivacke and Coolidge suggesting further collaboration. Only two days after Graham's letter quoted

Mrs. Coolidge with Harold Spivacke, chief of the Music Division of the Library of Congress, circa 1944

Library of Congress

above, he wrote to Coolidge, "May I tell you . . . how very happy I am about your commissioning the works for Martha. May I say from the bottom of my heart that it gave her an absolutely new lease on things. She has been a completely different woman since, and to have that work to look forward to in between time will bring her up marvelously. I can't wait to see what will come out of the collaboration with Copeland [*sic*] and Villa-Lobos."[24]

Coolidge had in fact at one time considered commissioning Villa-Lobos but gave up the notion fearing that communications with him in Brazil would have been unduly complicated during wartime. She asked Martha's permission instead to commission Hindemith to create a work to be performed on the same concert, but she expressed some doubt as to whether he would accept. By return mail Martha assured her that she would be delighted to have Hindemith compose a work for her, but added that in the event that he declined, she would suggest Carlos Chávez, with whom she was already acquainted. Coolidge knew Chávez too, for he had managed her Latin American Festival in Mexico City in 1937, and Copland, through his extended stays in Mexico, had become friends with Chávez and greatly admired his music. In the end, however, neither Villa-Lobos nor Chávez would be represented on the bill with Copland.

The genesis of *Appalachian Spring* can be thoroughly chronicled in the bulky correspondence of the various parties concerned. Their letters graphically document the obstacle course that separated the work's initial conception from its hugely successful premiere and provide a fascinating insight into the creative process of genius, here complicated by the fact that the ballet is the product of a collaborative effort. Since Martha Graham was at this time at Bennington College in Vermont and Copland was in Mexico City and New York, they left a paper trail of ideas—each sometimes rejected by the other—until from their gradual and mutual refinement of inspiration there comes the final invention, the ballet as it is known today.[25]

From the beginning, composer and choreographer agreed that this had to be something special, a truly American creation, a significant work by the dean of American composers for a uniquely American dance company. At the same time they were fully aware that they must work within certain practical constraints. The effectiveness of the lean, spare orchestration of the piece that has often been commented upon by music critics was actually a condition imposed on the composer by the terms of the commission as well as by Martha's desire that the ballet should be practical as a touring vehicle for her and her company. Moreover, they were creating a ballet limited by both the space of the Coolidge Auditorium and the budget, mindful also that in time of war any one of the musicians might suddenly be called up for military service.

Graham's letters to Coolidge, Copland, and Spivacke provide clear insights into her creative process. Immediately after Elizabeth offered the commission Martha wrote to ask her permission to "go ahead and think about the scripts, prepare a little draft to submit to you, and ask your opinion, of course." She explained that when asking a composer to write for her she always chose the subject herself and then "submitted to him the idea and a detailed script, not of the dance steps, etc., but of the idea and the action. The reason I have worked this way is that I find I only do things well when I can feel my way into them as a dancer. I have done those things only that I could feel and understand, not in a verbal sense, perhaps, but in my medium, my instrument, my body. . . . It usually takes me some time to prepare so I did want to talk to you soon."[26]

Graham's collaboration with the composers writing for her was much like that of a librettist and an opera composer. She supplied an initial story line and scenario for the composer and then the process of give and take would begin. Copland seems to have been a particularly compliant partner. Only a few days after offering the commission Elizabeth wrote to Martha, "I am glad to tell you that Aaron Copland has accepted our commission for writing a work for you under certain conditions, one of which is that he should learn from you just what you have in mind, how much time it is to occupy, what instruments etc."[27]

Since the piece was to be one of three works on the program, Coolidge herself imposed a time limit not to exceed half an hour and suggested that the instrumentation be limited to a small ensemble, one instrument of each kind, both wind and string, with piano. She left Martha to work out the choice of subject with the composers. In the meantime Coolidge did commission Chávez, and Graham completed the script for his piece first since communications with him in Mexico would necessarily take more time. However, by the beginning of August neither Martha nor Spivacke had received anything from him. Graham, who not only danced but also choreographed and usually designed the costumes for her productions herself, was understandably worried, for she had responsibilities to the dancers in her company as well. She appealed to Spivacke, who indicated that these delays would necessitate postponing the festival to the fall.

Working with Copland was easier. Their earliest correspondence reveals the various subjects that Martha was considering, some of which he objected to, others she found unsatisfactory. Among those discarded are parts of *Uncle Tom's Cabin* and some segments on Indian themes. Finally, Martha took some lines from Hart Crane's poem, *The Dance,* and fashioned a scenario set in rural Pennsylvania dealing with the marriage of a young pioneer couple. Its evocation of simple frontier life appealed to Copland and drew from him some of his best expressions of Americana in the form of hymnlike melodies and fiddle tunes, ending appropriately with variations on the Shaker hymn tune "Simple Gifts." Clearly, Martha was delighted that he approved of this last draft. In her autobiography published near the end of her life she recalls her letter to him: "I was so relieved to get your letter with your re-action to the revised script this morning. I will say that mildly I have been on pins and needles. I am glad you think it is better than the first one. I do know that when I hear your music it will give a new and different life to the script. Once the music comes I never look at the script. It is only to make a working base for the composer and myself. Now it exists in words, in literary terms only, and it has to come alive in a more plastic medium, which music is to me. So please feel free to let the music take its own life and urge."

Graham allowed her composers considerable latitude and was generous in acknowledging to Copland that "the ending will be better than I could devise as the music assumes its own life and character and that it will carry it through in a stronger way. Perhaps it is wrong to make you take that responsibility. But that is the way I work . . . to make a skeleton and then to be ready and willing to change when the music comes. The story is not so important, of course, as the inner life that emerges as the medium takes hold of the germ of the idea and proceeds to develop."[28]

Back in New York, Copland played the incomplete score for her, and she found it delightful. But she confided to Spivacke her reservations over the instrumentation requiring thirteen players, which would make it expensive and impractical for touring. "Aaron tells me it can be arranged for as few as two pianos or expanded to large orchestra but I had hoped to keep the original scoring intact as much as possible as I do feel the single piano is not adequate."[29]

As a practical consideration, Chávez was asked to limit his orchestra to the same instruments used by Copland. By January of 1944 he had had Martha's script for a year and had produced only a small amount of music, which she found "without stage awareness, bearing no relation to the script we had agreed upon." Fearing that she could not really go ahead, she posed the question to Spivacke, "If he does not get it to us soon what shall we do, give up the idea of a Chávez score or wait an indefinite period?"[30] The sketches of the staging and costumes were already complete, and the designers were ready to begin construction.

Coolidge sympathized completely with Martha's dilemma and indicated her own disappointment both with the music and with the delays. So when Chávez wrote to say that he would send the music soon she responded: "I must confess that his promises do not seem to mean much anymore, since the work was supposed to be in our hands on July 1, 1943."[31] In a subsequent letter she wrote, "I am sure you do not need to be told that I am not only deeply disappointed, but rather vexed at the irresponsible manner in which my commissions have been carried out, or, rather, neglected. I have told Dr. Spivacke that I am unwilling to wait any longer for the bare possibility that Mr. Chávez may ultimately fulfill his promise and that I think that there is nothing left but to offer someone else a commission."[32]

In response to Coolidge's request for some names of composers with whom Martha would find it desirable to work, Graham suggested Hindemith, Barber, Britten, Toch, or Stravinsky. They agreed upon Hindemith, who at first resisted the idea of working with a script and suggested to Martha something more abstract. In the end Martha agreed to do whatever he liked, and the product of their efforts was *Herodiäde*. In an interview with Agnes De Mille in 1985, Graham recalled how she went to call on Hindemith, who was by now teaching at Yale.

"He looked at me the whole time he sat at the piano and played. He never took his eyes off me. . . . By the time I got home the phone was ringing. It was Mrs. Hindemith. She said, 'Are you all right? I think we were too strong for you.' I said, 'You almost were. I almost fainted, I felt so weak.' It was the energy of the man." Hindemith promised that he would deliver the score precisely at noon on a certain Wednesday. Martha responded, "Well, if it's a day or two later, an hour or two later, you just let me know. He said, 'It will be there at noon on Wednesday.' At noon on Wednesday the door knock came and he gave me the score. I said how moved I was, and said, 'Oh, what will happen if I fail?' He said 'Then I will write you another piece.'"[33]

By mid-June 1944, Martha wrote to Hindemith that she was deeply moved by his music and admitted that "hearing it [the poem] in French, as Mrs. Hindemith read it to me, helped a great deal to understand the sonority that is in . . . the original which the English lacks."[34] Because of its incredibly demanding choreography, the piece, which was not published until 1955 and then only in piano reduction, is seldom danced today but is sometimes performed as a concert work.[35]

In the midst of all this travail Elizabeth had taken it upon herself to offer her old friend Darius Milhaud the choice of a commission, "a work for piano trio, string sextet, or a piece of dance music." By this time she had definitely made up her mind not to use the Chávez work even if it did arrive in time, and it is likely that she encouraged Milhaud to choose in favor of the dance. He did, and although he was the last of the three composers commissioned he was actually the first to complete his full score. In addition he attempted to solve Graham and Spivacke's worries over the instrumentation by announcing that he had limited himself to nine instruments (which was Spivacke's recommendation in the first place) and even offered to try a more reduced instrumentation "if Paul and Aaron do so and all of us use the same instruments." Spivacke passed the information on to Martha, adding, "I thought you might be glad to hear of his offer. If you do find the works suitable for touring, you must use this lever to get the other composers to do likewise."[36]

After many anxious moments of brokering by Spivacke and parleying of composers and choreographer, the pieces all came together in time for a triumphant celebration of Elizabeth's eightieth birthday, 30

October 1944, in an evening of ballet that combined the biblical account of Hindemith's *Herodiäde,* with Milhaud's favored subject of rebirth in *Jeux de Printemps,* and the evocative Americana of Copland's *Appalachian Spring.* The title of the Copland work was actually Graham's invention. He had simply called it "Ballet for Martha," and when they came together for the first rehearsals inquired what she had decided to call it.[37]

Graham had entrusted the design of the spare sets for the ballets to her friend and long-time collaborator, the sculptor Isamu Noguchi, and the costumes to Edythe Gilford. Hindemith came to the performance, though Martha admitted later that he did not much like what she had done. Copland, of course, was there to accept the bravos and the small stage of the Library of Congress groaned under a burden of talent. Martha danced the role of the bride, Erick Hawkins was cast as the husbandman, Merce Cunningham was the fire-and-brimstone preacher, and May O'Donell the pioneer woman. Martha, at age fifty, rose to the occasion "fresh and beautiful as the young bride and danced," as critic John Martin said, "like a 16-year-old." And to Erick, the bridegroom, she presented this role as a pledge of her devotion.[38]

Coolidge was delighted, and Spivacke, who had shielded her from much of the anxiety and uncertainty during the months of preparation, wrote to Martha to say, "As soon as I saw the first rehearsal I knew that this was what I was praying for, I never for a moment doubted that you would give us a marvelous performance but I must say that when I saw it, it exceeded even my greatest expectations and I still do not see how you overcame all the difficulties and obstacles which faced you."[39]

As a sort of postscript to the whole saga, Spivacke wrote to Graham in December to say that Chávez had, in fact, deposited his score at the American Embassy in Mexico City in August, and for some reason it had never been sent on to the Library of Congress. Spivacke was making every effort to locate it. The commission is dated 1944, but as late as 1950 Chávez wrote to Coolidge, "Some years ago the Elizabeth Sprague Coolidge Foundation of the Library of Congress commissioned me to write music for a ballet by Martha Graham. It was Martha's scenario, *Daughter of Colchis,* that served as a ground for the music, although later Miss Graham used my music for another ballet which she called *Dark Meadows.* In any event this is only to remind you of the commission."[40]

Elizabeth with Erik Hawkins and Martha Graham at the premiere of Appalachian Spring, *on the occasion of Coolidge's eightieth birthday in 1944*
Library of Congress

The Chávez piece was never performed at the Library of Congress, but Martha premiered it in New York in 1946. Agnes De Mille considers it one of Graham's finest choreographic inventions, the technical demands of which make it extremely difficult for both soloists and chorus. John Martin found the music of *Dark Meadow* "without theatrical or choreographic quality, pure paper-and-ink music, and long stretches of it sound like so many pages out of Czerny. . . . That Miss Graham has been able to make a dance composition against it is inexplicable."[41]

Of the three works commissioned for the 1944 festival only that of Copland has endeared itself to the public, and that largely in the form of the full symphonic orchestration done in 1945. With *Appalachian Spring* Copland created an American masterpiece and won for himself a Pulitzer Prize. For Elizabeth it was a matter of great satisfaction and pride to know that she had been the agent to set this creation in motion, and the success of it all was a welcome joy for her in a year that had otherwise been marked by a large measure of sadness and depression.

What the ballets had meant in the larger scheme of the history of dance in America can best be expressed in Martha Graham's own words: "American dance has . . . come of age."[42] By bringing together three major twentieth-century composers with the creative genius of Martha Graham, who brought to the perfection of her art a new technique and a new idiom, Coolidge had made a genuine contribution to the maturation of an American dance style that bore no resemblance to her first essay into the world of ballet with Stravinsky's *Apollon Musagète* in 1928. To return to the critics' observations of Adolph Bolm's direction of that earlier work is to recognize it as an anachronistic attempt to inject the obsolete elegance of an earlier, classical balletic style into the "underlying obstinacies of modernistic rhythm." As one unnamed critic had observed of *Apollon Musagète,* although their faces were wreathed in properly lyrical smiles, Stravinsky's muses—dancing on point in classical tutus—could be seen counting diligently as they executed steps originally devised for eight-bar measures now forced to fit into bars of three and seven or nine beats and "phrases that ended whenever the composer chose." No more graphic testimony of the coming of age of American dance could be found than in the comparison of these two Coolidge commissions.[43]

CHAPTER NINETEEN

Too Much Anno Domini

I have been feeling rather restless and aimless, but I think it is because I have outlived my generation and am feeling solitary and more or less alone.

– ELIZABETH SPRAGUE COOLIDGE TO ERNST TOCH, N.D.

AT AGE EIGHTY-FOUR Elizabeth wrote to Henry Spalding that she was "continuing in remarkable health, despite the relentless birthdays, and I sometimes quote to myself Tennyson's *Song of the Brook*, 'Men may come and men may go, but I go on forever.'"[1] There is a mellowness perceivable in the relationships of her later years, a growing degree of equanimity in her acceptance of the inevitable diminishing of energy, decline of health, and death of friends. Although she maintained the public countenance of success, fame, and satisfaction in her work, behind it there remained a persistent private pain of loneliness and fear. The demise of so many cherished friends was more than a mere reminder of her own mortality; it became the occasion of a retreat further and further into the consolation of treasured memories. "I have so long and interesting a past to remember that I find myself living largely in it and so, escaping a little from the present . . . I cling to the friendships which still remain to me."[2]

She had long ago learned the value of immersion in work, and to her personal credo of "doing for others and for Art" she added (like a cloak) a touch of bittersweet humor that she wore with grace. Although her letters to close friends with whom there was no need of keeping up a façade reflect a profound sense of loneliness and fear, they are tempered with a certain sage detachment, even whimsy. To those who inquired of her health and well-being her usual response was simply, "There is nothing wrong with me but too much anno Domini."

In rapid succession the 1940s had taken the lives of many of her closest friends, all much younger than herself—Alphonse Onnou and Edwin Rice in 1940, Frank Bridge in 1941, Henry Eichheim and Henry Prunières in 1942, Carl Engel in 1944, Alfredo Casella in 1947, and Jacques Gordon in 1948. Increasingly she turned to her close women friends who were dissociated from her professional dealings and opened her heart without fear of being thought weak or out of control. But the most cherished of these was already gone. With Gertrude Watson's death in 1938 Elizabeth had lost a boon companion and beloved friend who had been such a support throughout the years of Fred's illness. No one could ever fill the emptiness left by her death. Gertrude had continued to maintain her home in Pittsfield, and Elizabeth always found it a safe haven after her tiresome travels, but now, when faced with the prospect of returning there without Gertrude, she began to curtail her visits to the Berkshires. She took some comfort in the companionship of Lillian Littlehales and Gladys North, and her California friends Gladys Caldwell and Persis Coleman, but her letters to them suggest that Engel's death in May of 1944 had much to do with her sadness and the general depression that persisted well into the next year.

In the early Coolidge-Engel correspondence, Engel's wife, Helen, is frequently referred to and always figures in their social life outside the Library of Congress. But from late 1928 onward she vanishes from the picture, leaving one to suspect illness of some sort. There is no mention of her death, but vague references that suggest some tragedy. Elizabeth's letter written in early January of 1929 is particularly sympathetic: "I cannot tell you how saddened I am by the letter which you wrote on the 28th of December. . . . You must have seen by the tone of my letter how eager I was to know of your welfare and, alas, of your misfortune."[3] "It is indeed a cruel one, and I think no one can understand and sympathize more truly than I do."[4]

Whatever the nature of this unnamed suffering in Engel's life, Coolidge identified with it. She was well aware of his sadness at the loss of so dear a friend as Sonneck less than three months before, and the trauma of his facing the difficult decision to leave the Library of Congress just at this same time. In the ten remaining years of his life Engel suffered periodic bouts of ill health, discouragement, and dejection. Coolidge was aware of his depression, for he made no secret of it in his letters, especially one written just a few months before his death—the last of his letters contained in their correspondence files. It was sent just after his colleagues at Schirmer produced the Festschrift in honor of his sixtieth birthday, which clearly he had not appreciated: "I probably don't have to tell you that Schirmer's 'charming birthday memoir' annoyed me no end. As a visible token of friendship, composed by well-intentioned but ill-advised conspirators, it gratified me. But it merely served to emphasize, in my own mind, the fact that most of my sixty years have been wasted. . . . I do not have to look in the mirror to observe the ravage of time. I feel it in my bones."[5]

Coolidge's correspondence at the Library of Congress is suspiciously circumspect on the subject of Engel's death and, while letters and memorials to him are threaded with references to his "untimely demise," there is no mention of the cause of death. This and one of Engel's own essays entitled "Some Letters to a Namesake," have caused some to speculate that he may have taken his own life.[6] Tired, dispirited, and questioning the achievements of his life, Engel seems to have identified with this namesake who, in a like state of mind, had committed suicide at about the same age that Engel died. He wrote with sensitivity of the "craving for peace" that drove that earlier Carl Engel "to take the supreme, the irrevocable chance, not in a fit of cowardice, not in a frenzied moment of insanity, but with the calm deliberation of the Stoic. R.I.P."[7]

For Elizabeth the loss of loved ones was a familiar experience, but in the case of Engel's death her grief seemed intensified not only by her own general sense of isolation but also by the knowledge that his last days were so troubled. She has left no record of her most intimate response to his passing, but her sorrow must have been profound. Her public statement given on the occasion of a memorial concert the following March is a model of restraint, tracing only her professional association with Engel.[8]

Of the many testimonials of friends and colleagues at the time of Carl's death, the one that perhaps characterizes him best is that of Harold Bauer, who reflected that while there is some consolation in the statement that no man is truly indispensable and no loss irreparable, this is hard to believe when faced with the realization that "We shall not look upon his like again." Bauer identified the uniqueness of Engel's character as his capacity for deep and loving friendship. "I think that each one of us—his intimates and his associates—recognized in Carl Engel's friendship a unique quality that set it apart from any other relationship. 'He was *my* friend,' we all feel with the poignancy of strictly personal and private loss."[9]

If indeed Coolidge shared this most intimate sorrow with anyone she has carefully removed all trace of it from her correspondence; the only vestiges are the consoling letters that she wrote to other friends of Carl. To William Kroll, who had grown very close to Engel over the years, she confided, "I am sure that you and I both felt the same grateful and tender friendship for Carl Engel, who has left us so prematurely. I know from what he has said to me that he would not be sorry to go, for I think his life was a sad one, and he was not too well. For us who are left it is indeed a sorrowful loss, for nothing can compensate except the happy memories we both had of his help and sympathy."[10]

It is tempting to think that after such an enduring and intimate friendship Engel might have left some last testimony of his affection for her. We will never know. Elizabeth's silence is eloquent. It was for her perhaps a grief too personal to be shared and, after all, she well understood that love does not end at the grave, as Engel once reminded her. "Great loves die hard and some die never, thank heaven."[11]

A slight chink in the defenses of her interiorized grief is discernible in an outpouring of letters written less than two weeks after the memorial to Engel and just after her son's untimely announcement that the family would be spending the summer at his home in Vermont, where she felt she was unable to follow. On St. Patrick's Day of 1945 her depression seems to have reached an all-time low. When Lillian Littlehales attempted to console her with the knowledge of all the joy and pleasure she had brought to others, Elizabeth responded quite uncharacteristically, "I realize what you say about the privilege and blessedness of making other people happy, but I am selfish enough to wish sometimes to turn the tables and find once more what I used to have from Gertrude and my mother. . . . It is a questionable blessing to outlive one's generation to the point of domestic isolation."[12]

By the next paragraph, however, her tone quickly changes. "I see I am writing in a very self-centered and disagreeable mood so I will turn to pleasanter and more objective subjects," namely a recounting of the number of musical friends who had dropped by to play sonatas with her—Temianka, Prévost, Kroll, Schneider, and Kolisch.

That same gray St. Patrick's Day she apologized to Gladys Caldwell that her "rather monotonous and uneventful life this winter . . . does not make for good epistolary material."[13] She did, however, allude to a kind of half-hearted intention of writing her memoirs for which purpose "I have employed two women to file and catalog my enormous correspondence at the Library of Congress, which covers a period of twenty-five years or more and literally comprises thousands of letters." It is apparent, however, that she considered it more or less busywork and, though many had encouraged her to do it, her heart obviously was not in it. "I have not felt any interest or inspiration to do [it], but I imagine sometime the letters themselves will be published—which perhaps is more to the point, as I think any book that I should write would probably be nothing but a series of anecdotes."[14]

Other than her travel journals written as a young girl, Elizabeth never kept a diary as her mother had. Although she must have realized the historical significance of her work, in the early years of her patronage she did not even keep copies of her letters, and as late as 1951, when Spivacke learned that she was preparing to send to the Library only letters received, he remonstrated, "I am very shocked to find that you have separated the carbon copies of your own replies. Please send us all of them. I know that you are apt to minimize your own historical importance, but it is really essential for future understanding of the letters to have your replies so that people can tell what it is all about."[15]

Over the course of Coolidge's public life there were innumerable requests from aspiring authors who wished to write her life's story, as well as admonitions from such friends as Engel and Caldwell, who also urged her to write her autobiography. The answer was consistently and emphatically "no." Although she willing deposited her correspondence at the Library of Congress, where it is public record, she resisted all efforts of those who wished to publish them. When a certain Miss Gillette, who was hired in 1945 to index the letters, expressed a desire to write about them, Elizabeth refused, saying, "I am going to ask you to regard any such information as you may have gathered from filing of my material as more or less my personal property (and that of the Library of Congress to whom now the letters really belong) and at least wait until I have had a chance to look them over for myself. I am sure that you cannot misjudge my motive in saying that, and that you would feel the same about your own letters."[16]

Not even Carl Engel could convince her to publish the correspondence when in 1937 he wrote to tell her that Rolf Hoffmann proposed to publish a selection of her most important letters as part of a historical survey of chamber music. Engel expressed some hesitation about criteria for selection because "some of your most pertinent and humanly interesting remarks may have to be left out, because of references too frank—if only too just—to living persons. What should give spice and zest to these letters are precisely such passages that it would be a shame to omit. And yet, I feel sure that you would be the last one to wish to hurt anyone's feelings."[17]

She concurred that "it would be in very bad taste, if not actually illegal, to publish those more or less confidential expressions of my opinions about people and affairs which are still in existence."[18] Despite the privacy that she so ardently guarded, when she finally did go about setting down her memoirs the news leaked out, and Edward Weeks of the *Atlantic Monthly* requested publication rights to offer it in installments in the magazine. She must have sent him some rather bleached and laundered chapters, which provoked his complaint that they were too bland and compressed. "Again and again I wished that you might pause to tell in greater detail of the scenes which lived in your mind."[19] Nothing came of his efforts, nor did any of these notes survive, though it is likely that they formed the basis of her essay entitled "Da Capo," a paper that she read in 1951 for the Mother's Club of Cambridge.

Elizabeth's complaints about loneliness and the odd ache or pain should not be taken as a capitulation to age and infirmity or any lessening of interest in promoting her art. On the contrary, it is the very absence of this kind of personal revelation in most of her writing that causes these examples to stand out so strikingly now. The bulk of her correspondence from this late period actually provides many insights into the way that she invented her own trajectory over the hurdles and created an attitude of survival. Along with the passive retreat into memories, she resorted to the oft-tested restorative of hard work and the determination not to indulge in self-pity. To her old friend Persis Coleman, she once wrote of "the necessity of having an objective interest in life which entirely excludes dwelling upon the thought of one's self." And whether this interest be "a person or a cause, or any outside enthusiasm, I think it should be animated not by what you want for yourself but by what you want for it."[20] That she lived by this dictum is clearly echoed in words written a full twenty years later, when she reflected that "it makes old age worth while to have an impersonal object of enthusiasm and effort, and I feel that I have received probably more enjoyment than I have given to others in coming in contact with the best chamber music of our time."[21]

Her concern for others is admirably demonstrated by her great preoccupation with the safety of her many European friends who were in danger during World War II. Since her Italian friends, regardless of personal convictions, were on the side of the Axis powers, there was no possible communication with them, but she continued to write to those in England and to receive their letters, often left in ribbons by the censor's blades. The most poignant of these are the ones exchanged with the Bridges, who had left their home in Kensington to move to their country house in Eastbourne near the English Channel. There, "Frank actually saw from his window upstairs some destroyers catching a submarine. Horrible, but with such an awful excitement that one just had to watch."[22] By 1940, when the French channel ports were occupied by the Germans, both Royal Air Force and Luftwaffe planes roared overhead day and night and as many as a dozen bombs at a time were dropped only a few hundred yards from the Bridges' home.[23] Such news from England prompted Elizabeth to condole with a philosophical air: "[O]ne can only take refuge in what has already existed of beauty and happiness. This is sorry comfort; nevertheless, I feel that it is a comfort to know that the wonderful times which we have had together cannot be canceled, and that, come what may in the future, a rich and beautiful past is our inviolable possession."[24]

Harriet Cohen, too, cabled Elizabeth to report that her home, her library, and the precious Bechstein piano that she had brought to Chicago in 1930 were all lost when her house in London was hit by an incendiary bomb. The same indomitable spirit that sustained the Bridges and inspired Cohen to sign her cable "Rule Britannia" prompted Elizabeth to respond, "I think the world has never known such a magnificent display of spiritual force as is now exhibited by your nation, and I hope that you receive enough news from America to know how eagerly we wish to help you. . . . I am truly proud that my blood is entirely English."[25]

All the petty annoyances that Frank and Ethel Bridge had experienced in their early acquaintance with Elizabeth were long since forgotten, and Frank acknowledged, "My God, Souzanne dear, how much I owe to you for your spiritual and material help throughout these past years. It has helped me to face the present ghastly situation with less anxiety than would otherwise have been."[26] Unfortunately, Frank did not live to see the end of the war. Ethel's letter informing Elizabeth of his death elicited a tender expression of sympathy that unmistakably recalls the loss of her own dear Fred: "I do want to tell you one thought which possibly may comfort you a little, and that is, that you have already had longer and greater blessings in your many years of devoted married life than many people are permitted to enjoy, and that your memories of all those years must put into your present life a richness for which nothing can compensate." That she was speaking from experience is clear. "I know that this will seem difficult, perhaps even impossible, but I do know also how much better it is to lose something than never to have had it."[27]

Utterances such as these allow some insight into Coolidge's method of coping with tragedy and again emphasize her belief in the value of holding fast to memories, as she counseled Ethel: "It is my hope that as time goes on the beautiful past will somewhat outshine the dreadful present, and that you will be able to do, as I have so often done, revert in memory to the happiness and accomplishments which nothing can cancel."[28]

Coolidge's ability to commit to and to sustain deep friendships is one of her most admirable qualities. Those who could see past the hauteur that sometimes marked her demeanor were well rewarded, for once she had given her love in friendship she remained loyal and steadfast. It becomes quite evident now that her august age and genuine concern for her friends abroad permitted her to cast aside her usual Yankee reserve and to express her feelings with a greater openness.

On this side of the Atlantic the Coolidge family was doing its share for the war effort too. With America's entry into the conflict Elizabeth chose to spend most of her time in the East near Sprague and his family, who were "solidly embedded like Plymouth Rock, in Massachusetts soil."[29] She was too old to enter actively into relief efforts herself but did her part by arranging noon hour musical entertainment for workers in defense plants, sponsoring concerts for the benefit of relief organizations in the Allied countries, giving the automobiles that she kept in various parts of the country for the use of the Red Cross and Women's Auxiliary, and sending her chauffeur to drive, and one of her maids to sew, for the Red Cross. Although she missed her annual trips to California she was proud to report to Milhaud, "My family, too, are taking their share of the universal defense work. My son has been made one of the special Cambridge police, and his wife an air-raid warden and a first aid Red Cross worker. There is not much that I can do except to help others."[30]

Elizabeth would undoubtedly have been surprised had she known that during the war the auditorium that she built at the Library of Congress was pressed into services that were far from musical. It frequently became the scene of secret meetings of members of Congress and the armed forces. Although it is unknown exactly what transpired there, the staff of the Music Division of the Library was always aware of the meetings, and word was circulated sub rosa that "General Marshall is giving a concert today" or "the Senate Chorus is being conducted this afternoon by the Honorable Mr. Barkley."[31]

Despite her generosity and loyalty to democratic ideals Coolidge suffered the indignity of some public accusations in the press during the war years, branding her as a Socialist and even a Communist. These indictments were the result of her son's affiliation with the Socialist party. Sprague's Socialist leanings were well known ever since he took a public stand along with some prominent liberals in defense of Sacco and Vanzetti, the immigrant shoemaker and fishmonger whom he believed were unjustly convicted of murder in 1921 and executed in 1927. It was the case that more or less defined the term "liberal," and Sprague was among the many (including Felix Frankfurter) who believed the two men were persecuted for their political beliefs.[32]

Sprague's quest for political office on the Socialist ticket began as early as 1922 when he ran for secretary of state of Massachusetts. He was the party's nominee for state treasurer in 1926 and 1938, and campaigned for the United States Senate in 1934. He seems to have had no illusions about winning, but enjoyed the opportunity to promote Socialist views. Indeed, he admitted that "after each election . . . [I] still console myself after defeat by playing the viola, making photographs, or building model railways."[33] The same year as his unsuccessful bid for the Senate he made the news in Pittsfield when he joined the picket lines of the striking members of the Pittsfield local of the United Textile Workers of America. Police were prepared to rough up the mill workers when they walked out of the Berkshire Woolen and the Wyandotte Worsted Mills, but the presence of the son of one of Pittsfield's best-known and most respected citizens prevented any violence from occurring.[34] The strike, however, did mark the beginning of a powerful trade union movement in the city.

Several times during his ardent Socialist years, when his mother inquired what he wanted for his birthday, Sprague responded that he would like her to make a contribution to the Socialist Party in his name. It is these donations that have led to the mistaken belief that she was a member. Sprague became disenchanted with the pacifist stance assumed by the party when Germany invaded Norway, and found it so "irresponsible in the face of Nazi aggression" that he withdrew from the party.[35] Nevertheless, his association with the Socialists was a stigma that would come back to haunt him.

Sprague was strongly committed to the American Civil Liberties Union and was for a long time chairman of the Massachusetts branch. He also was a charter organizer of the Americans for Democratic Action, a group dedicated to the removal of communist influence from the old Union for Democratic Action. Sprague always insisted that the rights of communists should be respected, yet he spent much effort trying to thwart the attempts of communists to infiltrate liberal organizations. In view of these commitments, it is ironic that he and his mother should be accused of communist leanings. In 1934 a Senate committee under Martin Dies was established to investigate un-American activities, a kind of communist-hunting precursor of the later McCarthy Senate committee. In February of 1943 the *Washington Post* carried a full page advertisement under the banner "ABOLISH THE DIES COMMITTEE . . . as a step toward victory." Elizabeth's name appeared as a subscriber along with about a hundred others, including Adam Clayton Powell, Yehudi Menuhin, Albert Einstein, Helen Keller, and many prominent clergymen. One accusation against Mrs. Coolidge came in the form of an angry letter charging that "not even mother-love for a communist son can excuse or condone your action in signing your name to the attempted smear of the Dies Committee in today's *Washington Post.* Martin Dies and his committee are among the few safeguards of my loyalty in these dark times. . . . Why have you forsaken decency, honor, loyalty, patriotism? You are not worthy to have the protection of our flag. You and your like are a shame and a disgrace to this nation."[36]

Although Elizabeth undoubtedly found such accusations offensive, she has left no record of any recriminating thoughts. She seems rather to have treated it with the kind of detachment that characterized her attitude toward negative reviews of the avant-garde music that she sponsored. She would hardly have dignified such an uninformed and unjust accusation with a response, but she would always stand by her son even when he held opposite views or when she disapproved of some decision he had made.

After his discharge from the army with the rank of sergeant in 1919, Sprague moved with his family to Pittsfield, where he continued his experimentation in the laboratory that he had set up in his home there. He was by nature an intense person, easily absorbed in his work. It was a quality that obviously worried his mother, and she turned to Dr. William T. Councilman, Isa Coolidge's husband, and asked him to assume a paternal role toward Sprague who, in her opinion, was becoming much too isolated, "locked up with his own theories. . . . No man . . . can limit his life and his interests . . . without becoming warped and ineffectual. . . . I believe that you could render him a service which he has missed in missing the influence of a strong and active father."[37]

It is not known if Councilman actually did speak to Sprague, but shortly after Elizabeth's plea Sprague returned to Harvard to do graduate work and in 1924 received his Ph.D. He began teaching there while still a student, and after attaining the doctorate joined the regular faculty. Some critics have questioned the logic—if not the sincerity—of his espousal of Socialism, which, if followed to its ultimate philosophical ideal, would lead to abolition of all private wealth. His own words shed some light on the question. "I have been drawn rather deeply into the radical labor movement, first through the Socialist Party and now (1940) through the Teacher's Union. This originated in an abstract desire to see scientific methods applied to social problems, but has lately been actuated by a growing conviction that unless something effective and quick is done to solve the most pressing of these problems, society will collapse in an epidemic of depression, wars, and dictatorships, under which conditions neither science nor anything else worth doing will be possible."[38]

Sprague Coolidge could hardly deny his comfortable position, for destiny had placed him squarely in the company of the privileged and in a posture seemingly irreconcilable with the philosophy to which he was committed. But it is worth recalling that in the very year of his birth his mother and his Aunt Lucy had taken a similar stand at the time of the Pullman strike.

What most people would have no way of knowing was that Sprague's last thirty years at Harvard were spent in contributed services. Despite his unsalaried status he assumed a heavy load of graduate courses and administrative chores, including the initial organization of the Committee on the Ph.D. in Chemical Physics—all the while carrying on significant research in the field of quantum mechanics and publishing some landmark studies.[39]

Neither the false accusations nor the war kept Elizabeth from her music, and she continued to the end of her life to maintain a strict regimen. At seventy-four she was still practicing as much as six hours a day on such pianistically demanding repertoire as Beethoven's "Kreutzer" Sonata, the Schumann Piano Quintet, and the Brahms Trio in B Major that she was playing with members of the Kolisch Quartet. To a letter that she wrote to Ernst Toch when she was eighty Elizabeth's maid appended a note that gives an account of her daily routine. "We go for a drive for an hour each day in a taxi and she is practicing three hours daily and sometimes she composes at night for an hour or so."[40] It was during these last years that she returned to her earlier compositions and wrote a string quartet accompaniment to her Browning Cycle and an oboe obbligato to the Slumber Songs of the Madonna. Her only large new undertaking was the Oboe Sonata, her last composition, which, like her very first, was written for Sprague.

She still enjoyed listening to live music, though it could be done only with the help of increasingly cumbersome hearing aids. Henri Temianka recalls inviting her to an afternoon of chamber music at his home. "She arrived in her chauffeured limousine, a commanding six foot figure, . . . a bundle of imperious energy. . . . After she disembarked, the chauffeur emerged with an enormous box, large enough to have hidden a body. Staggering under its weight, somehow he managed to reach the music room, where he dumped it in front of the most comfortable armchair. Mrs. Coolidge soon followed, occupied her throne, produced a huge ear trumpet, and sat back expectantly. Seven string quartets later, she reluctantly agreed to a dinner break."[41]

It was especially those hours that she spent making music with others that brought the most sunshine into these otherwise gray autumnal days. She and Temianka became good friends in the 1940s and spent pleasant times playing sonatas together. On one occasion he called her just after arriving in Boston and was ordered to "come right over, and please bring your violin." He pleaded the need to bathe and unpack after his long trip from California. Although she reluctantly acquiesced, fifteen minutes later the telephone rang to say that Coolidge's chauffeur was waiting in the lobby with orders to transport him immediately to her.[42]

He understood Spivacke's dictum that "Mrs. Coolidge wants what she wants, when she wants it!" She had been practicing the Brahms D Minor Sonata and could not wait to play it with him and have him coach her. Whatever the quality of her playing at this time—when she admitted that sometimes she could hardly hear herself or her partner—she seems to have communicated in her music something beyond the mere notes on the page, which prompted Temianka to write, "It is claimed that you are about to celebrate your eightieth birthday. I, who played a Brahms Sonata with you in Washington as recently as last February, don't believe it. You are so miraculously young in spirit, you have so much vitality—enough to put all of us to shame—that it hardly ever occurs to me that you are older than I am, let alone that you are about to complete your eightieth year in this imperfect but exciting world." In the hours they spent together he had come to understand that the secret of her "remaining young through all these years lies in the fact that you have always been vitally interested in what others did. While others are moping about themselves, I think you never found time to mope."[43]

Even at eighty there were still new challenges, new fields to till, and some important new young talents to admit to her ever-widening circle of friends. The highlight of the year was, of course, the birthday festival and the success of *Appalachian Spring,* but it was also at this time that she began her association with William Primrose and Virgil Fox and renewed her earlier relationships with Roger Sessions and Roy Harris. She sponsored Fox in a series of organ recitals at the Library of Congress, and he in turn spent much of his free time in Washington squiring her around for rides and to movies.

When the war ended and gasoline was no longer rationed, Coolidge seems to have found a fountain of youth in the form of motoring, and by her own admission indulged in "a veritable orgy of driving." She began to attend concerts again, and although she found symphonic music increasingly difficult to listen to she made various attempts to overcome the problem by having hearing aids installed in the halls that she frequented. She claimed that she could hear best in motion picture theaters but that Radio City Music Hall had the most satisfactory system of all and she petitioned Koussevitzky to permit her to have such a system installed in Boston's Symphony Hall. That it was less than satisfactory is evident from the innumerable letters she wrote to the manager, G. E. Judd, recommending adjustments. Since the Boston hall had direct-current electricity and her instrument required alternating current, she offered $300 for the installation to accommodate her, and actually threatened to discontinue her subscription if this were not accomplished by the time of the opening concert, adding that she wanted to pay her subscription early in order to avoid the tax that would be added after 1 October. As demanding as she could be about such requests she was also sensitive to the possibility that her hearing aid might be offensive to the audience seated near her. For adjustment of this device when she was in Cambridge, she often called upon Jerome Weisner to come to her at once, ignoring the fact that he was the president of MIT and a busy man. In Washington her chauffeur, Sherman Warden, performed this service and was usually dispatched to the Library early to set up her equipment when she attended concerts there. By this time Gertrude Clarke Whittall was also quite deaf, and when the two great lady patrons of that institution attended concerts in the hall that one had built, played on instruments that the other had donated, they appeared as a pair of dowager queen bees, enthroned in their usual places in the auditorium, the wands of their respective hearing apparatus undulating in the air like great antennae seeking to reel in the soundwaves.

Deafness can impose a cruel isolation—doubly painful to one whose life is music—and although there is ample evidence that Elizabeth often found the affliction almost unbearable, she never conceded defeat to old age nor relinquished her acute interest in the affairs of the foundation that bore her name. While she could not ignore the effect of the unremitting accumulation of anno Domini upon her body, her mind and spirit seemed ageless, far too young to be confined and tended like some exotic marine specimen in an aquarium. Hers were the thoughts and schemes that require the freedom of the open seas. And to the unwary angler who might attempt to control her, at age eighty-four Elizabeth Sprague Coolidge could still prove to be Leviathan on a fishhook.

CHAPTER TWENTY

Finale Ultimo

Play out the play.

– SHAKESPEARE, *HENRY IV*, II, 539

OVER THE YEARS Elizabeth's Washington apartment had been the scene of much "musical jollification" as well as the site of some important creations. She had always been generous in offering the use of it to others when she was away, and so it is that one of Henry Spalding's books was written there, and on her dining room table Roy Harris produced one of his early symphonies as well as parts of his *History of Musical Materials.* But life in Washington during the war years was difficult for her, and she had become fearful of being alone, especially at night, so she was looking for another maid who could stay through these lonely hours. To make matters worse Sherman Warden was drafted in 1942. The absence of her faithful chauffeur and the rationing of gasoline meant the deprivation of daily outings that she so enjoyed. She admitted, "I find Washington pretty lonely, for all my friends who are worth-while are, of course, too essentially occupied to have much leisure, and my own society becomes very monotonous and unstimulating. . . . My chief occupation—other than superintending the mechanical routine of housekeeping, . . . has been practicing Brahms and Mozart."[1]

So in 1947 she moved back to Cambridge into modest accommodations at the Hotel Continental, minutes away from Sprague and Peg. She engaged Alicia Aspinwall to dismantle her Washington apartment and issued instructions to sell all her silver, china, and paintings, except family portraits, which she took care in her will to leave to her grandchildren. The Melcher painting of her with four-year-old Sprague was to go to the Library of Congress, where it now hangs in the foyer of the Coolidge Auditorium.[2] She seems to have systematically divested herself of superfluous material things and settled contentedly into a rather Spartan way of life. The most important appointment of her apartment was an old upright piano, where she still spent many contented hours. She owned no phonograph, so when Spivacke wrote in 1950 to say that he was sending her recordings of the festival of that year, she had to borrow one to hear them. There is much evidence that although she longed to be unencumbered by "the possession of things," as she put it, her inner life was lonely, and she longed for a spiritual equal.

But even in her seclusion she was far from idle. In 1949 she wrote to Henry Spalding, "I am continuing in the same direction but on a narrow and less active scale, as I advance toward my eighty-fifth birthday. Just now I am planning music in Washington and Pittsfield, . . . but I content myself largely with the planning and ask other people to do the executive work, while I remain rather quietly at home."[3]

By 1950 her health had deteriorated sufficiently that she could not make the trip back to Washington for the festival, though there is evidence that she considered doing so and attempted to engage her former maid, Bertha McCulloch, to accompany her there. McCulloch wrote confidentially to Spivacke, "She told me that money meant nothing if I would consent to go with her so I am depending on you to find a large comfortable room in a first class hotel. I shall feel uncomfortable because I must sleep in her room—she cannot be left alone for a minute. . . . She is as well as she will ever be, but is very unsteady and cannot rise without help."[4]

Despite many bodily ills, Elizabeth's mind was still clear and active, and 1951 found her making plans to engage Olga Averino to sing her Browning Cycle for a program that the Coolidge Foundation was mounting to celebrate her eighty-seventh birthday.

Ever since Alexander Schneider began his work with Casals, Elizabeth was busily looking for opportunities to present him to the public in performances of the Bach works he had studied with Casals. By now she could hardly separate her affection for him from her admiration of his talent and achievement. For her he was "a remarkable and adorable person, and one of the finest living artists." Quite apart from her delight in his professional achievements there is an unmistakably maternal quality in her forthright declaration to him: "I . . . think you are rather wonderful, and am glad that we have discovered each other."[5]

Among the performances she planned for him were some at Tanglewood, still at that time called the Berkshire Music Center. The Boston Symphony Orchestra had long since replaced the New York Philharmonic as the resident orchestra, and since the conductor was always the director of the festival, she was again dealing with Serge Koussevitzky who of course was no stranger to her. There was a feeling on the part of some of Coolidge's most loyal supporters that the Berkshire Music Center at Tanglewood had in some fashion usurped the title from Coolidge's early Berkshire Music Festivals. Mary Bristol, for years her secretary at Pittsfield, admitted that "Whenever I go to Tanglewood I think of you as the real founder of that great enterprise because if it had not been for you and your pioneer work in this locality, Tanglewood would never have existed as a musical center."[6]

If Coolidge in fact harbored any such thoughts she has left no written record of it. There is some suggestion that she felt a bit upstaged, but the purpose of Tanglewood was so different from her own emphasis on chamber music that she seemed to accept it with grace and even pride in the sense that she had thought of it first. In addition, at her advanced age she could only be happy that someone else was bearing the administrative burden of so large an undertaking. She generously financed chamber music concerts for Tanglewood and attended performances whenever she could. One of the most thrilling for her occurred 6 August 1946 when Britten's opera, *Peter Grimes,* was given its American premiere at Tanglewood and she was able to be in the audience with her dear Benji.[7]

When Sasha Schneider first wrote to Pablo Casals of his desire to visit the master in Prades in 1947, it was his intention simply to meet Casals. But encouraged by Diran Alexanian, an old friend and associate of Casals, he took along his fiddle.[8] He later admitted, "I arrived in Prades, still scared stiff, but was soon overwhelmed by the warmth and simplicity of Casals who first of all inquired after his friends in America [and then] said, 'I would like to hear you. Will you play?' I played one movement of a Bach Suite. He insisted that I play the whole Suite. After I finished I asked for his criticisms. He became charged [with] warmth and humanity and asked me not to leave." The prime object of Schneider's visit was not merely to meet Casals but to hear him play, and he was not disappointed. Casals obliged "with absolute naturalness, he played a Bach prelude I will never forget. . . . He asked me to come again the following day."[9]

Although Schneider stayed for only three days on this first visit to Prades, it was long enough to create a bond that would have important consequences for the world of music. He departed with a promise to return the next summer to study seriously with Casals all of the Bach Suites. So it was that with Coolidge's financial support he was able to spend three weeks in the summer of 1948 working several hours daily with Casals and eagerly relaying the experience to her in his grateful letters. It is evident that Schneider had discussed with Elizabeth the possibility of luring Casals out of his voluntary exile, for when he returned to Prades in 1948 it was not only to study but also to act as emissary and spokesman for some influential musicians who, in Casals's words, "considered it essential for me to come to America." Schneider did not go unarmed. He took with him promises of substantial amounts of money to coax Casals out of his seclusion to again perform in public. But the answer remained a firm "no." For Casals it was not a question of money, it was a moral issue. With great sensitivity to the older man's convictions Schneider took a different approach. Sensing his intense interest in young artists and also the deprivation of musical fellowship that resulted from his self-imposed exile, Sasha inquired why Casals did not play chamber music. Casals replied that "there was no one there with whom he could play. . . . He did not even have a piano—only a small upright on which he played his daily Bach Inventions and Fugues—which it is his custom to do as soon as he gets up in the morning."[10]

When the old gentleman seemed resolute and immovable in his decision to remain in seclusion, Sasha played his ace card. "You cannot condemn your art to silence. Since you don't wish to leave Prades, would you allow us to come here, a group of musicians, and give concerts with you?" With only some slight hesitation Casals agreed, believing that this was in line with his attitude. And so the idea of the Prades Festival was conceived.[11] Its realization, however, would require still another year of nurturing.

Mrs. Coolidge with Benjamin Britten at the American premiere of his opera Peter Grimes *at Tanglewood in 1946. The Coolidge signature pearls and hearing aid are clearly displayed.*

True to his promise Schneider returned in the summer of 1949, this time to spend seven glorious weeks doing nothing but playing chamber music with Casals and the musical friends he had recruited. In the meantime, through the agency of an unidentified "great American friend," Sasha was able to procure for Casals a fine concert grand piano.[12] Casals came alive with the excitement of again performing with others and the time was right for Schneider to approach the possibility of a festival in more concrete terms. Besides, 1950 would mark the 200th anniversary of the death of J. S. Bach, his idol. So before leaving Prades Schneider proposed "this music must continue, but on a much larger scale. I told Casals that I considered it a spiritual waste to deprive my colleagues of the opportunity of playing with him, listening to him play, hearing him talk and just being with him. Everyone felt that extraordinary warmth which I have tried to explain in words and cannot."[13] Indeed, Ivor Newton perhaps described it best when he observed that "to make music with Casals is to join in an act not far removed from religious ritual; showmanship and the exploitation of personality have nothing to do with it: he plays as though he were praying."[14]

It was clear that the issue required a different strategy, so Sasha suggested that if Casals would go nowhere to play would he object if Sasha could bring an orchestra to him in Prades? And would Casals agree to play and conduct this Bach festival? By this time Schneider could read Casals's reactions and noted, "I saw in his eyes a certain sparkle. I was encouraged by the fact that he did not refuse immediately. . . . He said 'All right, I will do it.' To be certain that he would not renege, I produced two witnesses. He was trapped—but happily trapped."[15]

Schneider set to work at once forming a committee to help fund a program for young American musicians to go to Prades in the summer of 1950 to celebrate the Bach bicentennial with concerts devoted entirely to his music.[16] He recruited an impressive assembly of patrons, most of them friends and associates of Coolidge—Mildred (Mrs. Robert Woods) Bliss, Mary Howe, Mrs. James Fesler, Cameron Baird, Rosalie Leventritt, Leopold Mannes, and Carleton Sprague Smith. Schneider and Casals both hoped that Elizabeth might be persuaded to come to the festival, but her age and declining health prevented her from making the arduous trip. She explained that she had neither a competent maid nor a traveling companion but would happily accept the title of honorary chairman of the committee that Casals wished to bestow on her. Her absence was a disappointment to Schneider, who admitted, "I only wish that you would be there too. How much I would like to see the two people I admire most and for whom I have the greatest respect come together."[17]

The response of musicians was heartening, and a distinguished roster of performers was assembled, including Serkin, Stern, Horszowski, Kirkpatrick, Leopold Mannes, and of course Sasha. Despite the presence of so many luminaries of the musical world, the very physical limitations of the location dictated simplicity. The choice of Prades for such a gathering was, in the opinion of some, sheer idiocy. There was no auditorium, so this first Prades Festival had to be held in the Church of St. Peter. Moreover, there was only one hotel, and practically everyone had to commute from seven to twenty-five miles in order to attend the programs, which were divided equally between the chamber and orchestral works of Bach and featured Casals in performance of the solo suites for cello. Not surprisingly, the festival received no publicity inside Spain. Nevertheless, the news leaked out and the emergence of Casals from seclusion elicited such excitement that a sizable number of Spaniards walked over the Pyrenees without exit permits in order to hear him play again.[18]

The festival was so successful that another was planned for the following year in Perpignan, with the repertoire enlarged to include Mozart and Beethoven. When Sasha reported that the proceeds of this second festival would go to a hospital in Perpignan that Casals was helping to support, Elizabeth—perhaps touched by the combination of being able to do something for both music and medicine at the same time—at once replied: "I should like to be one of the subscribers to your interesting project for the hospital in Perpignan. I had the interesting experience of visiting that old medieval town, together with the Respighis, and am very sympathetic with your wish to assist the Casals project. I am making the check in your name and you may transfer it as you please."[19]

Others joined the effort to bring Casals to the United States. Late in 1949 Harold Spivacke wrote to him, "In connection with the bicentennial celebration of Johann Sebastian Bach in 1950, we have decided that it would be particularly appropriate to present a special Bach Festival next spring in which for the first time both of these foundations (the Coolidge and the Whittall) would join forces and make presentation under joint sponsorship. We should like to invite you to come to Washington to take part in this celebration, both as a conductor and solo performer."[20]

Despite the possibility of personally renewing his friendship with Coolidge, Casals refused, but the fact that the suggestion came to naught did not prevent Schneider from another attempt. Realizing that 1950 was not only the bicentennial of the death of Bach but also the sesquicentennial of the capital of the United States, Schneider devised an added incentive to bring Casals to America. In the autumn after the first festival he wrote to inform Casals that he would be receiving a very important invitation to come to Washington to celebrate the 150th anniversary of the nation's capital, and while in this country he would be asked to perform and conduct a concert at the United Nations. The invitation would come from the honorary president of the National Sesquicentennial Commission, who was none other than President Harry S. Truman. Schneider undoubtedly thought that Truman's stand against Franco would help the cause along and wrote emphatically, "I want you to realize that this may be even more important than the Bach Festival in Prades. I honestly think that you should not refuse this invitation." Besides invoking the notion of such an appearance as a statement of his continued opposition to Franco, Sasha attempted to sweeten the pot with the promise that "you can have Rudi Serkin play with you, even God himself."[21] This too never materialized.

Coolidge's response to these failed invitations manifests her patience and sensitivity both to the master's conscience and to her protégé's disappointment. Regarding their inability to convince Casals to come to the United States at this time, she wrote to Schneider, "I think it is unwise to try to alter his decision, which amounts to a religious creed with him. To us it seems futile but to a Roman Catholic it is spiritually vital and imperative—which we must respect."[22]

The emergence of Pablo Casals from retirement was a matter of international news, and Schneider's role in this momentous musical event is well known, but what has never been publicly acknowledged is the part played by Coolidge. Reliable sources on Casals nearly all mention Schneider's role but make no mention of her.[23] It was, after all, her generous subsidy that enabled him to work with Casals in the first place and, in the course of repeated summers with him in Prades, to become instrumental in the creation of the festivals that brought an end to the great cellist's exile. Without this intervention Casals might have conceivably gone on living in silent seclusion for the remainder of his life. Although Elizabeth could not possibly have anticipated the eventual outcome of her initial grants to Schneider, her role in the playing out of this significant endeavor deserves more recognition.

This was not the last of her undertakings with Schneider. With characteristic energy and enthusiasm he had espoused a new cause, that of bringing classical music to a wider audience, reaching especially young people. His idea was to perform light classics and dance music in the eighteenth-century manner, the conductor with violin in hand, playing music that should leave the audience "gay and not gloomy." He envisioned a large out-of-door concert somewhere in New York and at first approached the Cloisters, but wrote to Elizabeth that "the director does not think Mozart appropriate."[24] With some trepidation, he took his cause to civic authorities, fully expecting opposition from the musicians union. But he went armed with a promise of $1,000 from Coolidge to underwrite the event. It appears that her name opened many doors, and he was at once promised fifteen musicians of his choice and the use of Washington Square. He wrote to Elizabeth triumphantly: "You will never realize what this meant to me. It happened the same way as with all my other ventures. First everybody laughed at me, saying you are crazy, it cannot be done. It will never be done, and here we are again, we two, doing something in this world which comes from the bottom of our hearts, and is so important at this moment, with the events going on in the world."[25]

This was to be one of Coolidge's last ventures. Earlier that summer she wrote to Schneider, "I am planning a bang-up festival in Pittsfield in September to celebrate the 35th anniversary of South Mountain."[26] But even in the midst of these plans Sasha and Washington Square were very much on her mind, and she wrote from Pittsfield, "As I remember, our concert in Washington Square is to take place on the 17th of August, and though I fear I cannot hear it in person, I . . . think perhaps you would like to have my contribution in advance, so I am sending you a check from my Chicago bank, which goes with love and all kinds of good wishes. Please let me have the publicity, both before and after the concert, and if possible, a signed program."[27]

The concert was a huge success and ended with Viennese waltzes that brought many in the audience to their feet to dance. There would be another Washington Square concert the following year, but without Elizabeth.

Throughout Elizabeth's last years, Spivacke was very attentive to her and kept in close contact. Aware of her failing health, he made use of these final days and months to elicit important recollections from her, for her mind was still undimmed and the associations of her long life were so extraordinarily rich that he used every opportunity to mine some last vivid recollections. She enjoyed reliving the past and at the same time was putting things in order for a longer journey. Mindful of the fact that she still retained the carbons of many of her letters, Spivacke pricked her memory on this issue, and finally, less than two weeks before her death, she sent to the Library of Congress the last carton of letters.

Only days before her last birthday Spivacke wrote to say that Samuel Barber had at last completed his commission and would be performing his *Hermit Songs* with Leontyne Price on the Founder's Day concert, which would be broadcast. On 2 November he again wrote, this time to say, "We missed you last Friday but I do hope you were listening. If you were you must have noted that we had one of the most successful Founder's Day Concerts that we have ever been privileged to present."[28] The letter was never sent—on 4 November 1953 Elizabeth Sprague Coolidge died. After a brief bout with pneumonia, her generous heart simply stopped. With her passing, the world of music lost not merely a benefactor, but a friend and an advocate. Newspapers and trade journals across the country and in Europe were filled with eulogies, and letters of condolence poured in from innumerable people whose lives were touched by hers. Among the most personal were those from Malipiero, who had heard the news through a newspaper clipping sent by a friend. To Spivacke he confided, "It was a real shock for me, for I owe so much to this true friend; before the war, so much of my life . . . was linked to her—you will be able to imagine all my affection if you think of my gratitude. I do not know the address of her son, nor his Christian name, nor of her many beloved grandchildren. How shall I be able to send them my profound condolence?"[29]

Sprague had received the Malipieros' birthday letters addressed to his mother, which clearly had reached Cambridge only after her death. He regretted "that she never saw them, for they would have brought a warm glow to her heart—indeed, something of the glow warms my own heart as I read them." From Sprague's letter we have some knowledge of Elizabeth's last illness. "The day before her birthday we took her to the hospital, gasping for breath. Oxygen made her more comfortable, but on November 4th she died. Her wedding anniversary was November 12th, and on that day I took her ashes to Pittsfield and put them beside my father's in the vault, and for the last time marked the date with my annual offering of white chrysanthemums."[30]

In the years immediately following Coolidge's death Anna and Gian Francesco Malipiero repeated to Sprague and to Spivacke a desire that they had earlier shared with Elizabeth, namely their wish to leave their property in Asolo to become a center where American musicologists might find "peace, comfort and working hours" to devote to musical studies.[31] Only a few weeks before Coolidge's death Anna reiterated their intentions that "we both want to leave all our belongings to some faculty in America. . . . It seems rather like an offering of a white elephant, but I am an inveterate optimist, and I know in my heart that a solution will be found and that a musicological and musical center for America will be here eventually in Casa Malipiero."[32] Coolidge had apparently approached Harvard with the idea of accepting the Malipiero villa, and Spivacke assured Anna that "although you may not have heard from Harvard yet, I can tell you that your proposal is receiving very serious consideration and I recently received a request for additional items of our correspondence which of course I am glad to place at their disposal. From what I hear they are quite interested to say the least."[33] Neither the Harvard plan nor the earlier offer to the Library of Congress came to pass. Today Casa Malipiero stands *rovinato,* empty and dilapidated.[34]

In 1949 Coolidge had agreed to sponsor another of Malipiero's ambitious editorial undertakings—a complete edition of Vivaldi. By the time of her death 150 volumes had been published, but the project was far from complete. It is clear from Sprague's correspondence that he assumed the support of the project that his mother had begun, and in the course of his correspondence with the Malipieros a genuine friendship developed. Sprague began to write to Francesco in Italian, a gesture that obviously touched the composer's heart, for he responded in his own language, "Il ricordo di sua madre è legato a più di trent'anni della mia vita . . . e penso spesso che cosa sarebbe accaduto se non fosse esistito un simile angelo protettore." (The memory of your mother is a bond of more than thirty years duration . . . and I think often of what might have happened had there not existed this guardian angel.)[35]

Aware that Sprague was a competent oboist and prompted by Spivacke's offer of a commission to write a memorial composition that would include a part for Sprague, the following year Malipiero wrote his *Sonata à quattro* for flute, oboe, clarinet, and bassoon.[36] Still another year later Anna wrote to tell Sprague that she was sending to Spivacke "for the shelves of the Elizabeth S. Coolidge Foundation, a copy of the libretto written by Pirandello for that opera which Francesco inscribed to your mother, because this copy is one of the 1933 edition now known to booksellers as among the 'unfindable.'"[37]

It is difficult to think of a major composer or performer of chamber music in the first half of this century whose life and career was not in some way touched by Elizabeth Sprague Coolidge. She was by her own admission driven by "the desire to serve Art, and through Art, to serve humanity," for it was her conviction "that the survival of the human spirit largely depends upon its artistic freedom; to lose the privilege of self-expression by which, through his Art . . . man has recorded his reaction to Truth and Beauty, would be to limit his spiritual nourishment." It was her belief and her hope that what she had done for her composers and their audiences would "ultimately result in a reaction which shall be beneficial to the whole world of music—creative, executive, critical and even managerial; for indeed I think that we are today in pitiful need of its tonic and healing support."[38]

There was no funeral for Elizabeth. Instead, on 6 December at the Library of Congress, Bach, Mozart, Beethoven and Brahms, "speaking through the willing fingers of Schneider and Kirkpatrick, Kroll and

Kahn, and the Berkshire Quartet, paid homage to her memory."[39] Even before the official memorial, on the evening following Coolidge's death, at a regularly scheduled concert in the Coolidge Auditorium the Budapest String Quartet offered a most appropriate memorial—one of which she undoubtedly would have approved. A simple card inserted in the program read, "Elizabeth Sprague Coolidge died on November 4, 1953. After the String Quartet by Haydn the Budapest String Quartet will play the *lento assai* from Beethoven's String Quartet in F Major, Op. 135."

The following summer the Coolidge Foundation, together with Sprague, Peg and their family, sponsored a memorial festival at South Mountain in Pittsfield. The program was inscribed to the memory of "one of the most imaginative and most generous patrons of music in the history of the art." Her goal in life had been very clear: "to serve Art and to serve humanity." In bidding her farewell the musical world could only say, "Well done, good and faithful servant."

CHAPTER TWENTY-ONE

Postlude: The Legacy

My faith in altruistic cooperation is strong, as is my belief in the civilizing discipline of culture. But we must put it to the test first, mustn't we? For, alas, altruism is of slow growth, and requires patience and forbearance, sometimes obstinacy. With all these to hope for what may we not achieve?

– ELIZABETH SPRAGUE COOLIDGE TO AURELIA HENRY REINHARDT, PRESIDENT OF MILLS COLLEGE, 10 AUGUST 1933

ALTHOUGH THE QUESTION may have been purely rhetorical, the sixty-odd years that have passed since 1933 not only invite but compel some attempt to evaluate the achievements which Elizabeth, by her own admission, awaited—and it is safe to say, expected. Admittedly, for Coolidge waiting was never easy and was often characterized by more "obstinacy" than "patience and forbearance." At least it must often have seemed so to her associates as she put her notion of "altruistic cooperation" to the test. Her belief in the "civilizing discipline of culture" was indeed a creed that undoubtedly owed much to the experiences of her earlier life, her own personal apprenticeship in self discipline. To attempt to separate the achievements of her professional life from the person she was would be to deny the influence of her hard-won formation of character.

One of the most intimate glimpses into this "school" in which she exercised the strength of will that would characterize so much of what she undertook to do later on comes from the pen of an unidentified friend with whom Elizabeth had obviously shared her private thoughts, one who had observed her at close range during the difficult years of Fred's last illness: "Do you remember how often that summer in Pittsfield we talked of life and our attitude towards it? I wanted the cup of oblivion and claimed I would rather be a vegetable type than pay so dearly for the power of enjoyment when the hour of suffering came. You always said you wanted to live at all costs, to drink the cup to its dregs rather than not feel it keenly."[1]

Every life has its share of craggy obstacles as well as its placid valleys, and even the most expansive and gregarious of personalities manage to keep to themselves bits and pieces from the heights as well as the abyss. Whether they were moments perhaps too precious to share or simply scraps so minuscule that they fell into the cracks does not matter in the long run. Despite the very public nature of her professional life, the occasional hiatuses in Coolidge's correspondence and the slight hints of silent beneficence only serve to remind one of Mark Twain's pronouncement that "Biographies are but the clothes and buttons of the man—the biography of the man himself cannot be written." Elizabeth undoubtedly would have agreed—indeed she probably would have wanted it so.

This by no means dispenses from an evaluation of her legacy, nor does it preclude some assessment of her unique personality. By no stretch of the imagination could one characterize Coolidge as a modest person, She was justifiably proud of her many accomplishments—even the thirty-one gallstones that she proudly displayed to visitors after her operation in 1943—but she was never arrogant or boastful. Nor was she immune to vanity, as is evidenced by her note to a woman who spied her in an audience and commented on her appearance. "I'm sure that you must realize that to speak of my becoming gown and youthful appearance was a feminine touch that gladdened my heart; for I love being thought of, not as an impresario exclusively, but also as a woman with the usual foibles of her sex."[2]

Above all she was honest and prized honesty in others highly. If she had one regret it was that her social station and the conventions of the period in which she reached maturity had conspired to deny her the opportunity of a college education. Although the honors that were heaped on her in later life may have assuaged her disappointment, she could not have failed to recognize a certain irony in their late bestowal.[3] In time she received honorary degrees from such notable institutions as Mount Holyoke (1926), Smith (1927), Yale (1927), Mills (1928), the University of California (1933), and Pomona (1938). In 1931 the government of France named her Chevalier of the Legion of Honor; in 1935 she was awarded the Order of the Crown of Belgium as well as a medal, "Hommage de gratitude," from the University of Liège, and the year 1937 brought the bestowal of the Order of Léopold, King of the Belgians. Once the accolades began they accumulated at an impressive pace, yet there is little evidence in her correspondence to suggest that, except for the Legion of Honor, she gave particular notice to these honors and decorations.

If there is any one word by which Coolidge could best be described, and perhaps would prefer to be remembered, it is "teacher."[4] She became and remained to the end of her days above all a teacher. Sometimes she fulfilled that role in the most traditional sense of pedagogue and tutor, as in the classes that she initiated for the Boys Club in Pittsfield, or in the teaching that she required of the resident ensembles that she supported in her later work. At other times she was in a broader sense an educator, guide, advisor, mentor, and counselor. In this capacity she related to both young and old, the unknown and the famous alike. Her interest in youth is symbolized by the fact that somewhere in Cagayan Valley, Philippine Islands, a Boy Scout troop was named for her and her portrait graced its club room. Those scouts half way around the world chose to honor her because she gave them a set of encyclopedias.

Her counsel could be stern at times, as is clear from her response to a young man who asked her for money and was told, "I am writing to you rather strongly, for I think it is a great mistake for a young man to contract the habit of soliciting money, especially from strangers, and I want to tell you for your own good that I do think you will go much further in your profession if you do not begin this habit."[5] Nor did she hesitate to catechize so hallowed an institution as Harvard University, when she objected to the school's use of her contribution to hire a renowned scholar whose work was in a rarefied area of musicology that in her opinion would benefit only a few. Instead, she stipulated that the money be spent for a basic course, Music 101, that would reach a much wider constituency.

Neither were her outspoken utterances limited to musical matters. When, for example, her favorite commentator was removed from the air she did not hesitate to voice her objections directly to the Federal Communications Commission: "As a citizen I presume I am entitled to an explanation of the withdrawal of Upton Close from the air. He is, without a doubt, one of the most intelligent and unbiased thinkers that the American public has ever had the good fortune to listen to. In comparison to the political clap-trap, sentimental twaddle, and singing jingles which you permit to go on endlessly, his words have been as refreshing as a good sea breeze. I shall appreciate an explanation of his withdrawal at your earliest convenience."[6]

It could never be charged that opposition ever intimidated Coolidge, for hers was the kind of conviction that wasted no time on doubts or perorations but moved into action swiftly. And like the best educators, she herself remained a perpetual student, always reading, practicing, and above all manifesting an incredible openness to the new in music. By her work she not only expanded her own intellectual horizons but manifestly contributed to the extension of musical knowledge in general. At the age of seventy-two, when Jerzy Fitelberg's Fourth Quartet was awarded the Coolidge Prize in 1936, she wrote to a friend, "I must confess that his idiom is as yet too strange to me to enable me to understand his work: therefore, I have not yet really enjoyed it. But I have recently received the score which I intend to study in the hope of being able to respond to his work."[7] And although she commissioned a quartet of Roy Harris she admitted, "I do not expect to like it much myself, but I consider that of no importance and am sincerely glad to have assisted in bringing to notice another serious American composer."[8] She was equally open to such unfamiliar sounds as the early excursions into electronic music, and after hearing the theremin for the first time she wrote to Carl Engel that "time and space are on their last legs, I think, and we shall all have to re-educate our senses to interpret a new set of sensory impressions."[9]

To those who complained of too much modernity in the Library of Congress concerts she replied, comparing them to an art exhibit.

"[L]iking or not liking the items in an exhibition seems irrelevant to its value as a display. Observation does not imply the necessity of enjoyment."[10] She made the point even more emphatically in an address to the National Federation of Music Clubs. "My plea for modern music is not that we should like it, nor necessarily that we should even understand it, but that we should exhibit it as a significant human document." In her opinion this meant more than merely listening to it, it meant "supporting the sincerity of its authors by placing their work upon our programs."[11]

This championing of modern music really represents an astounding degree of detachment on the part of the patron who, in her estimation, is the servant and must place the inviolability and integrity of art above personal pleasure. This lofty aim takes on special significance in the light of a private admission Coolidge made to Mabel Daniels near the end of her life. Daniels had invited her to a performance of what she rather apologetically described as some frankly "old fashioned and romantic music" of Paine, Chadwick, and MacDowell.[12] She was surprised when Elizabeth responded, "I assure you that the early music is really more to my taste than some of the ultra modern effusions to which I so often listen nowadays."[13] Indeed those who sat near her at Library of Congress performances could attest that from time to time Coolidge could be seen to turn off her hearing aid.

In much the same way that Coolidge respected art, she also reverenced justice—even in the smallest detail of her dealings. Despite her sometimes high-handed exchanges with merchants she was scrupulous in paying bills promptly and to the exact penny, never rounding off to the next dollar. No small service ever went unrewarded. After her festivals the doormen, bellhops, and maids of the hotels always received generous tips for their courtesy to her and her guests. And on more than one occasion she instructed her maid to return (with an apology) a towel that was inadvertently taken from a hotel. That she expected similarly prompt and exact justice to be rendered to her is obvious from her correspondence. By far the most amusing, and probably most extreme, example is the case of a young woman who took Coolidge's umbrella and narrowly escaped being sued for it, saved only by the intervention of Sprague and Peg who convinced her that the mere inconvenience of it would hardly balance out the cost in time, money, and aggravation.

More importantly this sense of justice precluded any sort of bigotry or prejudice, racial or religious. Although Coolidge and her mother before her were Colonial Dames, when the Daughters of the American Revolution denied Marian Anderson the privilege of performing in Constitution Hall in 1939 Elizabeth was vocal in her opposition to the action of the DAR, although not as dramatically so as Eleanor Roosevelt, who withdrew her membership. Elizabeth not only spoke out but lent her name and support to the concert that, in a symbolic gesture, was moved to the steps of the Lincoln Memorial. On a more personal note she at various times employed African-American maids, and often took her favorite, Annie Peterson, with her when she traveled, despite the problems that it caused when she visited certain schools (like Wellesley and Princeton) that did not permit blacks in their facilities.

Early in their association she told Engel, "I am not concerned whether or not the social register and the congressional directory are adequately represented in our audiences."[14] The ethnic and economic diversity apparent in the circle of her friends and associates suggests that neither bloodline nor investment portfolio were important to Coolidge. Many of those holding honored places in her circle were Jewish—Bloch, Milhaud, Castelnuovo, and Schönberg, for example. She encouraged Bloch's Hebraic works and Henry Eichheim's interest in Asian music by helping to finance his tours to the Far East to collect material for his *Oriental Impressions,* which she commissioned and programmed both here and abroad. She was open to the interests and ideologies of others as long as these did not violate human rights as did Fascism and Nazism, which she so vehemently opposed. And above all she supported her son's affiliation with the Socialist party even though it brought indignity upon her.

What would undoubtedly have saddened her in this regard fortunately occurred after her death. In February of 1954 Sprague received an invitation from the acting Librarian of Congress, Vernon W. Clapp, to apply for the place on the three-man board of the Coolidge Foundation that was left vacant by his mother's death. The other two members were, ex officio, the Librarian of Congress and the chief of the Music Division.

In compliance with standard government procedure of the time, Sprague was asked to submit his application in quadruplicate, with fingerprints, non-communist oath, and an exhaustive list of present and past associations, social as well as political. Among these he listed his membership in the North American Committee to Aid Spanish Democracy. It was the only one of his affiliations that was on the attorney general's list. No confirmation of his appointment could be made until the consummation of a clause in his mother's will under which she exercised power of appointment in favor of the Library. This was not settled until eighteen months later, by which time L. Quincy Mumford was appointed Librarian of Congress. Three months later a private courier arrived in Cambridge and "intimated unofficially" to Sprague that he should quietly withdraw his application rather than be confronted with the unpleasantness of having to justify incriminating evidence that would necessitate mounting a convincing rebuttal to charges of being a "security risk." All this was based upon information about him culled from FBI files. Certain of his ability to clear his name, Sprague chose to face the charges. In a letter to the *Berkshire Eagle* (carried by Associated Press and subsequently picked up by larger papers, among them the *New York Times*), he explained that he declined to withdraw, "feeling that I could furnish the needed rebuttal, that I was entitled to a chance to clear my record, and that Mr. Mumford should face the responsibilities of his office and make his own decisions. I therefore asked to be confronted with my dossier."[15]

This did not happen. Instead, by 1 February Mumford announced that the invitation to membership on the board had been extended to someone else and at the same time denied that Sprague had ever been considered a "security risk." He explained that "there is no formal hearing procedure for job applicants, so I simply decided he was not suitable for the position."[16] An unidentified correspondent for the predictably partisan *Berkshire Eagle* in turn raised the question, "In what respect is Mr. Coolidge not suitable for the position? Does this refer to qualifications, personality, or is Mr. Mumford simply trying to take the timid way out?"[17] He predicted that the whole affair would come back to haunt both Mumford and the Library.

This all occurred at the height of the McCarthy-era communist hunt, and heated opinions were exchanged in a polemical seesaw in the press, where Sprague attempted to explain his position as a member of the North American Committee to Aid Spanish Democracy. As he put it, instead of "running away yellow, for fear of being painted red," he carried on the battle to keep communism from infiltrating the group. He assumed a similar stance in other organizations in which he was active, especially the American Civil Liberties Union, the Massachusetts branch of which he was chairman. The situation was complicated by the fact that he had earlier signed a petition to commute the sentence of Earl Browder, the leader of the American Communist Party, because he believed it was excessive and vindictive punishment for passport forgery. He had likewise signed a petition to commute the sentences of some communists who were convicted under the Smith Act of 1940, an act that was strongly criticized by some as being an infringement of the rights of free speech and assembly. The issue was further complicated by the stand he had taken on the Sacco and Vanzetti case.

It was a trying time for anyone with liberal political tendencies. In the postwar years and so soon after the Alger Hiss case, Americans were falling victim to the specter of communist conspiracy all around. When independent thinking and nonconformism came under attack, men like Albert Sprague Coolidge were easy targets. It seemed no one was immune. "Congress, the presidency, the government bureaucracy, the news media, the entertainment world, veteran groups, school officials—competed to demonstrate their own patriotism by accusing others. Almost the only institution left to challenge them was the Supreme Court."[18]

In the end, Sprague Coolidge withdrew from the fray, saying that he did not need the job with its token stipend, nor did the job need him, adding that it was "outrageous and makes the government look ridiculous."[19] He felt he had accomplished something by exposing such paranoia. It was an opinion shared by others as well and sardonically expressed in an editorial in the *Berkshire Eagle* printed under the banner "ANTISEPTIC CHAMBER MUSIC": "[I]t is not easy to see how the security of the United States could be much imperiled by letting this amateur oboist—even if he was politically unsophisticated—serve as an advisor to the Library of Congress on chamber music. The injury done to the prestige of the United States by denying him the position is readily apparent, however. And it is made the more ludicrous and the more damaging because the action comes from the Library of Congress, which is supposed to be the repository of America's intellectual heritage and best traditions."[20]

The whole unfortunate incident is best summed up in Sprague's appraisal that "this episode does not measure up to the dignity with which my mother hoped to clothe her foundation by putting it under the auspices of the government of the United States. I deplore seeming to drag her name and her benefaction into the mud of politics but I feel even more strongly that we shall not get rid of McCarthyism by hushing up the unpleasant things to which it leads."[21]

Elizabeth would undoubtedly have been offended by the whole affair but at the same time would likely have applauded her son's fearless determination to stand up for what he believed in, for although she rarely spoke out publicly in matters of politics she often found herself swimming upstream against the current of popular opinion. She was not averse to expressing her thoughts to friends, however. When after World War II pianist Walter Gieseking was accused of cultural collaboration with the Nazis (of which accusation he was later cleared), she wrote to Alexander Schneider: "I cannot imagine that a piano recital could have very much political significance. If we were to estimate artists and composers from a political point of view, we should have to sacrifice much of the great music, and it seems to me we would lose more than we should gain. I believe the sooner this negative episode is forgotten in favor of some really positive value, the sooner we can all relax and enjoy art for its own sake."[22]

The achievements of the Foundation that Elizabeth had entrusted as the guardian of her legacy have countervailed any ill effects of the publicity over this unfortunate affair, which has long since been forgotten. The roster of composers commissioned in the years following the upheaval speaks for itself. It includes some of the major talents of the first half of this century. But even after the most scrupulous search of the files of the Library of Congress, it is not possible to construct a complete list of Coolidge's commissions and dedications. After her death Harold Spivacke acknowledged that "we know only definitely the works which were commissioned by the Coolidge Foundation. Strange as it may sound we have only a vague notion of Mrs. Coolidge's personal commissions since she did not keep any record of them."[23] Moreover, the catalog of names contained in the list of commissions raises some questions. Although some of the most brilliant lights among twentieth-century composers are found there, there are some notable absences; probably the most conspicuous is Charles Ives. His absence is all the more striking since his wife, Harmony, was a close friend of the Spragues.

Although Ives was one of the most original voices in American music, in his time he was apparently too outrageous for Elizabeth. It appears that Harmony attempted to act as an intercessor and in 1921 sent to Coolidge a copy of the *Concord Sonata* for study. In her response Elizabeth admitted that since she was unable to comprehend it she had sent it on to a friend whose opinion she respected and trusted. "I sent it to him because I did not in the least understand your husband's work myself, and I thought I could not judge of anything which to me was so foreign. I must confess that I found nothing in it which I liked, but there is so much nowadays that I do not like because I do not understand it that I did not wish to express my opinion about it."[24]

Although she does not identify this friend, whom she describes as having given up the European idiom in favor of studying Asiatic music, he is most certainly Henry Eichheim. It seems likely that she selected him to critique the Ives piece thinking that his rejection of the traditional "European idiom" might make him better qualified to understand Ives's untraditional method. However she withheld the report she received from him and simply informed Harmony: "I have today a response from this gentleman, and it is not encouraging to Charlie's work. I do not want to quote him because I think it would hurt you, but you see I am trying to be honest in responding to your request, and feel that it is more friendly to write in this way than not to write at all."[25]

Her description of Eichheim's evaluation of the piece as "not encouraging" is a kind understatement. His critique was harsh:

> *The sonata by Mr. Ives is pretentious drivel—I have no patience with such empty nonsense, and for such obvious reason. The rhythms are stupid, his vocabulary of chords is very limited. Counterpoint and structure are wholly absent so there remains only a mass of unorganized ugly sounds thrown together for no apparent reason. Wholesome contempt for*

> *[the] contemporary or tradition in art is admirable when felt by superb anarchists . . . but poking at established convention with such naive and terrible stuff either in music, painting or orchestration merely bores me, and is not good enough to make me angry.*[26]

Ives actually wrote to Coolidge to request a copy of the unidentified critic's comments, but the letter was never sent.[27] The degree of disappointment brought about by his exclusion from the ranks of those Coolidge favored with commissions is reflected in Ives's later comments about her. Still smarting a full twenty years after the fact, he recorded an incident from 1913 when Elizabeth frankly told him: "[Y]our music makes no sense to me. It is not, to my mind, music. How is it that—studying with Parker—you ever came to write like that?"[28] In turn Ives characterized Coolidge along with Clara Mannes, Max Smith (a New York critic), and David Stanley Smith as champions of the motto, "All things have a right to live and grow, even babies and music schools, but not *music.*"[29]

Such a statement is hardly consistent with Coolidge's record of supporting some of the most avant-garde works of the early twentieth century. Besides her forthright admission to his face that she did not understand his music, it is possible that Ives's absence from her circle had more to do with her perception of his "double life." Her view of him as a business executive first and composer only secondarily may have caused her to consider him less than entirely serious and committed. History would, of course, in time prove how committed he truly was, but in the 1920s and 1930s when these exchanges took place Coolidge was not alone in her failure to grasp his message. Few took him seriously until John Kirkpatrick's acclaimed performance of the *Concord Sonata* at Town Hall in 1939. Nonetheless, in the telling of this episode Coolidge has come under fire, especially in the work of David Wooldridge, whose commentary on the whole affair is an insult not only to Elizabeth but to the many other women patrons whose efforts great and small alike, have done so much to nourish the cause of the arts in this country. According to Wooldridge:

> *The Elizabeth Sprague Coolidges of this world are a perennial curiosity. Their presumable ancestors, the Charles Spragues, poets of awareness*

> *and sensitivity, beget descendants who inherit an awareness and sensitivity for business—like the Albert Spragues, close friends of the Joseph Twichells, who make fortunes in wholesale grocery trade. Fine. The world needs wholesale grocers. Then the Albert Spragues beget daughters who inherit (a) their money, and (b) a vague, uncomprehending awareness of who rather than what their ancestors have been—*viz., *"artists." That, plus daddy's money, gives them a sense of power: wealth* plus *art* = *"culture." They will become patrons of the arts. And the lady-bird artists respond, patronizing the patrons.*[30]

Coolidge needs no defense from such accusations, for her life and works are the ultimate and most eloquent rebuttal.

Inevitably the question arises whether some of the works written for her—most notably the string quartets—were done by composers for whom chamber music was not a congenial medium, but who created them because they recognized an opportunity to gain her favor and her money. The fact that much of this music has not been heard in the forty years since her death is not necessarily evidence of its quality. It may simply be too soon to make that judgment. On the other hand, it is possible that the absence of this music from the current repertoire bears out Virgil Thomson's belief that the string quartet does not always show a composer at his best, but it nearly always exposes his essential weaknesses.

In 1972 the BBC aired a broadcast featuring reminiscences of Coolidge in which it was noted that although she commissioned over fifty string quartets, the number that have found a place in the repertoire is relatively small. The commentator noted, however, that "a ten per cent success rate, regarding success as the evaluation of posterity, is in itself, a positive achievement." But perhaps even more importantly, "every work is a milestone in the life of its creator and often a commission of this sort could be of more importance biographically than musically, a leg up, a confidence booster, a real support which would lead to works of greater significance later."[31]

The unevenness in the quality of the manuscripts dedicated to Coolidge over the years is apparent, for although many of the greatest talents of the twentieth century are represented in the collection, some works are undeniably inferior. Quite apart from the matter of quality, there was also the problem of unsolicited compositions offered to her, with riders attached in the form of special requests or suggestions of monetary reward. The degree of her annoyance is evident in her complaint to Tibor Harsanyi: "[A]t least three times I have had offered me, in expectation of a gift of money, compositions (dedicated to me) which were openly intended for certain artists, and even accompanied by the request that I should arrange to give them the first performance." By this time the scope of her work had grown so vast that the contracting of artists and procuring of radio time necessitated plans made far in advance. She complained that this "did not always coincide with my own plans and I fear it has resulted in some annoyance and perhaps resentment, on the part of the players, who regarded these compositions as their own special property, although wishing to gain for the composers the cachet and the brilliant audience which they were hoping to attain from me." The solution was inevitable. "I have, therefore, come to the conclusion that I cannot well accept the multitude of dedications . . . unless with this acceptance goes the . . . ability to arrange for a first hearing and subsequent rights of performance by such artists as I may choose to engage, and at such times as suits my convenience. . . . I have been driven to this by the impossible situations in which I have found myself half a dozen times, by becoming responsible for compositions, without the corresponding control and authority which should go with such a commission."[32]

Even more difficult to assess are the motives of those artists who performed with her, especially in her later years, when her hearing was so severely impaired that she was tortured by an incessant jumble of noises raging inside her head. For some it may have been a ploy to gain her support, but for close friends like Sasha Schneider, Henri Temianka, Rudolf Kolisch, and William Kroll, it was more than likely a gesture of sincere gratitude and affection, since they understood how happy it made her.

Eventually the question must arise, "What if tragedy had not struck? Would Coolidge have lived the life of the idle rich?" It is difficult to imagine Elizabeth finding fulfillment solely within the confines of the women's clubs and the social life of Chicago—brilliant as it may have been. She was an activist at heart, restless without a project—or better still, a host of them. There is little to be gained from "what-if" speculation, especially if it diverts from demonstrable evidence. The undeniable fact remains that although Elizabeth matured to womanhood during the Victorian era (she was thirty-seven when Queen Victoria died), she had long since demonstrated an independence of thought that ran counter to many of the expectations heaped upon women of the period. It was an independence hard-won, however. When tragedy came she could have retired in comfort and succumbed to ennui and self-pity. But for Coolidge there were no acute attacks of "the vapors," and idleness was a word not to be found in her vocabulary.

It is more valuable by far to contemplate what can be learned from her example. The hallmark of Coolidge's philanthropy that sets her apart from most others was her intensely personal involvement in her work, even in her last years. What Ivor Newton once said of Lord Howard de Walden aptly describes Elizabeth Coolidge. "[T]he practical enthusiasm and personal interest of great patrons in the work of the artists they knew went far beyond anything an official cultural programme can give."[33]

In 1935, Eric Thacher Clarke observed that "organized activity in the arts, and especially in music, has rarely begun with the people. . . . [I]t is the wealthy who have made it possible and who have supported it, while leading the less wealthy, in emulation, to give their contributions too. Generations must always pass before the public takes things over from the patron, large and small."[34] The lesson that Coolidge taught is that patronage need not be the exclusive domain of the very wealthy. While her fortune was much smaller than that of Carnegie, Ford, or Rockefeller, the operative element in her equation of successful philanthropy was *creativity,* a creativity characterized by cooperation resulting from her inspiration of others, and by the fact that she did not believe in the dole. Her method of support nearly always required some service in return—often in the form of teaching. And over a period of time she gradually decreased the amount of her contribution, until the project was either being supported by others (often recruited by her) or had become self-supporting.

Clarke's theory is not unlike the thoughts contained in Coolidge's letter to Reinhardt quoted earlier. She understood that "altruism is of slow growth." Her endowment of the Library of Congress was a mere "mustard seed" compared with the Vanderbilt fortune, for example, which actually exceeded the treasuries of some sovereign states, yet the Coolidge Foundation has yielded rewards probably beyond any attempt to measure. Hers is a valuable lesson for the present time, when the arts must depend more and more upon individual private support.

Coolidge was not always successful, however. Her dream of a cabinet post in the arts and her hopes for a national conservatory and a national symphony orchestra that would be so not only in name, but would be government-subsidized, never came to pass. But the foundation that she established at the Library of Congress has become the instrument enabling her influence to reach out across this country and beyond. And through it she effectively created the mechanism enabling the Library to accept subsequent trusts. In the wake of her example there are today more than 150 such endowments, over twenty of them in the Music Division. The manuscript holdings of the Library have been significantly enriched through Coolidge's deposit of the works amassed by her dedications, commissions, and Berkshire competitions. Moreover, through their professional association with her, many of her composer-friends bequeathed their compositions and their personal papers to the Library.

The record of her life and work could and does speak for itself, but there were other voices even in her lifetime that recognized the greatness of her person and her contribution. On the occasion of her eightieth birthday, President Franklin D. Roosevelt issued this formal declaration. "Elizabeth Sprague Coolidge has done what none before her had found the means to do. No one has contributed more to the understanding of music in America, and no one has given greater encouragement to writers and performers of music in America than Mrs. Coolidge."

Probably the most eloquent testimony of all is contained in the words of Andrew W. Mellon, who stood up before the audience at the Library of Congress festival in 1931 and spoke words of prophetic import:

> *Six years ago a remarkable thing happened. A private citizen induced a government complacent in the efficiency of its operations to adopt an entirely new role . . . persuaded a government concerned only with the utilities to accept as an utility something far more subtle than those of the grosser sort which alone it had deemed within its province. And then,*

having inspired the necessary convictions, she herself provided the resources for giving them practical effect. She did all this without organization, without the exercise of any political influence—did it single handed. That is her habit—except when she gives, she gives with both hands. The consequences of all this may be such as no man can foresee—and only one woman.[35]

Appendix A

COOLIDGE MEDALISTS

1932	Walter Wilson Cobbett (English), musical activist and compiler of the *Cyclopedic Survey of Chamber Music.*
1933	Adolfo Betti (Italian), second violinist of the Flonzaley String Quartet.
1934	Alfredo Casella (Italian), composer, pianist, and critic.
1935	Carl Engel (American), composer, writer, critic, and chief of the Music Division of the Library of Congress.
1936	Edwin T. Rice (American), music patron and legal counsel to musicians.
1937	Gian Francesco Malipiero (Italian), composer.
1938	Frank Bridge (English), composer.
	Hugo Kortschak (Austrian/American), violinist and teacher.
	Jacques Gordon (American), violinist.
1939	Hans Kindler (Dutch/American), cellist, founder and conductor of the National Symphony.
	Alphonse Onnou (Belgian), founder and first violinist of the Pro Arte Quartet.
1940	Eugene Goossens (English), composer.
	Darius Milhaud (French), composer.
1941	Randall Thompson (American), composer and teacher.
	Alexandre Tansman (Polish), composer.
	Benjamin Britten (English), composer.
1942	Roy Harris (American), composer.
	William Kroll (American), violinist and composer.
1943	Quincy Porter (American), composer.

1944	No award. The Library of Congress and the Coolidge Foundation celebrated Mrs. Coolidge's birthday, and a special souvenir autograph album was given to her as the occasion's mark of distinction.
1945	Alexander Schneider (Russian/American), violinist.
1946	Robert Maas (Belgian), cellist of the Pro Arte String Quartet.
1947	Luther Marchant (American), music educator.
	Louis Speyer (American), oboist.
1948	Joseph Roisman (American), first violinist of the Budapest String Quartet.
	Erik Itor Kahn (American), chamber music pianist.

Appendix B

COMMISSIONS, DEDICATIONS, AND PRIZE-WINNING COMPOSITIONS

This compilation is based upon various partial lists of Coolidge's personal commissions, information culled from the correspondence, dedications indicated on the manuscripts themselves, and the official list of Coolidge Foundation commissions. It is at best an approximation. Nearly all works commissioned up to the time of Coolidge's death in 1953 were also dedicated to her. In addition it is likely that many of the works here indicated solely as dedications were actually also personal commissions, for Mrs. Coolidge was, especially in the early years, surprisingly casual about keeping records of her commissions.

LEGEND

ESC	Commissions offered personally
CF	Coolidge Foundation Commission
CP	Coolidge Prize
BP	Berkshire Prize
BPhm	Berkshire Prize, honorable mention
G	Gift
D	Dedication
PFhm	Pan American Festival, honorable mention

COMPOSER	TITLE	DATE	CATEGORY
Aitken, Hugh	*Fables: A Diversion for Soprano, Two Tenors, and Bass;* with flute, two oboes, bassoon, and string quartet	1974	CF
Alfano, Franco	*Per Santa Elizabetta*	1931	D
———.	*Sonata for Violoncello and Piano*	1926	D
Arma, Paul	*Concerto for String Quartet*	1948?	D
Babbitt, Milton	*String Quartet no. 4*	1970	CF
Balassa, Sandor	*A Daydreamer's Diary, op. 35*	1983	CF
Barati, George	*String Quartet*	1944	D
Barber, Samuel	*Hermit Songs*	1953	CF
Bartók, Béla	*String Quartet no. 5*	1934	CF
Bartolucci, Ernesto	*String Quartet in A, op. 25*	1945	D
Bax, Arnold	*Legend for Violin and Piano*	n.d.	D
———.	*Octet for Horn, Strings, and Piano*	1934	D
———.	*Sextet for Horn, Strings, and Piano*	1964	G
Beck, Conrad	*Concerto for String Quartet and Orchestra*	1929	D
Bedford, Herbert	*Lyrical Interlude: Pathways of the Moon;* for flute, oboe, violin, piano	1929	D
Bercerra, Gustavo	*Piano Quintet*	1962	CF
Berezowski, Nicolai	*Sextet, op. 26, for Three Violins, Two Violas, and Violoncello*	1940	CF
———.	*Theme and Fantastic Variation, op. 7*	n.d.	D
Bergsma, William	*Concerto for Wind Quintet*	1958	CF
Bettingen, Balthasar	*Concerto for Viola da Gamba and Orchestra*	1931	G
Beveridge, Thomas	*Serenade*	1978	CF
Bliss, Arthur	*Music for Oboe and Four Strings*	1927	CF
———.	*String Quartet*	1941	G
Bloch, Ernest	*Suite for Viola and Piano*	1919	BP
Bossi, Renzo	*Trio in 4 tempi concatenati in do maggiore*	1921	Bphm
Brescia, Domenico	*Ricercare and Fugue for Organ*	1931	D
———.	*Suite for Flute, Oboe, Clarinet, Horn, Bassoon, and Piano*	1928	D
———.	*Second Suite for Flute, Oboe, Clarinet, Horn, and Bassoon*	1922	D

Bridge, Frank	*Divertimenti for Flute, Oboe, Clarinet, and Bassoon*	1938	D
———.	*Dweller in My Deathless Dreams*	1925	D
———.	*Heart's Ease;* piano solo	1921	D
———.	*A Merry, Merry Xmas*	1934	D
———.	*The Pneu World, for Violoncello and Piano*	n.d.	G
———.	*Sonata for Piano and Violin*	1933	CF
———.	*String Quartet no. 3*	1927	ESC
———.	*String Quartet no. 4*	1937	ESC
———.	*Sextet for 2 Violins, 2 Violas, 2 Celli*	1922	ESC
———.	*Trio for Violin, Violoncello, and Piano*	1929	G
Britten, Benjamin	*String Quartet in D Major, no. 1, op. 25*	1941	ESC
Burian, Hans	*Five Lieder*	1925	D
Burton, Stephen Douglas	*Dances for Flute and Guitar*	1983	CF
Busch, Adolph	*Requiem for Mignon*	1945	D
———.	*Quartet in B Minor, op. 59*	1943	D
Caamaño, Roberto	*Quinteto para piano y cuarteto de cuerdas*	1962	CF
Carpenter, John Alden	*Quintet for Piano and Strings*	1933	ESC?
Casabona, Francisco	*String Quartet in G Minor*	1937	PFhm
Casella, Alfredo	*Partita for Piano and Small Orchestra*	1925	D
———.	*Per Santa Elizabetta*	1931	D
———.	*Sonata in C Major, Violoncello and Piano*	1927	D
———.	*Concerto Grosso in D Minor;* transcription of Vivaldi's "L'Estro armonico," no. 11	1936	D
———.	*Los Poema del Agua for nine instruments*	1931	D
———.	*Sonata à tre;* arrangement of the Trio Sonata from "The Musical Offering" of J. S. Bach	1933	D
———.	*Sonata à tre;* transcription of Sammartini	n.d.	D
———.	*Trio in D Major;* arrangement of Muzio Clementi's op. 27, no. 2	1932	D

———.	*Sinfonia per pianoforte, clarinette, tromba e cello*	19??	CF?
Castelnuovo-Tedesco, Mario	*Divertimento for Violin and Piano*	1945	G
———.	*Per Santa Elizabetta*	1931	D
———.	*Quartetto in Sol*	1929-30	ESC
Chávez, Carlos	*Ballet, Dark Meadow*	1944	CF
———.	*Il [segunda] invención, para violin, viola y violoncello*	1965	CF
Chevreuille, Raymond	*String Quartet no. 5*	1943	G
Clarke, Rebecca	*Rhapsody for 'Cello and Piano*	1923	ESC
———.	*Sonata for Viola and Piano*	1919	BPhm
———.	*Trio for Violin, Violoncello, and Piano*	1921	D
Collins, Anthony	*String Quartet no. 2*	1941	D
Copland, Aaron	*Appalachian Spring, ballet for Martha*	1944	CF
———.	*Appalachian Spring;* ballet, reduction for Piano	1944	CF
———.	*Quartet for Violin, Viola, Violoncello, and Piano*	1950	CF
Cordero, Roque	*String Quartet no. 1*	1960	CF
Corigliano, John	*Phantasmagoria* (on themes from *The Ghosts of Versailles*) for 'cello and piano	1992	CF
Corti, Mario	*Tartini Concerto in A Major for String Orchestra and Cembalo;* arranged for violin and piano	1924	D
Cowell, Henry	*String Quartet no. 5*	1956	CF
Creston, Paul	*Suite for Violoncello and Piano*	1956	CF
Crumb, George	*Ancient Voices of Children*	1970	C
Dallapiccola, Luigi	*Cinque canti per baritono e alcuni strumenti*	1957	CF
———.	*Parole di San Paolo, per una voce media e alcuni strumenti*	1964	CF
———.	*Sicut umbra, per una voce di cantate e quattro gruppi di strumenti*	1970	CF
Deak, Jon	*Vasilisa, A Young Girl Meets Baba-Yaga;* for flute, oboe, violin, viola, violoncello, and piano	1994	CF

De Lamarter, Eric	*Terzetto for Violin, Viola, and Violoncello*	1911	D
Dello Joio, Norman	*The Lamentation of Saul;* for flute, oboe, clarinet, viola, cello, piano, and baritone solo.	1954	CF
Dick, Marcel	*String Quartet no. 2*	1938	D
Domange, Mme. Albert	*Suite for Violin and Piano*	1926	G
Eichheim, Henry	*Oriental Impressions: Chinese Sketch;* for flute, oboe, violin, viola, harp and percussion	1921	G
———.	*Oriental Impressions: Japanese Nocturne;* for small orchestra	1921	G
———.	*Oriental Impressions: Japanese Sketch;* for flute, oboe, harp, and piano	1921	D
———.	*Oriental Impressions: Nocturnal Impression of Peking;* for violin, viola, flute, oboe, harp, and piano	1921	G
———.	*Sonata no. 2 for Violin and Piano*	1934	D
Eloy, Jean-Claude	*Faisceaux-Diffractions*	1970	CF
Enesco, Georges	*Quartet in D Minor, op. 30, no. 2, for Violin, Viola, Violoncello, and Piano*	1946	G
Farwell, Arthur	*String Quartet in A Major*	n.d.	G
Ficher, Jacobo	*String Quartet, op. 35, no. 2*	1937	D
Fine, Irving	*Romanza for Wind Quintet*	1963	CF
Fine, Vivian	*Ode to Henry Purcell*	1984	CF
Finney, Ross Lee	*Quartet for Violin, Viola, Violoncello, and Piano*	1948	D
———.	*String Quintet;* 2 violins, viola, 2 'celli	1959	CF
Fitelberg, Jerzy	*Quatrième quatuor à cordes*	1936	CP
Franco, Johan	*Serenade Concertante*	1938	D
Frischenlager, Friedrich	*Konzertante Musik, op. 51;* for piano and chamber orchestra	1931	D
Galindo, Blas	*Quinteto para instrumentos de arco y piano*	1960	CF
Gideon, Miriam	*Spirit Above the Dust*	1980	CF
Gilbert, Henry F.	*String Quartet*	n.d.	D
———.	*Suite for Chamber Orchestra*	1927	ESC
Ginastera, Alberto	*Bomarzo;* cantata for narrator, baritone and orchestra	1964	CF
———.	*Cuarteto de cuerdas, op. 26*	1968	CF

Goosens, Eugene	*Phantasy Sextet for Three Violins, Viola, and Two Violoncelli*	1923	ESC
———.	*String Quartet, op. 59, no. 2*	1940	D
Grandjany, Marcel	*Aria: Piece in the Classic Style for Harp and Organ, op. 19*	1940	D
———.	*Fantasie Chorale, op. 21, on the hymn "Pange lingua corporis mysterium,"* for harp and organ	1940	CF
Green, Ray	*Concertante for Viola and Piano*	n.d.	D
Gruenberg, Louis	*Quartet, op. 40, no. 2*	1937	CF
Guarneri, Camargo	*String Quartet no. 3*	1962	CF
Gubaydulina, Sofiya	*Dancer on a Tightrope;* for violin and piano	1993	CF
Halffter, Cristobal	*Quartet II: Memories*	1970	CF
Hamilton, Iain	*Hyperion*	1977	CF
Hanson, Howard	*Four Psalms*	1964	CF
———.	*Quartet, op. 23, in One Movement*	1923	ESC
Harris, Donald	*For the Night to Wear*	1978	CF
Harris, Roy	*Altissimi onnipotente (Canticle of the Sun)*	1961	CF
———.	*Quintet for Two Violins, Two Violas and Violoncello*	1940	CF
———.	*Sonata for Violin and Piano* (sketches)	n.d.	G
———.	*Three Variations on a Theme, Quartet no. 2*	1933	CF
———.	*Trio for Pianoforte, Violin and Violoncello*	1934	CF
Harsányi, Tibor	*Aria, Cadenza, and Rondo;* for violoncello and orchestra	1930	D
Henry, Leigh	*Mistress Coolidge's Coronal: Chamber Pieces for Strings*	1930	D
Hill, Edward Burlingame	*Sextet for Flute, Oboe, Clarinet, Bassoon, Horn, and Piano, op. 39*	1934	D
Hill, Mabel Wood	*Do Not Keep to Yourself, My Friend,* for voice and piano	19??	D
———.	*Quintette for Oboe, Violin, Viola, Piano, and Voice*	n.d.	G
Hindemith, Paul	*Canon à tre*	1949	D

———.	*Hérodiade de Stéphane Mallarmé, Récitation Orchestrale, a Ballet;* for chamber orchestra	1944	CF
———.	*Konzertmusik für Klavier, Blechbläser und Harfen*	1930	ESC
———.	*Four Part Songs to Old Texts*	n.d.	G
Honneger, Arthur	*Concerto da Camera;* for flute, English horn, and string orchestra	1948	D
———.	*Concerto da Camera;* reduction for flute, English horn, and piano	1948	D
———.	*String Quartet no. 3*	1936	D
Howe, Mary	*String Quartet*	n.d.	D
Hüttel, Joseph	*Divertissment grotesque;* for flute, oboe, clarinet, horn and piano	1929	CP
Huss, Henry Holden	*String Quartet in B Minor, op. 31*	1918	D
Huybrechts, Albert	*Sonate pour violon et piano*	1926	CP
———.	*Three Poems of Edgar Poe;* songs with piano	1928	D
Iarecki, Tadeusz	*Quartet for Strings, op. 21*	1918	BP
Jacobi, Frederick	*Hagiographa: Three Biblical Narratives For String Quartet and Piano*	1938	CF?
———.	*Two Assyrian Prayers;* for soprano (or tenor) and chamber orchestra	1924	BPhm
Kahn, Erich Itor	*Canon per Modum Speculi;* for soprano, alto, tenor and bass	1945	D
Kerntler, Jenö	*Sérénade for Violin, Violoncello, and Piano*	1932	G
Kirchner, Leon	*Trio for Violin, Cello and Piano*	1954	CF
Kolisch, Rudolph	*Happy Birthday to You;* for string quartet	1939	D
Kornsand, Emil	*String Quartet no. 2*	1944	D
Koutzen, Boris	*String Quartet no. 2*	1936	D
Kraft, William	*Music for String Quartet and Percussion*	1993	CF
Kroll, William	*Sextet for Two Violins, Two Violas, and Two Violoncellos;* arrangement of Beethoven *String Trio, op. 9, no. 3*	n.d.	D
Labroca, Mario	*String Quartet*	1923	D
Laderman, Ezra	*Double String Quartet*	1983	CF

Lajtha, Lázló	*String Quartet, op. 11, no. 3*	n.d.	D
La Violette, Wesley	*Octet for Oboe, Clarinet, Bassoon, Horn, Violin, Viola, Violoncello, and Double Bass*	1935	D
Llobet, Miguel	*Sept Chansons Populaires Espagñoles;* by Manuel de Falla, arranged for guitar accompaniment	1931	ESC
Lockwood, Normand	*Trio for Flute, Viola, and Harp*	1939	D
Loeffler, Charles Martin	*Canticum fratris solis;* for voice and chamber orchestra	1925	CF
———.	*Partita for Piano and Violin*	1930	CF
Lopatnikov, Nikolai	*String Quartet no. 2*	n.d.	D
Malipiero, Gian Francesco	*Cantàri alla Madrigalesca*	1931	D
———.	*Concerto for Orchestra*	1931	D
———.	*Epodi e Giambi*	1932	D
———.	*Cinque favole per una voce e piccola orchestra*	1950	CF
———.	*La Nave della Vittoria, Ricercare no. 2;* for flute, oboe, clarinet, bassoon, horn, three violas, and double bass	1926	D
———.	*Per Santa Elizabetta*	1931	D
———.	*Quattro Vecchie Canzoni;* for solo voice with flute, oboe, clarinet, bassoon, horn, viola and double bass	1940	D
———.	*Rispetti e strambotti;* for string quartet	1920	BP
———.	*Sonata à cinque;* for flute, violin, viola, violoncello, and piano	1934	D
———.	*Sonata à tre for Violin, Violoncello and Piano*	1927	D
———.	*Quartetto di Elizabetta*	1963	CF
———.	*Sonata à quattro per flauto, oboe, clarineto, e fagotto*	1954	CF
———.	*Stornelli e Ballate;* for string quartet	1923	D
———.	*String Quartet no. 4*	1934	D
———.	*I Trionfi d'Amore; tre commedie in una;* opera; vocal score with piano	1931	D
Malipiero, Riccardo	*In Time of Daffodils*	1964	CF
Martino, Donald	*String Quartet*	1983	CF
Martinů, Bohuslav	*Quintet for Two Violins, Two Violas, and Violoncello*	1927	D

———.	*Sextet for Two Violins, Two Violas, and Two Violoncelli*	1932	CP
Massarani, Renzo	*Pastorale for Oboe, Viola, Bassoon, and Violoncello*	1923	D
Matsudaira, Yoritsune	*Rhapsodie on a Theme of Gagaku*	1982	CF
Mennin, Peter	*Sonata Concertante for Violin and Piano*	1956	CF
Menotti, Gian Carlo	*The Unicorn, the Gorgon, and the Manticore*	1956	CF
Messiaen, Olivier	*Woodwind sextet*	1958	CF
Migot, Georges	*Le Premier Livre de Divertissements Français à deux et à trois*	1925	D
Milhaud, Darius	*Jacob's Dream, Suite chorégraphique en cinq parties;* for oboe, violin, viola, violoncello and double bass	1949	CF
———.	*Jeux de Printemps, Ballet suite;* for chamber orchestra	1944	CF
———.	*String Quartet no. 8*	1932	D
———.	*String Quartet no. 9*	1935	D
———.	*String Quartet no. 10*	1940	D
———.	*Septour à cordes*	1940	CF?
Mitchell, Lyndol C.	*String Quartet in E Minor*	1958	CF
Mojsisovics, Roderich von	*Es wird Früling!, op. 18, no. 3;* song with piano	1931	G
Nabokov, Nicolas	*Serenata estiva;* for string quartet	1937	D
Nono, Luigi	*Sará dolce tacere*	1960	CF
Ornstein, Leo	*Quintet for Two Violins, Viola, Violoncello and Piano, op. 92*	1929	D
Orrego-Salas, Juan	*Palabras de Don Quixote*	1970	CF
Page, George Nelson	*Sonata in F Minor, op. 7, for Piano*	1926	D
Palmer, Robert	*Quartet for Violin, Viola, Violoncello and Piano*	1946	D
———.	*Quintet for Two Violins, Viola, Violoncello, and Piano*	1950	CF
Perle, George	*Windows of Order, String Quartet no. 8*	1988	CF
Petit, Raymond	*Trois Récits des Evangiles;* for tenor voice and string quartet	n.d.	G
Petrassi, Goffredo	*String Trio*	1960	CF
Phillips, Burrill	*String Quartet no. 2*	1958	CF

Pierné, Gabriel	*Sonate da Camera, op. 48;* for flute, violoncello, and piano	1926	G
Piston, Walter	*Partita for Violin, Viola, and Organ*	1944	CF
———.	*Quintet for Wind instruments*	1956	CF
———.	*Sextet for Strings*	1964	CF
———.	*Trio for Violin, Violoncello, and Piano*	1935	CF
Pizzetti, Ildebrando	*Epithalamium;* cantata for solo voices, chorus, and small orchestra	1939	CF
———.	*String Quartet in D*	1933	D
———.	*Tre Canzoni;* for voice and string quartet	1928	D
———.	*Trio in A for Violin, Violoncello, and Piano*	1925	CF
Porter, Quincy	*String Quartet no. 7*	1943	D
Poulenc, Francis	*Sonata for Flute and Piano*	1957	CF
Powell, Mel	*Cantilena*	1970	CF
Prokofiev, Sergei	*String Quartet op. 50*	1930	CF
Raksin, David	*Oedipus Memneitai;* for baritone solo, chorus, and chamber orchestra	1986	CF
Ravel, Maurice	*Chansons Madécasses;* for voice, flute, cello, and piano	1925	CF
Reiser, Alois	*Quartet in E minor, op. 16*	1918	BP
———.	*String Quartet in C, op. 18*	1930	D
Respighi, Ottorino	*Concerto à cinque;* for oboe, trumpet, violin, double bass, piano, and string orchestra	1933	D
———.	*The Fountains of Rome* (sketches)	n.d.	G
———.	*Per Santa Elizabetta*	1931	D
———.	*Trittico Botticelliano;* for chamber orchestra	1927	D
Riegger, Wallingford	*La Belle Dame sans Merçi;* for strings, oboe, (English horn), clarinet, horn, and four solo voices (soprano, mezzo, tenor, and bass)	1924	BP
———.	*Three Canons for Woodwinds;* for piccolo, flute, clarinet, oboe and bassoon	1930	D
———.	*Two Canons for Woodwinds;* for piccolo flute, oboe, clarinet, and bassoon	1930	D
Rochberg, George	*Trio for Violin, Cello, and Piano*	1985	CF

Röntgen, Julius	*String Quartet. Heer Halewÿn Zong een Liedekÿn*	1922	BPhm
Rogati, George	*Sonata for Violin and Piano*	1924	D
Rogister, Jean	*Quintet for Clavecin, two Quintons, Viola d'Amor and Viola da Gamba*	1934	D
———.	*String Quartet in D, no. 4*	1927	D
Rootham, Cyril Bradley	*Septet for Viola, Oboe, Clarinet, Bassoon, Horn, Flute, and Harp*	n.d.	D
Rorem, Ned	*Nantucket Songs*	1979	CF
Rosé, Alfred	*String Quartet*	1927	D
Roth, Feri	*String Quartet in D*	1932	D
Roussel, Albert	*Trio for Flute, Viola, and Violoncello, op. 40*	1929	D
Rubinstein, Beryl	*String Quartet in Db, no. 2*	1933	D
Saygun, Adnan	*String Quartet op. 35*	1958	CF
Schönberg, Arnold	*String Quartet no. 3*	1927	CF
———.	*String Quartet no. 4*	1936	CF
Schuller, Gunther	*Music for Brass Quintet*	1961	CF
Schuman, William	*Amaryllis;* for string trio	1964	CF
———.	*Night Journey (Work for Martha Graham);* for orchestra	1948	CF
———.	*String Quartet no. 4*	1950	CF
Sessions, Roger	*String Quartet in E Minor, no. 1*	1936	D
Shapey, Ralph	*Trilogy: Song of Songs no. 1*	1980	CF
Siegmeister, Elie	*Ways of Love*	1983	CF
Simon, James	*Legende für Streichquartett in Drei Sätzen*	1930	D
Smith, David Stanley	*Sonata in A for Violin and Piano, op. 51*	1924	D
———.	*String Quartet in C, op. 46*	1920	D
———.	*String Quartet in Eb, op. 57*	1927	D
———.	*String Quartet in C, op. 71, no. 6*	1934	D
———.	*String Quartet in A, op. 77, no. 8*	1936	D
———.	*String Quartet, op. 90, no. 10*	n.d.	D
Sowerby, Leo	*Serenade for String Quartet*	1917	D
———.	*Trio for Flute, Viola, and Piano*	1919	G
Stock, Frederick	*Rhapsodic Fantasy for Orchestra*	1925	CF
———.	*Two Movements from String Quartet* (by Elizabeth Sprague Coolidge, arranged string orchestra)	1916	D

Stravinsky, Igor	*Apollon Musagète;* ballet in two scenes	1928	CF
Strube, Gustav	*Quintet for Flute, Oboe, Clarinet, Horn, and Bassoon*	1930	D
———.	*Sonata for Violoncello and Piano*	n.d.	D
Szántó, Théodore	*Nuits Blanches;* for small orchestra	1931	D
———.	*Suite Choréographique;* for string quartet	1929	G
Tal, Josef	*Imago;* for chamber orchestra	1982	CF
Tansman, Alexandre	*Serenade no. 3 for Orchestra*	1943	ESC
———.	*Sonata no. 4 for Piano*	1941	D
———.	*Triptyque for String Quartet*	1930	D
Tertis, Lionel	*Variations on the Passsacaglia of Händel;* (from Suite no. 7), for two Violas	1935	D
Thompson, Randall	*String Quartet no. 1*	1941	D
Thomson, Virgil	*Pervigilium Veneris;* (The Feast of Love)	1964	CF
Toch, Ernst	*Quintet for two Violins, Viola, Violoncello, and Piano, op. 64*	1938	ESC
———.	*Trio for Violin, Viola, and Violoncello, op. 63*	1938	D
Tuthill, Burnet Corwin	*Fantasy Sonata in One Movement for Clarinet and Piano, op. 3*	1932	D
Uray, Ludwig	*Suite in A Major for Violin and Piano*	n.d.	D
Vega, Aurelio de la	*Structures for String Quartet*	1962	CF
Villa-Lobos, Heitor	*Trio for Violin, Viola, and Violoncello*	1945	CF
Warner, H. Waldo	*Suite for Violin, Violoncello, and Piano, op. 22*	1921	BP
Webern, Anton	*Quartet, op. 28*	1938	CF
Weiner, Leo	*String Quartet no. 2 in F# minor*	1922	BP
Wellesz, Egon	*String Quartet, op. 60*	1943	G
Wernick, Richard	*String Quartet no. 3*	1989	CF
White, Eric Walter	*Three Songs for Medium Voice*	1925	D
White, Willy	*String Quartet in A Minor*	1938	D
Wigglesworth, F.	*Song for a Child;* with piano accompaniment	1943	G
Wildschut, Clara	*Sonata for Violin and Piano*	1926	D
Woollen, Russell	*Lines of Stephen Crane*	1981	CF

Notes

PREFACE

1 Anna Malipiero to ASC, 18 January 1954, C. Col.

2 ESC to Roy Harris, 26 July 1932, C. Col.

3 Donald Leavitt, "Mrs. Coolidge Goes to Washington," *Chamber Music Magazine* (Spring 1985), p. 15.

4 Oscar Sonneck to Carl Engel, 2 March 1924.

5 Carolyn G. Heilbrun, *Writing a Woman's Life* (New York: W. W. Norton, 1988), p. 59.

CHAPTER ONE

1 *Chicago Tribune,* 2 May 1865, p. 4.

2 NASD, 2 May 1865.

3 Henry S. Atwood, *The Atwood Family: ad 1599 to ad 1909* (privately printed, 1909), British Library. See also *The Little Red Book of Bristol,* I, p. 216, and *Wadley's Bristol Will,* p. 22, British Library, Department of Manuscripts.

4 PM, p. 30.

5 Benjamin Shurtleff, *The Descendants of John Atwood of Plymouth, Massachusetts* (Evanston, Ill.: National Society of the Daughters of the American Revolution, 1972), p. 5. See also Elijah Francis Atwood, *Ye Atte Wode Annals* (Sisseton, S. Dak.: Atwood Publishing Co., 1928), p. 9, and Evelyn Wood Lovejoy, *History of Royalton, Vermont, with Family Genealogies* (Burlington, Vt.: privately printed, 1911), p. 663.

6 Shurtleff, p. 35.

7 Lovejoy, p. 662.

8 Edward George Sprague, *The Ralph Sprague Genealogy* (Montpelier, Vt.: Capital City Press, 1913), pp. 25–26. See also *New England Historical and Genealogical Register* (Boston: New England Historical and Genealogical Society, 1909), pp. 137–51.

9 George Walter Chamberlain, *The Spragues of Malden, Massachusetts* (Boston: privately printed, 1923), p. 49.

10 Sprague, p. 71.

11 Ibid., p. 96.

12 Ibid., p. 132.

13 PM, p. 14.

14 Ibid., p. 34.

15 Ibid., p. 35.

16 Ibid., p. 72.

17 Ibid., p. 76.

18 Ibid., p. 41.

19 Ibid., p. 42.

20 *History of the Class of 1859, Yale College* (New Haven: Tuttle, Morehouse and Taylor, 1914), pp. 149–60.

21 Address given by John Haskell Hewitt, 25 November 1917. SMLA Miscellaneous Manuscripts, group 1258, box 9, folder 357.

22 *History of the Class of 1859, Yale College,* p. 160. It was here in Hartford that the fifth of his nine children, Harmony, married Charles Ives in 1908.

23 Will of Albert Arnold Sprague, 5 December 1913, p. 6, paragraph 12. SMLA, Treasurer's Records, YRG 5-B, series IV, box 386, folder 266.

24 NASD, [9 December] 1861.

25 AAS to NAS, 12 December 1861.

26 PM, p. 90.

27 "Death Calls Pioneer Grocer," *Modern Grocer* (16 January 1915), p. 6. Clipping, C. Col. NASD contains a promissory note dated 27 February 1862 that reads "$2,300, East Randolph. For value received I promise to pay Ziba Sprague on order twenty three hundred dollars on demand with interest annually." (The capital with which Sprague Warner was begun.)

28 TL, p. 31.

29 Joyce Antler, *Lucy Sprague Mitchell: The Making of a Modern Woman* (New Haven: Yale University Press, 1987), p. 21.

30 "Albert Arnold Sprague," *Retailer's Journal* (1 February 1915), p. 12, Clipping, C. Col.

31 This action predated the Pure Food and Drug Act of 1906.

32 NASD, 1871.

33 PM, p. 43.

34 NASD, 20 September 1872.

35 Ibid., 7 October 1871.

36 Ibid., 8 October 1871.

37 Ibid., 9 October 1871.

38 *Retailer's Journal,* p. 12. See also Antler, p. 7.

39 NASD, 29 November 1872 and July 1874.

40 Interview with Dr. John C. Coolidge, Cambridge, Massachusetts, 18 December 1988.

41 MDCP, box 74, contains correspondence, testimonials, memorials, and an undated letter introducing Regina to Joseph Joachim.

42 Ibid.

43 The title seems inspired by that of Tausig's school, which was known as the Schule der höhren Klavierspiele zu Berlin.

44 Amy Fay had also studied in Germany with Tausig, Kullak, and Deppe. She is better known than Watson because of the publication of her letters to her family, which appeared under the title *Music Study in Germany.*

45 Souvenir of Mrs. Watson's Class Reunions, Class of 1876, in NASD.

46 Ibid., 1877.

47 NASD, 12 March 1881.

48 NASD, 1 January 1881.

49 A. T. Andreas, *History of Chicago from the Earliest Period to the Present Time* (Chicago: A. T. Andreas Press, 1886), vol. 3, p. 405.

50 Ibid.

51 C. Col. contains the entire inventory of the Sprague Library, made 12 March 1915 by Fidelity Appraisal Company, Chicago.

52 Andreas, p. 649.

53 Ibid., p. 650.

54 Bessie Lou Pierce, *A History of Chicago,* vol. 2 (New York: Alfred A. Knopf, 1940), p. 485.

55 See Susan Dart, *The Friday Club: The First Hundred Years, 1887–1987* (Chicago: The Friday Club, 1987).

56 According to G. W. Orear (*Commercial and Architectural Chicago Illustrated,* Chicago: n.p., 1887, pp. 217–18), Sprague Warner was believed to be the second largest wholesale grocer and importer in the United States. Its business was so large that in order to meet demands it controlled the entire product of many manufacturing, canning, and preserving concerns. For a comprehensive description of the company with extensive photographs of the various departments, see *Sprague Warner and Co., 1862–1912* (Chicago: Rogers & Co., 1912).

57 It appears that the trip was a matter of real family council. NASD, 9 March 1882. "It has taken a good deal of talk and thought to bring us to this decision."

CHAPTER TWO

1 EPSD, n.p.

2 U.S. Visa, 1882, C. Col.

3 NASD, May 1882.

4 NAS Travel Diary, n.d.

5 EPSD, Munich, 21 August 1882. After Albert's death in 1915 Nan gave the painting *Virgin and Child with St. Catherine,* then thought to be an authentic Anthony Van

Dyck, to the Art Institute of Chicago as a memorial to her husband. She also made it possible for the Institute to buy El Greco's *Assumption of the Virgin.* I am indebted to John W. Smith, Archivist of the Art Institute of Chicago, for this information.

6 EPSD, Vienna, 11 August 1882.

7 Karen A. Shaffer and Neva Garner Greenwood, *Maud Powell: Pioneer American Violinist* (Ames: Iowa State University Press, 1988), p. 117.

8 EPSD, Paris, 14 October 1882.

9 NASD, Bayreuth, 14 August 1882. Nan's diary lists the entire cast.

10 EPSD, Vienna, 14 August 1882. Hermann Levi was the conductor on this occasion.

11 NASD, Bayreuth, 15 August 1882.

12 EPSD, Bayreuth, 15 August 1882.

13 NASD, Ibid.

14 Ibid., November 1882.

15 Ibid., Vienna, 19 August 1882.

16 Ibid., Paris, 9 October 1882.

17 EPSD, Paris, 9 October 1882.

18 Ibid., Marseilles, 18 December 1882.

19 EPS to Lucy Sprague, Rome, 24 June 1882.

20 EPS to Aunt Em Atwood, 18 September 1882, in NASD.

21 AAS to NAS, 30 September 1883, in NASD.

22 By the time Elizabeth went there, Mrs. Reed had expanded her school and changed the title to include the word *German.* See *Mrs. Sylvanus Reed's English, French, and German Boarding and Day School for Young Ladies* (New York: Baker and Godwin, Printers, 1870), NYCHS. Hereafter Reed, with date of edition.

23 Reed, 1879, p. 8.

24 Ibid., 1872, p. 10.

25 NASD, September 1883.

26 Reed, 1873, p. 9.

27 Grade Report in NASD.

28 Reed, 1873, p. 9.

29 EPS to parents, 13 October 1883, in NASD.

30 EPS to parents, 18 November 1883, in NASD.

31 Ibid.

32 Reed, 1870, p. 10.

33 EPS to parents, 16 March 1884, in NASD.

34 NASD, [December] 1884.

35 Emmett Dedmon, *Fabulous Chicago* (New York: Athenaeum, 1981), p. 114.

36 GJ, box 1, file 7, Sunday, 22 July 1883 (entry by John J. Glessner). The Glessner Journals cover a period from 1870 to 1921 and are contained in fifty-two leather-bound handwritten notebooks. Entries were written on Sundays, covering the previous week. They are written on the right-hand side of the page, with loose items such as letters, programs, and menus glued to the left side. About twenty percent of the entries are in Mr. Glessner's hand. All notes from the Glessner Journals in this study refer to the typed transcriptions and not the original manuscript pagination.

37 Daniel Burnham (1846–1912) was a prime mover in the Chicago school of architecture and an early experimenter with the concept of the skyscraper. In 1890 he was appointed chief of construction for the World Columbian Exposition and later became director of the works. He became known far and wide as a city planner and was employed in various cities of the United States. See Thomas S. Hines, *Burnham of Chicago: Architect and Planner* (Chicago: University of Chicago Press, 1979), p. xviii, and Louis H. Sullivan, *The Autobiography of an Idea* (New York: Dover, 1956 reprint of 1924 edition by the American Institute of Architects), p. 285ff.

38 Unidentified newspaper clipping, December 1885, GJ, box 1, file 12.

39 NASD, 5 December 1885. "E plays Chopin op. Polonaise in Ab and op. 38 Ballade."

40 GJ, box, 1, file [13] February 1882.

41 In addition to being an accomplished pianist, Fanny Glessner studied French, German, and Italian more or less seriously and also became a skilled botanist and apiarist. Later in life she took up the craft of silver smithing and created jewelry, some of which may be seen at the Glessner House at 1800 Prairie Avenue, which in 1970 was designated a Chicago landmark.

42 MDCP, Box 74, *Regina Watson Memory Book.* See letters of Teresa Carreño, 5 January 1913, and 29 October 1916.

43 While a student at Harvard, Charles Allerton Coolidge did sketches for the *Harvard Lampoon,* and after graduating he studied architecture at the Massachusetts Institute of Technology. Charles designed buildings for the University of Chicago, Harvard Medical and Law Schools, and Boston's North and South Stations. He also built numerous mercantile and academic buildings throughout the United States and Far East. When the firm of Shepley Rutan and Coolidge was dissolved in 1914, it was succeeded by Coolidge and Shattuck in Boston, and Coolidge and Hogden in Chicago. In time the Boston firm became Coolidge Shepley Bulfinch and Abbott, and is now Shepley Bulfinch Richardson and Abbott. See "A Century Completed, 1920–1956," *The Saturday Club,* eds. Edward W. Forbes and John H. Finley, Jr. (Boston: Houghton Mifflin Co., 1958). I am indebted to Mary Alice Molloy for assistance in locating this material.

44 ESC to parents, 19 August 1888.

CHAPTER THREE

1 Interview with Dr. John C. Coolidge, Cambridge, Massachusetts, 18 March 1989.

2 Emma Downing Coolidge, *Descendants of John and Mary Coolidge* (Boston:

Wright and Potter, 1930), pp. 32–35. See also George Walter Chamberlain, "The Early New England Coolidges and Some of their Descendants," *New England Historical and Genealogical Register* 77 (1923), pp. 271–75.

3 Chamberlain, *The Spragues of Malden,* pp. 270–99.

4 Emma Downing Coolidge, p. 306.

5 Since the Shurtleffs, like the Atwoods, came to the Plymouth Colony it is not surprising to find their genealogies linked several times. Barnabas, son of Nathaniel Atwood (1651–1724) married Lydia, daughter of Abiel Shurtleff (1666–1724), and Benjamin Shurtleff (1748–1821) married Abigail, the daughter of Lieutenant Nathaniel Atwood (1693–1767) by his second wife, Abigail Shaw.

6 Shurtleff, *Descendants of William Shurtleff,* p. 3.

7 *Frederic Shurtleff Coolidge: Some Letters Printed in Loving Memory* (Boston: George H. Ellis, 1917), letter of William Endicott, p. 4, and testimony of Dr. William T. Councilman, p. 5.

8 FSC to EPS, April 1890, from Squibnocket, Martha's Vineyard, C. Col.

9 FSC to EPS, 17 April [1890], C. Col.

10 FSC to EPS, 30 March 1890, C. Col.

11 GJ, box 2, file 6, 5 January 1890.

12 Ibid., file 5, 2 February 1889.

13 NAS to AAS, summer 1890, in NASD.

14 Ibid.

15 Undated fragment. AAS to NAS, in NASD.

16 In addition to being class president, Fred was a member of numerous clubs including the Art Club, Glee Club, Pierian Sodality, Rifle Club, and the Hasty Pudding Club. He was active in baseball and crew, and was an excellent marksman and enthusiastic hunter.

17 NAS to FSC, 23 September 1890.

18 NAS to FG, 21 September [1890], in GJ, box 2, file 8, insert, p. 102.

19 NASD, n.d., 1890.

20 Ibid., 2 August 1891.

CHAPTER FOUR

1 TL, p. 42.

2 Ibid., p. 30.

3 Carroll Smith-Rosenberg, "The Female World of Love and Ritual: Relations between Women in Nineteenth-Century America," *Signs* (1975), p. 16.

4 NASD, 13 November 1891.

5 Ibid., 28 February 1892.

6 Ibid., 25 February, 21 March, and 27 March 1893.

7 Ibid., 3 April 1893.

8 FSC to EPS, 9 October [ ].

9 *Rush Medical College, Forty-Ninth Annual Announcement, 1891–1892* (Chicago, 1891), p. 9, and *University of Chicago Bulletin of Information,* Courses in Medicine, June 1901, p. 7.

10 Beginning in 1894 he held various teaching positions and in 1900 was appointed dean. I am indebted to William Kona, Director of Archival Services, Rush–Presbyterian–St. Luke's Medical Center, for supplying this information.

11 Dedmon, p. 229.

12 On the changing name of the orchestra, see Ezra Schabas, *Theodore Thomas: America's Conductor and Builder of Orchestras, 1835–1905* (Urbana: University of Illinois Press, 1989), p. 183.

13 GJ, box 3, file 3, n.d.

14 Ibid., file 6, 10 January 1894.

15 NAS to ESC, 5 February [1892], C. Col.

16 See Edward W. Forbes and John H. Finley, Jr., "Charles Allerton Coolidge." pp. 189–93, and in the same source, "William Thomas Councilman, 1854–1944," pp. 60–72.

17 NASD, 6 March 1894.

18 NASD, 9 July 1894.

19 Ibid., 11 July 1894.

20 Dedmon, p. 249.

21 TL, p. 64 and Antler, p. 31.

22 TL, p. 64.

23 Ibid., p. 41.

24 NASD, 1 February 1894.

25 Ibid., 21 April 1897. It is clear from further entries that Amelia was hallucinating, seeing an animal on the closet shelf with eyes bigger than its ears, and making conversation with the bearskins on the floor.

26 Ibid., April 1894.

27 Clipping from unidentified newspaper in NASD, 22 October 1894.

28 AAS to ESC, 25 December 1895, C. Col.

CHAPTER FIVE

1 NASD, 8 April and 11 April 1895.

2 Ibid., 1 May 1895.

3 Ibid., 5 May 1895.

4 Ibid., 21 January 1896.

5 The lecture traces the history of dance from pagan through early Christian times, up to the inclusion of the minuet into the classical sonata form. She notes her sources as Riemann, Engel, Grove, and Böhm. Manuscript in C. Col.

6 She was rewarded with the discovery of a Mayflower connection on the Sprague side of the family in the person of the Elder Brewster, bailiff of the Archbishop of York, who came to Plymouth in 1620.

7 NASD, 11 January 1897.

8 Ibid., 12 November 1897.

9 The plates of the *After Supper Songs* were made at her father's expense and the copyright was then sold to Stone. It was later taken over from Stone by Duffield, from whom Elizabeth bought back the publishing rights in 1921 because she continually received requests for the collection and wanted to do another edition.

10 Amy Beach to ESC, 22 March 1902, C. Col.

11 On the relationship of the Brownings, see Margaret Forster's *Elizabeth Barrett Browning: A Biography* (New York: Doubleday, 1988), which draws upon a recently discovered diary and hitherto unknown letters.

12 ESC to Mrs. Charles Wright, 2 December 1951, C. Col.

13 Song no. 1 is based upon sonnet no. 1; Song no. 2, on sonnets 3, 4, and 6; Song no. 3 on sonnets 25 and 23; Song no. 4 on sonnet 16; Song no. 5 on sonnets 7, 8, 9, and 10; Song no. 6 on sonnet 14; Song no. 7 on sonnet 21; Song no. 8 on sonnet 22; Song no. 9 on sonnet 12; and Song no. 10 on sonnet 43.

14 Amy Beach to ESC, 17 November 1902, C. Col.

15 Ibid.

16 Ibid.

17 Ibid.

18 Ibid.

19 Ibid.

20 Amy Beach to ESC, 26 April 1904, C. Col.

21 NASD, entries for 28 January, 18 February, and 26 February 1900. I am indebted to John Collins Harvey, M.D., Ph.D., for his critical reading of the portions of this study that deal with medical problems.

22 FSC to AAS, 8 June 1901, in NASD. He was receiving as much as 700 grams of iodides at a time.

23 Information for the following portion of the text is based largely on Allan M. Brandt, *No Magic Bullet: A Social History of Venereal Disease in the United States since 1880* (New York: Oxford University Press, 1985); David Riesman, *Medicine in Modern Society* (Princeton: Princeton University Press, 1938); Temple S. Hoyne, A.M., M.D., ed., *Venereal and Urinary Diseases,* 2nd ed. (Chicago: Halsey Bros., 1894); and Harrie Sheridan Baketel, A.M., M.D., *The Treatment of Syphilis* (New York: Macmillan, 1920).

24 See Hoyne, *Venereal and Urinary Diseases,* p. 18.

25 NASD, 7 April 1895, and GJ, box 1, file 10, letter, FSC to FG, [May] 1895.

26 NASD, 26 June 1900.

27 Ibid., 7 September 1900.

28 Ibid., 14 June 1901.

29 Ibid., 10 September 1901. "Lucia will not see Otho or anyone but the nurses and me. Otho miserable and unhappy not to see Lucia." She did, in fact, finally allow him in before she died.

30 Trudeau speaks of the erroneous notions that obscured even the medical profession's perception of the disease.

31 Dr. Henry Sigerist, *American Medicine,* trans. Hildegard Nagel (New York: Norton, 1934), p. 248. Under Trudeau, the Saranac Lake/Adirondack region became one of the greatest world centers for the treatment and study of tuberculosis. See also Robert Taylor, *Saranac: America's Magic Mountain* (Boston: Houghton Mifflin, 1986).

32 ESC to NAS, 19 July 1902, in NASD.

33 ESC to AAS, 9 June 1903, in NASD.

34 NASD, 20 and 22 April 1903.

35 Ibid., 31 May 1902. "Fred plays golf with his brother Charles which is a hazardous thing to do. He is a bit willful and hard to control."

36 Interview with Dr. John C. Coolidge, 17 March 1988.

37 Elizabeth Barrett Browning, *Sonnets from the Portuguese,* Sonnet no. 8.

CHAPTER SIX

1 George F. Willison, *The History of Pittsfield, Massachusetts, 1916–1955* (Pittsfield: Sun Printing Co., 1957), p. 2. See also Edward Boltwood, *The History of Pittsfield, Massachusetts, 1876–1916* (Pittsfield: The Eagle Printing and Binding Co., 1916).

2 A. Scott Berg, *Goldwyn: A Biography* (New York: Knopf, 1989), pp. 21–22.

3 On industry in Pittsfield, see Willison, especially pp. 2–3 and pp. 7–8.

4 Ibid., pp. 334–35.

5 ESC to NAS, 30 October 1905, in NASD.

6 *Frederic Shurtleff Coolidge: Letters,* p. 14.

7 Ibid., p. 15.

8 Daniel Gregory Mason, *Music in My Time* (Westport, Conn.: Greenwood Press, 1970 reprint of original Macmillan edition, 1938), p. 182.

9 See Shaffer and Greenwood, pp. 223, 225.

10 Mason, *Music in My Time,* p. 180.

11 ESC to parents [30 October 1904], in NASD.

12 Pittsfield Department of Public Records, Registry of Deeds, Book 330, p. 171, 10 April 1905.

13 Willison, p. 10. Watson's estate is often referred to as the Onata Stock Farm, so named because her grandfather, Elkanah Watson, introduced to the Berkshires the

Merino breed of sheep, the superior quality of whose fleece was important to the development of Pittsfield's textile industry.

14 NASD, 10 May 1905.

15 Ibid. [24 November 1905].

16 In a letter of 14 April 1946, Elizabeth indicates that some of the texts were her own invention, some were from *Mother Goose Rhymes,* and some from William Blake's *Songs of Innocence.*

17 Francis Rogers to ESC, 26 September 1901 and 6 January 1902, C. Col.

18 Gustave Schirmer to ESC, 15 February 1902, C. Col.

19 Percy Goetschius to ESC, 21 February 1910, C. Col.

20 NASD, 23 January 1906.

21 FSC to ESC [1906], C. Col.

22 FSC to ESC, 28 February 1906, C. Col.

23 NASD, 4 June 1906.

24 For the architect's elevations see *Architectural Review* 13 (1906), plates 74 and 77.

25 "Albert Sprague Coolidge, Memorial Minute Adopted by the Faculty of Arts and Sciences, Harvard University, April 10, 1979," *Harvard University Gazette* 74: 25 May 1979, n.p.

26 NASD, 28 October 1906 and 30 September 1906.

27 ESC to NAS [1906], in NASD.

28 The Boys' Club had been founded in 1900 with the financial support of Zenas Crane, who made his fortune in the manufacture of high-quality paper used by the Bureau of Engraving for printing U.S. currency and securities. From Crane's modest beginning, the club grew rapidly so that by the time of Fred's association the membership numbered more than 800.

29 Pittsfield historians Willison and Boltwood are in disagreement with regard to both the founding date and the identity of the founder of the Anti-Tuberculosis Society. See Boltwood, p. 225ff and Willison, p. 340. It is worth noting that both books abound in inaccuracies, especially regarding dates that refer to the Coolidges' life in Pittsfield.

30 ESC to the Anti-Tuberculosis Association, 30 November 1938, C. Col.

31 NASD, 22 December 1906.

32 NAS to Otho, 25 December 1906, C. Col.

33 NASD, December 25 1906.

34 Ibid., 1 January 1907.

35 Ibid., 15 January 1907.

36 Ibid., 24 March 1907.

37 ESC to NAS, February 1908, in NASD.

38 NASD, 25 July 1907. An entry of 1 August indicates that Elizabeth paid $700 of the cost of the painting, and Albert the other $400. At approximately the same time

Nan was also sitting for a portrait by Ipsen. Her painting now hangs in the foyer of Sprague Hall at Yale.

39 NASD, 10 June 1908.

40 Ibid., 22 September 1908.

41 Ibid., 8 September 1910. This is a curious comment in view of Ives's reputation as a skilled keyboard player. See Jan Swafford, *Charles Ives: A Life with Music* (New York: Norton, 1996), especially pp. 48–53, 118–21, and 150–51.

42 FSC to AAS and NAS, 7 December 1908, C. Col.

43 ESC to AAS and NAS, [31] December 1908, C. Col.

CHAPTER SEVEN

1 ESC to NAS, 25 March 1909, in NASD.

2 NASD, 17 June 1909.

3 Ibid., 6 April 1909. See also Antler, p. 126.

4 Daniel Gregory Mason to ESC, 14 June 1909, C. Col.

5 Mason, *Music in My Time,* pp. 181–82.

6 Gustave Dannreuther to ESC, 28 June 1909, and 1 July 1909, C. Col.

7 Daniel Gregory Mason to Percy Goetschius, 9 December 1909, and Regina Watson to Rafael Joseffy, 12 December 1909. Amy Beach also wrote a letter to Goetschius that has not survived, but to which Goetschius refers in his letter to ESC, 15 December 1909, C. Col.

8 Frederick Stock to ESC, 31 May 1911 and 17 September 1911, C. Col.

9 Percy Goetschius to ESC, 19 December 1909, C. Col.

10 Percy Goetschius to ESC, 30 October 1910, C. Col.

11 These and numerous other manuscript notebooks filled with exercises are a part of the Coolidge Collection at the Library of Congress.

12 Although Coolidge did compose a Sonata for Oboe and Piano it is a much later composition. On the basis of both chronology and later diary entry it is quite clear that the work being referred to here is her String Quartet in E Minor which is written in sonata form.

13 ESC to AAS, 2 November 1909, in NASD.

14 NASD, 23 January 1910.

15 Ibid., 31 January 1910. One of Elizabeth's associates in the Boys' Club at this time was James Keegan, who functioned as superintendent. On Elizabeth's birthday in 1943, Keegan wrote, "I recall how you, with your intense love of music and desire to be helpful to others, actually instructed boys in the art of playing the piano." 30 October 1943, C. Col.

16 NASD, 6 July 1910.

17 Minutes of the Pittsfield Community School, 18 October 1940. See also Clifford Peasles to ESC, n.d., C. Col. Peasles was one of Elizabeth's former students who

wrote to say that he was receiving his Master's degree in music from Columbia University. See also his letter of 1950: "I have thought recently how 40 years ago you were in the prime of life, and while there were many things you could have done and enjoyed, you chose to run the Music School at the Club and teach us, not too eager boys."

18 Ehrlich was a Nobel Laureate who worked together with Sahachiro Hata. The popular term "magic bullet" stems from Ehrlich's explanation that "the antibodies are magic bullets which find their targets by themselves." The arsenic compound, arsphenamine, had many side effects, and some patients even died from its toxicity. It required intravenous injection, a technique involving surgical procedures unfamiliar to many American general practitioners. See Brandt, p. 40ff.

19 NASD, 3 January 1911.

20 FSC to ESC, [January] 1911, C. Col.

21 ESC to NAS, 27 January 1911, in NASD.

22 FSC to NAS, 19 February 1911, in NASD.

23 NASD, [February] 1911.

24 Ibid., 22 July 1911.

25 Ibid., 15 August 1911.

26 Ibid., 12 September and 3 October 1911.

27 Ibid., 1 September and 5 September 1911.

28 William T. Councilman to ESC [1911], C. Col.

29 ESC to NAS, 11 November 1911, in NASD.

30 ESC to AAS, 28 October 1911, in NASD.

31 ESC to NAS, 26 December 1911, in NASD.

32 Gertrude Watson to NAS [1911], in NASD.

33 Regina Watson in ESC, 6 November 1911, C. Col.

34 ESC to NAS, 22 January 1912, in NASD.

35 AAS to ESC, 23 March 1912, C. Col.

36 ESC to AAS, 31 March [1912], in NASD. Albert gave $5,000 toward the new TB home, which opened on 20 September 1913, and Elizabeth loaned Fred's portrait to be placed there. David Twichell, the brother of Harmony, was a physician at the Trudeau Institute in Saranac.

37 Unidentified newspaper clipping, C. Col.

38 Mason, *Music in My Time*, p. 180.

39 FSC to ESC, 12 November 1912, C. Col.

40 GJ, box 6, file 2. See insert, p. 74, clipping from unidentified newspaper with detailed description of the festivities.

41 NASD, 13 July 1913.

42 Ibid., 8 September 1913.

43 FSC to ESC, 19 September 1913, C. Col.

44 NASD, 30 October 1913.

45 Ibid., 1 December 1913.

46 Ibid., 14 August 1913. The quartet has been recorded by the Manhattan String Quartet.

47 Percy Goetschius to ESC, 12 April 1914, C. Col.

48 ESC to Harris Danziger, 19 December 1933, C. Col.

49 ESC to NAS, 23 March 1914, in NASD.

CHAPTER EIGHT

1 NASD, 3 September 1912.

2 NAS to AAS, 12 December 1861, C. Col.

3 ESC to parents, 22 March 1914, in NASD.

4 NASD, 17 June 1914.

5 Ibid., 11 September 1914.

6 ASC to NAS, 24 October 1914, in NASD.

7 GJ, box 5, file 3, p. 115, 17 January 1915.

8 *Modern Grocer,* 16 January 1915, p. 6.

9 13 January 1915, n.p., C. Col.

10 18 January 1915, n.p., C. Col. The corporations for which Sprague served as director include the Chicago Telephone Co., Commonwealth Edison Co., the Liverpool and London and Globe Insurance Co., the Elgin National Watch Co., and the Northern Trust Co. He was a member of the board of trustees of Rush Medical College and the Art Institute of Chicago, served as president of the Relief and Aid Society, and belonged to numerous fraternal clubs.

11 The *Christian Science Monitor,* 15 March 1915, reports that the $50,000 bequest was used to purchase El Greco's *Assumption of the Virgin,* which had hung in the Art Institute since 1906 and would now be a memorial to Mr. Sprague.

12 Will of Albert Arnold Sprague, 7 June 1905; first codicil, 3 February 1906; second codicil, 31 January 1911; third codicil, 5 December 1913. Northern Trust Co. of Chicago, Executor and Trustee. SMLA, Treasurer's Reports, YRG 5-B, series IV, box 417, folder 903.

13 Charles Hamill to ESC, 30 January 1915, C. Col.

14 Charles Hamill to ESC, 5 February 1915, C. Col.

15 ESC to FG, 16 March 1915, GJ, box 6, file 4, insert, p. 183.

16 Frederick Stock to ESC, 14 November 1915, C. Col.

17 Frederick Stock to ESC, 1 December and 22 December 1915, C. Col.

18 Frederick Stock to Charles Martin Loeffler, 23 June 1916, C. Col.

19 Death Certificate No. 16417, State of New York, Department of Health of the City of New York Bureau Records, Department of Records and Information Services, Municipal Archives. Several newspaper accounts report conflicting dates, and the death certificate actually places Fred's death on 14 May. Elizabeth's statement that she stayed with him until he died in the early hours of 15 May would seem to be more reliable.

20 Will of Frederic Shurtleff Coolidge, 29 February 1913. On 13 March 1915 Elizabeth filed a request in Probate Court for the County of Berkshire, Massachusetts, to be appointed conservator by reason of her husband's "mental weakness." On 16 March Fred signed the agreement.

21 Unidentified newspaper clipping, C. Col.

22 Ibid.

23 Ibid.

24 *Wholesale Grocer,* June 1915, p. 12.

25 After Nan's death the memoirs were published along with notes for the unfinished portions as *Pleasant Memories of My Life* (New York: privately printed, 1916).

26 Typescript in C. Col.

27 GJ, box 6, file 4, 9 February 1915, and insert, p. 180.

28 ESC to Arthur Hadley, 5 July 1915, SMLA, Treasurer's Reports, YRG 5-B, series III, box 157, folder 2470.

29 Philo Adams Otis, *The Chicago Symphony Orchestra: Its Organization, Growth, and Development 1891–1924* (Chicago: Clayton F. Summy Co., 1925), pp. 179–80.

30 See letter of Frank Billings, M.D., to ESC, 11 May and 3 October 1916, C. Col.

31 See letter of Wyllye Andrews, M.D., to ESC, 5 April 1917, C. Col.

32 ESC to George Parmly Day, 7 March 1916, and letter of George Parmly Day to John W. Bristol, 19 July 1916, SMLA, Yale University, Treasurer's Reports, YRG 5-B, Series III, box 357, folder 1468.

33 Regarding the portraits see letters of George Parmly Day to ESC, 2 July, 20 July, and 18 September 1917, and letters of ESC to Day, 6 July and 10 September 1917. SMLA, Treasurer's Report, Ibid., folders 2469 and 2470. The portraits that now hang in Sprague Hall are not the ones that were originally placed there. The original painting of Albert Arnold Sprague done by Gari Melcher was replaced by the portrait by Louis Betts, and the Melcher portrait of Nancy Ann Sprague was replaced by Ernest Ipsen's painting done in 1911. These were given to Yale by Coolidge in 1927.

34 John Haskell Hewitt, address given at the dedication of Sprague Hall, 25 November 1917. SMLA, MMS, group 1258, folder 357.

35 Willison, p. 116.

36 W. R. MacAusland to ESC, 17 December 1917. With the decline in the number of patients in later years the maintenance of the Home for Crippled Children became unrealistic, and the director, Dr. George Reynolds, reported that the endowment could be used to better advantage elsewhere. He recommended that it

be applied to the House of Mercy Hospital, which was in real need of money to build a new operative wing and to provide better orthopedic care. Elizabeth agreed, though not without some regret at "having to give up all the educational work which was so successfully done at Upway Fields." See letter from ESC to George S. Reynolds, M.D., 28 February 1942, C. Col.

37 See letters of Nicholas Murray Butler, president of Columbia University, to ESC, 17 February and 1 March 1915, 3 April 1916, and 1 April 1918. See also letter of John B. Pine, clerk of the trustees of Columbia University, to ESC, 3 April 1816, C. Col.

38 John B. Blake to ESC, 21 November 1916, C. Col.

39 Arthur Farwell to ESC, 5 January 1916, C. Col.

40 Leo Sowerby to ESC, 12 September 1916, C. Col.

41 Unidentified newspaper clipping, MDCP, box 74. Library of Congress Manuscript Division.

42 See Antler, p. 218ff.

43 TL, pp. 272–73.

44 Lucy Sprague Mitchell to ESC, 15 April 1916, C. Col.

45 TL, p. 455.

CHAPTER NINE

1 Typescript of a speech delivered by ESC on NBC radio, 13 February 1936, C. Col. Coolidge's refusal to allow James Bennison Corcoran to include her in his book on American composers (1949) clearly reflects her views as expressed here.

2 Cobbett was actually an inventor who retired from business at the age of sixty to devote himself to fostering the study, appreciation, and performance of chamber music. In 1924 he created a medal to be awarded for distinguished service to chamber music. Elizabeth was the second recipient. A few years later she would follow suit by establishing the Coolidge Medal, the first award of which was made to Cobbett.

3 Published by Oxford University Press, 1929. An enlarged and revised edition by Colin Mason appeared in 1963.

4 The other members of the quartet were Emmanuel Fiedler, second violin, Louis Svenčenski, viola, and Fritz Giese, violoncello. The second violin and cello chairs changed quite frequently over the years, but the first violin and viola remained constant from the time of the quartet's formation until its disbanding.

5 It was a coup on the part of Damrosch to obtain the services of the Kneisel Quartet in residence and as heads of the string department. The immediate success of the school is attributed to the outstanding faculty that Damrosch was able to recruit. See George Martin, *The Damrosch Dynasty* (Boston: Houghton Mifflin, 1983), pp. 296–98. It is worth noting that Elizabeth was closely associated with most of the faculty in one way or another; she knew Damrosch well, studied composition with Goetschius, piano with Stojowski, and frequently hired Barrère to perform at her festivals.

6 One noteworthy example is Schönberg's *Verklärte Nacht,* which the Kneisels took into their repertoire after Rice performed it with his group and called it to the attention of Kneisel. Their repertoire also included such recent works as the quartets of Debussy, Franck, Ravel, Enesco, Glazunov, and Kodaly, as well as the works of the Second New England School.

7 Marianne (Mädie) Kneisel Kahn established a quartet that Elizabeth helped to support. Mädie was the wife of Erich Itor Kahn who, with Alexander Schneider (violin) and Benar Heifitz (cello), formed the Albeneri Trio in 1945, which was also subsidized by Coolidge.

8 See Mason, *Music in My Time,* p. 196.

9 Much of the success of the quartet that de Coppet founded was the result of the remarkable stability of its personnel. Adolfo Betti, Alfred Pochon, and Iwan d'Archambeau remained for the entire life of the quartet. Ugo Ara had to leave in 1917 to join the Italian army. He was replaced first by Louis Bailly, in 1924 by d'Archambeau's brother Felicien, and finally by Nicholas Moldavan.

10 GJ, box 6, file 4, 17 May 1916, entry by John Glessner. "Dinner was delayed a few minutes because of Mr. de Coppet. Just as it was announced he complained of a pain in his left eye and extreme pain in the back of his head. He asked us to pay no attention to him, that the pain would pass off in a few minutes, so we looked away, but he swayed a little, was supported to sofa, and lay down, became unconscious almost immediately. Three physicians were summoned. We stepped with the Flonzaleys into the Music room and soon slipped away to our hotel taking Mr. Betti and Mr. d'Archambeau."

11 Hugo Kortschak to ESC, May 1916, C. Col.

12 ESC to Hugo Kortschak, 10 May 1916, C. Col.

13 Ibid.

14 Ibid.

15 Ibid.

16 Ibid. The personnel of the Berkshire Quartet changed fairly quickly. Felber was drafted in 1917 and was replaced by Sergei Kotlarsky. By 1919 Jacques Gordon was the second violinist and the name of Louis Bailly appears in place of Clarence Evans on the program of the Berkshire Festival in 1919, though he was still a member of the Flonzaley Quartet. It appears that he may have been a substitution, for Evans again is with the group for the festival in 1920.

17 ESC, "Da Capo," p. 3.

18 *New York Times,* 12 February 1918, p. 9. On the disbanding of the Kneisel Quartet, see *Musical America* 25 (April 1917), p. 1.

19 Stoeckel was a German immigrant who came to this country in 1848 at the time of the revolution in Germany and was for many years on the faculty of Yale University. On the Lichfield Festival see Pamela J. Perry, "Premieres of Sibelius and Others in the Connecticut Hills" in *Cultivating Music in America,* Ralph Locke and Cyrilla Barr, eds. (Berkeley and Los Angeles: University of California Press, 1997), pp. 124–28, specifically 125.

20 ESC, "Da Capo," p. 3.

21 Ibid.

22 Typescript of the citation on the occasion of the awarding of the Coolidge Medal to Edwin T. Rice, 30 October 1936, C. Col.

23 See typescript of Rice's biographical notes supplied to the Library of Congress at the time of the award, 1936, C. Col.

24 See especially the letters of Edwin T. Rice to ESC, 27 January 1935, 31 October 1935, and 4, 6, and 11 November 1935, with reference to South Mountain, C. Col.

25 See Martin, *The Damrosch Dynasty*, pp. 50, 111, 123.

26 ESC, "Da Capo," p. 4.

CHAPTER TEN

1 Pittsfield Office of Public Records, Registry of Deeds, book 384, p. 481, 21 October 1916.

2 The cottages have since been torn down, but the auditorium is still in use and has been entered in the Massachusetts Registry of Historic Buildings.

3 On Coolidge's perception of art as her religion, see ESC to Roy Harris, 26 July 1932. "[T]he love and fidelity which I feel toward art are high priestesses in the service of the only religion I know." C. Col.

4 Daniel Gregory Mason, "The Berkshire Festival of Chamber Music," *New Music Review* 17 (1918), p. 372.

5 Alfredo Casella, *Music in My Time,* trans. Spencer Norton (Norman: University of Oklahoma Press, 1955), pp. 201–2.

6 Hugo Kortschak to ESC, 2 April 1918, C. Col.

7 Alfred Human, "Hold America's First Chamber Music Festival," unidentified newspaper clipping, 1918, C. Col.

8 ESC, "Da Capo," p. 4.

9 Willem Willeke to ESC, 15 August 1918, C. Col.

10 Typescript, "Memorial to Willem Willeke," address by Paul Manship, Juilliard School of Music, C. Col.

11 "Romantic History of Willeke's Amati Violoncello," unidentified newspaper clipping, Williams College Collection.

12 Hugo Kortschak to ESC, 13 November 1921, C. Col.

13 On the difference between Mannes's school and the Institute of Musical Art established by his brother-in-law Frank Damrosch, see Martin, p. 237.

14 Clara Mannes to ESC, 21 September 1916, C. Col.

15 Clara Mannes to ESC, 8 May 1917, C. Col.

16 Clara Mannes to ESC, 27 September 1917, C. Col.

17 See letters of Rubin Goldmark to ESC, 17 April 1919, 10 May 1919, 26 August 1919, and 2 May 1920, C. Col. On 30 July 1919 Goldmark wrote, "Your exercises are

remarkably good—the slips unimportant and very few. I am convinced you will have benefited a great deal for having gone through this laborious work so conscientiously. . . . It will make everything that comes later on so much more fluent."

18 Ernest Bloch to ESC, 12 September 1919, C. Col.

19 Ernest Bloch to ESC, 5 September 1920, C. Col.

20 Ernest Bloch to ESC, 14 February 1924, C. Col. It has been suggested that much of his depression at this time was caused by the Cleveland Institute's rejection of the reforms in curriculum and policy that he had recommended.

21 ESC to Ernest Bloch, 19 February 1924. See also letter of 24 February 1924 for enclosure of her letter to Eastman. C. Col.

22 Loudon Charlton to ESC, 13 December 1917, C. Col. His letter of 12 February 1918 lists all of the subscribers and reveals that Coolidge's was the largest contribution.

23 Frederick Stock to ESC, 27 August 1919, C. Col.

24 Rebecca Clarke to ESC, 17 August [1919], C. Col.

25 Rebecca Clarke to ESC, 29 September [1919], C. Col.

26 Between 1916 and 1935 Coolidge contributed a total of $31,000 to the general fund of the MacDowell Colony as well as smaller amounts to the scholarship fund. For all except three of those years her contribution was the largest single gift to the colony. See MDCP, reports, box 72, LC Manuscript Division.

27 Marian MacDowell to ESC, 17 May [1924?], C. Col.

28 Typescript address by Louis K. Anspacher, p. 3, C. Col.

29 Hugo Kortschak to ESC, 23 May 1920, C. Col.

30 Loudon Charlton to ESC, 23 May 1921, C. Col.

31 Ibid.

32 Loudon Charlton to ESC, 11 January 1927, C. Col.

33 Ugo Ara to ESC, 5 May 1921, C. Col.

34 Ugo Ara to ESC, 25 October 1921, C. Col.

35 Oscar Sonneck to ESC, 29 August 1921, C. Col.

36 Mukle had also at one time concertized with Maud Powell. See Shaffer, pp. 222–23.

37 Rebecca Clarke to ESC, 28 September [1922], C. Col.

38 ESC, "Da Capo," p. 5.

39 On Coolidge's reactions to the English presence at the sixth Berkshire Festival in 1923, see Steven Banfield, "'Too Much of Albion'? Mrs. Coolidge and Her British Connections," *American Music* 4 (1986), pp. 61–88.

40 ESC, "Da Capo," p. 6.

CHAPTER ELEVEN

1 See OS to CE, 4 September 1920, Engel Papers, LC.

2 OS to CE, 21 October 1921, Engel Papers, LC.

3 See *Oscar Sonneck and American Music,* William Lichtenwanger, ed. (Urbana: University of Illinois Press, 1983), p. xiv.

4 Ibid., p. 112.

5 Ibid., p. 114.

6 Ibid., p. 115.

7 Ibid., pp. 175–80.

8 OS to HP, 1 December 1921, C. Col.

9 Ibid.

10 ESC, "Da Capo," p. 6.

11 CE to ESC, 5 October 1922, C. Col.

12 ESC to CE, 9 December 1922, C. Col.

13 CE to ESC, 13 December 1922, C. Col.

14 CE to ESC, 7 November 1923, C. Col.

15 See *Smithsonian Annual Report,* 1906, pp. xvi–xvii, 226.

16 Mary Howe, *Jottings* (Washington: privately printed, 1959), p. 109ff.

17 ESC to CE, 26 January 1924, C. Col.

18 Composers represented on the program were Ernest Bloch, Gian Francesco Malipiero, H. Waldo Warner, Leo Weiner, Julius Röntgen, Eugene Goossens, and Henry Eichheim.

19 HP to ESC, 10 February 1924, C. Col.

20 Typescript of prefatory and concluding remarks, n.d., p. 3, C. Col.

21 CE to ESC, 2 November 1924, C. Col.

22 Ibid.

23 CE to ESC, 7 April 1926, C. Col.

24 ESC to CE, 19 February 1924, C. Col.

25 CE to ESC, 20 February 1924, C. Col.

26 CE to ESC, 13 November 1923, C. Col.

27 ESC to HP [12 November 1924], C. Col. Reprinted as Appendix iv-a in *United States Library of Congress, Report of the Librarian for the Fiscal Year Ending June 30, 1925* (Washington, D.C.: Government Printing Office, 1925), pp. 286–87.

28 The sum was later increased to $90,000.

29 HP to ESC, 15 November 1924, C. Col.

30 *United States Library of Congress, Report of the Librarian of Congress for the Fiscal Year Ending June 30, 1924* (Washington: Government Printing Office, 1924), p. 5.

31 Harold H. Rockwell to ESC, 10 December 1924, C. Col.

32 Report of the Librarian of Congress, 1924, p. 5.

33 Herbert Putnam, "Tributes to Carl Engel," *Musical Quarterly* 31 (1945), p. 138.

34 Frank Bridge to ESC, 26 June 1928, C. Col.

35 CE to ESC, 15 May 1926, C. Col.

36 See sketch in letter, CE to ESC, 14 August 1926, C. Col.

37 CE to ESC, 14 December 1924, C. Col.

38 CE to ESC, 4 December 1924, C. Col. Although Engel never identifies the "personality almost as strong and extraordinary" as ESC, there is considerable evidence to suggest that it was Amy Lowell. Percy Lee Atherton gives credit to Lowell for broadening Engel's intellectual horizons. See "Boston Days (1909–1922): Some Engeliana," in *A Birthday Offering to C. E.,* Gustave Reese, ed. (New York: G. Schirmer, 1943), p. 27. For a discussion of Lowell's role in Engel's naturalization process, see William Bedford, "A Musical Apprentice: Amy Lowell to Carl Engel," *Musical Quarterly* 58 (1972), pp. 519–42. See also Willis Wager, "Amy Lowell and Music," in *A Birthday Offering,* pp. 209–13.

CHAPTER TWELVE

1 Carl Engel, untitled, unpublished speech [1925] on the occasion of the first festival, C. Col.

2 ESC to CE, 30 January 1925, C. Col.

3 CE to ESC, 21 May 1925, C. Col.

4 CE to ESC, 29 October [1924], C. Col. The idea of the circular stage that Engel envisioned was abandoned on the advice of the acoustical consultant, Melville Swan. The courtyard was built and later embellished by the addition of a pool, and the bas-relief that still graces the foyer is the work of Brenda Putnam, daughter of the Librarian of Congress, Herbert Putnam.

5 ESC to CE, 12 November 1925, C. Col.

6 See *A Birthday Offering,* p. 7.

7 CE to ESC [1926], C. Col.

8 CE to ESC, 9 March 1926, C. Col.

9 CE to ESC, 26 June 1926, C. Col.

10 CE to ESC, 23 January 1928, C. Col.

11 Ibid.

12 CE to ESC, 4 December [1924], C. Col.

13 CE to ESC, 1 September 1926, C. Col. The decision not to engage Ravel is to be regretted, for Coolidge wanted him to compose another string quartet.

14 On the "English Festival" see p. 151.

15 ESC to Persis Coleman, 29 December 1928, C. Col.

16 CE to ESC, 4 December [1924], C. Col.

17 CE to ESC, 2 March 1925, C. Col.

18 CE to ESC, 27 May 1924, C. Col.

19 CE to ESC, 21 November 1924, C. Col.

20 ESC, "Da Capo," p. 8.

21 CE to ESC, 5 March 1925, C. Col.

22 Richard Aldrich, "Open Washington's New Music Hall," *New York Times,* 29 October 1925.

23 Kate Scott Brooks, "Schubert Opus in Musical Festival," *Washington Herald,* 31 October 1925.

24 Aldrich, "Play Old Masters as Festival Ends," *New York Times,* 30 October 1925.

25 Henry Taylor Parker, "Washington Festival," *Boston Evening Transcript,* 30 October 1925.

26 CE to ESC, 14 April 1926, C. Col.

27 *Washington Herald,* 3 April 1925.

28 CE to ESC, 11 January 1926, C. Col.

29 Only two of the original members of the quartet remained: Kortschak, the founder, and Emmeran Stoeber, cellist. Jacques Gordon, who played with the group briefly in 1919, was again second violinist, and Clarence Evans was the violist.

30 On the Chicago festival see p. 205.

31 Interview with Dr. John C. Coolidge, Cambridge, Massachusetts, 6 December 1989.

32 CE to ESC, 1 February and 28 February 1928, C. Col. See also Vera Stravinsky and Robert Craft, *Stravinsky in Pictures and Documents* (New York: Simon and Schuster, 1978), pp. 274–75.

33 CE to ESC, 1 February 1928, C. Col.

34 CE to ESC, 18 February 1928, C. Col.

35 Lawrence Gilman, *New York Tribune,* 30 April 1928.

36 CE to ESC, 23 March 1928, C. Col.

37 CE to ESC, 28 February 1928, C. Col.

38 Ibid.

39 ESC to CE, [September] 1926, C. Col. For more detailed treatment of their disagreement over policy, see Cyrilla Barr, "'The Faerie Queene' and the 'Archangel': The Correspondence of Elizabeth Sprague Coolidge and Carl Engel," *American Music* 15 (Summer 1997), pp. 159–182.

40 CE to ESC, 8 September [1926], C. Col.

41 ESC to CE, 20 March 1928, C. Col.

42 CE to ESC, 7 November 1928, C. Col.

43 For fuller discussion of the failed Sonneck scholarship, see Cyrilla Barr, "The Musicological Legacy of Elizabeth Sprague Coolidge," *Journal of Musicology* 11 (1993), pp. 250–68.

44 The obverse of the medal depicts the eagle with a lyre and an encircling legend reading "The Elizabeth Sprague Coolidge Medal for Eminent Services to Chamber Music." The reverse reads "Awarded by the Elizabeth Sprague Coolidge Foundation to (recipient's name) on Founder's Day (year)." For a list of Coolidge Medalists, see Appendix A, p. 351.

45 ESC to CE, 5 July 1931, C. Col.

46 CE, unpublished speech on occasion of first festival, C. Col.

CHAPTER THIRTEEN

1 Meridian Mansion opened in 1918 as a luxury apartment featuring, among other things, a penthouse, formal dining room, and its own power plant. By the time Coolidge moved in it was nicknamed "The Senatorial Beehive" because it was the residence of so many diplomats and members of Congress. It is now called The Envoy. See James M. Goode, *Best Addresses: A Century of Washington's Distinguished Apartment Houses* (Washington, D.C.: Smithsonian Institution Press, 1988), pp. 151–57.

2 Dr. John C. Coolidge relates that on several occasions she confided to him her suicidal thoughts. Interview, 20 December 1988, Cambridge, Massachusetts.

3 ESC to ASC, 13 February 1931, C. Col.

4 Margaret Deneke to ESC, 4 February 1953, C. Col.

5 ESC to Hans Kindler, 3 June 1933, C. Col.

6 ESC to Frank Bridge, 28 February 1928, C. Col.

7 ESC to ASC, 29 January 1924, C. Col.

8 ESC to ASC, 2 February 1924, C. Col.

9 ESC to Gladys Caldwell, 24 March 1942, C. Col.

10 ESC to Frank Bridge, 29 November 1922, C. Col.

11 Ethel Bridge to Marjorie Fass, 20 August 1923, BPLA.

12 Ethel Bridge to Marjorie Fass, 1 September 1923, BPLA.

13 Ethel Bridge to Marjorie Fass, 2 September 1923, BPLA.

14 Frank Bridge to Marjorie Fass, 4 September 1923, BPLA.

15 Frank Bridge to Marjorie Fass, 3 September1923, BPLA.

16 Ethel Bridge to Marjorie Fass, 4 September and 19 September 1923, BPLA.

17 Ibid.

18 Frank Bridge to ESC, 7 December 1923, C. Col.

19 Frank Bridge to ESC, 29 April 1924, C. Col.

20 Richard W. Hale to ESC, 19 November 1924, C. Col.

21 *Musical Times,* November 1927, quoted in Jay Rosenfeld, *Elizabeth Sprague Coolidge: A Tribute on the One Hundredth Anniversary of Her Birth* (privately printed, 1964), p. 9.

22 Bloch was extremely pleased with Kindler's performance. Over the years the two men became good friends, and Kindler did much to popularize Bloch's music.

23 Coolidge was always very proud that Kindler's first conducting experience was in her service. When in Paris she appealed to him to find a conductor for her, and he responded shyly, "I haven't done it but I should like to try if you are willing." Typescript of testimonial from presentation of Coolidge Medal to Kindler in 1939, C. Col.

24 In later tours, where performances were in cities far removed from one another, she used local contacts to procure concert halls—Malipiero in Venice, Prunières in Paris, and Bridge in London.

25 Quoted in Sister Mary Virginia Butkovich, "Hans Kindler, 1892–1949" (Ph.D. diss., Catholic University of America, 1965), p. 99. It is worth noting that it was Kindler who suggested commissioning Bartók and Szymanowski and began negotiating with Sibelius to compose a cello concerto. Sibelius indicated that he would "do his best this summer." Hans Kindler to ESC [7 February 1927], C. Col. It is not known why the work never materialized.

26 CE to ESC, 22 February 1933, C. Col.

27 ESC to Henry Prunières. 28 December 1925, C. Col.

28 Hans Kindler to ESC [July 1927], C. Col.

29 Hans Kindler to ESC, February 1927, C. Col. The "problematical Bridge" refers to the extreme technical demands of his string quartet, which caused negative reactions from some of the performers. Bridge revised the piece and "excised a good many of the things that required a super technique." He recommended giving it to the Pro Arte to premiere rather than the Rosé or Flonzaley Quartets so "steeped in the classics." Frank Bridge to ESC, 29 April 1927 and 1 August 1927, C. Col.

30 Hans Kindler to ESC [May 1927], C. Col.

31 ESC to Hans Kindler, 8 June 1927, C. Col.

32 Hans Kindler to ESC [1927], C. Col.

33 Hans Kindler to Miss Lawton, 23 December 1928, C. Col.

34 ESC to Hans Kindler, 6 January 1929, C. Col.

35 See *A New Era in Music* (Oakland, Calif.: Mills College, 1928), pages unnumbered.

36 ESC to ASC, 27 January 1929, C. Col.

37 ESC to ASC, 20 February 1924, C. Col.

38 ESC to ASC, 14 May 1932, C. Col.

39 ESC to CE, 7 February 1928, C. Col.

40 CE to ESC, 30 September 1930, C. Col.

41 ESC to CE, 2 March 1930, C. Col.

42 ESC to Robert Maas, 6 May 1930, C. Col.

43 ESC to Frank Bridge, 2 January 1934, C. Col.

44 Although Elizabeth received unoffical word of Claudel's actions in 1930 the actual presentation of the award did not occur until the following year. The ambassador

of France had conveyed the news to Engel, who passed the announcement on to her. See letters, ESC to Henry Prunières, 8 July and 12 July 1931, C. Col.

45 Anna Malipiero to ESC, 15 June 1930, C. Col.

46 Luther Noss, *Paul Hindemith in the United States* (Urbana: University of Illinois Press, 1989), p. 8ff. By September Kortschak was able to report to Elizabeth that he had had a good session with Hindemith on the interpretation of the music and that "Hindemith is very happy over it and terribly anxious that it might please you too." Hugo Kortschak to ESC, 1 September 1930, C. Col.

47 25 October 1930.

48 25 October 1930.

49 17 October 1930.

50 See letters of Prunières to ESC, 19 October and 27 November 1930, 1 January and 21 January 1931, C. Col.

51 Karleton Hackett, 13 October 1930.

CHAPTER FOURTEEN

1 ESC to Walter Fischer, n.d., C. Col.

2 Harvey Sachs, *Music in Fascist Italy* (London: Weidenfeld and Nicolson, 1987), p. 10. Sachs's book is the best comprehensive study of the subject available in English. For a thorough treatment of it in Italian see Fiamma Nicolodi, *Musica e musicisti nel ventennio fascista* (Fiesole, Italy: Discanto Edizioni, 1984). One of the virtues of Nicolodi's book is the substantial section containing transcripts of documents from various Italian archives, including the *Archivio centrale dello stato,* Rome.

3 ESC to Richard Hale, 19 January 1925, C. Col.

4 Casella, p. 131ff.

5 Casella to ESC, 22 August 1923, C. Col.

6 Casella to ESC, 13 July 1924, C. Col.

7 Malipiero to ESC, 21 August 1929, C. Col.

8 Ibid. Malipiero's second wife, Anna Wright, was English and functioned as his secretary and translator much of the time.

9 ESC, "Da Capo," p. 11.

10 "The Prisoner of Vittoriale," *Washington Times-Herald,* 6 March 1938, quoted in Butkovich, p. 105.

11 Ibid.

12 ESC, "Da Capo," p. 11.

13 GJ, box 6, file 5, 26 April 1915.

14 Scrapbook of 1931 European Tour, C. Col. The scrapbook contains translations of all the reviews from the German and Hungarian papers, possibly the work of Kortschak.

15 Hugo Kortschak to ESC, 4 November 1931, C. Col.

16 Scrapbook. It is amusing to note that the *Kölnisches Zeitung* identified her as "the parent of the former president."

17 Scrapbook.

18 Ibid.

19 Translated by Jay Rosenfeld and reprinted in the *Berkshire Evening Eagle,* 27 October 1931, C. Col.

20 Casella, p. 162.

21 ESC to Malipiero, 5 December 1926, C. Col.

22 For more detailed treatment of Coolidge's financing of the Malipiero and Prunières editions, see Cyrilla Barr, "The Musicological Legacy of Elizabeth Sprague Coolidge." *Journal of Musicology* 11 (1993), pp. 250–68.

23 In addition to his Lully editions Prunières produced numerous articles on Lully's works.

24 ESC to Malipiero, 7 September 1935, C. Col.

25 ESC to Malipiero, 5 October 1941, C. Col.

26 ESC to Malipiero [1940], FCV.

27 Frank Bridge to ESC, 9 November 1931, C. Col.

28 ESC, "Da Capo," p. 13.

29 ESC to Frank Bridge, 26 September 1935, C. Col.

30 Sachs, p. 94.

31 Ibid., p. 10.

32 Ibid., p. 182.

33 D'Annunzio to Mussolini, 27 May 1929, Nicolodi, p. 350.

34 For a list of the compositions presented to Mussolini, see *Appunto della Segreteria particulare di Mussolini,* 5 June 1931, Nicolodi, p. 352.

35 ESC to Malipiero, 26 November [1933], FCV.

36 Sachs, p. 132.

37 Anna Malipiero to ESC, 18 October 1945, C. Col.

38 See ESC to Santoliquido, 24 October 1928, 26 February, and 7 April 1932. See also Santoliquido to ESC, 2 April 1932, C. Col.

39 *Il Tevere* XVI–40, p. 3. I am indebted to Mary DiQuinzio for obtaining for me the complete text of the article. See also Sachs, p. 180ff.

40 Casella, p. 161.

41 ESC to CE, 25 January 1934. See also ESC to CE, 3 May 1934. "May I ask *en passant* whether you have ever concluded the purchase of that Berg manuscript for the Friends of Music, and if so when you would like me to pay my share of it, which I promised you last winter." C. Col.

42 CE to ESC [1934]. "[T]he Library share from the Friends of Music will be about $640." C. Col. The remaining $400 was paid by Coolidge.

43 Quoted in Butkovich, p. 106, n. 79.

44 Testimonial speech on the occasion of a dinner honoring ESC by the trustees of Mills College, Oakland, California, 19 April 1928, C. Col.

45 Review of Paris performance translated by Jay Rosenfeld, in *Berkshire Evening Eagle,* 27 November 1931, C. Col.

CHAPTER FIFTEEN

1 ESC to Frank Bridge, 6 May 1932, C. Col.

2 ESC to ASC, 6 March 1932, C. Col.

3 ESC to Frank Bridge, 6 May 1932. She also expressed fear of kidnapping at the time of her Mexican festival in 1929.

4 CE to ESC, 7 May 1934, C. Col.

5 ESC to CE, 8 May 1934, C. Col.

6 Oliver Strunk to ESC, 16 July 1934, C. Col.

7 ESC to Oliver Strunk, 19 November 1934, C. Col.

8 ESC to Oliver Strunk [January 1936], C. Col.

9 Oliver Strunk to ESC, 17 January 1936, C. Col.

10 ESC to CE, 1 May 1937, C. Col.

11 CE to ESC, 3 May 1937, C. Col.

12 CE to ESC, 25 January 1938, C. Col.

13 Hindemith wrote chapter 6 of the *Unterweisung im Tonsatz* on board the ship coming to America and completed the last chapter while he was in Washington. See Noss, pp. 17, 19.

14 Ibid., p. 16.

15 HJ, 9 April 1937.

16 Noss, p. 26.

17 HJ, 11 April 1937.

18 Noss, p. 19.

19 HJ, 10 April 1937.

20 HJ, 11 April 1937.

21 Ibid.

22 HJ, 29 April 1937.

23 Mary Howe, *Jottings,* p. 109ff.

24 Butkovich, pp. 117–20.

25 Ibid., p. 129.

26 ESC to Walter Bruce Howe, 3 February 1933, C. Col.

27 Mary Howe to ESC, 11 March 1936, C. Col.

28 Mary Howe to ESC, 17 February 1939, C. Col.

29 Mary Howe to ESC, 19 February 1939, C. Col.

30 Unidentified clipping, n.d., C. Col.

31 Mary Howe to ESC, 7 January 1940 and ESC to Mary Howe, 9 January 1949, C. Col.

32 Mabel Daniels to ESC, 3 July 1943, C. Col.

33 Amy Beach to ESC, 14 January 1921, C. Col.

34 ESC to Philip Hale [1924?], C. Col.

35 Ethyl Smyth to ESC, 14 May 1926, C. Col.

36 Mabel Daniels to ESC, 18 February 1934, C. Col.

37 Ellen Knight, *Charles Martin Loeffler: A Life Apart in American Music* (Urbana: University of Illinois Press, 1993), pp. 240–41.

38 ESC to CE, 26 January 1938, C. Col.

39 ESC to Gertrude Clarke Whittall, 4 April 1936, C. Col.

40 Gertrude Clarke Whittall to ESC, 6 December 1936, C. Col.

41 CE to ESC, 18 October 1937, C. Col.

42 ESC to CE, 25 October 1937, C. Col.

43 CE to ESC, 9 April 1934, C. Col.

44 Ibid.

45 Ibid.

46 ESC to Henry Eichheim, 14 April 1934, C. Col.

47 ESC to Katherine Savage, 4 June 1940, C. Col.

48 Bruce Howe to Dorothy Indenbaum, 1 June 1987. I am indebted to Ms. Indenbaum for this information and to Mr. Howe for permission to quote his account of the incident.

CHAPTER SIXTEEN

1 Articles of Incorporation, in letter of Edwin T. Rice to ESC, 14 November 1935, C. Col.

2 ESC to Willem Willeke, 20 February 1935, C. Col.

3 Willem Willeke to ESC, 2 March 1935, C. Col.

4 ESC to Willem Willeke, 5 March 1935, C. Col.

5 Ibid.

6 Ibid.

7 Typescript of Coolidge's speech to the board of the South Mountain Association, 4 September 1936, C. Col.

8 ESC to Edwin T. Rice, 15 August 1937, C. Col.

9 Ibid.

10 ESC to Hugo Kortschak, 15 December 1937, C. Col.

11 ESC to Charles W. Power, 1 June 1938, C. Col.

12 ESC to Willem Willeke, 15 August 1937, C. Col.

13 Kathleen Parlow to ESC, 27 August 1941, C. Col.

14 ESC to Charles W. Power, 18 November 1941, C. Col.

15 ASC to Sally Willeke, 27 October 1941, C. Col. Sprague would have known this from experience—he had performed with the South Mountain Quartet for the 1938 Berkshire Festival, when he played the added viola part in the Brahms Quintet in G Minor.

16 Ibid.

17 Kathleen Parlow to ESC, 17 August 1941, C. Col.

18 Samuel Colt to ESC, 9 June 1940, C. Col.

19 Samuel Colt to ESC, 24 October 1949, C. Col.

20 Ibid.

21 ESC to Mary Bristol, 2 August 1941, C. Col.

22 Willem Willeke to ESC, 9 September 1948, C. Col.

23 ESC to Samuel Colt, 6 March 1946, C. Col.

24 Aurelia Henry Reinhardt to ESC, 22 August 1933, C. Col.

25 ESC to Aurelia Henry Reinhardt, 30 August 1933, C. Col.

26 Lou Henry Hoover to Mrs. Baldwin, 14 August 1937, Lou Henry Hoover Papers, HHPL. I am indebted to Elise Kirk for materials concerning Mrs. Hoover's association with Coolidge.

27 ESC to Lou Henry Hoover, 14 July 1937, Lou Henry Hoover Papers, HHPL.

28 ESC to Lou Henry Hoover, 16 September 1939, Lou Henry Hoover Papers, HHPL.

29 Ibid.

30 Typescript report of Lou Henry Hoover to the Friends of Music, Lou Henry Hoover Papers, HHPL.

31 Ibid.

32 Luther Marchant to ESC, 28 July 1934, C. Col.

33 ESC to Luther Marchant, 4 August 1934, C. Col.

34 ESC to Luther Marchant, 30 July 1936, C. Col.

35 Ibid.

36 Luther Marchant to ESC, 24 May 1938, C. Col.

37 Ibid.

38 ESC to Harold Spivacke, 30 April 1950, C. Col.

CHAPTER SEVENTEEN

1 Leonardo Pinzauti, *Il Maggio Musicale fiorentine* (Florence, 1938), p. 64, quoted in Sachs, p. 186.

2 Sachs, p. 184.

3 Castelnuovo, *Una vita di musica,* quoted in Sachs, p. 14.

4 Ibid., p. 185.

5 Mario Castelnuovo to ESC, 25 November 1938, C. Col.

6 Darius Milhaud to ESC, 23 June [1940], C. Col. It appears that Pierre Monteaux also used his influence. See Roger Nichols, *Conversations with Madame Milhaud* (London/Winchester, 1996).

7 Luther Marchant to ESC, 4 November 1940, C. Col.

8 ESC to Darius Milhaud, 29 April 1942, C. Col.

9 Ernst Toch to ESC, 11 September 1938, C. Col.

10 ESC to Ernst Toch, 30 January 1940, C. Col.

11 Frank Bridge to ESC, 4 July 1939, C. Col.

12 Beth Britten, *My Brother Benjamin* (Abbotsbrook, Bourne End, Buckinghamshire, England: Kensal House, 1986), p. 29.

13 Ibid., p. 172.

14 Ethel Bridge to whom it may concern, 7 October 1942. Frank Bridge–Benjamin Britten Correspondence, BPLA.

15 Henry Eichheim to ESC, 16 December 1940, C. Col.

16 Gunnar Johansen to ESC, 19 May 1940, C. Col. For a treatment of the Pro Arte Quartet's history see Martha Blum, *The Pro Arte Quartet: 50 Years* (Madison, Wis.: The University of Wisconsin-Madison Anonymous Fund, 1991). I am indebted to Ms. Blum for assistance with the Pro Arte portion of this work.

17 Gunnar Johansen to ESC, 17 May 1940, C. Col.

18 Carl Bricken to ESC, 22 May 1940, C. Col.

19 ESC to Luther Marchant, 23 October 1940, C. Col.

20 Carl Bricken to ESC, 5 November 1940, C. Col.

21 ESC to Carl Bricken, 10 November 1940, C. Col.

22 ESC to Laurent Halleux, 8 December 1940, C. Col.

23 Warwick Evans to Carl Bricken, 26 May [1941], Pro Arte files, University of Wisconsin Archives.

24 ESC to Carl Bricken, 6 November 1940, C. Col.

25 Carl Bricken to ESC, 8 November 1940, C. Col.

26 Henri Temianka to ESC, 28 June 1945, C. Col.

27 ESC to Carl Bricken, 3 June 1941, C. Col.

28 Darius Milhaud to ESC, [1940], C. Col.

CHAPTER EIGHTEEN

1 Typescript of speech before broadcast, 7 August 1936, C. Col.

2 Boris Schwarz, *Great Masters of the Violin* (New York: Simon and Schuster, 1983), p. 511.

3 Blum, p. 1.

4 ESC to Nicolas Moldavan, 20 January 1941, C. Col.

5 Carol June Bradley, *American Music Librarianship: A Biographical and Historical Survey* (New York: Greenwood Press, 1990), pp. 56–57.

6 Margaret Chanler to ESC, 28 January 1937, C. Col.

7 Schwarz, p. 393.

8 Alexander Schneider to ESC, 16 November 1944, C. Col.

9 Alexander Schneider to ESC, 15 May 1948, C. Col.

10 Alexander Schneider to ESC, 4 January 1948, C. Col.

11 Alexander Schneider to ESC, 9 September 1948, C. Col.

12 ESC to Arthur Judson, 16 January 1925, C. Col.

13 ESC to William Popper, 25 April 1937, C. Col.

14 ESC to Howard Hinners, 29 December 1937, C. Col.

15 Private H. Carlisle Estes to E. Power Biggs, 11 November 1943, American Guild of Organists Library, Boston University.

16 Unsigned letter, to Mills College, n.d., C. Col.

17 ESC to Juliet Noehren, 6 February 1944, C. Col.

18 ESC to Carolyn Cushing, 4 March 1936, C. Col.

19 Bradley, pp. 46–47.

20 ESC to ASC, 6 November 1938, C. Col.

21 See also Aaron Copland and Vivian Perlis, *Copland since 1943* (New York: St. Martin's Press, 1989).

22 ESC to Martha Graham, 8 August 1941, C. Col.

23 Martha Graham to ESC, 2 August 1942, C. Col.

24 Erick Hawkins to ESC, 4 August 1942, C. Col.

25 I am grateful to Philip Tacka for sharing his research on the creation of *Appalachian Spring.*

26 Martha Graham, 8 August 1942, C. Col.

27 ESC to Martha Graham, 8 August 1942, C. Col.

28 Martha Graham. *Blood Memory* (New York: Doubleday, 1991), p. 228.

29 Martha Graham to Harold Spivacke, 25 October 1943, C. Col.

30 Martha Graham to ESC, 16 January 1944, C. Col.

31 ESC to Martha Graham, 19 January 1944, C. Col.

32 Ibid.

33 Quoted in Agnes De Mille, *Martha: The Life and Work of Martha Graham* (New York: Random House, 1991), pp. 260–61.

34 Martha Graham to Paul Hindemith, 19 June 1944, C. Col.

35 Noss, p. 122.

36 Harold Spivacke to Martha Graham, 7 July 1944, C. Col.

37 Graham, p. 230.

38 Quoted in De Mille, p. 261.

39 Harold Spivacke to Martha Graham, 2 November 1944, C. Col.

40 Carlos Chávez to ESC, 6 January 1950, C. Col.

41 Quoted in De Mille, p. 268.

42 Martha Graham to ESC, 2 August 1943, C. Col.

43 Unidentified newspaper clipping, C. Col.

CHAPTER NINETEEN

1 ESC to Henry Spalding, 11 December 1948, C. Col.

2 ESC to Ernst Toch, 24 August 1942, C. Col.

3 ESC to CE [January 1929], C. Col.

4 ESC to CE, 30 March 1929, C. Col.

5 CE to ESC, 16 August 1943, C. Col.

6 Engel's death certificate reports that he died of natural causes: hypertensive cardiovascular disease, coronary arteriosclerosis and chronic myocarditis. Certificate of Death, No. 10811, Bureau of Vital Records and Statistics, Department of Health, City of New York.

7 Carl Engel, "Some Letters to a Namesake," *Musical Quarterly* 28 (1942), pp. 337–79.

8 In Putnam, "Tributes to Carl Engel," p. 139.

9 Harold Bauer, "Carl Engel, July 21, 1883–May 6, 1944," *Musical Quarterly* 30 (1944), p. 249.

10 ESC to William Kroll, 20 May 1944, C. Col.

11 CE to ESC, 14 April 1926, C. Col.

12 ESC to Lillian Littlehales, 17 March 1945, C. Col.

13 ESC to Gladys Caldwell, 17 March 1945, C. Col.

14 ESC to Lillian Littlehales, 17 March 1945, C. Col.

15 Harold Spivacke to ESC, 21 October 1951, C. Col.

16 ESC to Florence Gillette, 1 August 1945, C. Col.

17 CE to ESC, 24 May 1937, C. Col.

18 ESC to CE, 26 May 1937, C. Col.

19 Edward Weeks to ESC, 4 April 1951, C. Col.

20 ESC to Persis Coleman, 12 January 1930, C. Col.

21 ESC to Mrs. E. M. Tenney, 22 March 1950, C. Col.

22 Ethel Bridge to ESC, 3 December 1939, C. Col.

23 Frank Bridge to ESC, 10 October 1941, 21 February 1940, and 11 March 1940, C. Col.

24 ESC to Ethel Bridge, 16 September 1939, C. Col.

25 ESC to Ethel Bridge, 29 December 1940, C. Col.

26 Frank Bridge to ESC, 18 May 1940, C. Col.

27 ESC to Ethel Bridge, 31 March 1941, C. Col.

28 ESC to Ethel Bridge, 5 June 1941, C. Col.

29 ESC to Gladys Caldwell, 25 May 1942, C. Col.

30 ESC to Darius Milhaud, 28 February1942, C. Col.

31 "Work of Coolidge Foundation," unsigned article in *New York Times*, 5 February 1956. Berkshire Athenaeum, Local History File.

32 On Frankfurter's position see Leonard Baker, *Brandeis and Frankfurter: A Dual Biography* (New York: Harper and Row, 1984), pp. 256–71.

33 "Albert Sprague Coolidge," *Harvard Class of 1915, 15th Annual Report* (Cambridge: Tolman University Press, 1930).

34 Willison, p. 178.

35 Robert Cooke, Albert Sprague Coolidge obituary, clipping from *Boston Globe* [August 1977].

36 Mrs. W. R. Hare to ESC, 8 February 1943, C. Col.

37 ESC to William. T. Councilman, 12 December 1921, C. Col.

38 "Albert Sprague Coolidge," *Harvard University 25th Annual Report* (Cambridge: Cosmos Press, 1940), p. 162.

39 For a discussion of Sprague's scientific research and publications see "Albert Sprague Coolidge, Memorial Minute," adopted by the Faculty of Arts and Sciences, Harvard University, 10 April 1979. Reprinted from the *Harvard University Gazette* 74, no. 34 (25 May 1979). See also Hubert M. James and Albert Sprague Coolidge, "The Ground State of the Hydrogen Molecule," *Journal of Chemical Physics* 1 (1933), pp. 825–832.

40 Bertha Palmer to Ernst Toch, 19 January 1944, C. Col.

41 Henri Temianka, "Elizabeth Sprague Coolidge," unpublished typescript, 1 July 1984, C. Col.

42 Ibid.

43 Henri Temianka to ESC, 27 October 1944, C. Col.

CHAPTER TWENTY

1 ESC to Ernst Toch, 3 February 1945, C. Col.

2 ESC's will, codicil of 28 June 1952, SMLA, Treasurer's Records, 5-B, series IV, box 386, folder 266.

3 ESC to Henry Spalding, 23 April 1949, C. Col.

4 Bertha McCulloch to Harold Spivacke [1950], C. Col.

5 ESC to Alexander Schneider, 15 September 1944, AS Col.

6 Mary Bristol to ESC, 20 August 1940, C. Col.

7 *Peter Grimes* was actually commissioned by the Koussevitzky Foundation and premiered at Sadler's Wells in London on 7 June 1945.

8 Alexanian was a renowned cellist and teacher, and a long-time associate and friend of Casals. Jointly they produced the *Traité théorique et pratique du violoncelle.*

9 Interview with Alexander Schneider [1950], unidentified typescript, p. 1, AS Col. Hereafter, Schneider interview.

10 Schneider interview, p. 2.

11 Ibid.

12 Ibid. Casals was living in Spartan conditions, so the musicians took up a collection to give him a refrigerator as well. Also his "cello had not been cleaned or worked on for years; its condition was near-ramshackle, the fine old instrument being held together with little more than baling-wire and spit: the Maître was using a piece of matchstick to steady the pitch of one string, and a scrap of paper to raise one side of the bridge." See Paul Moor, "Casals at Prades," *Theater Arts* (October 1950), p. 23.

13 Schneider interview, p. 3.

14 Ivor Newton, *At the Piano* (London: Hamish Hamilton, 1966), p. 147.

15 Schneider interview, p. 3.

16 "I am very busy getting the Fulbright Bill support to organize a Bach Festival next summer. The Fulbright Bill will enable some exceptional young musicians to go to Europe to study, financing this with blocked money in Europe." Alexander Schneider to ESC, 18 October 1949, AS Col.

17 Alexander Schneider to ESC, 10 January 1949, AS Col.

18 Moor, p. 23.

19 ESC to Alexander Schneider, 5 February 1949, AS Col.

20 Harold Spivacke to Pablo Casals, 7 October 1949, AS Col.

21 Alexander Schneider to Pablo Casals, 7 September 1950, AS Col.

22 ESC to Alexander Schneider, n.d., AS Col.

23 It is surprising that Lillian Littlehales, Elizabeth's close friend, makes no mention of either Coolidge or Schneider in her book on Casals. While Forsee and Kahn do speak of Schneider, they overlook Coolidge entirely.

24 Alexander Schneider to ESC, 26 May 1953, AS Col.

25 Alexander Schneider to ESC, 19 June 1953, C. Col.

26 ESC to Alexander Schneider, 19 May 1953, C. Col.

27 ESC to Alexander Schneider, 3 August 1953, C. Col.

28 Harold Spivacke to ESC, 2 November 1953, C. Col.

29 Gian Francesco Malipiero to Spivacke, 23 November 1953, FCV.

30 ASC to Gian Francesco Malipiero, 7 December 1953, FCV.

31 Anna Malipiero to ESC, 29 March 1946. See also 8 June 1952. C. Col.

32 Anna Malipiero to ESC, 28 September 1953, C. Col.

33 Harold Spivacke to Gian Francesco Malipiero, 9 December 1953, FCV.

34 Interview with Maria Giulia Malipiero, third wife and widow of Gian Francesco, 20 June 1987.

35 Gian Francesco Malipiero to ASC, 15 April 1955, C. Col.

36 Harold Spivacke to Gian Francesco Malipiero, 3 March 1954, FCV. The work was premiered at the thirteenth Festival of Chamber Music at Pittsfield on 21 August 1954.

37 Anna Malipiero to Harold Spivacke, 24 March 1956, C. Col.

38 ESC, undated typescript of address to a meeting of the National Federation of Music Clubs, C. Col.

39 ASC to Gian Francesco Malipiero, 7 December 1953, FCV.

CHAPTER TWENTY-ONE

1 Anon. to ESC, n.d., C. Col.

2 ESC to Hortense Berry, 6 October 1940, C. Col.

3 Although Elizabeth left no written record of disappointment, Engel was outspoken in his criticism of Yale for taking so long to honor her and especially of Harvard for never recognizing her with an honorary degree.

4 "We always said that grandmother should have run a school for boys." Elizabeth Coolidge Winship, interview, 20 December 1988.

5 ESC to Thomas King, 16 September 1922, C. Col.

6 ESC to the Federal Communications Commission, 1 July 1945, C. Col.

7 ESC to Bruno David Ussher, 22 April 1937, C. Col.

8 ESC to CE, 14 May 1932, C. Col.

9 ESC to CE, 7 February 1928, C. Col.

10 *Bulletin of the Friends of Music, Library of Congress,* 15 February 1939, reprint, *Berkshire Eagle,* 3 April 1939, C. Col.

11 Undated typescript, C. Col.

12 Mabel Daniels to ESC, 18 April 1951, C. Col.

13 ESC to Mabel Daniels, 24 April 1951, C. Col.

14 ESC to CE, 23 March 1926, C. Col.

15 Quoted in *Berkshire Eagle,* 27 January 1956, and *New York Times,* 1 February 1956, *Berkshire Eagle* files, Pittsfield, Mass.

16 *Information Bulletin, Library of Congress,* vol. 15, 6 February 1956.

17 *Berkshire Eagle,* undated clipping, *Berkshire Eagle* files, Pittsfield, Mass.

18 Baker, *Brandeis and Frankfurter,* p. 453.

19 "Dr. Sprague Coolidge Obituary," *Boston Globe,* 1 September 1977, C. Col.

20 *Berkshire Eagle,* undated clipping, C. Col.

21 ASC letter to *Berkshire Eagle,* 27 January 1956, *Berkshire Eagle* files.

22 ESC to Alexander Schneider, 5 February 1949, C. Col.

23 Harold Spivacke to Anna Malipiero, 26 January 1954, FCV.

24 John Kirkpatrick, ed. *Charles E. Ives Memos* (National Institute of Arts and Letters, 1972; New York: Norton paperback, 1991), p. 99.

25 Ibid., p. 100.

26 Henry Eichheim to ESC [1921], C. Col.

27 Sketch of reply is blue-penciled "Not sent." *C. E. Ives Memos,* p. 100, n. 8.

28 Ibid., p. 99.

29 Quoted in David Wooldridge, *From the Steeples and the Mountains* (New York: Knopf, 1972), p. 166.

30 Ibid., p. 172. The Charles Sprague to whom Wooldridge refers is not related to Elizabeth.

31 Transcription from the Recorded Sound Archive, London.

32 ESC to Tibor Harsanyi, 28 July 1930, C. Col.

33 Newton, *At the Piano,* p. 171.

34 Eric Thacher Clarke, *Music in Everyday Life* (New York: Norton, 1935), p. 14.

35 Typescript, October 1931, C. Col.

Bibliography

SECONDARY SOURCES

Agajanian, Shaakeh S. *Sonnets from the Portuguese and the Love Sonnet Tradition.* New York: Philosophical Library, 1985.

"Albert Sprague Coolidge." *Harvard University 25th Annual Report.* Cambridge: Cosmos Press, 1940.

"Albert Sprague Coolidge, Memorial Minute adopted by the Faculty of Arts and Sciences, Harvard University; April 10, 1979." *Harvard University Gazette* 74 (25 May 1979): unnumbered.

Aldrich, Richard. "Old English Airs Given at Festival." *New York Times,* 30 October 1925.

———. "Open Washington's New Music Hall." *New York Times,* 29 October 1925.

———. "Play Old Masters as Festival Ends." *New York Times,* 31 October 1925.

Ammer, Christine. *Unsung: A History of Women in American Music.* Westport, Conn.: Greenwood Press, 1980.

Anderson, Dorothy M. *The Era of the Summer Estates: Swampscott, Massachusetts, 1870–1940.* Canaan, N.H.: Phoenix Publishing, 1985.

Andreas, A. T. *History of Chicago from the Earliest Period to the Present Time.* 3 vols. Chicago: A. T. Andreas Press, 1886.

Andrews, Wayne. *Battle for Chicago.* New York: Harcourt Brace and Co., 1946.

Anschutz, Edward Pollock. *Sexual Ills and Diseases.* Philadelphia: Boericke and Tafel, 1896.

Antler, Joyce. *Lucy Sprague Mitchell: The Making of a Modern Woman.* New Haven: Yale University Press, 1987.

Architectural Record (1896). Great American Architects Series, no. 3, part 1. "Shepley, Rutan and Coolidge," 12–15.

Atherton, Percy Lee. "Boston Days (1909–1922): Some Engeliana." In *A Birthday Offering to C. E.,* edited by Gustave Reese, 27–34. New York: G. Schirmer, 1943.

Atwood, Elijah Francis. *Ye Atte Wode Annals.* Sisseton, S. Dak.: Atwood Publishing Co., 1928.

Atwood, Henry S. *The Atwood Family: AD 1599 to AD 1909.* Privately printed [1909].

Baker, Leonard. *Brandeis and Frankfurter: A Dual Biography.* New York: Harper and Row, 1984.

Baker, Liva. *The Justice from Beacon Hill.* New York: Harper Collins, 1991.

Baketel, Harrie Sheridan. *The Treatment of Syphilis.* New York: Macmillan, 1920.

Bancroft, Herbert Howe. *The Book of the Fair.* Chicago: Bancroft Co., 1893.

Banfield, Steven. "'Too Much of Albion'? Mrs. Coolidge and Her British Connections." *American Music* 4: (1986) 61–88.

Barr, Cyrilla. *The Coolidge Legacy.* Washington: Library of Congress, 1997.

———. "The Faerie Queene and the Archangel: The Correspondence of Elizabeth Sprague Coolidge and Carl Engel." *American Music* 15 (1997): 159–82.

———. "The Musicological Legacy of Elizabeth Sprague Coolidge." *Journal of Musicology* 11 (1993): 250–68.

———. "A Style of Her Own: The Patronage of Elizabeth Sprague Coolidge." In *Cultivating Music in America: Women Patrons and Activists since 1860,* edited by Ralph P. Locke and Cyrilla Barr, 185–203. Berkeley: University of California Press, 1997.

———, annotator. "Coolidge on Gowns, Dedications, and American Chauvinism." In *Cultivating Music in America: Women Patrons and Activists since 1860,* edited by Ralph P. Locke and Cyrilla Barr, 204–8. Berkeley: University of California Press, 1997.

Barzun, Jacques. *Music in American Life.* Bloomington: Indiana University Press, 1962.

Bauer, Harold. "Carl Engel, July 21, 1883–May 6, 1944." *Musical Quarterly* 30 (1944): 249–54.

Bedford, William. "Elizabeth Sprague Coolidge: The Education of a Patron of Chamber Music: the Early Years." Ph.D. diss., University of Missouri, 1964.

———. "A Musical Apprentice: Amy Lowell to Carl Engel." *Musical Quarterly* 58 (1972): 519–42.

Berg, A. Scott. *Goldwyn: A Biography.* New York: Alfred A. Knopf, 1989.

Berkshire Festivals of Chamber Music, 1918–1938. Pittsfield, Mass.: South Mountain, 1938.

Bissell, Arthur. "The Original Gold Coast." *Chicagoan* (25 August 1928): 9–13.

Block, Adrienne Fried, and Carol Neuls-Bates. *Women in American Music: A Bibliography of Music and Literature.* Westport, Conn.: Greenwood Press, 1979.

Block, Geoffrey. *Charles Ives: A Bio-Bibliography.* Westport, Conn.: Greenwood Press, 1988.

Blum, Martha. *The Pro Arte Quartet: 50 Years.* Madison, Wis.: The University of Wisconsin-Madison Anonymous Fund, 1991.

Boltwood, Edward. *The History of Pittsfield, Massachusetts, 1876–1916.* Pittsfield: The Eagle Printing and Binding Co., 1916.

Borowski, Felix. "Coolidge Chamber Festival." *Christian Science Monitor,* 25 October 1930.

Bowers, Jane, and Judith Tick, eds. *Women Making Music: The Western Art Tradition, 1150–1950.* Urbana: University of Illinois Press, 1987.

Bradley, Carol June. *American Music Librarianship: A Biographical and Historical Survey.* New York: Greenwood Press, 1990.

Brandt, Allan M. *No Magic Bullet: A Social History of Venereal Disease in the United States since 1880.* New York: Oxford University Press, 1985.

Bray, Trevor. "Frank Bridge and Mrs. Coolidge." *Music and Musicians* 26 (1977–78): 28–30.

Bremner, Robert H. *American Philanthropy.* Chicago History of American Civilization Series. Edited by Daniel J. Boorstin. Chicago: University of Chicago Press, 1960.

Brigham, William E. "Mrs. Frederick S. Coolidge Offers a Building for Music." *Boston Transcript,* 5 December 1924.

Britten, Beth. *My Brother Benjamin.* Abbotsbrook, Bourne End, Buckinghamshire, England: Kensal House, 1986.

Brooks, Kate Scott. "Schubert Opus in Musical Festival." *Washington Herald,* 31 October 1925.

Burg, David F. *Chicago's White City of 1893.* Lexington: University of Kentucky Press, 1976.

Butkovich, Sister Mary Virginia. "Hans Kindler, 1892–1949." Ph.D. diss., Catholic University of America, 1965.

Carnegie, Andrew. *The Gospel of Wealth and Other Timely Essays.* Edited by Edward F. Kirkland. Cambridge: Harvard University, Belknap Press, 1962.

Casella, Alfredo. *Music in My Time.* Translated and edited by Spencer Norton. Norman: University of Oklahoma Press, 1955.

A Century of Progress—Official Guide Book of the Fair, 1933. Chicago: Century of Progress, 1933.

Chamberlain, George W. "The Early New England Coolidges and Some of Their Descendants." *New England Historical and Genealogical Register* 77 (1923): 270–304.

———. "Records of the Coolidges of Cambridgeshire, England." *New England Historical and Genealogical Register* 80 (1926): 401–15.

———. "Some Records of the Vermont Coolidges." *New England Historical and Genealogical Register* 78 (1924): 28–33.

———. *The Spragues of Malden, Massachusetts.* Boston: privately printed, 1923.

Chase, Gilbert. *America's Music from the Pilgrims to the Present.* 3d ed. Urbana: University of Illinois Press, 1987.

Chicago, Highlights in History. Chicago: Chicago Historical Society, n.d.

Chotzinoff, Samuel. *Toscanini: An Intimate Portrait.* New York: Alfred A. Knopf, 1956.

Clarke, Eric Thacher. *Music in Everyday Life.* New York: Norton, 1935.

Clark, Herma. *The Elegant Eighties When Chicago Was Young.* Chicago: A. C. McClurg, 1941.

Coolidge, Albert Sprague. "The Function of the National Executive Committee." *American Socialist Monthly* 5 (1936): 12–16.

Coolidge, Elizabeth Sprague. "Da Capo." A paper read before the Mother's Club, Cambridge, 13 March 1951. Washington: Library of Congress, 1952.

———. "The Order of the Garden." *Atlantic Monthly* 107 (1922): 771–77.

Coolidge, Emma Downing. *Descendants of John and Mary Coolidge.* Boston: Wright and Potter, 1930.

Copland, Aaron, and Vivian Perlis. *Copland since 1943.* New York: St. Martin's Press, 1989.

Corredor, José Maria. *Conversations with Casals.* Translated by André Mangeot. New York: E. P. Dutton, 1957.

Cromie, Robert. *The Great Chicago Fire.* Introduction by Paul M. Angle. New York: McGraw Hill, 1958.

Curti, Merle. "The History of American Philanthropy as a Field of Research." *American Historical Review* 62 (January 1957): 352–63.

Cushing, Harvey. "William Thomas Councilman." In *The Saturday Club: A Century Completed, 1920–1956.* Edited by Edward W. Forbes and John H. Finley, Jr. Boston: Houghton Mifflin, 1956.

Damrosch, Walter. *My Musical Life.* New York: Charles Scribner's Sons, 1940.

Dart, Susan. *The Friday Club: The First Hundred Years, 1887–1987.* Chicago: The Friday Club, 1987.

Dedmon, Emmett. *Fabulous Chicago.* New York: Athenaeum, 1981.

De Mille, Agnes. *Martha: The Life and Work of Martha Graham.* New York: Random House, 1991.

DeSantis, Mila. "Elizabeth Sprague Coolidge e i concerti di musica italiana contemporanea." *La Musica* 4 (September 1988): 49–59.

Douglas, Ann. *The Feminization of American Culture.* New York: Alfred A. Knopf, 1977.

Dreiss, Joseph G. *Gari Melchers, His Works in the Belmont Collection.* Edited by Richard S. Reid. Charlottesville: University Press of Virginia, 1984.

Dubos, René, and Jean Dubos. *The White Plague, Tuberculosis, Man and Society.* New Brunswick: Rutgers University Press, 1987.

Duncan, Hugh Dalziel. *The Rise of Chicago as a Literary Center from 1885–1920: A Sociological Essay in American Culture.* Totowa, N.J.: The Bedminster Press, 1964.

Edgell, George H. "Charles Allerton Coolidge." In *The Saturday Club: A Century Completed 1920–1956,* edited by Edward W. Forbes and John H. Finley, Jr. Boston: Houghton Mifflin, 1956.

Ehrenreich, Dr. "Neue Musik im alten Römer." *Gross-Frankfurter Volksstimme,* 26 October 1931.

Ellmann, Richard. *Oscar Wilde.* New York: Alfred A. Knopf, 1986.

Engel, Carl. "Charles Martin Loeffler." *Musical Quarterly* 11 (1925): 311–30.

———. "Concert A.D. 2025 in the Library of Congress." In *Essays Offered to Herbert Putnam,* 140–45. New Haven: Yale University Press, 1929.

———. "The Eagle is Learning to Sing." Typescript, C. Col., n.d.

———. "George W. Chadwick." *Musical Quarterly* 10 (July 1924): 438–547.

———. "Some Letters to a Namesake." *Musical Quarterly* 28 (1942): 337–79.

———. "View and Reviews." *Musical Quarterly* 8 (October 1922): 611–32.

———. "What Great Music Owes to Women." *Etude* 97 (November 1929): 797.

Entrikin, Isabelle. *Sarah Josepha Hale and Godey's Lady's Book.* Philadelphia: Lancaster Press, 1946.

Epstein, Dena J. "Frederick Stock and American Music." *American Music* 10 (1992): 20–52.

"Europe Will Hear Coolidge Concerts." *Musical America* 51 (September 1931): 4.

Forsee, Aylesa. *Pablo Casals: Cellist for Freedom.* New York: Thomas Y. Crowell Co., 1965.

Forster, Margaret. *Elizabeth Barrett Browning: A Biography.* New York: Doubleday, 1988.

Frederic Shurtleff Coolidge: Some Letters Printed in Loving Memory. Boston: George H. Ellis, 1917.

French, Florence. *Music and Musicians in Chicago.* Chicago: published by the author, 1899.

Garland, Joseph E. *Boston's North Shore: Being an Account of Life Among the Noteworthy, Fashionable, Wealthy, Eccentric and Ordinary 1823–1890.* Boston: Little Brown, 1978.

Gilbert, Paul, and Charles Lee Bryson. *Chicago and Its Makers.* Chicago: Felix Mendelsohn Publishers, 1929.

Gilman, Lawrence. "St. Francis Set to Music." *New York Herald Tribune,* 24 November 1929.

Glessner, John J. *Some Friends of Mine Among the Earlier Members of the Commercial Club.* Chicago: privately printed, n.d.

Goode, James M. *Best Addresses: A Century of Washington's Distinguished Apartment Houses.* Washington, D.C.: Smithsonian Institution Press, 1988.

Graham, Martha. *Blood Memory.* New York: Doubleday, 1991.

Gunn, Glenn Dillard. "Chicago Festival of Chamber Music Set for October 12–16." *Chicago Herald Examiner,* 16 June 1930.

———. "Chicago Owes Much to Mrs. Coolidge for the Music Festival." *Chicago Herald Examiner,* 17 October 1930.

———. "Mme. Averino Stirs Public Response in Pizzetti Songs." *Chicago Herald Examiner,* 15 October 1930.

Hackett, Karleton. "Mrs. Coolidge Gives Feast to Music Lovers." *Chicago Post,* 13 October 1930.

Hallowell, Davis, M.D. *Hearing and Deafness: A Guide for Laymen.* New York: Murray Hill Books, 1947.

Handbook of the World's Columbian Exposition. Chicago: Rand, McNally and Co., 1893.

Heilbrun, Carolyn G. *Writing a Woman's Life.* New York: W. W. Norton, 1988.

Herter, Norton, M.D. "Haydn in America." *Musical Quarterly* 18 (April 1932): 309–37.

Hindmarsh, Paul. *Frank Bridge: A Thematic Catalogue, 1900–1941.* London: Faber Music, in association with Faber and Faber, 1983.

Hines, Thomas S. *Burnham of Chicago: Architect and Planner.* Chicago: University of Chicago Press, 1979.

History of the Class of 1859, Yale College. New Haven: Tuttle, Morehouse and Taylor, 1914.

Horowitz, Joseph. *Understanding Toscanini.* New York: Alfred A. Knopf, 1987.

"The House of Dr. F. S. Coolidge, Pittsfield, Massachusetts." Photographic plates. *Architectural Review* 13 (1906).

Howe, Mary. *Jottings.* Washington, D.C.: privately printed, 1959.

Hoyne, Temple S., ed. *Venereal and Urinary Diseases.* 2nd ed. Chicago: Halsey Bros., 1894.

Hyde, James Nevins, M.D., and Frank Hugh Montgomery, M.D. *A Manual of Syphilis and the Venereal Diseases.* Philadelphia: W. B. Saunders and Co., 1900.

James, Hubert M., and Albert Sprague Coolidge. "The Ground State of the Hydrogen Molecule." *Journal of Chemical Physics* 1 (1933): 825–32.

Jezic, Diane Peacock. *The Musical Migration and Ernst Toch.* Ames: Iowa State University Press, 1989.

Kahn, Albert A. *Joys and Sorrows: Reflections by Pablo Casals.* New York: Simon & Schuster, 1970.

King, Nick. "Further Protection for South Mountain." *Berkshire Eagle,* 23 August 1973, p. 19.

———. "South Mountain Gets Protection." *Berkshire Eagle,* 22 August 1973.

Kirk, David. *Pablo Casals: A Biography.* New York: Holt, Rinehart and Winston, 1974.

Kirkpatrick, John, ed. *Charles E. Ives Memos.* New York: National Institute of Arts and Letters, 1972; Norton paperback reprint, 1991.

Knight, Ellen. *Charles Martin Loeffler: A Life Apart in American Music.* Urbana: University of Illinois Press, 1993.

Krenek, Ernst. "America's Influence on its Emigré Composers." *Perspectives of New Music* (Spring-Summer 1970): 115.

Lauber, John. *The Inventions of Mark Twain: A Biography.* New York: Hill and Wang, 1990.

Leavitt, Donald. "Mrs Coolidge Goes to Washington." *Chamber Music Magazine* (Spring 1985).

Lerner, Gerda. *The Majority Finds Its Past: Placing Women in History.* Oxford: Oxford University Press, 1979.

Levine, Lawrence W. *Highbrow/Lowbrow: The Emergence of Cultural Hierarchy in America.* Cambridge: Harvard University Press, 1988.

Lewis, Lloyd. *Chicago: The History of Its Reputation. Part I. Introduction* and *Part II* by Henry Justin Smith. New York: Harcourt Brace and Co., 1929.

Lichtenwanger, William, ed. *Oscar Sonneck and American Music.* Urbana: University of Illinois Press, 1983.

Littlehales, Lillian. *Pablo Casals.* New York: W. W. Norton, 1948.

Locke, Ralph P., and Cyrilla Barr, eds. *Cultivating Music in America: Women Patrons and Activists since 1860.* Berkeley: University of California Press, 1997.

Longstreet, Stephen. *Chicago: 1866–1919.* New York: David McKay Co., 1973.

Lovejoy, Evelyn Wood. *History of Royalton, Vermont with Family Genealogies.* Burlington, Vt.: privately printed, 1911.

Mahan, Sheila A. "South Mountain's Driving Force." *Berkshire Eagle,* 28 August 1981.

Martin, George. *The Damrosch Dynasty.* Boston: Houghton Mifflin, 1983.

Mason, Daniel Gregory. "The Berkshire Festival of Chamber Music." *New Music Review* 17 (1918): 372–75.

———. *Music in My Life.* Westport, Conn.: Greenwood Press, 1970; reprint of original Macmillan edition, 1938.

Mayer, Harold M., and Richard C. Wade. *Chicago: Growth of a Metropolis.* Chicago: University of Chicago Press, 1969.

McCarthy, Kathleen D. *Women's Culture, American Philanthropy and Art, 1830–1930.* Chicago: University of Chicago Press, 1991.

Menzies, Ian. "Coolidge's Famed Music Lecture." *Boston Daily Globe,* 28 January 1960.

Milhaud, Darius. *Notes Without Music: An Autobiography.* New York: Alfred A. Knopf, 1953.

Milinowski, Marta. *Teresa Carreño: "By the Grace of God."* New Haven: Yale University Press, 1940; reprinted by Da Capo Press, 1977.

Miller, Margo. "Musical Virtuosity in the Physics Lab." *Berkshire Eagle,* 29 January 1960.

Mitchell, Lucy Sprague. *Two Lives: The Story of Wesley Claire Mitchell and Myself.* New York: Simon and Schuster, 1953.

Moers, Ellen. *Literary Women.* London: The Women's Press, 1978.

Moor, Paul. "Casals at Prades," *Theater Arts* (1950): 21–24.

Moore, Edward. "Music Festival Offers Lively Italian Songs, Not Exactly Merry." *Chicago Tribune,* 15 October 1930.

Morrison, Marjorie. "Homage to Elizabeth Sprague Coolidge." *Peabody Conservatory Bulletin* (May 1937): 13–16.

Mrs. Sylvanus Reed's English, French, and German Boarding and Day School for Young Ladies. New York: Baker and Godwin, 1864, 1870, 1872, 1873, 1879, and 1883.

The Musical Woman: An International Perspective. Edited by Judith Lang Zaimont, Catherine Overhauser, and Jane Gottlieb. Westport, Conn.: Greenwood Press,1983.

Neuls-Bates, Carol, ed. *Women in Music: An Anthology of Source Readings from the Middle Ages to the Present.* New York: Harper and Row, 1982.

New England Historical and Genealogical Society. *New England Historical and Genealogical Register.* Boston: New England Historical and Genealogical Society, 1909.

Newton, Ivor. *At the Piano.* London: Hamish Hamilton, 1966.

Newton, William Monroe. *History of Barnard, Vermont.* 2 vols. Montpelier, Vt.: Vermont Historical Society, 1928.

Nicolodi, Fiamma. *Musica e musicisti nel ventennio fascista.* Fiesole, Italy: Discanto Edizioni, 1984.

Noss, Luther. *Paul Hindemith in the United States.* Urbana: University of Illinois Press, 1989.

Oakley, Ann. *Subject Women.* New York: Pantheon Books, 1981.

Olmsted, Stanley. "Season's First Founder's Day Concert Given." *Washington Herald,* 31 October 1930.

O'Meara, Alice. "Mrs. Willem Willeke Carries on South Mountain Tradition." *Berkshire Eagle,* 9 July 1854, p. 10.

Orear, G. W. *Commercial and Architectural Chicago Illustrated.* Chicago: 1887, pp. 217–18.

Otis, Philo Adams. *The Chicago Symphony Orchestra: Its Organization, Growth, and Development, 1891–1924.* Chicago: Clayton F. Summy Co., 1925.

———. "The Development of Music in Chicago, An Historical Sketch." *Papers and Proceedings of the Music Teachers National Association for 1920,* 109–27. Hartford: Music Teachers National Association, 1921.

Pachter, Marc, ed. *Telling Lives: The Biographer's Art.* Washington, D.C.: New Republic Books/National Gallery of Art, 1979.

Parker, Henry Taylor. "From the Berkshires Even Unto Washington." *Boston Evening Transcript,* 30 October 1925.

Patrick, Hugh T., and William Allen Pusey. "Sanger Brown." In *Proceedings of the Institute of Medicine of Chicago* 7, no. 5 (15 May 1928): 52–54.

Pendle, Karen, ed. *Women and Music: A History.* Bloomington: Indiana University Press, 1991.

Perry, Pamela J. "Premieres of Sibelius and Others in the Connecticut Hills." In *Cultivating Music in America,* edited by Ralph Locke and Cyrilla Barr, 124–28. Berkeley and Los Angeles: University of California Press, 1997.

Pierce, Bessie Louise. *A History of Chicago.* Vol. 2. New York: Alfred A. Knopf, 1940.

Poole, Ernest. *Giants Gone: Men Who Made Chicago.* New York: Whittlesey House, McGraw Hill Co., 1943.

Prunières, Henry. "Le Festival international de musique de chamber à Chicago." *La Revue Musicale* (January 1931): 74–77.

———. "Gian Francesco Malipiero." *Musical Quarterly* 6 (July 1920): 326–41.

Putnam, Herbert. "Tributes to Carl Engel." *Musical Quarterly* 31 (1945): 137–140.

"Records of the Coolidges of Cambridgeshire, England." *New England Historical and Genealogical Register* 80 (1926): 401–15.

Reese, Gustave, ed. *A Birthday Offering to Carl Engel.* New York: G. Schirmer, 1943.

Rice, Edwin T. *Musical Reminiscences.* New York: Friebele Press, 1943.

Riesman, David. *Medicine in Modern Society.* Princeton: Princeton University Press, 1938.

Rogers, Bernard. "'English Invasion' at Berkshire Event." *Musical America* 38 (October 1923): 13.

Rosenfeld, Jay. *Elizabeth Sprague Coolidge: A Tribute on the One Hundredth Anniversary of Her Birth.* Privately printed, 1964.

———. "Festival." *Berkshire Eagle,* 7 November 1964.

———. "Music Festival at Chicago Opens." *Berkshire Eagle,* 12 October 1930.

Rossiter, Frank R. *Charles Ives and His America.* New York: Liveright, 1975.

Rush Medical College Forty-Ninth Annual Announcement, 1891–1892. Chicago: 1891.

Sachs, Harvey. *Music in Fascist Italy.* London: Weidenfeld and Nicolson, 1987.

Santoliquido, Francesco. "La piovra musicale ebraica." *Il Tevere* 16 (14–15 December 1937): 1–2.

Schabas, Ezra. *Theodore Thomas: America's Conductor and Builder of Orchestras, 1835–1905.* Urbana: University of Illinois Press, 1989.

Schwarz, Boris. *Great Masters of the Violin.* New York: Simon and Schuster, 1983.

Shaffer, Karen A., and Neva Garner Greenwood. *Maud Powell: Pioneer American Violinist.* Ames: Iowa State University Press, 1988.

Shepherd, Arthur. "'Papa' Goetschius in Retrospect." *Musical Quarterly* 30 (July 1944): 307–18.

Shirley, Wayne. "Ballet for Martha, the Commissioning of *Appalachian Spring.*" *Performing Arts Annual* 1987 (Library of Congress), pp. 102–23.

Shurtleff, Benjamin. *Descendants of William Shurtleff of Plymouth and Marshfield, Massachusetts.* Revere, Mass.: privately printed, 1912.

———. *John Shaw of Plymouth.* Edited and indexed by Margaret Johnson Drake. Evanston, Ill.: published by the author, 1972.

———. *The Descendants of John Atwood of Plymouth, Massachusetts.* Evanston, Ill.: National Society of the Daughters of the American Revolution, 1972.

Shurtleff, Harold Robert. *The Log Cabin Myth.* Cambridge: Harvard University Press, 1939.

Sigerist, Dr. Henry. *American Medicine.* Translated by Hildegard Nagel. New York: W. W. Norton, 1934.

Smith, Cecil. "Coolidge Festival Silver Anniversary Honors Benefactor." *Musical America* 70 (15 November 1950): 3, 6, 37.

Smith-Rosenberg, Carol. "The Female World of Love and Ritual: Relations Between Women in Nineteenth-Century America." *Signs* (1975): 1–29.

Sonneck, Oscar George. "A Survey of Music in America." In *Suum Cuique: Essays in Music.* New York: G. Schirmer, 1916.

Soule, Richard, Jr. *Memorial of the Sprague Family.* Boston: James Munroe and Co., 1847.

Spivacke, Harold. "Carl Engel, Librarian." In *A Birthday Offering to C.E.*, compiled and edited by Gustave Reese, 13–19. New York: G. Schirmer, 1943.

Sprague, Augustus Brown Ried. *Genealogy in Part, of the Sprague Families as Descended from Edward Sprague of England, from 1614 to 1902.* Worcester, Mass.: published by the compiler, 1902.

Sprague, Edward George. *The Ralph Sprague Genealogy.* Montpelier, Vt.: Capital City Press, 1913.

Sprague, Hosea. *The Genealogy of the Spragues in Hingham, Arranged in Chronological Order.* Hingham, Mass.: published by the author, 1828.

Sprague, H. H. *The Founding of Charlestown by the Spragues.* Boston: published by the author, 1910.

Sprague, Frank William. "The Brothers Ralph and William Sprague and Some of Their Descendants." In *New England Historical and Genealogical Register* 63 (1909): 147–58.

Sprague, Nancy Ann Atwood. *Pleasant Memories of My Life.* Boston: privately printed, 1916.

Sprague, Seth. *Memorial of the Sprague Family.* Boston: James Munroe and Co., 1847.

Sprague Warner and Co. Fine Groceries and Table Luxuries. Chicago: 1885.

Sprague, Warren Vincent, M.D. *Sprague Families in America.* Rutland, Vt.: Tuttle, 1913.

Stehman, Dan. *Roy Harris: A Bio-Bibliography.* New York: Greenwood Press, 1991.

Stiller, Richard. *The Love Bugs: A Natural History of the Venereal Diseases.* Nashville: Thema Nelson, Inc., 1974.

Stinson, Eugene. "Italian Music Pleases Guests of Mrs. Coolidge." *Chicago Tribune*, 15 October 1930.

Stone, James H. "Mid-Nineteenth-Century American Beliefs in the Social Value of Music." *Musical Quarterly* 63 (January 1957): 38–49.

Stravinsky, Vera, and Robert Craft. *Stravinsky in Pictures and Documents.* New York: Simon and Schuster, 1978.

Sullivan, Louis H. *The Autobiography of an Idea.* New York: Dover, 1956; reprint of American Institute of Architects edition, 1924.

Swafford, Jan. *Charles Ives: A Life with Music.* New York: W. W. Norton, 1996.

Taylor, Robert. *Saranac: America's Magic Mountain.* Boston: Houghton Mifflin, 1986.

Thomas, Rose Fay. *Memoirs of Theodore Thomas.* New York: Books for Libraries Press, 1971; reprint of Moffat, Yard and Co., 1911.

Tuthill, Burnet C. "Fifty Years of Chamber Music in the United States." *Papers and Proceedings of the Music Teachers National Association for 1928.* 23rd series. Hartford: Music Teachers National Association (1929): 163–75.

United States Library of Congress, Report of the Librarian for the Fiscal Year Ending June 30, 1922. Washington, D.C.: Government Printing Office, 1923.

United States Library of Congress, Report of the Librarian for the Fiscal Year Ending June 30, 1924. Washington, D.C.: Government Printing Office, 1924.

United States Library of Congress, Report of the Librarian for the Fiscal Year Ending June 30, 1925. Washington, D.C.: Government Printing Office, 1925.

University of Chicago Bulletin of Information. Vol. 1. Chicago: The University of Chicago, 1901.

Wager, Willis. "Amy Lowell and Music." In *A Birthday Offering to Carl Engel,* edited by Gustave Reese. New York: G. Schirmer, 1943.

Waters, Edward. "The Wa-Wan Press." In *A Birthday Offering to C.E.,* edited by Gustave Reese, 214–33. New York: G. Schirmer, 1943.

Watson, Leland A., and Thomas Tolan, M.D. *Hearing Tests and Hearing Instruments.* Baltimore: The Williams and Wilkins Co., 1949.

Weaver, William. *Duse: A Biography.* New York: Harcourt Brace Jovanovich, 1985; reprint of Thames and Hudson edition, 1984.

Wells, H. G. *The Future in America.* New York: Harper and Brothers, 1906.

Whitesitt, Linda. "Women's Support and Encouragement of Music and Musicians." In *Women and Music: A History,* edited by Karin Pendle, 301–13. Bloomington: Indiana University Press, 1991

Willison, George F. *The History of Pittsfield Massachusetts, 1916–1955.* Pittsfield: Sun Printing Co., 1957.

Wooldridge, David. *From the Steeples and the Mountains.* New York: Knopf, 1972.

REFERENCE WORKS

Encyclopaedia Britannica. Toronto: William Benton, 1958.

Hitchcock, H. Wiley, and Stanley Sadie, eds. *New Grove Dictionary of American Music.* 4 vols. New York: Macmillan, 1986.

Malone, Dumas, ed. *Dictionary of American Biography.* New York: Charles Scribner's Sons, 1958.

Sadie, Stanley, ed. *New Grove Dictionary of Music and Musicians.* 2 vols. London: Macmillan, 1980.

PRIMARY SOURCES

Archivio Contemporaneo Bonsanti, Florence, Italy

Private papers of Luigi Dallapiccola

British Library

MS Harl 1543

Britten-Pears Library, Aldeburgh, England

Britten-Bridge correspondence
Bridge–Marjorie Fass correspondence

Chicago Historical Society

Glessner journals

Coolidge Private Collections

Elizabeth Coolidge Winship, Lincoln, Massachusetts
Dr. John C. Coolidge, Cambridge, Massachusetts

Florence, Italy

Alfredo Casella papers, private collection of Fiamma Nicolodi

Fondazione Giorgio Cini, Venice, Italy

Coolidge-Malipiero correspondence

Herbert Hoover Presidential Library

Lou Henry Hoover papers

Harvard University, Pusey Archives

Frederic Shurtleff Coolidge papers

Library of Congress

Alexander Schneider collection
Coolidge correspondence with Otto Albrecht, Putnam Aldrich, Franco Alfano, Gabriele D'Annunzio, Martha Baird, Georges Barrère, Béla Bartók, Marion Bauer, Amy Beach, Nicolai Berezowski, Arthur Bliss, Ernest Bloch, Lucrezia Bori, Nadia Boulanger, Antonia Brico, Frank Bridge, Benjamin Britten, John Alden Carpenter, Teresa Carreño, Alfredo Casella, Mario Castelnuovo-Tedesco, George Chadwick, Carlos Chávez, Chicago Historical Society, Chicago Newberry Library, Chicago Symphony Orchestra, Chicago Women's Symphony Orchestra, Walter Wilson Cobbett, Albert Sprague Coolidge, Margaret Coit Coolidge, Aaron Copland, Frank Damrosch, Walter Damrosch, Mabel Daniels, Gustav Dannreuther, Archibald T. Davison, Emma Claude Debussy, Edward J. Dent, Rudolf Dolmetsch, Henry Drinker, Henry Eichheim, Georges Enesco, Carl Engel, Lehman Engel, David Ewen, Edmund Fellowes, Arthur Foote, Carlo Gatti, Giulio Gatti-Casazza, Karl Geiringer, Martha Graham, Cecil Gray, Donald Jay Grout, Erick Hawkins, Glen Haydon, Edward Burlingame Hill, Paul Hindemith, Helen Hopekirk, Mary Howe, Charles Ives, Gunnar Johansen, Hans Kindler, Otto Kinkeldy, Rudolf Kolisch, Hugo Kortschak, Henry Krehbiel, Fritz Kreisler, William Kroll, Jan LaRue, Sigmund Levarie, Charles Martin Loeffler, Alma Mahler, Gian Francesco Malipiero, Clara Mannes, Bohuslav Martinů, Daniel Gregory Mason, Lowell Mason, Emerson Meyers, Darius Milhaud, Lucy Sprague Mitchell, Horatio Parker, Carl Pfatteicher, Ildebrando Pizzetti, Maud Powell, Henry Prunières, Maurice Ravel, Gustave Reese, Ottorino Respighi, Paul Robeson, Carlos Salzedo, Robert Schauffler, Alexander Schneider, Arnold Schönberg, Percy Scholes, Rudolph Serkin, Roger Sessions, Ted Shawn, Carleton Sprague Smith, David Smith, Oscar Sonneck, Alice Sprague, Harriet Sprague, Frederick Stock, Igor Stravinsky, Oliver Strunk, Rose Fay Thomas, Oscar Thompson, Ernst Toch, Leon Vallas, Joseph Wagner, Felix Warburg, Anton Webern, Gilles Whittaker, Gertrude Clarke Whittall, Edith Bolling Wilson, Felix Winternitz.

Miscellaneous uncataloged coolidge materials
MacDowell Colony papers

New York City Historical Society

Records of Mrs. Sylvanus Reed's English, French, and German Boarding and Day School

Pittsfield, Massachusetts

Athenaeum, Local History File
Pittsfield Department of Public Records
Berkshire Eagle. *Clipping file.*

Radcliffe College, Schlesinger Library

Nancy Ann Atwood Sprague diaries

University of Wisconsin-Madison Archives

Pro Arte Quartet papers

Vermont Historical Society, Montpelier, Vermont

Atwood and Sprague genealogies

Williams College

Clipping file

Yale University, Sterling Memorial Library Archives

Records of Probate Court
Treasurer's records
Yale picture collection
Records of the Secretary
Miscellaneous manuscript collection

Index

Numerals in *italic* face indicate references to illustrations. Elizabeth Sprague Coolidge's name is abbreviated as ESC.